# THE FLOW OF CAPITAL FUNDS
# IN THE POSTWAR ECONOMY

NATIONAL BUREAU OF ECONOMIC RESEARCH

STUDIES IN CAPITAL FORMATION AND FINANCING

# The
# Flow of Capital Funds
# in the Postwar Economy

*by*

RAYMOND W. GOLDSMITH

YALE UNIVERSITY

PUBLISHED BY

NATIONAL BUREAU OF ECONOMIC RESEARCH

NEW YORK

DISTRIBUTED BY

COLUMBIA UNIVERSITY PRESS

NEW YORK AND LONDON

1965

# NATIONAL BUREAU OF ECONOMIC RESEARCH
## 1964

## RELATION OF THE DIRECTORS TO THE WORK AND PUBLICATIONS OF THE NATIONAL BUREAU OF ECONOMIC RESEARCH

1. The object of the National Bureau of Economic Research is to ascertain and to present to the public important economic facts and their interpretation in a scientific and impartial manner. The Board of Directors is charged with the responsibility of ensuring that the work of the National Bureau is carried on in strict conformity with this object.

2. To this end the Board of Directors shall appoint one or more Directors of Research.

3. The Director or Directors of Research shall submit to the members of the Board, or to its Executive Committee, for their formal adoption, all specific proposals concerning researches to be instituted.

4. No report shall be published until the Director or Directors of Research shall have submitted to the Board a summary drawing attention to the character of the data and their utilization in the report, the nature and treatment of the problems involved, the main conclusions, and such other information as in their opinion would serve to determine the suitability of the report for publication in accordance with the principles of the National Bureau.

5. A copy of any manuscript proposed for publication shall also be submitted to each member of the Board. For each manuscript to be so submitted a special committee shall be appointed by the President, or at his designation by the Executive Director, consisting of three Directors selected as nearly as may be one from each general division of the Board. The names of the special manuscript committee shall be stated to each Director when the summary and report described in paragraph (4) are sent to him. It shall be the duty of each member of the committee to read the manuscript. If each member of the special committee signifies his approval within thirty days, the manuscript may be published. If each member of the special committee has not signified his approval within thirty days of the transmittal of the report and manuscript, the Director of Research shall then notify each member of the Board, requesting approval or disapproval of publication, and thirty additional days shall be granted for this purpose. The manuscript shall then not be published unless at least a majority of the entire Board and a two-thirds majority of those members of the Board who shall have voted on the proposal within the time fixed for the receipt of votes on the publication proposed shall have approved.

6. No manuscript may be published, though approved by each member of the special committee, until forty-five days have elapsed from the transmittal of the summary and report. The interval is allowed for the receipt of any memorandum of dissent or reservation, together with a brief statement of his reasons, that any member may wish to express; and such memorandum of dissent or reservation shall be published with the manuscript if he so desires. Publication does not, however, imply that each member of the Board has read the manuscript, or that either members of the Board in general, or of the special committee, have passed upon its validity in every detail.

7. A copy of this resolution shall, unless otherwise determined by the Board, be printed in each copy of every National Bureau book.

*(Resolution adopted October 25, 1926,*
*as revised February 6, 1933, and February 24, 1941)*

*This report is one of a series emerging from an investigation of postwar capital market developments in the United States aided by a grant to the National Bureau from the Life Insurance Association of America. Supplementary grants by the Research and Educational Trust Fund of the Mortgage Bankers Association of America and the Commission on Money and Credit aided the preparation of the present report. The Life Insurance Association of America, the Mortgage Bankers Association, and the Commission on Money and Credit are not, however, responsible for any of the statements made or views expressed in the report.*

# Contents

## Contents

# Tables

# Tables

## Tables

# Tables

# Tables

## Tables

# Charts

# Charts

# Foreword

THIS report discusses the main features of the American capital market on the basis of annual statistics of fund flows and balance sheets for the postwar period (from the end of 1945 through 1958). These statistics, the development of which constitutes a substantial part of the Bureau's Postwar Capital Market Study, are utilized freely throughout this volume, and the details of their sources and derivation are given in Volume II of *Studies in the National Balance Sheet of the United States*.[1] As explained there, the figures bear a close relationship to those utilized in the Federal Reserve Board's Flow-of-Funds Section despite some important differences.[2]

The limitation of this study to a presentation of the basic statistics is most pronounced in Chapters 3 and 4. Chapters 6 through 10, which deal with the flow of funds through the five main sectors of the capital market—U.S. Treasury securities, state and local government securities, corporate bonds, corporate stock, and residential mortgages —go somewhat beyond these limits by providing sketches of the main institutional and operational features of these five markets because the statistics of fund flows would otherwise be hardly understandable. It must be emphasized, however, that these five chapters are not substitutes for monographs that adequately analyze, or even exhaustively describe, these markets during the postwar period. Chapters 7 and 10, which deal with state and local government securities and residential mortgages, suffer less from these defects because they draw on the studies by Robinson and Klaman,[3] which form parts of the Postwar

---

[1] *Basic Data on Balance Sheets and Fund Flows,* Princeton for NBER, 1963.

[2] See *ibid.,* Introduction.

[3] Roland I. Robinson, *Postwar Market for State and Local Government Securities,* Princeton for NBER, 1960, and Saul B. Klaman, *The Postwar Residential Mortgage Market,* Princeton for NBER, 1961.

Capital Market Study. No equally thorough sources exist for the three other markets.[4] Lack of adequate previous studies was felt particularly in the case of the market for corporate stock.

This volume does not deal in a systematic manner with the inter-relations among fund flows, balance sheets, and interest rates for the different capital market instruments, partly because of the lack of adequate previous studies of these complicated relationships and partly because a substantial study of interest rates is now in progress at the National Bureau.[5] Nor does it discuss systematically the many political and legislative forces, e.g., in taxation, that have impinged upon the various sectors of the capital market during the postwar period. This study thus is not a comprehensive analysis of the American postwar capital market in all its aspects, but a preparatory step to such an ambitious undertaking. The book's title indicates the limitations of its scope, perhaps to a somewhat exaggerated degree.

Since the primary function of this study is the presentation of basic data on fund flows and balance sheets in one integrated set of statistics, references to other similar bodies of data are generally omitted in the text. For the same reason the literature is specifically cited only where needed to supplement the basic set of data utilized.

As the study depended to a large extent on the flow-of-funds and balance-sheet statistics of the Postwar Capital Market Study, the acknowledgments made in that connection in the preface to *Studies in the National Balance Sheet of the United States* apply here, too, particularly the acknowledgment of the assistance of the staff of the Flow-of-Funds Section of the Federal Reserve Board and of the National Bureau's staff headed by Rachel Floersheim, Robert E. Lipsey, and Morris Mendelson. A special acknowledgment, however, is due here to Rachel Floersheim who for over two years supervised the preparation of the tables and the checking of tables and text. Without her devoted assistance the study could not have been carried to completion. Assisting Rachel Floersheim in the statistical work and checking were Yvette Binder, Amy F. Hoagland, Susan Horowitz, Anita S. Martin, Christine Mortensen, and Carol H. Schwartz. Christine Culbert greatly

[4] Eli Shapiro's monograph on "The Postwar Market for Corporate Securities and Loans," which also forms part of the Postwar Capital Market Study, was not yet available when this study was written.

[5] See *Tested Knowledge of Business Cycles,* Forty-Second Annual Report, National Bureau of Economic Research, New York, 1962, pp. 78, 82.

improved the original text by her painstaking editing. The charts were drawn by H. Irving Forman with his usual skill.

Thanks are also due to the Staff Reading Committee of the National Bureau consisting of Roger F. Murray, Thomas R. Atkinson, and James S. Earley; to the Directors' Reading Committee of Willis J. Winn, Donald B. Woodward, and Theodore O. Yntema; and to Saul B. Klaman and Eli Shapiro who read the chapters dealing with their special fields but are not responsible for the remaining defects. I am also indebted to Bertrand Fox and Eli Shapiro, while Director and Deputy Director of the Research Staff of the Commission on Money and Credit, for assistance in numerous ways. Grateful acknowledgment is also made to the members of the Advisory Committee on the Study of the Postwar Capital Market.

Publication of this study, which was substantially completed in 1962, has been delayed for various reasons, among them checking and revision of figures in the light of new information.

RAYMOND W. GOLDSMITH

*May 1964*

# THE FLOW OF CAPITAL FUNDS
# IN THE POSTWAR ECONOMY

# Summary

This summary is arranged in two parts. The first deals with the general characteristics of the American capital market during the postwar period; the second with the flow of funds through the five main sectors of the capital market which constitute the core of the study —the markets for Treasury and state and local government securities, for corporate bonds and stocks, and for residential mortgages. Whereas the second part is limited to a brief summary of the main findings presented in Chapters 6 through 10, the first part covers some aspects that were not specifically discussed in the report, but may be helpful in understanding postwar capital market developments. Emphasis here is on the characteristics of the American capital market in the postwar period that distinguish its structure and operation from the prewar periods that were not affected by war or the Great Depression, i.e., in particular between the turn of the century and World War I and the 1920's. The report deals with the years 1946 through 1958, generally referred to as the postwar period, but the first part of the summary occasionally also takes account of developments during 1959–61, which are not covered in the tables.

## General Characteristics of the Postwar Capital Markets

1. On a national scale the financing task is measured by the volume of gross capital formation, since funds equal in size to gross capital formation must be withheld from current consumption out of national product. During the postwar period gross capital formation averaged $39 billion a year under the narrowest concept, which covers only business structures (excluding residences), business equipment, and net foreign balance; $66 billion under the standard concept, which also includes residential structures and government civilian capital

formation; and $108 billion under a broader concept, which is more consistent in that it separates durable from nondurable output and therefore also embraces consumer durables and military construction and equipment. These figures amount to 12 per cent of gross national product for the narrow concept, 20 per cent for the standard concept, and 29 per cent for the broad concept, including consumer durables and government tangible assets.

2. Measured by the share of civilian gross or net capital formation, the relative size of the financing task in the postwar period was about the same as over the previous fifty years, excluding periods affected by war or the Great Depression (see Tables 16 and 19). Gross capital formation under the standard definition averaged slightly above one-fifth of gross national product for most decades since the turn of the century (and indeed since 1869)—a ratio about the same as that observed during the postwar period. If consumer durables are included, the ratio for the postwar years is even slightly above that for the earlier periods. On a net basis, the ratio of capital formation to national product in the postwar period is somewhat below the level prevailing before 1930, particularly if consumer durables are excluded. This points to a shift between internal and external financing, but does not influence the relative size of the total financing task.[1]

3. For the operation of the capital market, great importance attaches to the forms which capital formation takes and to the sectors which undertake it. While all of the three main sectors—business, households, and government—use both internal and external funds to finance their capital expenditures, the ratios of the two types of funds differ, as do the factors which affect the distribution and the total volume of capital expenditures. Similarly, the forms of external financing differ among sectors—governments and households, for instance, being unable to issue equity securities. Within sectors the forms of external financing also differ, depending on the character of capital expenditures, capital structure, the cost of funds of different types, and many other factors.

4. The sectoral distribution of capital expenditures during the postwar period showed a continuation of trends observed for more than half a century before 1930, namely, an increase in the share of households and governments and a decrease in the share of business in total national capital expenditures. During the postwar period, households

---

[1] See Tables 12–16 for gross capital expenditures and Tables 17–20 for net investment.

accounted for well over two-fifths of total capital formation if consumer durables are included (about one-fourth if they are excluded), business for a little less than two-fifths, and civilian government for one-tenth. This compares with shares in the last three decades of the nineteenth century and the first three decades of the twentieth century of 40 per cent for households (23 and 18 per cent excluding consumer durables), 56 and 54 per cent for business, and 3 and 6 per cent for government.[2] Within the business sector, a substantial increase took place in the share of equipment at the expense of that of structures. Thus there was a considerable increase in the share of expenditures on capital goods of relatively short life—machinery, vehicles, and consumer durables—in the private economy, partly offset in national capital formation by an increase in the share of government construction.

5. For the economy as a whole, gross capital expenditures (including military) absorbed nearly two-thirds of all capital funds used during the postwar period if the sources-and-uses-of-funds statements of the seven main sectors (nonfarm households, agriculture, unincorporated business enterprises, nonfinancial corporations, financial institutions, state and local governments, federal government) are combined. Among the acquisition of financial assets and accounting for the remaining one-third of total uses of capital funds, short-term claims were lower than long-term claims, absorbing 15 and 19 per cent of total uses of capital funds, respectively. Net purchases of equity securities by the different sectors absorbed only 2 per cent of total funds used (see Table 21). The smallness of this ratio is due partly to the breadth of the sectors used; e.g., all net purchases and sales of equity securities within the nonfarm household sector are eliminated in the consolidated figures for the sector.

6. On a national scale the distribution of capital funds among sources is necessarily closely connected with that of uses. Thus about two-thirds of total sources represented gross saving and slightly over one-third external financing. Of gross saving, in turn, about two-thirds were provided by earned depreciation allowances if the latter are calculated uniformly for all sectors on a straight-line basis and at replacement cost. The remaining one-third of total internal sources represented the net saving of the various sectors. The importance of the

---

[2] The figures for 1869–1929 are from unpublished worksheets underlying the R tables in Simon Kuznets, *Capital in the American Economy: Its Formation and Financing,* Princeton for NBER, 1961.

distribution of internal financing among earned depreciation allowances and net saving obviously differs among and within sectors; it also depends on how conscious the different economic units are of the distinction between gross and net saving and capital formation, and on how much this distinction influences their investment and saving decisions.

7. Substantial differences in the structure of uses and sources of capital funds are apparent between the main sectors. The share of gross capital expenditures in total funds used varied (excluding financial institutions) between two-thirds for nonfarm households and nearly 100 per cent for the federal government. Unincorporated business devoted nearly nine-tenths of the available funds to gross capital expenditures, agriculture 93 per cent, and nonfarm business 83 per cent (see Table 27).

8. The importance of external financing was largest for nonfinancial corporations, for which it accounted for more than two-fifths of all funds used (again excluding financial institutions). State and local governments and nonfarm unincorporated business enterprises were next with about one-third of total funds used, but this ratio does not have a very precise meaning for unincorporated business enterprises. External financing was relatively least important for nonfarm households for which it furnished less than one-fifth of total capital funds, for agriculture with one-eighth, and for the federal government with one-twentieth (see Table 27). Differences among sectors existed also in the structure of external financing. Examples are: first, nonfinancial corporations, which in the postwar period were by far the largest users of external funds, raised nearly one-half of total outside funds in the form of short-term liabilities, two-fifths through long-term debt, and about one-seventh through the sale of new equity securities; second, nonfarm households secured one-third of them on a short-term and two-thirds on a long-term basis, the latter in the form of home mortgages (see Table 24).

9. Possibly as important as the level and distribution of financing during the postwar period is a comparison with financing in earlier periods not affected by wars or the Great Depression. Such a comparison shows that changes in the structure of uses and sources of funds have been relatively small for the whole economy or the seven main sectors for which the statistics are available.

On a national basis, the shares of gross capital expenditures in total uses and of internal and external financing in total sources were about the same in 1901–12 and 1923–29 as in the postwar period.[3] Within external financing, however, some substantial and significant changes occurred. The share of equity financing, not more than 5 per cent of total external financing in the postwar period, was not even half as large as in the two prewar periods when it is estimated at one-seventh and one-fifth. The near equality between short- and long-term borrowing observed in the postwar years was also found in 1901–12, and in 1923–29. However, in comparison to the 1920's, the relative importance of long-term liabilities increased in the postwar period.

Similar trends are found in the financing of nonfinancial corporations. The share of external financing in total capital funds was about the same in 1901–12 and 1923–29 as in the postwar years. Recourse to the issuance of equity securities, however, was sharply lower, a ratio to total external financing of one-sixth in the postwar period compared with about one-third for 1901–12 and more than two-fifths for 1923–29. In the case of nonfarm households, financing methods in the postwar period were very similar to those observed in the 1920's, but quite different from those prevailing between the turn of the century and World War I. Both in the postwar period and the 1920's, external financing provided something more than one-sixth of total funds, and long-term borrowing accounted for over three-fifths of total external financing. From 1901 to 1912, on the other hand, external financing was responsible for only one-twelfth of total funds used and long- and short-term borrowing were of about equal importance.

10. The postwar period is characterized by a fairly steady rise in the level of interest rates, evidencing an excess demand for funds over the available supply. This rise reflects only in part the fact that until 1950 the Federal Reserve System supported the price of long-term Treasury securities, and thus kept their rates somewhat lower than they otherwise would have been and indirectly also influenced the level of other interest rates. If there are long swings of forty to fifty years' duration in the level of interest rates, as is possible though far from proven, the postwar period probably constitutes the major part of a long upswing, following the long downswing of 1920–45, and parallels the preceding long upswing from the late 1890's to 1920.

Interest rates were at historically extremely low levels at the beginning of the postwar period, but by 1958 they had reached the highest levels witnessed since the early 1930's, although not the peaks of the

[3] Kuznets, *Capital in the American Economy*, pp. 490, 558, and unpublished worksheets underlying R tables. See also Table 23 of this book.

7

early 1920's or the 1870's. New issues of long-term, high-grade corporate bonds ended the period at over 4 per cent compared to 2½ per cent in 1945, nearly 6 per cent at the peak of 1920, and somewhat less than 4 per cent at the trough of the 1890's. No sharp changes occurred during the postwar period in the differentials among the main types of long-term interest rates. Short-term rates, however, rose relatively more than long-term rates, Treasury bills advancing from the pegged level of less than ½ per cent in 1945 to an average of 2¼ per cent during the 1954–58 cycle. The more relevant bank rates on short-term business credits nearly doubled, rising from 2.34 per cent in 1945 to 4.34 per cent in 1958.

The second characteristic of the yield structure of the postwar period is the divergent development of the yields of fixed interest-bearing securities and of equities of the 1950's. Common stock yields (dividend-price ratios) advanced from approximately 4 per cent in 1945 to 6½ per cent in 1949–50, a movement parallel to that of bond yields. Then, however, they declined steadily to about 4 per cent in 1958, and continued downward through 1959.[4] As a result, common stock yields fell below the yields on new issues of high-grade bonds beginning in 1958, a position duplicated only in 1929.[5] These historically abnormal yields relations, however, had no pronounced effect in the 1950's on the ratio of gross or net new issues of bonds to flotations of stocks.

11. An important basic characteristic of the capital market is the extent of the participation of financial institutions, i.e., primarily the banking system, thrift institutions, and private and government insurance organizations.

Between the end of 1945 and 1958, the assets of financial institutions (excluding government lending agencies and personal trust funds administered by banks) increased from about $352 billion to $704 billion, or at a rate of slightly more than 5½ per cent per year. (During the next three years they rose by another $100 billion or about 15 per cent.) This rate of growth is considerably below the 7½ per cent a year which was observed between 1900 and 1929, and also below the average rate from 1929 to 1945.

Economically more relevant is the relation of the assets of financial institutions to either national product or all financial assets. By these

---

[4] *Business Statistics,* Washington, 1961, p. 102.

[5] *Historical Statistics of the United States,* Washington, 1960, p. 656, Series X-333, X-335, X-339.

tests, financial institutions during the postwar period just about kept pace with the growth of the economy. The assets of financial institutions were about 1.6 times gross national product in both 1945 and 1958. They were equal at both dates to somewhat more than one-third of all financial assets in the United States.

12. The influence of financial institutions on individual sectors of the capital market is reflected in the proportion of the main capital market instruments held by these institutions. During the postwar period financial institutions increased their share in four of the five main instruments (state and local government securities, corporate bonds and stocks, and residential mortgages), while their share in Treasury securities outstanding showed no substantial change. Throughout the period the role of financial institutions was dominant in the market for corporate bonds where their net purchases accounted for more than nine-tenths of the net increase in supply, in the market for residential mortgages where their share was almost as high, and, of course, in the market for short-term credit. Their influence was very great also in the market for state and local government securities since they absorbed about three-fifths of the net increase in supply, and in the market for Treasury securities, where statistical measurement is difficult, since net changes over the postwar period as a whole were very small in both the total amount outstanding and in the holdings of financial institutions which remained at approximately two-thirds of the total. While financial institutions held less than one-tenth of common stock outstanding at any time during the postwar period, their role in the market for stock, except the stock of investment companies and of closely held corporations, was much more substantial, and their net purchases represented a large and increasing fraction of total new issues.

13. The relatively small change in the position of financial intermediaries in the postwar capital market contrasts with the substantial advance over the preceding fifty or more years, particularly between the Great Depression and World War II. Thus the share of the financial assets of financial institutions in all financial assets outstanding in the United States was somewhat less than one-fourth in 1900 and in 1929, and increased to somewhat over one-third in 1939 and 1945.[6] Similarly, the assets of financial institutions, which had been nine-tenths of gross national product at the turn of the century, increased

[6] Raymond W. Goldsmith and Robert E. Lipsey, *Studies in the National Balance Sheet of the United States,* Princeton for NBER, 1963, Vol. II, Table Ia.

to 1.3 times GNP in 1929 and to twice GNP in 1939,[7] compared to the level of about 1.6 times GNP that prevailed throughout the postwar period. It is, therefore, possible that the importance of financial institutions in the capital market, which has been increasing since the middle of the nineteenth century, is reaching a peak, and that the share of the main types of financial institutions in capital market instruments is stabilizing, at least in the case of claims which constitute the great majority of financial assets outstanding.

14. As a result of differences in the rate of growth of assets, considerable shifts occurred during the postwar period in the distribution of the aggregate assets of all financial institutions and, correspondingly, in the role of the various groups of financial institutions in the capital market.

The outstanding change was the decline in the share of the assets of the banking system from three-fifths at the end of World War II to two-fifths in 1958 or 1961. The share of commercial banks alone fell from a little over two-fifths to not more than one-third of the assets of all financial institutions. The decline of the share of the banking system was due primarily to a reduction in the ratio of money to national product or to financial assets. The ratio of time and savings deposit departments in commercial banks to the total assets of financial institutions actually increased slightly, from 9 to 10 per cent, so that the decline of the assets of the monetary system proper (Federal Reserve System plus check deposit departments of commercial banks) was even sharper.

Among the main groups of financial institutions other than the monetary system, insurance organizations held their share between 1945 and 1958 at 48 per cent of the assets of all nonmonetary institutions. The share of miscellaneous financial institutions remained at about 17 per cent of the assets of all nonmonetary institutions, and the share of thrift institutions, including the saving departments of commercial banks, at above one-third (Table 5).

15. The shift between the monetary system and the nonmonetary institutions is partly an offset to the extraordinary increase, in absolute and relative terms, in the assets of the monetary system that occurred during World War II accompanying the repressed inflation of that period. The share of the monetary system in the total assets of financial institutions in 1958 of about one-third, however, was con-

7 For GNP figures in 1900–29 and 1939, see Kuznets, *Capital in the American Economy,* pp. 558 and 486 (Variant III).

siderably below the proportion of 1939 of two-fifths. While it was about the same as the 1929 ratio, it was substantially below that of 1900 (see Table 5). The stability of the share of thrift institutions during the postwar period at one-third of the total assets of non-monetary institutions contrasts with the downward trend observed between 1900 and 1939. Even more significant is the stability in the share of insurance organizations in the postwar period, which contrasts sharply with the increase between 1929 and 1945, an increase due largely to the sharp rise in the assets of government insurance and social security organizations.

16. Throughout the study, figures for averages of the three cycles observed during the postwar period (1946–49, 1949–54, 1954–58) are presented, compared, and commented upon. It is not possible to summarize here the results of these comparisons, but the most important fact is that the main relationships are very similar in the second and third cycles, but are considerably different in the first cycle which was strongly influenced by the transition from a war to a peacetime economy. In the financial sphere, this change meant primarily the rapid disappearance of the overhang of liquid assets in excess of requirements which had accumulated during World War II, the end of the retirement of substantial amounts of Treasury securities and the sharp reduction of their holdings by banks and insurance companies, and the abandonment of price support for Treasury securities by the Federal Reserve System. These three developments were essentially completed during or shortly after the end of the first cycle. Other differences between the first cycle, on the one hand, and the second and third, on the other, were the increasing share of external financing, and the decrease in the relative importance of short-term credit among the sources of external financing.

17. In capital market techniques—as distinct from the size and direction of capital market flows—the changes during the postwar period, although numerous, were not far-reaching, at least not compared with the innovations during the 1920's or the 1930's. Changes in the character of capital market instruments, in the nature of the operations of the different types of financial institutions, and in the structure of the investment banking machinery were all in the same direction as during the thirty years before World War II, and sometimes even earlier.

An interesting example is the direct placement of corporate bonds, one result of the increasing predominance of large institutional investors in the market for corporate bonds and the registration provisions of the Securities Act of 1933. During the postwar period, about 48 per cent of all corporate bonds offered were placed privately. This is a very substantial proportion, but the share had already been as high as 24 per cent from 1936 to 1940.[8]

In this and other instances, techniques initially developed during the 1920's and 1930's became more commonly accepted and were in many ways refined, but there was no basic change in the developments during the postwar period.

18. There are, however, a few important features of postwar capital market techniques, the increasing use or modification of which are sufficiently pronounced that these techniques can be reasonably regarded as postwar innovations.

The first of these is the widespread use of lease-back financing, under which a financial institution acquires a building or plant and simultaneously leases it for a long term to an industrial or commercial enterprise to operate, and it becomes the property of the operator after the stipulated lease payments have been made. Lease-back transactions transform a loan into the purchase and sale of tangible property, and transfer the physical assets involved from the balance sheet of the operator and lessee to that of the owner and lessor, while leaving no trace of the lease payment obligations on the balance sheet of either lessee or lessor. (Since lease-back transactions do not give rise to the issuance or retirement of financial instruments, they are not included in the statistics on which this study is based.) No comprehensive data exist of the volume or terms of lease-back financing, but it was no doubt substantial compared to related forms of loan financing, i.e., private placements of corporate bonds and long-term loans of commercial banks.

The second innovation is embodied in the specialized credit arrangements developed for financing oil production, the construction of oil and gas pipelines, service stations, tankers, and the erection and operation of petro-chemical plants. These projects, mostly of large size and involving lease-back transactions or assignments of revenues in one form or another, were initiated largely by industrial groups and involved primarily direct financing by institutions, chiefly commercial banks, life insurance companies, and pension funds, without or with only delayed recourse to a public offering of securities.

[8] For postwar period, Table 71. For 1936–40, *25th Annual Report of the Securities and Exchange Commission,* Washington, 1959, pp. 222 and 226.

## Summary

19. While it is not possible to mention minor changes in capital market techniques during the postwar period, it may be noted that most of them reflect two general tendencies. The first of these is an increasing flexibility in capital market instruments, such as repayment schedules and substitution of collateral. The motive and effect of these innovations were to tailor the contracts more and more closely to the specific requirements of certain groups of borrowers and lenders. The issuance of Treasury securities or finance company paper with maturity dates that coincide with corporate tax instalments is a simple example. Tax-exempt securities with unusually high or low initial or final coupons are a more complicated one.[9]

The second tendency is the substitution of professional for lay management of security portfolios and, more generally, of financial assets. Examples are the purchase of investment company securities or the participation in common trust funds instead of owner-management of small and medium-sized holdings; the substitution of investment advisory or trust department management of larger estates, both involving continuous supervision for a fee, instead of usually haphazard and discontinuous management by the owner or a casual adviser; or the use of Treasury bills and other more risky short-term securities in lieu of part of the large amounts of demand deposits in excess of day-to-day needs formerly held by the treasurers of large corporations.

## Flow of Funds Through the Five Main Capital Market Sectors

An idea of the absolute and relative magnitude of the five sectors of the capital market with which this report deals may be gathered from the fact that, at the end of 1958, the amounts outstanding of these five generally marketable instruments amounted to $1004 billion, or almost one-half of the $2082 billion of financial assets then in existence in the United States. These five instruments showed a substantial increase in outstandings in the course of the postwar period, the annual rate of growth between 1945 and 1958 averaging 5.8 per cent. The share of the five instruments in total financial assets, however, remained unchanged at approximately one-half. Of the increase of $523 billion in the value of the five instruments outstanding, more than one-half reflected the sharp rise in stock prices during the second

[9] See Roland I. Robinson, *Postwar Market for State and Local Government Securities,* Princeton for NBER, 1960, pp. 112 ff.

part of the period. The net amount of funds raised through these five instruments amounted to only $246 billion, or nearly $20 billion a year.

The market for Treasury securities occupied a special, and particularly important, position in the American postwar capital market. Short-term Treasury securities came to constitute one of the most important forms of holding the liquid reserves of business and financial institutions, competing here primarily with demand and time deposits in commercial banks and with certain other short-term instruments. After World War II Treasury securities—primarily those of a maturity up to one year—became the balancing item in the portfolios not only of most financial institutions, but also of many large nonfinancial corporations. This means that Treasury securities are usually not the first choice of any substantial group of private investors, but are acquired when the assets in which financial institutions or nonfinancial corporations prefer to invest their funds are not available in sufficient amounts or on satisfactory terms, and that Treasury securities are liquidated when the demand for these other assets is high.

Only in the postwar period did this role of Treasury securities as the balancing item in the portfolios of most investor groups become evident, although a trend in that direction could be detected since World War I. The development, of course, was caused by the sharp increase during World War II in the volume of Treasury securities outstanding, both in absolute and relative terms.

While the amount of Treasury securities outstanding changed but little over the entire postwar period, three investor groups expanded their holdings substantially, both in absolute and relative terms: government insurance and pension funds, which absorbed $30 billion of Treasury securities, and thus increased their holdings by 125 per cent; state and local governments, whose net purchases of $6 billion enlarged their holdings by about 120 per cent; and foreigners, who tripled their holdings acquiring on balance fully $5 billion of Treasury securities. The Federal Reserve banks, although making net purchases of $2 billion, increased their holdings by only 9 per cent. Among domestic private financial institutions, only two groups added appreciably to their holdings: fire and casualty insurance companies, which increased their holdings by two-thirds by adding nearly $2¼ billion, and savings and loan associations which increased them by 60 per cent through net acquisition of less than $1½ billion of Treasury securities.

All these purchases were almost offset by the massive net sales of commercial banks, totaling more than $24 billion, or 27 per cent of their holdings, at the end of 1945; and of life insurance companies, which liquidated 65 per cent of their holdings at the beginning of the period by net sales of $13.5 billion of Treasury securities. Substantial sales, absolutely or relatively, were also made by mutual savings banks and nonfinancial corporations. The holdings of nonfarm households in 1958 were smaller by $1 billion compared to 1945, but this amounted to a relatively small decline of 2 per cent in their holdings.

The differences among investor groups were most pronounced in Cycle I when large liquidation of Treasury securities by banks and life insurance companies, totaling $18 billion and $5 billion for the full cycle, were absorbed almost exclusively by the U.S. government, either by retirement of securities or by acquisitions on behalf of its pension and insurance funds. The net sale or purchase balances of the different groups were smaller in Cycle II and still smaller in Cycle III. Government funds continued to be the main net buyers of Treasury securities, while life insurance companies and mutual savings banks were the main sellers, joined in Cycle III by commercial banks and nonfinancial corporations.

### STATE AND LOCAL GOVERNMENT SECURITIES

The demand for state and local government securities during the post-war period was limited essentially to three investor groups—commercial banks, fire and casualty insurance companies, and individuals with high incomes—and depended on the funds available for investment by these groups, on interest rate differentials, and on income tax rates. The supply of tax-exempt securities, on the other hand, was mainly determined by the difference between the capital expenditures of the state and local government and their gross savings (current income minus current expenditure, excluding capital consumption allowances).

Of total net purchases of state and local government securities of $40 billion, households absorbed only 32 per cent, compared to their share in holdings of well over one-half at the beginning of the postwar period. More than 60 per cent of the net supply of state and local government securities remained to be absorbed by financial institutions. Commercial banks alone took more than 30 per cent and fire and casualty insurance companies 15 per cent; these are the two groups among financial institutions for which the tax exemption of state and local government securities is of the greatest value because their income is subject to the full corporate income tax.

Compared to the differences in the trend of holdings and net acquisitions of state and local government securities over the entire postwar period, differences in the distribution among the main holder groups from one of the three postwar cycles to another were moderate. Thus, the share of all financial institutions together in the net supply of state and local government securities in the three cycles varied only from 61 to 65 to 54 per cent. Variations were, of course, more pronounced for individual groups of financial institutions. Thus, the share of commercial banks declined from two-fifths of the total in the first cycle to only one-fifth in the third cycle, while that of fire and casualty insurance companies rose from one-twelfth in the first cycle to about one-sixth in the second and third cycles.[10]

### CORPORATE BONDS

Between 1945 and 1958 the volume of corporate bonds more than tripled, from $27 to $89 billion, an average annual rate of increase of $9\frac{1}{2}$ per cent; the intercyclical changes point toward an upward trend. Reflecting the substantial rate of growth of corporate bonds outstanding, the average annual increase rose from $3.6 billion in Cycle I to $4.2 billion in Cycle II and to $6.5 billion in Cycle III. The volume of new bond offerings, of course, was considerably higher because some of the new issues were used to retire outstanding issues. The ratio between net increase in bonds outstanding and bond offerings was two-thirds in 1946–49 and 1949–54 and three-fourths in 1954–58.

Of total bond offerings of about $90 billion, approximately 30 per cent each were issued by manufacturing companies and by electric and gas utilities. Communication enterprises, primarily the Bell system, accounted for 10 per cent, and the railroads for 5 per cent. The last fourth of corporate bond offerings was divided among finance companies, and real estate, trade, and miscellaneous corporations. The distribution of bond offerings among the main industries did not differ significantly from one cycle to the other.

Corporate bonds provided approximately one-tenth of total financ-

[10] State and local government securities are discussed in greater detail in Chapter 7.

ing, over one-fifth of external financing, and over one-fourth of debt financing of nonfinancial corporations. These ratios would be slightly higher if term loans by banks were included. The relative importance of corporate bonds as a means of financing was fairly stable during the three cycles, particularly if bonds are related to total net sources of funds.

The proportion of corporate bonds placed directly with institutional investors came close to one-half for the entire postwar period. It was highest, at slightly above 50 per cent, in Cycle II. Most industrial subdivisions followed the main pattern. The share of private placements, however, varied widely among industries, ranging from 3 per cent for railroads to about 90 per cent for other transportation. Of the two most important issuer groups, electric utilities had an average ratio of direct placements of about 30 per cent since many regulatory agencies prescribe offerings through competitive bidding, while direct placements accounted for almost two-thirds of the bond offerings of manufacturing corporations.

The outstanding characteristics of the distribution of net purchases of corporate bonds during the postwar period was the dominance of financial institutions. For the period as a whole, holdings of corporate bonds by financial institutions increased by $57 billion, while the total amount outstanding rose by $61 billion. Financial institutions absorbed only about three-fourths of the total increase in Cycle III after their purchases had been virtually as large as the entire increase in the supply in Cycles I and II.

Among financial institutions, the insurance sector was the predominant buyer of corporate bonds, and here again private life insurance companies were the decisive source of demand. For the entire postwar period the increase in the holdings by life insurance companies amounted to slightly more than one-half of the total increase in corporate bonds outstanding. Inclusion of private and government insurance funds brings the share to four-fifths of the total, and to about nine-tenths of the absorption of corporate bonds for all financial institutions. Net purchases by commercial banks were virtually nil, but at least part of their term loans are very similar in character to directly placed corporate bonds. If term loans with a maturity of more than five years are included, the share of commercial banks in the net issuance of corporate bonds would rise to about one-tenth of the total.[11]

[11] Corporate bonds are discussed in greater detail in Chapter 8.

# Summary

## COMMON STOCK

The market for common stock in the postwar period had two outstanding features. First, new common stock issues were remarkably small compared to the issuance of other capital market instruments, to the volume of internal and external finance of corporations, to the value of common stock outstanding, and to the total assets of most investor groups. Second, trading in common stock was very large, and the resulting shifts in the portfolios of the different investor groups were substantial and of considerable importance for the smooth functioning of the capital market.

Net issues of corporate stock from 1946 through 1958 amounted to nearly $34 billion (excluding $7 billion of investment company issues), of which $29 billion represented common stock. These figures include both marketable and nonmarketable issues of small and new corporations. The statistics of the Securities and Exchange Commission, which are limited to marketable issues, show stock issues of only $17 billion excluding investment companies.[12]

New issues of common stock showed a considerable upward trend throughout the postwar period, the annual average rising from $1.6 billion in Cycle I to $2.5 billion in Cycle II and $3.9 billion in Cycle III. This increase, however, was smaller than the expansion in the rate of absorption of other main capital market instruments, other than U.S. government securities, by investors. As a result, the share of common stock in the net issuance of the five main capital market instruments declined from one-fifth in Cycle I to one-ninth in Cycle II and it was one-seventh in Cycle III.

For the entire postwar period, common stocks provided 5 per cent of the total funds absorbed by all nonfinancial corporations and the ratio was approximately the same for all three cycles. In relation to total external financing, common stocks contributed about one-eighth, again without substantial changes among the three cycles. Common stocks supplied nearly three-fifths as large a volume of funds as corporate bonds did, and an even smaller proportion if bank term loans of five years' maturity or longer are included with bonds.

Stocks accounted for only 2 per cent of the aggregate financing of manufacturing and mining corporations, and 24 per cent of that of public utilities and communications, but contributed virtually nothing

---

[12] This does not include convertible bonds exchanged for common stock.

to the funds secured by corporations in transportation and trade. The share of stock in the external financing of these groups was similarly varied. It amounted to only 5 per cent for manufacturing and mining corporations, to 38 per cent among public utilities, and was negligible again for transportation and trade. Compared, finally, to the total of issuance of securities and long-term debt, stocks contributed 12 per cent for manufacturing and mining and 43 per cent for public utilities.

For the entire postwar period, financial institutions, other than the personal trust departments of commercial banks, had a net purchase balance of common stock of $14 billion, equal to nearly one-half of total net issues excluding that of investment companies which are rarely acquired by other financial institutions.

It may be more appropriate, however, to compare the $14 billion of net acquisition of common stock by financial institutions with the $17 billion [13] of new issues of marketable common stock (excluding investment company issues), since financial institutions acquire only relatively small amounts of the nonmarketable issues of small corporations. The share of financial institutions in the absorption of new marketable common stock issues, then, is nearly 80 per cent. Since stockholders other than financial institutions undoubtedly acquired a substantial proportion of the new marketable issues of common stock, particularly of those offered under subscription rights, other stockholders must, for the postwar period as a whole, have been net sellers to financial institutions of seasoned marketable common stock other than investment company issues.

Net purchases of common stock were concentrated in two groups of financial institutions—private pension plans and investment companies—which accounted for more than two-fifths and for nearly one-third, respectively, of all net institutional purchase of common stock.

The share of the net purchases of common stock by institutions increased very markedly over the postwar period. While net institutional purchases were equal to more than two-fifths of net new marketable common stock issues (other than those of investment companies) in Cycle I, they rose to one-half in Cycle II, and advanced further to about four-fifths in Cycle III.

The predominance of financial institutions as net buyers of marketable common stock other than investment company issues is still more dramatically illustrated by the fact that net noninstitutional

[13] This figure includes cash issue alone and not the common stock issue resulting from bond conversion.

absorption of such securities averaged only $0.6 billion a year over the postwar period, and that, contrary to most capital market measures, this absorption did not increase from cycle to cycle.

Although little is known definitely about net purchases and sales of common stock, and hence about shifts of holdings, among groups of domestic individual investors, there are some indications that investors of moderate means and in the younger age groups made net acquisitions while large and older investors had either no net purchase balance or a net sales balance. The shift involved is probably small compared to the total value of total stock outstanding and is not likely to have changed the degree of concentration of ownership of common stock substantially. Both in 1958 and in 1945 a very large proportion of all common stock was in the hands of a relatively small proportion of families.

For the period 1946–58 aggregate net purchases of common stock of all types represented 3 per cent of total nonfarm households' savings. Net purchases of marketable common stock alone were equivalent to 2 per cent of individual saving. Exclusion of investment company stock reduces the share to 1 per cent. Net purchases of common stock of whichever scope thus constituted only a minor outlet of all current saving for all individuals taken together.[14]

### RESIDENTIAL MORTGAGES

The flow of capital funds in the market for residential mortgages during the postwar period is characterized by five developments: (1) the extraordinarily rapid rise of the volume of residential mortgage debt, slowed only from 1951 to 1953 because of the Korean War and government limitations on residential construction and mortgage lending; (2) a persistent rise in interest rates; (3) a marked increase in the position of financial institutions as mortgage lenders; (4) the pervasive influence of the federal government on many aspects of the market and the resulting tendency toward standardization of many aspects of the residential mortgage as a capital market instrument; (5) the development of new techniques adapted to the special environment created by government interference and institutionalization.

Between the end of 1945, when the residential mortgage debt was not higher than in the mid-1920's, and 1958, the total mortgage debt on residential real estate increased from $23 to $133 billion. The rate

---

14 Common stock is discussed in greater detail in Chapter 9.

of increase of 14½ per cent per year was one of the highest, and the absolute increase in the volume of residential mortgages of $110 billion was by far the largest, among the main capital market instruments.

Life insurance companies and mutual savings banks were the main buyers of insured home mortgages, each accounting for more than one-fourth of the total. Commercial banks and savings and loan associations followed with about one-seventh and one-fifth, respectively, and federal agencies with about one-twelfth. This left not much for all other holders. Savings and loan associations were by far the most important lenders on uninsured home mortgages, accounting for more than one-half of the total. Commercial banks and life insurance companies have followed at a great distance, holding about 15 per cent of the total each. Noninstitutional lenders are credited with one-eighth of all uninsured home mortgages, a considerable part of which was represented by junior liens. Mutual savings banks were the most important factor in the market for multifamily mortgages, absorbing over one-third of the postwar period total. Life insurance companies and noninstitutional lenders absorbed one-fifth each, and savings and loan associations supplied one-sixth of the funds to this market.

The main change in the sources of funds for residential mortgages during the postwar period is the high share of life insurance companies during the first part, particularly 1948–51, of commercial banks particularly in 1946–47, and of savings and loan associations particularly during the second part of the period. In 1948–51 life insurance companies absorbed about 30 per cent of total net residential mortgage loans, savings and loan associations less than 25 per cent, and commercial banks about 15 per cent. From 1952 through 1958, on the other hand, life insurance companies accounted for under 20 per cent of the absorption of residential mortgages, their share even declining to 10 per cent in 1957–58, while savings and loan associations increased their share to an average of over 40 per cent and to nearly one-half in 1957–58.

# CHAPTER 1

# Scope and Function of the Capital Market in the American Economy

---

### *Origin of the Capital Market in the Separation of Saving and Investment*

A MARKET for new capital, apart from transactions in existing financial and real assets, exists because in a modern economy saving (the excess of current income over current expenditures on consumption) is to a large extent separated from investment, i.e., expenditures on durable assets usually defined as new construction, equipment, and additions to inventories and excluding education, research, and health.[1]

In any given period every economic unit either saves or dissaves—if we ignore the relatively few units whose current expenditures exactly balance their current income; and most units make capital expenditures, which usually involve payments to other units for finished durable goods, materials, or labor, but which may also be internal and imputed (e.g., Crusoe building his boat). Both saving and investment may be calculated gross or net of capital consumption allowances or retirements. Since these diminish saving and investment equally, the difference between saving and investment is the same whether calculated on a gross or net basis.

The relation between saving and investment varies considerably among economic units. For some, saving is regularly in excess of

[1] For an individual economic unit, investment also includes the acquisition of existing tangible assets, but such acquisitions are offset by equivalent sales in a closed economy.

CHART 1

CHARACTERISTICS OF FINANCIAL SURPLUS
AND DEFICIT UNITS

Saving = increase in net assets of all types

Capital expenditures = net increase in tangible assets

Financial surplus = increase in financial assets
(or decrease in liabilities and contributed capital)

Financial deficit = decrease in financial assets
(or increase in liabilities and contributed capital)

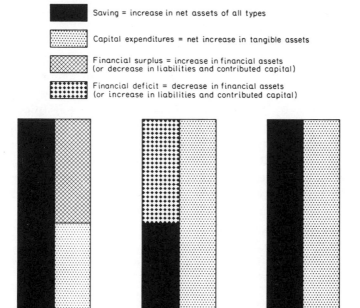

Surplus units          Deficit units          Neutral units

investment. These units, which may be designated as saving surplus units (Chart 1), make funds available to the capital market, either by acquiring financial assets—money, other claims, or equities—or by reducing their own liabilities through repayment. The fact that a unit has a surplus status does not, of course, mean that it does not have any investment during the period, i.e., that it makes no capital expenditures; it only indicates that the unit's investment is smaller than its saving during the period. For other units, designated as saving deficit units,[2] capital expenditures are in excess of saving. These units absorb funds from the capital market by increasing their liabil-

[2] The terms surplus and deficit units indicate the difference between saving and investment, not, as might be suggested by the words, the difference between current income and current expenditure which, of course, is equal to saving or dissaving.

ities, including the sale of their own equity securities or by reducing their financial assets, including their holdings of money. In the third type of unit, which may be called neutral, saving is equal to investment. These units, therefore, neither supply funds to nor demand funds from the capital market.

If all the economic units in a country were constantly neutral, no capital market would exist and money would be used only as a medium of exchange, as a means of immediate payment for transactions undertaken in markets for commodities and services. Such an economy is characterized by the absence of financial assets or liabilities.

At the other conceptual extreme stands a society in which saving (or dissaving) and investment are completely separated, i.e., in which the investment of all saving surplus units and the saving of all saving deficit units are zero. Such a society is entirely compatible with the basic characteristics of a modern economy. It would only require that all homes and consumer durables, as well as the structures and equipment used by the government and nonprofit organizations, be rented from business enterprises, which in turn rely entirely on external financing supplied by ultimate economic units either directly or through financial institutions.

All the societies which we know, and particularly all modern economies, lie between these two extremes. In them, saving surplus units account for most of saving, and saving deficit units account for a large proportion of investment. There are well-defined groups that have more or less regularly a saving surplus or deficit status. Within a modern economy, nonfarm households are commonly saving surplus units, while nonfinancial business enterprises and governments as a group generally have a saving deficit status, and financial institutions are close to a neutral position. This is evident for the United States in Table 1, which shows for each of the seven main sectors aggregate saving and aggregate investment, as well as the excess of saving for the period 1946–58 as a whole.

The total saving surpluses and deficits of all sectors together comes to $270 billion for 1946–58, as shown in Table 1. This figure, to repeat, is not a measure of the volume of primary capital market transactions—i.e., new loans made and new securities issued—because the saving surpluses of some units are netted against the saving deficits of other units within sectors, and because many units simultaneously save and make capital expenditures.

TABLE 1

SAVING AND INVESTMENT, BY SECTOR, 1946-58
(billion dollars)

| Sector | Saving | | Capital Consumption Allowances (3) | Investment | | Excess Saving: Surplus (+) or Deficit (−) (6) |
|---|---|---|---|---|---|---|
| | Gross (1) | Net (2) | | Gross (4) | Net (5) | |
| 1. Nonfarm households | 680 | 334 | 346 | 554 | 208 | +126 |
| 2. Agriculture | 89 | 21 | 69 | 95 | 26 | −6 |
| 3. Nonfarm unincorp. business | 62 | 12 | 49 | 75 | 26 | −13 |
| 4. Nonfinancial corporations | 278 | 91 | 186 | 359 | 173 | −81 |
| 5. State and local govts. | 82 | 29 | 54 | 106 | 52 | −24 |
| 6. Federal government (civil) | 17 | 1 | 16 | 20 | 4 | −3 |
| 7. Financial intermediaries | 22 | 19 | 3 | 5 | 2 | +17 |
| 8. Total (civil) | 1,230 | 506 | 724 | 1,215 | 491 | +15 |
| 9. Federal government (military) | 156 | −28 | 184 | 156 | −28 | 0 |
| 10. Total (including military) | 1,386 | 478 | 909 | 1,371 | 462 | +15 |

Source: National Balance Sheet, Vol. II.

Col. 1: Table VIII-d-3.
Col. 2: Table VIII-d-3b.
Col. 3: Difference between gross and net investment.
Col. 4: Table VIII-a-7.
Col. 5: Table VIII-a-7b.
Col. 6: Col. 1 minus col. 4.

Note: Components may not add to totals because of rounding here and elsewhere in this chapter.

Among the sectors, virtually the only net suppliers of funds are non-farm households, their saving being far in excess for their capital expenditures. This sector's saving surplus is about one-fifth of its gross saving and more than two-fifths of its net saving.

Financial institutions, which hardly make sizable capital expenditures, represent the only other sector with a saving surplus, but it amounts to less than one-seventh of that generated by nonfarm households.

The largest saving deficit is shown by nonfinancial corporations, which alone account for more than three-fifths of the aggregate saving deficits of all sectors. Their saving deficit—which measures the net absorption of funds from other sectors—amounts to three-tenths of their own gross saving but to 90 per cent of their net saving. Unincorporated business, farm and nonfarm, also absorb net funds from other sectors, the saving deficit of these two sectors together being about one-seventh of the saving deficits of all sectors and nearly one-fourth of that of nonfinancial corporations.

State and local governments also show a substantial excess of investment over saving, amounting to more than one-sixth of the net saving deficit of all sectors. The deficit, however, amounts to only about three-tenths of their own gross saving and four-fifths of their net saving, thus being smaller relatively than for nonfinancial corporations but greater than for the other two business sectors.

The federal government had during the postwar period only a negligible excess of investment over saving, so that it neither absorbed funds from other sectors nor supplied funds to them (Chart 2).

It is unfortunately impossible to prepare tables similar to Table 1 for narrower sectors or to show for any given period the number of saving surplus, saving deficit, and neutral units, and the amounts of aggregate surpluses and deficits. This is because the usual statistics of corporations and governments do not classify units by the existence or size of a saving surplus or deficit. Even households have not been tabulated by the size of their saving surplus or deficit, although the information could be obtained by retabulating the basic data collected in some of the sample surveys of consumer income and expenditure.[3]

---

[3] Some inferences can, however, be drawn from average saving and average investment for groups of households classified by total income and expenditures, aggregate saving or dissaving, age and occupation of head of household, or other characteristics by which the data have been tabulated.

It is, therefore, impossible to judge how large the average proportion of saving surplus, saving deficit, and neutral units is in the different sectors and subsectors, how it varies with the business cycle, how

CHART 2

SECTORAL SAVING AND INVESTMENT. 1946–58

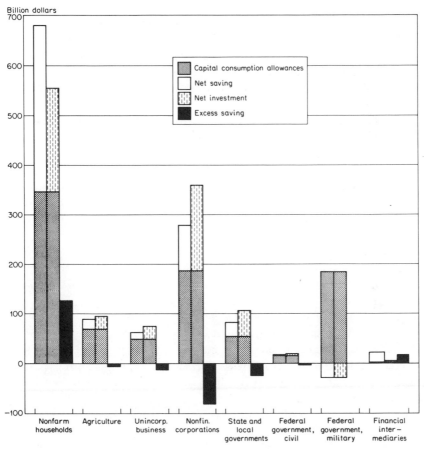

Source: Table 1.

concentrated surpluses and deficits are within groups, and how regularly the same units show saving surpluses or deficits. This severely reduces our ability to analyze the usual aggregative statistics of savings and investment.

## *Two Functions of the Capital Market* [4]

The capital market of a modern economy has two basic economic functions: first, the allocation of a period's current saving among users and uses, or the supply of financing for the period's investment; second, the facilitation of the transfer of existing assets, tangible and intangible, among individual economic units, groups of them, sectors, and countries. These two functions are closely connected in theory as well as in practice. Modern market economies could not operate without discharging both functions reasonably effectively. In both cases, the main instrument and guide of allocation is the price, in the sense of the yield of a tangible asset or a financial instrument and of yield differentials among assets. [5]

Allocation operates primarily through three devices: first, the pattern of yield differentials among capital market instruments; second, institutional restrictions on the flows of funds which are not expressed in yield differentials—often referred to as capital rationing, i.e., the fact that no borrower except possibly the central government can secure any amount of funds by simply offering a higher price; and third, government controls which have effects similar to institutional capital rationing.

Yield differentials reflect primarily three factors: relative cost, relative risk, and relative liquidity. All three factors influence the supplier as well as the user of the funds, but they do so in somewhat different ways.

From the point of view of the lender, it is the relative cost of acquiring a capital market instrument and of servicing it that is relevant. Obviously if it is more expensive for a lender to acquire and administer, directly or indirectly through an agent, one type of capital market instrument than another, then the yield he requires will be higher by the difference in cost, other characteristics of the instruments being equal. This factor explains part of the differential between large and

---

[4] The word "function" is used here solely to describe an existing situation, not to claim that the allocation resulting from the operation of the capital market is optimal.

[5] The term "yield" is used instead of the more familiar "interest rate" in order to emphasize that what influences the allocation of funds is not the nominal interest rate (the relation of the contractual interest payment to the face value of the claim), but the relation of income—fixed or variable; contractual, actual, or expected; gross or net of capital consumption allowances, depending on the situation under study—to the market value of the asset.

small commitments and between commitments close to or far from the lender's base of operation, although it may not explain the actual size of the differential which, of course, is influenced by many other factors. Even apart from these other factors, the actual yield differential may be larger or smaller than the cost differential unless the market is perfect.

Cost differentials are not constant over time. In particular, costs are likely to be high when a specific capital market instrument is new, is applied to new types of transactions or uses, or is acquired by lenders unfamiliar with it. In other words, in addition to the well-known simultaneous economies of scale, there are historical economies of habituation which are independent of, or complementary to, economies of scale.

In a perfect market where participants act rationally and take the long view, the risk component in interest rate differentials would be equal to the expected average loss on a specific type of commitment.[6] Loss here is to be interpreted broadly, including not only ultimate out-of-pocket cost after tax, but also making allowance for the cost of liquidating the commitment, the foregone opportunities of using the funds otherwise, the loss of actual or potential business because of adverse publicity connected with losses, even if covered by reserves, and similar indirect effects of commitments that get into difficulties. Hence an entirely rational risk allowance by the lender may well be above the strictly actuarial evaluation of losses. If participants do not act rationally and do not take the long view, in which reserves established on some commitments are regarded as balancing losses of other commitments, the risk allowance reflected in yield differentials is indefinite and erratic.

Even if they try to act rationally, different lenders will differ in their evaluation of the risk inherent in the same commitment, particularly of the nonactuarial component of risk. So much has been written recently about different attitudes toward risk that it does not seem necessary to elaborate on this point. These differences in the evaluation of the risk on identical commitments would drive the risk component in yield differentials up to the risk allowance of the lender who rates the risk highest and who is still needed to satisfy demand.

---

[6] To the extent that repayment provisions reduce this risk, e.g., by providing for gradual repayment or callability at the borrower's choice, they improve an instrument's liquidity and may reduce its yield.

## Scope of the Capital Market

In this report the broadest and simplest limitation of the boundaries of the capital market will be used. It will cover all financial assets and liabilities and all transactions in such assets except those which involve the exchange of money for a nonfinancial consideration, i.e., except monetary payments in exchange for commodities and for labor and capital services. For statistical convenience, gross transactions in money and money market instruments (federal funds, Treasury bills, bankers' acceptances, commercial and finance company paper), though not the holdings or net changes in them, will be disregarded.

The capital market so defined includes transactions not only in organized markets—securities exchanges or the over-the-counter markets —but also in nonmonetary financial assets effected among financial institutions, between a financial institution and a member of another sector of the economy, or among members of nonfinancial sectors. The capital market also covers imputed transactions of a financial character, the most important of which are retained earnings (internal saving) accruals and capital consumption allowances, and interest accrued. These are sometimes called nonmarket capital fund flows to distinguish them from actual capital market transactions.

This definition of the capital market entirely ignores the distinction often made between the capital market and the money market, i.e., the separation of liquid short-term claims and liabilities from other financial assets. There seems to be no sound reason for making this distinction as no sharp boundary exists between short-term claims, on the one hand, and long-term claims and equities, on the other. Instead, a fairly continuous spectrum extends from claims that can be immediately exchanged for cash—whether legally or actually—to claims with a very distant, or even without any final, maturity. There is more economic meaning in the distinction between financial assets which are a general medium of exchange—i.e., the U.S. currency and deposits with the Federal Reserve or commercial banks subject to check—held outside the banking system and other financial assets. Under this distinction, however, the scope of the "money market" becomes small in comparison to the capital market and little reason remains for the separation, particularly in view of the existence of financial assets of near-money character.

## Capital Market Instruments

The capital market has two aspects—flows of financial transactions and stocks of financial assets and liabilities—which are closely related because stocks may be looked upon as the sum of net previous flows and net flows can be regarded as first differences in stocks.[7]

There are as many categories of financial flows as there are types of financial instruments, i.e., types of intangible assets and liabilities that are reasonably homogeneous internally and distinguishable from each other. Within financial stocks and flows, the basic distinction is between claims, which are expressed in terms of a definite number of monetary units and usually carry a fixed interest rate, and equities which embody fractional right to profits (i.e., certain residuals between income and expenditures or between assets and liabilities) and which fluctuate in value. Among claims, in turn, at least five main categories can usefully be distinguished, despite gradual transitions between them: money, nonmonetary short-term claims against financial institutions, other short-term claims, long-term claims against financial institutions, and other long-term claims. Each of these categories, as well as equities, can be further divided according to their marketability under normal conditions. This leads to the establishment of nine chief categories of financial assets and the corresponding types of financial transactions, which are shown in Table 2 together with rough estimates of their size in 1958 in the United States to indicate orders of magnitude. For practical purposes, a finer and somewhat different breakdown of financial assets is needed, one which will vary with time and place and will be strongly influenced by the prevailing legal and institutional arrangements.

## Capital Market Participants

Three basically different groups must be distinguished among the owners and issuers of financial instruments and among the partners to the transactions in financial assets: financial institutions, nonfinancial business enterprises, and ultimate economic units (i.e., households and governments). Financial institutions are those whose assets are predominantly financial (i.e., claims against other sectors and equities

---

[7] This is a simplified formulation which disregards difficulties introduced by valuation changes, difficulties that are discussed in some detail in Chapter 2.

TABLE 2

MAIN CAPITAL MARKET INSTRUMENTS, 1958

| | Order of Magnitude (billion dollars) | Per Cent of Total |
|---|---|---|
| 1. Money (monetary metals, currency, checking deposits) | 222 | 11 |
| 2. Nonmonetary short-term claims against financial institutions | 150 | 7 |
| 3. Other marketable short-term claims (Treasury securities with maturity of less than one year, commercial paper) | 69 | 3 |
| 4. Other nonmarketable short-term claims (bank loans, loans on securities, other loans, trade receivables, consumer receivables, other intangible assets) | 295 | 14 |
| 5. Marketable long-term claims (marketable Treasury securities with maturity of more than one year, state and local government securities, publicly offered corporate bonds) | 223[a] | 11 |
| 6. Nonmarketable long-term claims against financial institutions (represented by assets of life insurance companies and private and government pension funds) | 200 | 10 |
| 7. Other nonmarketable long-term claims (other U.S. government securities, other bonds, mortgages, bank term loans, investments in rest of world) | 351[a] | 17 |
| 8. Marketable equities (corporate stock including corporate stock listed on exchanges or actively traded in over-the-counter markets) | 372 | 18 |
| 9. Nonmarketable equities (equities in financial nonprofit organizations and in unincorporated nonfarm business, other corporate stock) | 200 | 10 |
| 10. All financial assets | 2,082 | 100 |

Source: All table references below are to <u>National Balance Sheet</u>, Vol. II, unless otherwise specified.

Line 1: Table I, line II 1.
Line 2: Table I, line II-2.
Line 3: Table I, line II-13a, and Table III-5$\ell$-a, col. 1.
Line 4: Short-term bank loans are from Table I, line II-9, minus bank term loans (Table IV-c-9b) and Table III-5$\ell$a, sum of cols. 3, 7, and 10 (commercial paper held by banks). Other items are from Table I, lines II-6, 7, 8, and 10, and Table IV-b-20, line 11.
Line 5: U.S. government securities are from <u>Treasury Bulletin</u>, February 1959, p. 25, minus Table I, line II-13a. State and local government securities from Table I, line II-14. Publicly offered corporate bonds represent 60 per cent of other bonds and notes (Table I, line II-15) minus other commercial paper (Table III-5$\ell$-a, sum of cols. 4, 8, and 11).
Line 6: Table I, lines II-3, 4, and 5.
Line 7: U.S. government securities are from Table I, line II-13, minus Table I, line II-13a, and U.S. government securities included in line 5. Other bonds are 40 per cent of other bonds and notes (Table I, line II-15) minus other commercial paper (Table III-5$\ell$-a, sum of cols. 4, 8, and 11). Mortgages are from Table I, lines II-11 and 12. Bank term loans are from Table IV-c-9b. Investments in rest of world are from Table IV-b-20, lines 9 and 10.

NOTES TO TABLE 2 (concluded)

Line 8: 25th Annual Report, SEC, pp. 62 and 67.
Line 9: The sum of equities in other business (Table I, lines II-18 and
II-19), corporate stock (Table I, lines II-16 and II-17) minus market-
able corporate stock (line 8 of this table).

[a]If government-insured mortgages were considered marketable long-term
claims, line 5 would equal $278 billion and line 7 (excluding government-
insured mortgages) would equal $296 billion, since FHA- and VA-insured
mortgages equal $55   billion (Tables IV-b-11a-6 and IV-b-11a-4).

of other business enterprises not their own subsidiaries and affiliates),
and whose liabilities are in general regarded as liquid assets by the
creditors, predominantly nonfinancial business enterprises and households. Ultimate economic units are distinguished from both financial
institutions and nonfinancial business enterprises in that their net
worth cannot under present legal arrangements become the property
of another economic unit as does that of business enterprises.

In a modern economy financial institutions hold a considerable
proportion of all financial assets outstanding, even excluding claims
against other financial institutions. In the United States the share of
financial institutions in such financial assets (chiefly business and consumer loans, mortgages, and securities) is now on the order of two-
fifths.[8] At the same time the liabilities of financial institutions constitute a large proportion of the financial assets and a substantial share
of the total assets of nonfinancial business enterprises as well as of
household and governments. These relationships are illustrated in
Chart 3 for the end of 1958.

This chart shows that claims against financial institutions represent three-tenths of the total assets of households and account for almost one-half of nonfarm household financial assets. At the same time
liabilities to financial institutions represent nine-tenths of all nonfarm
household debt. The link to financial institutions is less pronounced
in business enterprises (including farm business). Claims against financial institutions constitute about one-fifth of financial assets and about
6 per cent of total assets, while liabilities to financial institutions (including bonds and stocks held by financial institutions) represent
about one-half of the total debt of nonfinancial enterprises, and financial institutions hold one-twentieth of their equity. In the case of federal, state, and local governments, claims against financial institutions

[8] Raymond W. Goldsmith, Robert E. Lipsey, and Morris Mendelson, *Studies in
the National Balance Sheet of the United States*, Vol. II: *Basic Data on Balance
Sheets and Fund Flows*, Princeton for NBER, 1963, Table I (1958).

CHART 3

BALANCE-SHEET RELATIONS BETWEEN FINANCIAL INSTITUTIONS AND NONFINANCIAL SECTORS, 1958

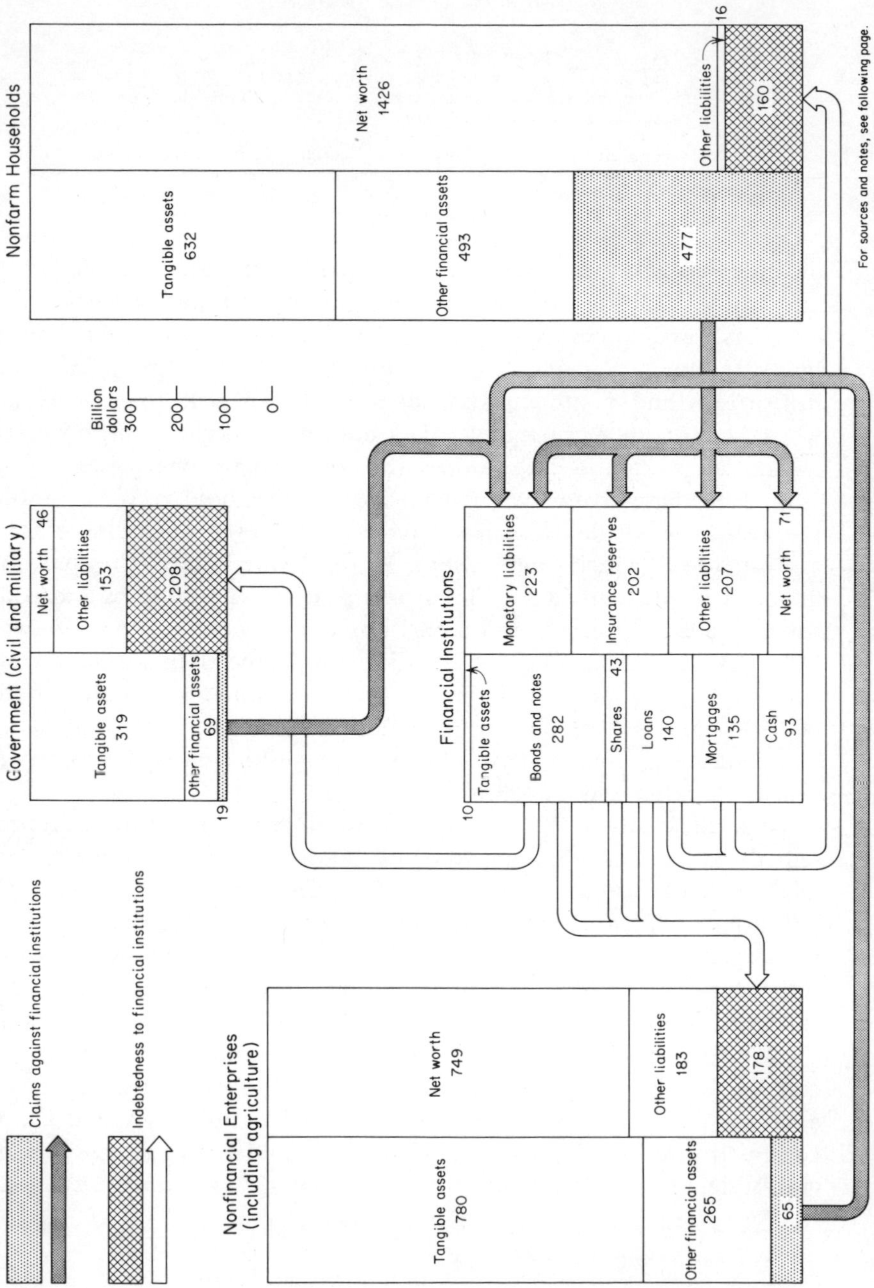

**Nonfarm Households**

Tangible assets
632

Net worth
1426

Other financial assets
493

477

Other liabilities 160

16

Billion dollars

300
200
100
0

**Government (civil and military)**

Tangible assets
319

Net worth 46
Other liabilities
153

208

Other financial assets
69

19

**Financial Institutions**

Tangible assets 10

Monetary liabilities
223

Bonds and notes
282

Insurance reserves
202

Shares 43

Loans
140

Other liabilities
207

Mortgages
135

Net worth 71

Cash
93

Claims against financial institutions

Indebtedness to financial institutions

**Nonfinancial Enterprises**
**(including agriculture)**

Tangible assets
780

Net worth
749

Other financial assets
265

Other liabilities
183

178

65

For sources and notes, see following page.

34

## NOTES TO CHART 3

Source: *National Balance Sheet*, Vol. II, Table I, 1958; and, for federal government, also Table III-7a. The following detailed explanation refers to the columns and lines in Table I, 1958, unless otherwise specified.

### Nonfarm Households

Net worth: Col. 1, line IV.
Other liabilities: Col. 1, line III-14, less indebtedness to financial institutions.
Indebtedness to financial institutions: Sum of col. 1, lines III-8, III-9, and III-10, and col. 5, lines II-6 through II-11a.
Tangible assets: Col. 1, line I-7.
Other financial assets: Col. 1, line II-21, less claims against financial institutions.
Claims against financial institutions: Sum of col. 1, lines II-1, II-2, II-3, II-4, II-5, II-10, and II-18, and col. 5, line IV.

### Nonfinancial Enterprises

Net worth: Cols. 2, 3, and 4, line IV, less col. 5, lines II-16 and II-17. (Lines II-16 and II-17 of col. 5 are treated as indebtedness of nonfinancial corporations to financial institutions.)
Other liabilities: Cols. 2, 3, and 4, line V, less net worth and indebtedness to financial institutions.
Indebtedness to financial institutions: Sum of col. 5, line II-7; cols. 2, 3, and 4, line III-9; a quarter of col. 5, line II-10; col. 5, line II-11b and II-12; col. 5, line II-15 less line III-12; and col. 5, lines II-16 and II-17.
Tangible assets: Cols. 2, 3, and 4, line I-7.
Other financial assets: Cols. 2, 3, and 4, line II-21, less claims against financial institutions.
Claims against financial institutions: Cols. 2, 3, and 4, lines II-1, II-2, and II-3.

### Financial Institutions

Net worth: Col. 5, line IV.
Monetary liabilities: Col. 5, line III-1.
Other liabilities: Col. 5, line III-14, less monetary liabilities and insurance reserves.
Insurance reserves: Col. 5, lines III-3, III-4, and III-5.
Tangible assets: Col. 5, line I-7.
Shares: Col. 5, lines II-16 and II-17.
Bonds and notes: Col. 5, lines II-13, II-14, and II-15.
Mortgages: Col. 5, lines II-11 and II-12.
Loans: Col. 5, line II-21, less shares, bonds and notes, mortgages, and cash.
Cash: Col. 5, line II-1.

### Government

Net worth: Sum of col. 6, line IV, and Table III-7a, line IV.
Other liabilities: Cols. 6 and 7, line III-14, less indebtedness to financial institutions.
Indebtedness to financial institutions: Sum of col. 7, line III-9, and col. 5, lines II-13 and II-14.
Tangible assets: Sum of col. 6, line I-7, and Table III-7a, line I-7.
Other financial assets: Cols. 6 and 7, line II-21, less claims against financial institutions.
Claims against financial institutions: Cols. 6 and 7, lines II-1 and II-2.

35

are relatively unimportant, accounting for one-fifth of financial and about 5 per cent of total assets.

Financial institutions thus are of particular importance among capital market participants. A summary picture of the main types of financial institutions operating in the United States in 1958 is, therefore, given in Table 3.

At that time all financial institutions, broadly defined, had $800 billion of assets, which was more than one-fifth of the total national assets, i.e., the aggregate of the assets of all independent economic units in the United States. Use of the narrower definition, which is employed in most of this report and excludes personal trust funds and a few other minor types of financial institutions, reduces the amount and the share to slightly below one-fifth. Since the assets of financial institutions consist primarily of claims, their share in these

TABLE 3

SYNOPSIS OF FINANCIAL INSTITUTIONS, 1958 AND 1945

|  | Type of Institution | Total Assets | | Annual Rate of Growth (per cent) (3) |
|---|---|---|---|---|
|  |  | 1958 (billion dollars) (1) | 1945 (billion dollars) (2) |  |
| 1. | Monetary authorities | 79.2 | 69.8 | 1.0 |
| 2. | Commercial banks | 241.3 | 160.4 | 3.2 |
|  | Demand deposit business | 167.7 | 128.0 | 2.1 |
|  | Time and saving deposit business | 73.6 | 32.4 | 6.5 |
| 3. | Mutual savings banks | 38.1 | 17.0 | 6.4 |
| 4. | Savings and loan associations | 55.4 | 8.8 | 15.2 |
| 5. | Credit unions | 4.4 | 0.4 | 20.0 |
| 6. | Life insurance organizations | 111.6 | 46.6 | 7.0 |
|  | Companies | 108.8 | 44.9 | 7.0 |
|  | Fraternal orders | 2.8 | 1.7 | 3.9 |
| 7. | Private pension funds | 27.8 | 2.7 | 19.7 |
| 8. | Govt. insur. and pension funds | 66.1 | 25.8 | 7.5 |
|  | Federal | 49.9 | 22.8 | 6.2 |
|  | State and local | 16.2 | 3.0 | 13.9 |
| 9. | Fire and casualty insurance | 25.6 | 7.6 | 9.8 |
| 10. | Investment companies | 20.4 | 3.6 | 14.3 |
| 11. | Finance companies[a] | 20.8 | 2.0 | 19.7 |
| 12. | Security brokers and dealers | 6.3 | 5.0 | 1.8 |
| 13. | Govt. lending agencies | 29.9 | 18.4 | 3.8 |
| 14. | Personal trust departments | 55.4 | 29.0 | 5.1 |
| 15. | Miscellaneous finance[b] | 6.6 | 2.5 | 7.8 |
| 16. | Total | 788.9 | 399.6 | 5.4 |

Source: <u>National Balance Sheet</u>, Vol. II, Tables III-5a through III-5m, III-1a, and III-7c.

[a]Includes mortgage companies.

[b]Includes banks in possessions, agencies of foreign banks, agricultural credit organizations, group health insurance, and savings bank life insurance.

is, of course, considerably higher. It amounted in 1958 to about one-third of the national total for short-term claims and to half of all long-term claims. In contrast, financial institutions held only one-tenth of corporate stock outstanding and less than 1 per cent of tangible assets.

As a comparison of columns 1 and 2 in Table 3 shows, the assets of financial institutions grew rapidly during the postwar period, nearly doubling. This increase is in line with the expansion of gross national product during the postwar period, but is somewhat smaller than the rise in the market value of national assets. The relative size of financial institutions in 1958 thus was equal to or, in comparison to national assets, slightly below the level of 1945. It was, however, throughout the postwar period above the predepression level.[9]

The doubling of the assets of all financial institutions resulted from considerable differences in growth among the main types of institutions. On the one hand, money-issuing institutions, i.e., the Federal Reserve System and the demand deposit departments of commercial banks, increased their assets only by one-fourth between the end of World War II and 1958. All other financial institutions together expanded their assets by 170 per cent, or even by 180 per cent if personal trust funds are excluded. Among these other financial institutions, two groups need to be distinguished. Growth was relatively moderate, amounting to between 115 and 140 per cent over the postwar period, for the saving departments of commercial banks, mutual savings banks, life insurance companies, and federal insurance and pension funds. At the other extreme, savings and loan associations, investment companies, and state and local government insurance and pension funds increased their assets by from 400 to over 500 per cent. Trusteed private pension funds, credit unions, and finance companies were even able to expand their assets tenfold. Some of these differences reflect stagnation or shrinkage during World War II, for instance, in the case of finance companies and savings and loan associations. Other institutions may be regarded as still being in the early phases of development during which the rate of growth is usually considerably more rapid than among old established institutions.

[9] For a comparison of the share of financial institutions in national assets since the turn of the century, see my *Financial Intermediaries in the American Economy Since 1900,* Princeton for NBER, 1958, Chapter IX, e.g., Table 95, p. 319.

## *Historical Background*

Developments in the capital market and in the financial structure of the United States in the postwar period cannot be understood without consideration of the earlier history of the system, at least as far back as World War I. Tables 4 through 6 are intended to provide in summary form the information required on financial institutions and tie in with similar data provided earlier for the postwar period. Obviously an adequate discussion of the trends in the American capital

TABLE 4

ASSETS OF FINANCIAL INSTITUTIONS, SELECTED DATES, 1900-58
(billion dollars)

|  | | 1900 (1) | 1929 (2) | 1939 (3) | 1945 (4) | 1958 (5) |
|---|---|---|---|---|---|---|
| 1. | Federal Reserve System |  | 5.5 | 21.0[a] | 69.8 | 79.2 |
| 2. | Commercial banks | 10.0 | 66.2 | 66.3 | 160.4 | 241.3 |
|  | Demand deposit business[b] | 8.4 | 37.6 | 47.7 | 128.0 | 167.7 |
|  | Saving and time deposit business[b] | 1.6 | 28.6 | 18.6 | 32.4 | 73.6 |
| 3. | Mutual savings banks | 2.4 | 9.9 | 11.9 | 17.0 | 38.1 |
| 4. | Savings and loan associations | 0.5 | 7.4 | 5.4 | 8.8 | 55.4 |
| 5. | Credit unions |  | 0 | 0.2 | 0.4 | 4.4 |
| 6. | Finance companies |  | 2.6 | 3.0 } | 2.0 | 20.8 |
| 7. | Mortgage companies | 0.2 | 0.8 | 0.4 | | |
| 8. | Life insurance companies | 1.7 | 17.5 | 29.2 | 44.9 | 108.8 |
| 9. | Fraternal order insurance | 0 | 0.8 | 1.2 | 1.7 | 2.8 |
| 10. | Private pension funds |  | 0.5 | 1.0 | 2.7 | 27.8 |
| 11. | Property insurance companies | 0.5 | 4.7 | 4.8 | 7.6 | 25.6 |
| 12. | Other private insurance | 0 | 0 | 0 | 0.2 | 1.1 |
| 13. | Investment companies |  | 3.0 | 1.6 | 3.6 | 20.4 |
| 14. | Govt. insur. and pension funds |  | 1.5 | 6.3 | 25.8 | 66.1 |
| 15. | Govt. lending agencies |  | 0.4 | 9.8 | 18.4 | 29.9 |
| 16. | Other finance[c] | 0.6 | 10.0 | 2.0 | 7.3 | 11.8 |
| 17. | Total | 15.9[d] | 130.8[d] | 164.1[d] | 370.5 | 733.5 |

Source: 1900-39: Goldsmith, *Financial Intermediaries*, Table 10, p. 73; subdivision of line 2 derived from *ibid.*, Table A-3c. 1945 and 1958: *National Balance Sheet*, Vol. II, Tables III-5a through III-5m, III-1a, and III-7c.

[a]Including $2.0 billion in Exchange Stabilization Fund.

[b]Allocated in proportion to total deposits of commercial banks.

[c]Includes security brokers and dealers.

[d]The difference between these figures and the corresponding ones in *National Balance Sheet*, Vol. II, Table III-5o, may be partly accounted for as follows: First, Table III-5o includes monetary metals held by the Treasury (*A Study of Saving*, Vol. III, Table W-43, line 9), which are not included in this table. Second, Table III-5o includes assets only of unincorporated security brokers and dealers (*A Study of Saving*, Vol. III, Table W-37, line V), while this table includes assets of all security brokers and dealers.

Note: A blank space indicates that the given type of financial institution did not exist in that year (see my *Financial Intermediaries*, Chart 3, p. 61).

TABLE 5

DISTRIBUTION OF ASSETS OF FINANCIAL INSTITUTIONS,
SELECTED DATES, 1900–58
(per cent)

|  |  | 1900 (1) | 1929 (2) | 1939 (3) | 1945 (4) | 1958 (5) |
|---|---|---|---|---|---|---|
| 1. | Federal Reserve System |  | 4.2 | 12.8[a] | 18.8 | 10.8 |
| 2. | Commercial banks | 62.9 | 50.6 | 40.4 | 43.3 | 32.9 |
|  | Demand deposit business[b] | 52.8 | 28.7 | 29.1 | 34.5 | 22.9 |
|  | Saving and time deposit business[b] | 10.1 | 21.9 | 11.3 | 8.7 | 10.0 |
| 3. | Mutual savings banks | 15.1 | 7.6 | 7.3 | 4.6 | 5.2 |
| 4. | Savings and loan associations | 3.1 | 5.7 | 3.3 | 2.4 | 7.6 |
| 5. | Credit unions | | 0 | 0.1 | 0.1 | 0.6 |
| 6. | Finance companies | | 2.0 | 1.8 } | 0.5 | 2.8 |
| 7. | Mortgage companies | 1.3 | 0.6 | 0.2 | | |
| 8. | Life insurance companies | 10.7 | 13.4 | 17.8 | 12.1 | 14.8 |
| 9. | Fraternal order insurance | 0 | 0.6 | 0.7 | 0.5 | 0.4 |
| 10. | Private pension funds | | 0.4 | 0.6 | 0.7 | 3.8 |
| 11. | Property insurance companies | 3.1 | 3.6 | 2.9 | 2.1 | 3.5 |
| 12. | Other private insurance | 0 | 0 | 0 | 0 | 0.2 |
| 13. | Investment companies | | 2.3 | 1.0 | 1.0 | 2.8 |
| 14. | Govt. insur. and pension funds | | 1.1 | 3.8 | 7.0 | 9.0 |
| 15. | Govt. lending agencies | | 0.3 | 6.0 | 5.0 | 4.1 |
| 16. | Other finance[c] | 3.8 | 7.6 | 1.2 | 2.0 | 1.6 |
| 17. | Total | 100.0[d] | 100.0[d] | 100.0[d] | 100.0 | 100.0 |

For source and notes, see Table 4.

market in the half century before the end of World War II is not intended.[10] Similar brief sketches of the historical background will be found in Chapters 3 and 4 about capital market flows and the participation of sectors other than financial institutions.

It will immediately be seen from these figures that the rate of growth of the assets of financial institutions during the postwar period of 5.4 per cent was not extraordinary in historical perspective. In fact, this rate was considerably lower than that observed from 1900 to 1929, when it averaged 7.5 per cent, and was below the average rate of 6.7 per cent for 1929–45 (see Table 4). Similarly it is seen that differences in the rates of growth of the different types of financial institutions during the postwar period are not more pronounced than, but generally are in the same direction as, differences in the two earlier periods. This is evident from the character of the changes in the distribution of total assets among financial institutions in Table 5.

The outstanding development of the postwar period—the decline in the share of monetary organizations (Federal Reserve Banks and de-

[10] More detailed figures and some discussion of the trends may be found in my *Financial Intermediaries*.

mand deposit business of commercial banks) from 53 to 34 per cent of the assets of all financial institutions—is found to agree in direction with the decline between 1900 and 1929 from 53 to 33 per cent. The rate of decline, however, was considerably less rapid, at 0.7 percentage points per year, during the first three decades of the century than during the postwar period, when it averaged 1.5 percentage points per year. The increase in the share of monetary organizations between 1929 and 1945 may be regarded as an interruption of a long-term trend, caused primarily by the extraordinary expansion of the money supply during World War II. The upward movement in the share actually is greater during the war period though the share stood at about 42 per cent in 1939, which represents a considerable increase over 1929 and 1958. Thus the decline during the postwar period to a certain extent counteracted the upswing during World War II. It remains to be seen whether the downward trend observed between 1900 and 1929, as well as during the second half of the nineteenth century, will continue.

The postwar increase in the share of thrift institutions (savings departments of commercial banks, mutual savings banks, savings and loan associations, and the credit unions) from 16 to 23 per cent only restored their position to the 1939 level, which was still 6 percentage points below the level of 1900 and 13 percentage points below that of 1929. Considerable shifts, however, occurred in the distribution of the total share among the four types of thrift institutions. The savings departments of commercial banks and savings and loan associations gained between 1900 and 1929; the latter also gained in the postwar period. Mutual savings banks continued declining: their share in the total declined from more than one-half in 1900 to not much over one-fifth in 1929 and remained at about one-fifth in 1958, with only a temporary interruption between 1929 and 1945 when their share climbed back to 33 per cent.

On the other hand, the sharp advance in the share of life insurance companies and pension organizations from one-fifth to over one-fourth between 1945 and 1958 continued an upward trend which had been in evidence since 1900, when their share stood at only one-tenth of the assets of all financial institutions. While the increase in the postwar period was about equally distributed among life insurance companies, private pension funds, and government insurance and pension funds, any rise between 1929 and 1945 was attributable to government insurance and pension funds, whereas the larger increase between 1900 and 1929 was accounted for almost exclusively by life insurance companies.

Table 6 confirms that the tendency for the assets of financial institutions to grow without a substantial increase in the number of units, which can be observed in most branches for the postwar period, was also in effect for the half century before World War II. The

TABLE 6

TRENDS IN GROWTH OF MAIN FINANCIAL INSTITUTIONS, 1900–58

| | Commercial Banks (1) | Mutual Savings Banks (2) | Savings and Loan Assoc. (3) | Life Insurance Companies (4) | Fire and Casualty Insurance Companies (5) |
|---|---|---|---|---|---|
| I. NUMBER OF ENTERPRISES (THOUSANDS) | | | | | |
| 1900 | 12.9 | 0.6 | 5.4 | 0.1 | 0.7 |
| 1912 | 26.3 | 0.6 | 6.3 | 0.3 | n.a. |
| 1929 | 24.3 | 0.6 | 12.3 | 0.4 | 1.4 |
| 1945 | 14.1 | 0.5 | 6.1 | 0.5 | n.a. |
| 1958 | 13.5 | 0.5 | 6.2 | 1.4 | n.a. |
| II. NUMBER OF PERSONS EMPLOYED (THOUSANDS) | | | | | |
| 1900 | 25 | n.a. | 11 | 70 | |
| 1912 | 90 | n.a. | 12 | 180 | |
| 1929 | 328 | n.a. | 48 | 242 | 291 |
| 1945 | 314 | n.a. | 14 | 293 | 277 |
| 1958 | 605 | n.a. | 51 | 510 | 530 |
| III. ASSETS (BILLION DOLLARS) | | | | | |
| 1900 | 10.0 | 2.4 | 0.5 | 1.7 | 0.5 |
| 1912 | 21.8 | 4.0 | 1.0 | 4.4 | 1.0 |
| 1929 | 66.2 | 9.9 | 7.4 | 17.5 | 4.7 |
| 1945 | 160.4 | 17.0 | 8.8 | 44.9 | 7.6 |
| 1958 | 241.3 | 38.1 | 55.4 | 108.8 | 25.6 |

Source

Section I
1900, 1929: Goldsmith, Financial Intermediaries, p. 65.
1912: Historical Statistics, 1960, pp. 399, 630, 631, 672. Averages of June 30 of current and following year.
1945, 1958: Statistical Abstract, 1959, pp. 440, 456, 472.
Section II
1900, 1912: Values for 1929 extrapolated on basis of unpublished estimates by S. Lebergott.
1929, 1945, 1958 (except Col. 3): S. M. Robbins and N. E. Terleckyj, Money Metropolis, Cambridge, Mass., 1960, p. 266; for 1958, Survey of Current Business, July 1960, Table 52 (columns 4 and 5 divided in accordance with 1956 ratio shown in Robbins and Terleckyj).
1929, 1945: For savings and loan associations, a rough estimate.
1958: Savings and Loan Fact Book, 1961, Chicago, U.S. Savings and Loan League, 1961, p. 101.
Section III
1900, 1912, 1929: Goldsmith, Financial Intermediaries, pp. 73–74.
1945, 1958: National Balance Sheet, Vol. II, Table II.

number of commercial and mutual savings banks in the United States in 1958 was hardly larger than at the turn of the century. Even the number of savings and loan associations, whose assets increased approximately a hundredfold between 1900 and 1958, was in 1958 less than one-fifth above that of 1900. Only in the case of life insurance companies was the number of independent units in 1958 considerably larger than in 1900 or 1929, but the increase consists primarily of very small companies.

Two measures of the growth of financial institutions compared to that of the entire economy are available—total assets and total employment. By both measures, financial institutions have gained in importance within the economy.[11] The share of financial institutions in total assets (excluding personal trust funds and government lending agencies) increased from approximately one-tenth in 1900 to one-seventh in 1929 and to one-fifth in 1939. By 1958 the share had returned to the 1939 level, after a slight bulge during World War II which left the ratio slightly below one-fourth in 1945.

In the case of employment, an increase in the share of financial institutions occurred between 1900 and 1929 when the proportion of the labor force employed by financial institutions rose from 0.5 to 2.6 per cent.[12] By the end of World War II, the share had declined to 2 per cent. Thereafter the upward trend resumed and increased the share to about 3.5 per cent by 1958. Thus the postwar increase was about in line with that observed during the first decades of the century when financial institutions underwent a rapid extensive and intensive development.

[11] For more detail, see my *Financial Intermediaries*, Chapter IX.

[12] These are rough estimates based on data in *Historical Statistics of the United States, Colonial Times to 1957*, series D-65, D-57, D-4; Sidney Robbins and Nestor Terleckyj, *Money Metropolis*, Cambridge, Mass., 1960, p. 266; and *Statistical Abstract of the U.S.: 1960*, pp. 205 and 211.

# CHAPTER 2

# A Framework for Capital Market Analysis

THE purpose of a framework is to provide a systematic, comprehensive, and consistent description and analysis of the facts in order to establish functional relationships that permit us to understand the modus operandi of the capital market. The selection of the specific framework is a matter of choosing among alternatives the one that makes best use of the available data, that embodies the maximum of internal checks against errors and omissions, that is flexible enough to permit multiple analytical uses, that requires the least effort on the part of the user, and that can be most easily adapted to testing the various economic theories of the subject without being indissolubly wedded to any one of them.

The flow-of-funds approach treated as an intrinsic part of a comprehensive system of national accounts seems to come closest to meeting these requirements. It is flexible; it provides safeguards against omissions of relevant transactions; it embodies considerable internal checks on the accuracy of the primary data utilized; and it does not prejudge to a dangerous extent the substantive answers to the questions that may be asked of the figures. Moreover, it supplies an integrated framework for the two basic aspects of the capital market—the flows of capital market transactions and the stocks of capital market instruments—by providing a systematic presentation of transactions in a flow-of-funds statement and of stocks in a balance sheet. It is for these reasons that this report is based on a national accounting framework of the capital market.

A framework is, it must be stressed, an organizing device. In its ideal form, it is a flexible instrument rather than a strait jacket; it is not, however, an economic or econometric model—a difference to which we shall return later in this chapter. It may help to answer questions, but it does not by itself provide the answers. It is primarily descriptive and an aid to analysis, but not a substitute for theory. It provides the means for testing hypotheses, but is not a device for producing them.

## General Characteristics of a National Accounting Framework [1]

Before constructing a statistical framework of the capital market as part of a comprehensive system of national accounts, it is necessary to settle six basic questions, in addition to delimiting its geographical scope and time span: (1) the assets and liabilities [2] to be covered by the framework with respect to stocks (holdings) and to flows (transactions); (2) the classification of these assets; (3) the valuation of the flows and stocks; (4) the entities (economic units) to be covered by the framework; (5) the grouping of these economic units; and (6) the method whereby the transactions and holdings of individual economic units shall be combined into flow and stock accounts for sectors and ultimately for the nation.

Each of these six questions presents difficult problems which are not specific to the statistical framework for capital market analysis, but are common to the entire field of national accounting. Since these problems have been treated quite exhaustively in the literature, it is not necessary to discuss them here. All that is required is an understanding of the framework and its application to the American capital market in the postwar period, which can be provided by a brief summary of the solutions to the six problems that have been adopted in the flow-of-funds statements and the balance sheet underlying this report.[3]

---

[1] As this section covers a subject very similar to that discussed in Chapter 2 of Goldsmith and Lipsey, *Studies in the National Balance Sheet of the United States* (Princeton for NBER, 1963), I have not hesitated occasionally to borrow from that slightly more detailed treatment.

[2] Liabilities which may algebraically be regarded as negative assets are intended to include net worth items. In future, the term "assets" is used for all three categories in order to avoid unnecessary verbiage and to have a partner to the term "transactions" which applies to flows of assets, liabilities, and net worth items.

[3] Readers interested in the basic problems of national accounting as they refer to flow-of-funds statements and national balance sheets may consult the following publications: Petter Jakob Bjerve and Mikael Selsjord, "Financial Accounting within a System of National Accounts" (*The Measurement of National Wealth,* Income and

# A Framework for Capital Market Analysis

In accordance with the basic tenet of national accounting to extend the system as far as the "measuring rod of money" reaches, the framework for capital market analysis includes all assets that have a market value which can be expressed in monetary terms. The scope of assets is thus limited to items that can be appropriated under the legal system of the day and place. The framework is not limited, however, to items that actually change hands for a monetary consideration; like national accounting, it includes imputed items, i.e., items that reflect economically relevant events even though they do not give rise to actual money transactions. A prime example is allowances for capital consumption.

### CLASSIFICATION OF ASSETS

The arrangement of the many separate types of assets into a relatively small number that can be handled within a system of national accounts depends primarily on the purpose of the system. When it is the analysis of the capital market, two main criteria may be applied: first, the importance of a given asset within the entire flow-of-funds or national balance-sheet picture; and second, homogeneity,

Wealth Series VIII, London, 1959); *Flow of Funds in the United States, 1939–53* (Washington, Federal Reserve System, 1955, Chapter I); "A Quarterly Presentation of Flow of Funds, Saving, and Investment" (*Federal Reserve Bulletin*, August 1959, pp. 828–849, 1046–1062); Morris A. Copeland, *A Study of Moneyflows in the United States* (New York, NBER, 1952); J. Denizet, "Les Problèmes Téchniques Posés par l'Etablissement des Comptes d'Opérations Financières" (*Studies in Social and Financial Accounting*, Income and Wealth Series IX, London, 1961); Graeme S. Dorrance, "Balance Sheets in a System of Economic Accounts" (*International Monetary Fund Staff Papers*, October 1959); Raymond W. Goldsmith, "The National Balance Sheet of the United States of America, 1900–1949" (*Income and Wealth Series IV*, London, 1955); Goldsmith and Lipsey, *National Balance Sheet* (Chapter 2); William C. Hood, *Financing of Economic Activity in Canada* (Ottawa, 1959, Parts I and VI); M. Hsing, "The Construction of Social Accounting Models" (*Weltwirtschaftliches Archiv*, Vol. 83, 1959); *The National Economic Accounts of the United States: Review, Appraisal, and Recommendations* (New York, NBER, 1958, Chapters XII and XIV); Ingvar Ohlsson, *On National Accounting* (Stockholm, 1953); John P. Powelson, *National Income and Flow-of-Funds Analysis* (New York, 1960, Part III); L. M. Read, "The Development of National Transactions Accounts" (*Canadian Journal of Economics and Political Science*, February 1957); Stanley J. Sigel, "A Comparison of the Structure of Three Social Accounting Systems" (*Input-Output Analysis: An Appraisal*, Studies in Income and Wealth 18, Princeton for NBER, 1955); Stanley J. Sigel, "An Approach to the Integration of Income and Product and Flow-of-Funds National Accounting Systems: A Progress Report" (*The Flow-of-Funds Approach to Social Accounting: Appraisal, Analysis, and Applications,* Studies in Income and Wealth 26, Princeton for NBER, 1962).

i.e., the behavioral similarity of the items combined in one category and their differentiation from other categories.

In applying these principles, it is impossible to rely entirely on a few distinctive characteristics of the whole spectrum of assets (already existing at the beginning of the period or created during the period), such as liquidity, maturity, or age. Rather it is necessary to follow conventional distinctions which are based on the actual operation of the capital market and which use as primary criteria the type of issuer, the nature of the instrument—claim or equity, the maturity, and the object of financing. This leads to the following main primary classification of assets and of transactions in them:

Tangible Assets
Claims
    Cash (currency and checking deposits)
    Other short-term claims against financial institutions
    Short-term claims (not securities) against other sectors, distinguishing claims against consumers and against business
    Claims arising from insurance and pension contracts, distinguishing those against private and government insurance organizations
    Mortgages, separating farm and nonfarm mortgages and residential and nonresidential mortgages
    Debt securities, distinguishing Treasury securities (short- and long-term), state and local government securities, and corporate and other bonds and notes
Equities
    Corporate stock, distinguishing preferred and common stock
    Equities in unincorporated business enterprises
    Equities in nonprofit organizations

In building up balance sheets and flow-of-funds statements, many of these categories are further subdivided and most of these subdivisions are preserved in the tables used in this study, if only in order to permit users to rearrange items to suit their specific purposes.

#### VALUATION

The valuation of flows generally presents no conceptual problems, although difficulties are encountered in practice because of insufficient basic data. In principle, all flows are entered in the framework at the valuation at which the transactions actually take place. Imputed items are valued as closely as possible to the actual value of identical or similar transactions. This is one of the reasons why capital consumption allowances, the most important of all imputed items, are valued at replacement cost rather than at original cost, as is customary in business accounting. The same principle calls for a valuation of inventories in which additions and withdrawals are taken into account at current valuation, i.e., a method similar to LIFO. Actually inventory transactions have not been derived from flow figures, but have been obtained as first differences of inventory holdings that are customarily valued at original cost or market value, whichever is lower. However, adjustment for inventory profits provides figures that reflect only the current value of the physical changes in inventories.

The problems are more difficult in the valuation of stocks. The principle adopted here is valuation at current (market) values at balance-sheet dates. Where no market value exists, the closest practical approximation is used. This means replacement cost as is (i.e., taking account of the proportion of useful life expired) for most categories of reproducible tangible assets, and book value for inventories. In the interest of simplicity, face value is used for all claims since the difference between face value and market value or its equivalent is negligible for short-term claims. The difference is substantial and ascertainable only for long-term marketable securities. These, however, constitute only about one-tenth of all claims.[4]

### COVERAGE OF ECONOMIC UNITS

In principle all separate decision-making units that participate in the economic process are to be regarded as independent entities having a balance sheet and a flow-of-funds statement of their own. Hence the framework includes the balance sheets and flow-of-funds statements of all households, nonprofit organizations (such as educational institutions, foundations, churches, fraternal organizations, and labor unions), all business enterprises, and all government units. Only business enterprises or government organizations that are owned or controlled by other business enterprises (i.e., majority-owned subsidiaries of corporations) or by other government organizations are denied independent status, i.e., their holdings or transactions are consolidated with those of the controlling unit.

Problems arise, however, in two important cases. First, are unin-

---

[4] This ratio excludes mortgages, term loans, and privately placed corporate bonds as not subject to regular market price fluctuations, although the price realized on an occasional nonscheduled transaction may not always be the par or book value.

corporated business enterprises (and possibly closely held family corporations) to be regarded as economic units independent of their owners, i.e., sole proprietors, partners, and shareholders? The decision depends on whether or not the enterprise as such can be regarded as a decision-making unit, and hence can be made only the basis of the circumstances of each case. Since usually not enough direct information is available, the following rough general rule has been adopted. All corporations, even if closely held, and all unincorporated nonfarm business enterprises, even sole proprietorships, have been regarded as independent economic units with their own balance sheets and flow-of-funds statements. Consequently, the equity in these enterprises has been treated as an asset of the owners. The operation of a farm, on the other hand, has not been regarded as an independent economic activity, and hence the balance sheets and flow-of-funds statements of farm households include both the household and the farm business assets and transactions.

Secondly, which of the numerous organizations and agencies of the federal government and which of the more than 100,000 other government units enumerated in the Census of Government are to be regarded as economically independent entities with their own balance sheet and flow-of-funds statements? Though partly arbitrary, the answer has been formulated here in such a way as to preserve as far as possible the unity of different sectors of the capital market. This has sometimes required abandoning the principle of consolidating the balance sheets and flow-of-funds statements of all organizations which are under common ownership and control in that they respond to a single set of decisions. Such a separation is probably easiest to justify in the allocation of the Federal Reserve System (as well as other federal monetary funds) to the monetary sector rather than to the federal government sector. More doubtful is the separation of the insurance and pension funds, administered as trustee by the federal, state, and local governments, from the other activities of these governments, and their allocation to the financial sector. In this case the nature of the operations and the identifiability of the beneficiaries were regarded as justifying a violation of the rule against separating the activities of one decision-making unit. The same considerations might have justified separating some of the business-type enterprises of governments and their allocation to the business sector. Such a separation was, however, foregone, first because of the great difficulty in segregating the assets and transactions connected with these activities, and, secondly, because the management of these activities was less independent of the other activities of the government owners.

SECTORING

In grouping sixty million economic units into the limited number of sectors that can be accommodated within a system of social accounts and for which sufficiently reliable annual data are available, we are theoretically guided by the principle of homogeneity. This principle instructs us, first, to combine in one sector all those units which are similar in behavior, in this case similar in their asset and liability structure and in their reactions to capital market developments. It instructs us, secondly, not to divide assets or transactions under the control of one decision-making unit among two or more sectors. The two instructions unfortunately sometimes conflict in the real world and a choice must be made, often rather arbitrarily. As already indicated in the previous section, the first instruction has been regarded as overriding for nonfarm enterprises and government financial institutions, while the second has prevailed for agriculture and government nonfinancial enterprises. Consequently no distinction has been made between assets and transactions of a business type and those of a household or government type for agriculture and government nonfinancial enterprises, respectively. On the other hand, the business-type assets and transactions of nonagricultural unincorporated enterprises and of government financial institutions have been separated from those of their owners, with only the difference between business-type assets and liabilities (or between investment in and withdrawals from business) shown in the owners' balance sheet or flow-of-funds statement. The framework is, however, flexible enough to let users who disagree with these decisions adopt a treatment more in line with their preferences.

The statistics contained in the basic tables make it possible to treat agriculture in the same way as unincorporated business, i.e., as an intermediary. This means including in the flow-of-funds statement and the balance sheet of agriculture only those items that are connected with business operations, while regarding the net worth in the balance sheet as an asset of the owners and transferring it to the nonfarm household sector, together with the holdings of, and the transactions in, consumer-type assets of agriculture. These assets—farm homes, consumer durables, life insurance, time deposits and U.S. sav-

49

ings bonds—are now included in the balance sheet or the flow-of-funds statement of agriculture.

We may also go to the other extreme and combine the assets and transactions of the agriculture and unincorporated business sectors with the nonfarm household sector on the grounds that all three sectors are owned and operated by individuals and that any separation of their household and business activities is artificial. In that process, the net worth of nonfarm unincorporated business enterprises disappears, an item that is now shown separately on the right-hand side of the balance sheet of unincorporated business and on the left-hand side of that of nonfarm households.

Table 7 shows the effects of these alternative treatments of agricul-

TABLE 7

EFFECTS OF ALTERNATIVE TREATMENT OF UNINCORPORATED FARM AND NONFARM
BUSINESS, 1945 AND 1958
(billion dollars)

|  |  | 1945 | | | 1958 | | |
|---|---|---|---|---|---|---|---|
|  |  | A | B | C | A | B | C |
|  | **TOTAL ASSETS** | | | | | | |
| 1. | Nonfarm households | 739 | 623 | 720 | 1,851 | 1,602 | 1,789 |
| 2. | Nonfarm unincorporated business | 0 | 53 | 53 | 0 | 138 | 138 |
| 3. | Agriculture | 0 | 104 | 86[a] | 0 | 208 | 165[a] |
| 4. | All households (1+2+3) | 739 | 780 | 859 | 1,851 | 1,948 | 2,092 |
| 5. | Nonfinancial corporations | 251 | 251 | 251 | 766 | 766 | 766 |
| 6. | All nonfinancial business (2+3+5) | 251 | 408 | 390 | 766 | 1,112 | 1,069 |
| 7. | National assets | 1,491 | 1,533 | 1,611 | 3,640 | 3,735 | 3,881 |
|  | **TOTAL NET WORTH** | | | | | | |
| 1. | Nonfarm households | 689 | 592 | 689 | 1,613 | 1,426 | 1,614 |
| 2. | Nonfarm unincorporated business | 0 | 41 | 41 | 0 | 97 | 97 |
| 3. | Agriculture | 0 | 97 | 79[a] | 0 | 187 | 144[a] |
| 4. | All households (1+2+3) | 689 | 730 | 809 | 1,613 | 1,710 | 1,855 |
| 5. | Nonfinancial corporations | 163 | 163 | 163 | 508 | 508 | 508 |
| 6. | All nonfinancial business (2+3+5) | 163 | 301 | 283 | 508 | 792 | 749 |
| 7. | National net worth | 714 | 755 | 834 | 2,150 | 2,247 | 2,392 |

Source: <u>National Balance Sheet</u>, Vol. II, Table I.

A = both farm and nonfarm business treated as unsegregated part of the activities of nonfarm households.

B = agriculture treated as an ultimate sector and nonfarm business as an intermediate sector. (Same treatment as in basic tables.)

C = both farm and nonfarm business treated as intermediate sectors, the net worth of which is included among the assets of nonfarm households.

[a]Residences, consumer durables, saving deposits, and life insurance reserves of agriculture shifted from line 3 to line 1.

ture and unincorporated business on the assets and total net worth of these three sectors and on the national totals for 1945 and 1958. The flow-of-funds statements of these three sectors, and particularly the calculation of their saving, would be affected similarly by this alternative treatment.

The detailed basic tables also permit transfer of government pension and trust funds from the finance to the government sector. Data are not sufficient for the reverse operation, i.e., the transfer of other government enterprises to the finance and nonfinancial business sectors.

The actual sectoring adopted in this report is a compromise based on the availability of sufficiently reliable annual data throughout the postwar period and the desire to maintain as much continuity and comparability as possible with related bodies of data, primarily the Federal Reserve Board's flow-of-funds statistics, the saving statistics of the Securities and Exchange Commission, the long-range series of *A Study of Saving in the United States*,[5] and the balance sheets of *Financial Intermediaries in the American Economy since 1900*.[6] As a result, the following seven main sectors were distinguished, which means that separate balance sheets and flow-of-funds statements were prepared for each of them for each year:

Nonfarm households
Unincorporated nonfarm business enterprises
Agriculture
Nonfinancial corporations
Financial enterprises
State and local governments
Federal government

In a framework designed specifically for the analysis of the capital market and hence intended to provide as much information as possible on the participants and the transactions in the various segments of that market, sectoring must be more detailed in fields in which capital market activities are concentrated. For this reason, the finance sector, which includes all institutions closely associated with the capital market, was divided into the following subsectors, for which annual balance sheets and flow-of-funds statements were provided:

[5] By Raymond W. Goldsmith, Princeton, 1956.
[6] By Raymond W. Goldsmith, Princeton for NBER, 1958.

Monetary institutions
   Federal Reserve banks and Treasury monetary funds
   Check banks [7]

Nonmonetary depositary institutions
   Credit banks [7]
   Mutual savings banks
   Saving and loan associations
   Credit unions

Insurance and pension funds
   Life insurance companies
   Noninsured pension plans
   Fire and casualty insurance companies
   Other private insurance companies
   Federal government pensions and retirement funds
   State and local government pensions and retirement funds

Other financial institutions
   Investment companies
   Finance companies
   Common trust funds
   Other financial institutions [8]

The main shortcomings of the sectoring used in this report from the point of view of capital market analysis are: (1) the inclusion of

[7] No separate figures exist for "check banks" and "credit banks" since commercial banks do not report separately on these two main activities. Such figures could be derived by allocating demand deposits to "check banks" and time deposits to "credit banks" and matching these deposits with assets from among those held by commercial banks. This theoretically very important and desirable separation could not be made with the resources available for this study.

[8] It may be argued quite cogently that the personal trust departments of commercial banks should also be included in the financial institutions sector. This was not done because there are no reliable figures available before 1959 for the value and composition of personal trust funds administered by these departments. Personal trust funds were, therefore, implicitly included in the holdings of nonfarm households. Rough estimates of the size of personal trust funds administered by commercial banks are, however, shown in *National Balance Sheet*, Volume II, Table III-1a. It is thus possible to shift these funds from the nonfarm household to the financial sector if one is willing to accept the estimates. The amounts involved in such a shift are not negligible—the personal trust departments administered about $50 billion worth of assets in 1959—and are particularly important in comparison to the total holdings in nonfarm households in the case of tax-exempt securities and of corporate stock.

nonprofit organizations in the nonfarm household sector; (2) the lack of separation of the more than fifty million nonfarm households into at least a few groups based on size of assets, net worth, or other characteristics significant for their capital market behavior such as homeowners and renters; (3) the impossibility of separating the holdings and activities of owner operators, absentee owners, and tenants in agriculture; (4) the failure to provide separate balance sheets and flow-of-funds statements for at least the main groups of nonfinancial corporations, such as manufacturing and mining, public utility, trade, services, and real estate, and for closely held (mostly small) and publicly held and financed (mostly large) corporations; and (5) the failure to separate the assets and transactions of business-type activities of the federal, state, and local governments.

Of these shortcomings, the first was partly remedied by providing a rough balance sheet of nonprofit organizations for a few benchmark dates. Since total assets of these organizations now amount to only about 6 per cent of those of nonfarm households, the failure to segregate them obviously is not likely to obscure the activities of nonfarm households, except possibly for a few types of financial assets such as Treasury securities other than savings bonds. Separate flow-of-funds statements for half a dozen groups of nonfinancial groups until 1956 may be found in a monograph being prepared by Eli Shapiro on "The Postwar Market for Corporate Securities and Loans," which forms part of the Postwar Capital Market Study. The material to remedy shortcomings (2), (3), and (5) is not yet at hand. The only thing that could be done would be to separate, on the basis of estate tax returns, the balance sheet of nonfarm households with assets of more than $60,000 for a few benchmark dates.[9]

### DEGREE OF NETNESS

Flow-of-funds statements and balance sheets can be drawn up at different degrees of grossness and netness. Three aspects of this difference are relevant in the statistical framework for capital market analysis: first, the use of net sales and purchase balances in lieu of separate figures for purchase and sales flows; second, the offsetting of liabilities against the assets with which they are connected; third, the

---

[9] Estimates are available, as yet, only for 1953 (Robert J. Lampman, *The Share of Top Wealth-Holders in National Wealth, 1922–56,* Princeton for NBER, 1962), and they would require further study before being fitted into the framework.

degree to which units are consolidated rather than combined in constructing balance sheets or flow-of-funds statements for sectors and subsectors.

In principle, separation of a sector's purchase and sales flows for a given capital market instrument is much to be preferred to the use of only the undivided net purchase or sales balance. Use of the net basis washes out many relevant transactions and makes it much more difficult to explain the movements of net balances as well as of interest rates.[10] Unfortunately, however, separate figures on purchase and sales flows are available only for a few capital market instruments —sales and retirement of corporate securities by their issuers, primary transactions (i.e., borrowing and repayment) in residential mortgages, and incurrence and repayment of consumer debt—and even for these not for all sectors. For this reason all the basic tables in this report are drawn up on a net basis, as is unavoidable when flows must be obtained as first differences of stocks. (In analyzing the individual sectors of the capital market, however, use can be made of data on gross purchase and sales flows whenever they are available.)

In principle, liabilities are not netted against assets with which they may be regarded as connected. Thus policy loans are not deducted from policyholders' equity, or individuals' borrowing on common stock from their holdings of common stock. Similarly, an attempt is made to avoid offsetting a sector's accounts payable against its accounts receivable, except in a few cases where the material is available only in the form of the net excess of receivables or payables. It is obvious that offsets of this type greatly diminish the value of flow data for capital market analysis since the movements in the minuend and subtrahend may differ substantially and may depend on quite different factors.

---

[10] Home mortgages may be used as an example. The net flow of home mortgages is the result of new loans made and repayments on old loans among which, in turn, two flows may be distinguished: regular (scheduled) amortizations and unscheduled prepayments. While new loans are subject to substantial cyclical and other fluctuations, repayments follow a much more regular course, particularly amortization payments. Obviously much less information on the modus operandi of this segment of the capital market can be obtained if we are limited to one net flow series, which is the result of three heterogeneous gross flows, than from the three or more gross flow series themselves. It would be desirable to analyze separately the series on new loans made, scheduled amortizations, and nonscheduled prepayments, further distinguishing, if possible, flows to and from the main types of financial institutions, and connecting the movements in these series with explanatory variables specifically applicable to them.

54

In accordance with the principles discussed in the section on coverage above, sectoral balance sheets are gross in that they are the aggregation of the separate balance sheets of all units in the sector without elimination of claims and liabilities, or equity security holdings and issuance, among units that belong to the same sector. Similarly, the national balance sheet or flow-of-funds statement is simply the sum of those for all separate sectors. The use of consolidated rather than combined statements for parents and subsidiaries in the corporate business sector cannot be regarded as an exception since subsidiaries are not independent economic entities in the sense of constituting separate decision-making units. The same argument applies to the consolidation of the accounts of all federal government agencies, insofar as they are left in the federal government sector and not transferred to the financial institution sector.

## Unit Equations

### BASIC RELATIONS

The stocks and flows of any economic unit that are relevant for the operation and analysis of the capital market can be summarized in three basic expressions: a balance-sheet equation and two forms of a sources-and-uses-of-funds equation. The balance-sheet equation expresses the equality between the sums of all assets, on the one hand, and of all liabilities and net worth, on the other. This expression is an identity which holds under all circumstances (even if varying and inconsistent methods of valuation are used for different assets and liabilities) as long as net worth is defined as the difference between the book value of assets and that of liabilities.

The sources-and-uses-of-funds equation has two forms because a flow can be visualized either as a transfer of an asset (including money) or as the difference in the stock before and after the transfer. In its first (flow) form it reflects the necessary equality of the sum of all sources and all uses of funds, both of which may be limited to cash flows or enlarged by imputed items to serve the purposes of analysis. More specifically, it asserts that the sum of saving (the excess of current income over current expenditure), borrowing, receipts on account of repayments, issuance of equity securities, and sale of assets, on the one hand, equals the sum of lending, repayments, increase in holding of money, purchase of new equity securities, acquisition of existing assets, and capital expenditures, on the other.[11] The flow version of the sources-and-uses-of-funds equation, expressed above in gross terms, can also be presented in net form. In that case, the left-hand side contains, in one of several possible arrangements, saving, net borrow-

TABLE 8

RELATION OF NET FLOW TO CHANGE IN HOLDINGS: ILLUSTRATIVE EXAMPLE

| Item | Number of Units (1) | Original Cost to Owner (2) | Book Value to Owner (3) | Market Value (4) |
|---|---|---|---|---|
| 1. Holdings, beginning of period | 100 | 150 | 200 | 300 |
| 2. Purchases during period | 30 | 100 | 100 | 100 |
| 3. Sales during period, FIFO | 15 | 23 | 30 | 55 |
| 4. Sales during period, LIFO | 15 | 50 | 50 | 55 |
| 5. Net purchases during period, FIFO | 15 | 77 | 70 | 45 |
| 6. Net purchases during period, LIFO | 15 | 50 | 50 | 45 |
| 7. Write-ups | | 0 | 20 | 0 |
| 8. Holdings, end of period, FIFO | 115 | 227 | 290 | 460 |
| 9. Holdings, end of period, LIFO | 115 | 200 | 270 | 460 |
| 10. Change in holdings, FIFO | 15 | 77 | 90 | 160 |
| 11. Change in holdings, LIFO | 15 | 50 | 70 | 160 |
| 12. Realized capital gains, FIFO | | 32 | 25 | 25 |
| 13. Realized capital gains, LIFO | | 5 | 5 | 5 |
| 14. Unrealized appreciation, beginning of period, FIFO | | 150 | 100 | 100 |
| 15. Unrealized appreciation, end of period, FIFO | | 233 | 190 | 190 |
| 16. Unrealized appreciation, end of period, LIFO | | 260 | 210 | 210 |
| 17. Change in unrealized appreciation, LIFO | | 83 | 90 | 90 |
| 18. Change in unrealized appreciation, FIFO | | 110 | 110 | 110 |
| 19. Flow | 15[a] | 45[b] | 45[c] | 45[d] |

[a] Line 6.

[b] Lines 10 minus 12 (or 11 minus 13).

[c] Lines 10 minus 12 minus 7 (or 11 minus 13 minus 7).

[d] Lines 10 minus 12 minus 17 (or 10 minus 13 minus 18).

ing (borrowing less repayments made), and net issuance of equity securities, while the right-hand side shows net lending (lending less repayments received), increase in holding of money, net acquisition of existing assets (purchasing less sales), and capital expenditures.

In the second (change-of-holding or balance-sheet-differential) form,

[11] If net transfers (receipts and outlays without economic counter-value such as gifts, bequests, and inheritances) are not included in saving, a separate item must be added on both sides to those listed above.

exactly the same items appear on both sides as in the flow form. However, all items are now expressed as first differences between the value
of holdings at the beginning and at the end of the period. They are,
therefore, equivalent to net flows rather than gross flows. The values
that are required to make this form equivalent to the flow form are
not the unadjusted first differences, which are obtained by subtracting
the book value at the beginning of the period from that at the end.
To fit the equation, the unadjusted first differences must be adjusted
for those changes in book value which reflect realized capital gains
and losses or other valuation changes (write-ups and write-downs) that
have occurred during the period. Specifically, the difference in book
(original cost) values must be diminished by net capital gains realized
during the period (or increased by realized capital losses) and by write-
ups (or increased by write-downs) to become equal to the net purchase
balance, i.e., the excess of the cash value of purchases over that of sales.
In cases where balance-sheet valuations are based on current market
prices rather than on book values, allowance must also be made for
the change in unrealized capital gains or losses. The equation then
becomes: net purchase balance equals difference in market value of
holdings minus realized net capital gains minus net write-ups minus
net increase in unrealized capital gains.[12] These relationships are illustrated in a simple numerical example in Table 8, which also shows
that the equation is valid irrespective of the method of valuing sales,
particularly for both FIFO and LIFO accounting for inventories.

### EXPLANATION OF SYMBOLS

The relationships just described can be expressed more precisely and
more clearly when translated into simple algebraic symbols. All flows
are indicated by small letters and all stocks by capital letters, while
small Greek letters are used to indicate ratios, and bars or dots above
the symbols differentiate between alternative bases of valuation of
stocks and flows. Subscripts, in the form of small letters to the right
of the symbol, identify the two parties that take part in a transaction,
the first subscript representing the seller or debtor (issuer) and the
second the buyer or holder (creditor). In the case of internal transactions, such as saving or capital consumption allowances, the two subscripts are identical. Similarly, in the case of tangible assets and net

---

[12] All capital gains, realized and unrealized, and valuation changes are calculated
on the basis of book values.

worth in the balance sheet, the subscript identifying the owner is repeated.

For simplicity and to preserve a fairly close connection with the statistics actually used in the body of the report, only seven sectors are distinguished: nonfarm households $(h)$; business $(b)$, comprising nonfinancial corporations, unincorporated nonfarm enterprises, and agriculture; monetary institutions $(m)$; other financial institutions $(f)$; state and local governments $(l)$; federal government $(t)$; and the rest of the world $(x)$.

It is more difficult to reduce the numerous types of assets distinguished in the statistics to a number that is small enough to keep the formulae from becoming unwieldy but still preserves the essential economic differences. Similar problems arise in limiting the number of types of transactions to be distinguished symbolically. By way of compromise, the symbols used have been reduced to just over a dozen,

TABLE 9

SYMBOLS FOR ITEMS IN BASIC CAPITAL MARKET EQUATIONS

| | Flow* | | | Stock** |
| Item | Purchase (1) | Sale (2) | Net (3) | (4) |
|---|---|---|---|---|
| 1. Saving, gross | -- | $s + d$ | -- | $S + D$ |
| 2. Saving, net | $-\bar{r}^b$ | -- | $s$ | $S$ |
| 3. Borrowing | $r$ | $b + {}_\ell r^h$ | $b$ | $B$ |
| 4. Lending | $1 + r^\ell$ | $r$ | $\ell$ | $\dagger$ |
| 5. Cash transactions | $-m$ | $+m$ | $m$ | $M$ |
| 6. Issuance of money | $r^n$ | $n + {}_e r^n$ | $n$ | $N$ |
| 7. Acquisition of new equity securities | $e + {}_i r^e$ | $r$ | $e$ | $\dagger$ |
| 8. Issuance of equity securities | $r^i$ | $i + r^i$ | $i$ | $I$ |
| 9. Existing financial assets | -- | -- | $f$ | $F$ |
| 10. New capital expenditures | $k$ | -- | $k - d^k$ | $K - D^k$ |
| 11. Capital consumption allowances | -- | -- | $d$ | $D$ |
| 12. Existing tangible assets | -- | -- | $j$ | $T - D$ |
| 13. Realized capital gains and losses | -- | -- | $g$ | -- |
| 14. Unrealized capital gains and losses | -- | -- | $v$ | $V$ |
| 15. Foreign assets | -- | -- | $x$ | $X$ |

*Flows include accounting accruals.
**Stock net of capital consumption but gross of valuation changes unless contrary specifically indicated. Stocks (at market) are *not* equal to sum of flows.
†Holdings of newly acquired loans and equities are included in F (line 9, col. 4).
Lines 1-2, col. 4: Earned surplus.
Lines 3,4,7,8: Transactions in which original lender or borrower (issuer) is involved.
Lines 4,5,7,9,12, col. 4: On asset side of balance sheet.
Lines 4,7,9,12, col. 4: In the balance sheet no distinction is made between assets acquired during accounting period and those held at start of period.
Line 14, col. 4: Unrealized net appreciation.
Line 15, col. 4: Net foreign balance (foreign assets minus liabilities to foreigners).

which are brought together for easy reference in Table 9. A few additional symbols which occur rarely are explained when first used.

### FLOW EQUATIONS

We may then start by expressing in these symbols the first of the four forms of the basic flow-of-funds equation. This may be called the un-identified flow form because it does not identify the other unit (or group of units) which participates in the transaction or, in the case of stocks, acts as creditor (holder) or debtor (issuer). The equation uses net flows for financial assets, $f$, and existing tangible assets, $j$, because the statistical data are predominantly in this form, but for the same reason uses gross flows for capital expenditures. The equation [13] then is for any unit $j$:

$$\underbrace{k_j + j_j + l_j + m_j + e_j + f_j + x_j}_{\text{Uses}} = \underbrace{\underbrace{s_j + d_j}_{\text{Internal}} + \underbrace{b_j + n_j + i_j}_{\text{External}}}_{\text{Sources}}. \tag{1}$$

For any given unit or period, some of the items may, of course, be equal to zero, either because no transaction of the indicated type has occurred, or because acquisitions and dispositions happened to be equal. The equality is obviously unaffected if saving and capital expenditures are expressed in net instead of gross form, since this simply means substitution of $s$ for $(s + d)$ on the right and of $(k - d)$ for $k$ on the left side.

Equation (1) yields, by a slight readjustment, the formula for one of the two basic estimates of saving, viz., saving calculated from changes in assets and liabilities, the method used by the Securities and Exchange Commission, by the Federal Reserve Board, and in *A Study of Saving:*

$$s_j = (l_j - b_j) + (e_j - i_j) + (m_j - n_j) + f_j + (k_j - d_j) + j_j + x_j. \tag{1a}$$

Another rearrangement, more relevant to capital market analysis, leads to

---

[13] Reversing predominant practice, uses are shown on the left and sources on the right side of the equation, in order to preserve the parallelism between flows and stocks, assets (cumulated uses) being traditionally shown on the left—at least in the United States—and liabilities and net worth (cumulated sources) on the right side of the balance sheet.

$$s_j = \underbrace{(l_j + m_j + e_j + f_j + x_j')}_{\substack{\text{Gross saving} \\ \text{through} \\ \text{financial assets}}} - \underbrace{(b_j + n_j + i_j)}_{\text{Borrowing}} + \underbrace{(k_j + j_j)}_{\substack{\text{Gross saving} \\ \text{through} \\ \text{tangibles}}} - d_j. \quad \text{(1b)}$$

$$\underbrace{\phantom{xxxxxxxxxxxxxxxxxxxxxxxxxxxxxxxxxxxx}}_{\substack{\text{Net saving through} \\ \text{financial assets}}} \quad \underbrace{\phantom{xxxxxxxxxx}}_{\substack{\text{Net saving} \\ \text{through} \\ \text{tangible assets}}}$$

$$\underbrace{\phantom{xxxxxxxxxxxxxxxxxxxxxxxxxxxxxxxxxxxxxxxxxxxxxxxx}}_{\text{Total net saving}}$$

If the other party to the transaction, or the sector to which the other party belongs, is identified, we obtain the second form of the equation, the identified flow form. Even when only seven sectors are distinguished, the equation becomes unwieldly in its general form. In actual application, many of the terms of the equation, of course, are equal to zero and disappear for a given unit and period. Equation (2), which is written in a form that applies to any individual unit in any of the seven sectors, is based on reasonable assumptions about such eliminations.

$$
\left.
\begin{aligned}
& k_{hj} + k_{bj} + k_{mj} + k_{xj} \\
& + l_{hj} + l_{bj} + l_{mj} + l_{fj} + l_{lj} + l_{tj} + l_{xj} \\
& + m_{mj} \\
& + c_{bj} + c_{mj} + c_{fj} + c_{xj} \\
& + f_{hj} + f_{bj} + f_{mj} + f_{fj} + f_{lj} + f_{tj} + f_{xj} \\
& + j_{hj} + j_{bj} + j_{mj} + j_{fj} + j_{lj} + j_{tj} + j_{xj} \\
& + x_{hj} + x_{bj} + x_{mj} + x_{fj} + x_{lj} + x_{tj}
\end{aligned}
\right\} =
$$

$$
\left[
\begin{aligned}
& (s + d)_{jj} \\
& + b_{jh} + b_{jb} + b_{jm} + b_{jf} + b_{jl} + b_{jt} + b_{jx} \\
& + n_{jh} + n_{jb} + n_{jm} + n_{jf} + n_{jl} + n_{jt} + n_{jx} \\
& + i_{jh} + i_{jb} + i_{jm} + i_{jf} + i_{jx}
\end{aligned}
\right.
$$

$$\quad (2)$$

In equation (2), $k_{fj}$, $k_{lj}$, and $k_{tj}$ are assumed to be zero since capital expenditures usually consist of purchases from business, households or foreigners but not from other sectors. Similarly the $e$ items can be limited to business sectors—nonfinancial business ($b$), financial institutions ($f$), monetary organizations ($m$), and foreigners ($x$)—as there are no transferable equities in the three household and government sectors.

In the case of money, the net increase in holdings is treated as limited to one partner—monetary organizations. This treatment deviates from the usual procedure of designating the immediate partner in a transaction by the second subscript. In other words, money flows are treated with a higher degree of netness. The $n$ (issuance of money) line, of course, is applicable only to monetary institutions and disappears for all other units which by definition are not in a position to issue money

### CHANGE OF HOLDING EQUATIONS

Before turning to the two alternative forms of the basic equation in which flows during a period are represented by changes in stocks between the beginning and the end of the period, it is necessary to introduce the balance-sheet equation initially in its unidentified form because of the importance it has in its own right in capital market analysis and because it is the fount of the second form of the flow equation.

$$T_j - D_j + M_j + F_j + X_j = B_j + N_j + I_j + S_j \qquad (3)$$

As long as $S$ (surplus) is treated as a residual, the other terms in the equations may use any basis of valuation, even inconsistent ones. Where, as is common in business accounting, all terms are on an original cost basis and no revaluations have taken place, $S$ is equal to earned net worth understood as the sum of past saving (both, however, including net realized capital gains), while $I$ is equal to the sum of contributed capital at original values. If all other terms reflect market or replacement values, then $S$ is no longer equal to accumulated saving (current income less current expenditures), but includes all realized and unrealized net capital gains.

The equation is written in the net unidentified form. In the gross form, $T$ would be substituted for $(T - D)$ and $(S + D)$ for $S$. Other terms remain unchanged.

The unidentified change-of-holdings form of the basic equation then becomes equation (4), if we use book values throughout and gross values in the case of tangible assets and keep in mind that if assets are carried at book value the change in holdings must be diminished by net realized capital gains and net write-ups to yield the net purchase balance of the flow form.[14]

---

[14] In case assets are carried at market value, the reported change in holdings must also be adjusted for the change in the net unrealized appreciation in order to equal the net purchase balance of the flow form.

$$\left.\begin{array}{l} \Delta T_j - g^j{}_j - v^j{}_j) + (\Delta F_j - g^f{}_j - v^f{}_j) \\ + \Delta M_j + (\Delta X_j - g^x{}_j - v^x{}_j) \end{array}\right\}$$

$$= \left[\begin{array}{l} (\Delta S_j - g^s{}_j - v^s{}_j) + (\Delta D_j - g^d{}_j - v^d{}_j) \\ + (\Delta B_j - g^b{}_j - v^b{}_j) \\ + \Delta N_j + (\Delta I_j - g^i{}_j - v^i{}_j) \end{array}\right. \tag{4}$$

In the identified change-of-holdings form, the subscript for the other party to the transaction usually identifies the ultimate issuer or debtor instead of, as the rules require and as shown in equation (2) for the identified flow form, the party from whom the asset was acquired or to whom it was sold. For instance, a change in holdings of Treasury securities by life insurance companies is indicated by $\Delta F^t{}_{ft}$, irrespective of the sector from whom the Treasury securities were bought or to whom they were sold.[15] The reason for this deviation from the rule, of course, is the near impossibility of obtaining the required data.

It is possible, however, to set up an identified change-of-holdings form in an alternative way which identifies the immediate partner in the transaction. In that case, to keep to the example just used, net transactions in Treasury securities by life insurance companies with each other sector are entered as a separate item. Then $\Delta F^t{}_{hf}$, for instance, identifies the net purchase of Treasury securities by financial institutions from nonfarm households.[16] Since the statistical data are practically never available in this detail, this form is not yet in general use, nor would it be of much value unless separate figures for purchases and sales were available, in which case the gross flow rather than any variant of the change-of-holding form of the equation is needed.

For those instruments in which transactions in existing stock are absent, limited to transactions between issuer and different holder groups, or of negligible size, there is no difference between the two versions of the identified change-of-holdings form of the flow equation. These conditions are practically met for instruments like mortgages and trade debt, but are most conspicuously inapplicable to marketable securities and money.

Realized and unrealized capital gains and valuation adjustments

[15] The right-hand superscript $t$ is used to distinguish transactions in outstanding Treasury securities from those in other outstanding financial assets.

[16] This form practically requires separation of all main types of financial assets by type of issuer. Thus Treasury securities would be treated as a separate category ($G$) and the expression would become $\Delta G_{jh}$.

(write-ups and write-downs), being internal accounting items, are identified by doubling the subscript of the affected unit and by a right-hand superscript indicating the type of asset involved. Thus $g^e{}_{hh}$ is a symbol for net capital gains on corporate stock realized by households.

The identified change-of-holdings form [17] of the basic equation then becomes for any unit $j$ in the gross version which includes $D_{jj}$:

$$
\begin{aligned}
(\Delta T_{jj} - g^j{}_j - v^j{}_{jj}) & \\
+ (\Delta F_{hj} + \cdots + \Delta F_{xj} - g^f{}_{jj} - v^f{}_{jj}) & \\
+ (\Delta M_{hj} + \cdots + \Delta M_{xj}) & \\
+ (\Delta X_{hj} + \cdots + \Delta X_{tj} - g^x{}_{jj} - v^x{}_{jj}) & = \\
= (\Delta S_{jj} - g^s{}_{jj} - v^s{}_{jj}) & \quad\quad\quad (5)\\
+ (\Delta D_{jj} - g^d{}_{jj} - v^d{}_{jj}) & \\
+ (\Delta B_{jh} + \cdots + \Delta B_{jx} - g^b{}_{jj} - v^b{}_{jj}) & \\
+ (\Delta N_{jh} + \cdots + \Delta N_{jx}) & \\
+ (\Delta I_{jh} + \cdots + \Delta I_{jx} - g^i{}_{jj} - v^i{}_{jj}) &
\end{aligned}
$$

where $(F_{hj} + \cdots + F_{xj})$ and similar expressions are abbreviations of

$$(F_{hj} + F_{bj} + F_{fj} + F_{mj} + F_{lj} + F_{tj} + F_{xj}),$$

and realized capital gains or losses are lumped together in one term $(g_{jj})$ without identifying the other party involved in the transaction giving rise to the gains or losses.

## Sector Equations

Sector equations are simply the sum of the unit equations of all the units that belong to the sector, without elimination of intrasector transactions or holdings.

Sector equations also appear in four versions: the unidentified and the identified flow form and the unidentified and the identified change-of-holdings form. It is, therefore, unnecessary to repeat the

[17] It is thus assumed that the immediate partner in the transaction is identified. If the equation is based on the sector of the ultimate issuer or debtor, the number of terms is considerably reduced. In particular, the third line reduces to $M_{mj}$ on the left and $N_{jm}$ on the right side and the terms involving the subscripts $h$, $l$, and $t$ disappear in the fourth line.

four equations as they apply to sectors rather than to individual economic units. The only way in which they differ from the unit equations described in the preceding section is that, in the subscripts, sector symbols ($h$, $b$, etc.) are substituted for the subscript $j$, which was used in the preceding section to identify the unit in any sector for which the equations were drawn up.

## Market Equations

If the sectoral equations for all sectors are combined, a system is obtained from which it is possible to derive market equations for any

TABLE 10

REDUCED (UNIDENTIFIED) SEVEN-SECTOR MODEL OF CAPITAL MARKET, FLOW FORM

| Sector | Market |
|--------|--------|
| 1. | $l_h + e_h + m_h + j_h + k_h + f_h = (s+d)_h + b_h +$ |
| 2. | $l_b + e_b + m_b + j_b + k_b + f_b = (s+d)_b + b_b + \qquad i_b$ |
| 3. | $l_1 + e_1 + m_1 + j_1 + k_1 + f_1 = (s+d)_1 + b_1 +$ |
| 4. | $l_t + e_t + m_t + j_t + k_t + f_t = (s+d)_t + b_t +$ |
| 5. | $l_f + e_f + m_f + j_f + k_f + f_f = (s+d)_f + b_f + \qquad i_f$ |
| 6. | $l_m + e_m + m_m + j_m + k_m + f_m = (s+d)_m + b_m + n_m + i_m$ |
| 7. | $l_x + e_x + m_x + j_x + h_x + f_x = (s+d)_x + b_x + \qquad i_x$ |
| 8. | $\Sigma l + \Sigma e + \Sigma m + \Sigma j + \Sigma k + \Sigma f = \qquad \Sigma s + \Sigma b + \Sigma n + \Sigma i$ |

flow, i.e., any capital market instrument, that is separately represented in all the sector equations. The procedure is illustrated in Table 10, which is drawn up in the unidentified flow form. The same procedure can be applied when the unidentified change-of-holdings form is used although the table would be more complicated since, e.g., $(L_h - g^l{}_h - v^l{}_h)$ would replace $l_h$, etc.

The derivation of the market equations from the sector equations is based on the fact that all transactions between two domestic units appear twice with identical value in the sector equations, once in the equation of the sector for which the transaction constitutes a source of funds and again in the equation of the sector for which it represents a use of funds.

Thus the following market equation for new domestic lending can be derived from the reduced seven-sector model of Table 10.[18]

[18] If the equation is to cover all lending and borrowing and not only domestic lending and borrowing, terms must be added for lending to foreigners, i.e., bor-

$$l_h + l_b + l_m + l_f + l_i + l_t = b_h + b_b + b_m + b_f + b_i + b_t \qquad (6)$$

This equation is self-evident if it is recalled that each transaction appears once in the form of one sector's borrowing and again as lending by either the same or another sector. Exactly the same relationships obtain for money ($m$ item on the left-hand side and $n$ on the right-hand side of the equation) and for new equity securities ($e$ and $i$ items).

To be practically useful, the equations must generally be drawn up for capital market instruments of narrower scope, e.g., for new mortgage lending or even for new home mortgage lending, or for transactions in outstanding state and local government securities. The form and basic characteristics of the equation, however, are not affected by the lesser or greater number of flows, i.e., capital market instruments, or of sectors distinguished in the system of equations.

The derivation of market equations from the sector equations may become clearer when all items involving flows of the same type, i.e., all transactions in the same instrument, indicated by the symbol $j$, are brought together in an item flow matrix as is done in Table 11.

In practice, no item matrix will have all its cells filled since none of the assets and liabilities, except money, will in any given period show transactions between each pair of sectors—as well as within sectors —in the seven-sector model forty-nine pairs. Generally the narrower the scope of the item, the shorter the period covered, and the more imperfect the statistics, the larger is the proportion of cells remaining empty. Furthermore, when the matrix relates to transactions in new assets and liabilities (i.e., assets created during the period) rather than to transactions in existing (outstanding) assets and liabilities, it often shrinks to one column. The matrix for new corporate bonds, for instance, is necessarily reduced to one column, that representing the business sector.

Market equations for any given instrument reflect the obvious and necessary equality between the sum of all sales and that of all purchases since the transactions are registered at actual values. To preserve this feature, security transactions must be entered consistently either gross or net of commissions, brokerage fees, etc. If they are en-

---

rowing by foreigners ($b_x$), and for borrowing from foreigners ($l_x$). The equation, however, now no longer balances since $l_x \neq b_x$. To restore the balance, we must add a term for net lending or borrowing ($l_x - b_x$) on the appropriate side.

TABLE 11

ITEM FLOW MATRIX, SEVEN-SECTOR MODEL

| Buying Sector | Selling Sector | | | | | | | | |
|---|---|---|---|---|---|---|---|---|---|
| | h | b | f | m | l | t | d* | x | n** |
| h | $j_{hh}$ | $j_{bh}$ | $j_{fh}$ | $j_{mh}$ | $j_{lh}$ | $j_{th}$ | $j_{dh}$ | $j_{xh}$ | $j_{nh}$ |
| b | $j_{hb}$ | $j_{bb}$ | $j_{fb}$ | $j_{mb}$ | $j_{lb}$ | $j_{tb}$ | $j_{db}$ | $j_{xb}$ | $j_{nb}$ |
| f | $j_{hf}$ | $j_{bf}$ | $j_{ff}$ | $j_{mf}$ | $j_{lf}$ | $j_{tf}$ | $j_{df}$ | $j_{xf}$ | $j_{nf}$ |
| m | $j_{hm}$ | $j_{bm}$ | $j_{fm}$ | $j_{mm}$ | $j_{lm}$ | $j_{tm}$ | $j_{dm}$ | $j_{xm}$ | $j_{nm}$ |
| l | $j_{hl}$ | $j_{bl}$ | $j_{fl}$ | $j_{ml}$ | $j_{ll}$ | $j_{tl}$ | $j_{dl}$ | $j_{xl}$ | $j_{nl}$ |
| t | $j_{ht}$ | $j_{bt}$ | $j_{ft}$ | $j_{mt}$ | $j_{lt}$ | $j_{tt}^{\dagger}$ | $j_{dt}$ | $j_{xt}$ | $j_{nt}$ |
| d* | $j_{hd}$ | $j_{bd}$ | $j_{fd}$ | $j_{md}$ | $j_{ld}$ | $j_{td}$ | $j_{dd}$ | $j_{xd}$ | $j_{nd}$ |
| x | $j_{hx}$ | $j_{bx}$ | $j_{fx}$ | $j_{mx}$ | $j_{lx}$ | $j_{tx}$ | $j_{dx}$ | -- | -- |
| n** | $j_{hn}$ | $j_{bn}$ | $j_{fn}$ | $j_{mn}$ | $j_{ln}$ | $j_{tn}$ | $j_{dn}$ | -- | $j_{nn}$ |

*All domestic sectors.
**All sectors.
†Empty if all Treasury accounts consolidated.

tered on a net basis, the commissions, etc., are regarded as part of the current income of the sectors providing the service and part of the current expenditure of the sectors acquiring or disposing of the asset. If a gross basis is adopted, commissions, etc., must be treated as capitalizable expenditures and become part of investment in the national accounts.[19]

For illustration, the market equation for new home mortgages made and incurred (symbols $b^h$ and $l^h$ respectively) is shown in flow form, on the fairly realistic assumption that all borrowers belong to the household or unincorporated business sectors while all lenders are part of the household, business, financial, or monetary institutions sectors.

$$\left. \begin{array}{l} l^h{}_{hh} + l^h{}_{hb} + l^h{}_{hf} + l^h{}_{hm} \\ + l^h{}_{bh} + l^h{}_{bb} + l^h{}_{bf} + l^h{}_{bm} \end{array} \right\} = \left\{ \begin{array}{l} b^h{}_{hh} + b^h{}_{hb} + b^h{}_{nf} + b^h{}_{hm} \\ + b^h{}_{bh} + b^h{}_{bb} + b^h{}_{bf} + b^h{}_{bm} \end{array} \right. \quad (7)$$

If repayments are included in the equation, because the equation covers all direct transactions between mortgagors and mortgagees, and

[19] Cf. *A Study of Saving*, Vol. II, pp. 59–62.

repayments are indicated separately, the number of terms in the equation is doubled since in principle there is an $r^h$ corresponding to each $b^h$ and $l^h$. All the basic features of the equation, however, remain unchanged.

It may be worthwhile to return briefly to the last line of Table 10 which is the sum of all sector equations. This line indicates that

$$\Sigma l + \Sigma m + \Sigma e + \Sigma j + \Sigma k + \Sigma f = \Sigma(s + d) + \Sigma b + \Sigma n + \Sigma i. \quad (8)$$

Now on a national basis obviously: (a) $\Sigma l = \Sigma b$; (b) $\Sigma m = \Sigma n$; (c) $\Sigma e = \Sigma i$; (d) $\Sigma j = 0$.

Thus line 8 of Table 10 reduces to $\Sigma k + \Sigma f = \Sigma(s + d)$, where $\Sigma k$ includes $\Sigma x$. In other words, the sum of the saving of all units within the national territory is equal to the sum of capital expenditures and foreign balance. The equation can, of course, be drawn up either on a gross or a net basis, the difference being the deduction from both sides of the sum of capital consumption allowances ($\Sigma d$).

The four identities (a) to (d) that were eliminated in consolidating the sector accounts into the final equation $\Sigma k + \Sigma f = \Sigma(s + d)$ represent the market equations for new domestic lending, money, new equity securities, and outstanding assets, respectively. If more types of new and existing assets had been distinguished, the number of terms in each sectoral equation would be larger. So would be the number of identities of the type (a) to (d), and hence the number of market equations. Nothing, however, would be changed in principle, and the final consolidated capital market equation would be the same as before, namely $\Sigma k + \Sigma f = \Sigma(s + d)$.

Exactly the same procedure can be applied to the change-of-holdings form of the equations. In this case we shall end up with a parallel to line 8 in Table 10 in the form:

$$\left.\begin{array}{l}\Sigma\Delta M + \Sigma\Delta F + \Sigma\Delta T \\ + \Sigma\Delta X - \Sigma g - \Sigma v\end{array}\right\} = \left\{\begin{array}{l}\Sigma\Delta S + \Sigma\Delta D - \Sigma g - \Sigma v + \Sigma\Delta B \\ + \Sigma\Delta N + \Sigma\Delta I.\end{array}\right. \quad (8a)$$

If we eliminate those items on both sides that are necessarily equal, because they represent the two sides of the same relation, (8a) is reduced to

$$\Sigma\Delta T + \Sigma\Delta X = \Sigma\Delta S + \Sigma\Delta D \quad (8b)$$

on a gross basis, and on a net basis to

$$\Sigma\Delta T - \Sigma\Delta D + \Sigma\Delta X = \Sigma\Delta S. \quad (8c)$$

## Implementation of Framework

Since the framework of the unit, sector, and market equations was drawn up with the statistics actually used in this report in mind, the question of implementation, i.e., of substituting numbers for the symbols in the equations, can be dealt with briefly.

The statistical material now available, taken for financial assets primarily from the Federal Reserve Board's flow-of-funds statistics and for tangible assets from the National Bureau's Postwar Capital Market Study, makes it possible to implement the equations for the seven sectors annually for 1946–58 in somewhat greater item detail than in the preceding sections. This implementation is briefly described in the section on the actual framework. Material is also available to implement sector equations quarterly from 1953 on, although somewhat more roughly, by using the Federal Reserve Board's flow-of-funds tabulations.[20] These quarterly figures, however, have not been used in this report chiefly because resources were not available to extend the data back to at least 1950 to bring them in line with the annual data, primarily by the addition of transactions in tangible assets, and to adjust the quarterly data for seasonal variations.

It is thus possible to draw up market equations annually from 1946 through 1958. The tables in Section VIII of Volume II of *National Balance Sheet* provide all the necessary basic data by showing for each year net purchases or sales by each of the seven main sectors and by the subsectors of the financial sector.

The sector or market equations that can be derived from the statistics now available fail, however, to meet the conceptual requirements of the framework on a number of points, some of which are important for analysis of the capital market and some of which are not.

First, the equations constitute a hybrid combination of equations in change-of-holdings form for claims and a few tangible assets with net flow form equations for most tangible assets and for corporate stock. Such a combination has no serious disadvantages from the viewpoint of either accuracy or usability in capital market analysis compared to a framework consisting exclusively of either flow-of-funds or change-of-holdings form equations. The absence of two complete sys-

[20] For 1953–55 use could also be made of the tabulations prepared by Morris Mendelson (*The Flow-of-Funds Through the Financial Markets, 1953–1955*, New York, NBER, 1959).

stems of equations derived from different basic data means, however, the loss of an important accuracy check.

A second and more serious problem was that, in calculating flows from changes in reported holdings, it proved impossible in most cases within the given time and resource limitations to adjust the difference in the book value of holdings at the end and the beginning of the period for net realized capital gains and, less important, for net write-ups and write-downs. Treasury securities are the only capital market instrument for which such adjustments are possible, at least for some important groups of holders.[21] Corporate stock, for which differences in book values of holdings are likely to diverge most widely from net purchase or sales balances, is not affected by this drawback since the flow figures for the most important groups are derived from primary information on the value of purchases and sales. The figures shown in the tables as net purchase or sales balances of claims are thus too high for most groups by net realized capital gains or too low by net capital losses. Since interest rates rose during the postwar period and bond prices fell, this deficiency probably leads to an overstatement of the increase in holdings of financial institutions, which are calculated from differences in the book values of holdings. Net purchases of nonfarm households are, therefore, probably understated (or net sales overstated) because this sector is treated as a residual for virtually all capital market instruments. It is not likely that the errors introduced by this inability to adjust for net realized capital gains or net write-ups has distorted any of the main capital market movements over the period, but it may have done so for some years, some capital market instruments, and some sectors.

Thirdly, most flows are on a net rather than a gross basis. The only important exception is capital expenditures. It would have been possible to use gross figures for several additional flows, primarily the incurrence and repayment of consumer debt and home mortgage debt, but this was not done since it could not be achieved for most other flows and sectors.

The framework should be implemented in the following directions:

1. Primary data are needed on purchases and sales separately to supplement the indirect calculation of flows from changes in reported holdings.

---

[21] These adjustments are also ignored (except for Treasury securities) in the Federal Reserve Board's flow-of-funds statistics.

2. More information is required on realized capital gains and losses and on write-ups and write-downs, so that changes in reported holdings will approximate more closely true net flow figures when they are not available or can be used more effectively as a check against the available net flow data.

3. The transactions of nonprofit organizations should be separated from those of nonfarm households, and the transactions of nonfarm households thus adjusted should be divided into a few subsectors.

4. Data should be developed to permit a division of the nonfarm business sector into about half a dozen subsectors each with its balance sheet and flow-of-funds statement.

5. Supplementary subsector accounts should be developed for large, small, closely held and financed, and publicly held and financed nonfinancial corporations.

6. In the case of some capital market instruments, particularly Treasury securities and corporate bonds, holdings of and transactions in marketable and nonmarketable instruments should be separated.

7. Full quarterly accounts, comparable with the annual balance sheets and flow-of-funds statements, should be developed both on an unadjusted and a seasonally adjusted basis.

## From a National Accounting Framework to a Complete Model of the Capital Market

The unit, sector, and market equations which have been discussed hitherto are descriptive and refer to a period in the past.[22] They do not say anything about the functional or causal relationships that

[22] The equations are equally valid if all terms are interpreted as referring to an identical period in the future, so that each term reflects the planned or expected magnitude, under the constraint for each unit, each sector, and ultimately the nation as a whole, among others, of equality of sources and uses of funds, or of assets and liabilities plus net worth. These conditions are probably met for planned figures since we may assume that the planner takes the constraints into account in his plans. However, they are not met for market equations when the figures are regarded as values anticipated by decision-making units, whether or not they are interpreted as point estimates or as the range of a probability distribution. In either case, the constraints could be met only by a change in anticipations. Even if it were possible to ascertain the values of flows or stocks expected or anticipated by all decision-making units, the resulting sectoral or national equations would show residuals, which might be of great value in process analysis. The possibility of quantifying anticipated values is still so remote for most types of flows and stocks—capital expenditures constitute the most important possible exception—that the specific problems arising in this field need not be discussed here.

may exist among terms of the equation beyond the obvious constraint of equality of both sides. Nor do they indicate the factors which have made the values of each term in the equations what they happen to be. The equations, finally, give no information on the interrelations among sectors and among instruments. This does not mean that the framework is of no help in capital market analysis, either in its empty form or when actual numbers have been substituted for the symbols. All empirical capital market analysis must start from such a framework, or some body of data essentially similar to it.

The objective of capital market analysis, however, is to go beyond the basic equations as they stand, and to explain the relative size of the various items in the equations and the movements in the items over time. This can be done in very different ways: by relying on advanced methods of statistical analysis of equations for a number of periods, or for a number of subsectors; by making use of the tools of economic theory; and by putting emphasis on psychological and institutional explanations. In this respect capital market analysis poses exactly the same problems as the study of any broad topic in applied economics. There is, consequently, not one high road of capital market analysis. Any method that contributes to an understanding of the modus operandi of the capital market is acceptable, and the more it contributes, the more intensively it should be used.

Of the many possibilities of breathing life into a framework, one deserves special attention, if only because it has become prominent in economic analysis in the postwar period—the use of a model of the capital market. A model may in this connection be defined as a set of equations in which each term is expressed as a function of one or more variables, variables which in turn may be endogenous (i.e., contained within the system of equations that make up the framework) or exogenous (not thus contained).[23] Like a framework, a model can be empty (all terms being expressed as algebraic symbols only), full (containing numerical values for all terms), or mixed (combining numerical and symbolic terms).

The difference between model and framework is best illustrated by an example. The market equation for any given period for home

[23] There is sometimes a difference of opinion as to whether a given system of equations is to be treated as a framework or as a model. Input-output tables, for example, are regarded by some skeptics as a framework for interindustry transactions, while others treat them as a model having explanatory value. (Cf. introduction to *Input-Output Analysis,* Studies in Income and Wealth 18, Princeton for NBER, 1955, pp. 4–6.)

mortgages (symbols: $l$ for new mortgages made, $b$ for new mortgages incurred, $a$ and $r$ for repayments made and received, and $f$ for existing mortgages acquired and sold) in the framework looks as follows in the identified flow form, omitting for the sake of simplicity terms likely to be of relatively small size, and assuming the absence of capital gains or valuation changes:

$$l_{hh} + l_{hf} + a_{hh} + a_{hf} + f_{ff} = b_{hh} + b_{hf} + r_{hh} + r_{hf}.$$

For the builder of the framework—at least in its full numerical form—the job is done as soon as he has substituted numbers for the four independent terms [24] in this equation, and has satisfied himself that these numbers are the best the primary data will yield and are not in conflict with other relevant figures. It is at this point that the model builder's work begins. If he is content with an empty (non-numerical) model, he will indicate in symbolic language the endogenous or exogenous variable on which each term of the equations of the framework depends. He might, to use a very simplified case in our example, assume that the term $b_{hf}$ (nonfarm households' borrowing on home mortgages from financial institutions) depends in some unspecified way on the current volume of home construction and the relationship between current interest rates on home mortgage and prime corporate bonds $(\rho^h - \rho^b)$ symbolically

$$l_{hf} = b_{hf} = f(c;\rho^h - \rho^b).$$

Or he might assume, now introducing exogenous variables from other (earlier) periods, that repayments depend somehow on the volume of mortgage loans outstanding, i.e., made previously $(H)$, and on the difference between original and current home mortgage interest rates $(\rho_t - \rho_{t-n})$. Then

$$r_{hf} = a_{hf} = f(H;\rho_t - \rho_{t-n}).$$

Such a procedure need not be limited to relatively small components of the flow of funds. It can equally well be applied to flows as broad as a sector's or even the nation's total saving. Thus it could be, and has been assumed, that a given year's aggregate personal saving depends on various combinations of independent variables, such as the current year's total or disposable income or possibly nonwage income only, the income of one or more years in the past, future ex-

---

[24] Only four of the nine terms are independent because $b_{hh} = l_{hh}$; $b_{hf} = l_{hf}$; $r_{hh} = a_{hh}$; $r_{hf} = a_{hf}$; and $f_{ff} = 0$.

pected income, the highest previous income, the stock of liquid assets variously defined or of total assets, and the level of interest rates, present, past, or expected. The latter set of independent variables is particularly relevant since every fund flow is actually associated with an interest rate—exactly as commodity flows are associated with commodity prices—and there is a theoretical presumption that some functional relation exists between the direction and size of fund flows and the absolute and, probably more relevant, the relative level of the associated interest rate.

The model builder may even go one step further, without as yet sullying his hands with statistics, and indicate the general form of the relationship between the term to be explained and the explanatory independent variables. This may be done by indicating—through specification of the sign of the first or higher derivatives of the function or by other mathematical devices—whether the relationship is positive or negative, arithmetic or logarithmic, simultaneous or lagged, periodic or irregular, etc.

The model builder may finally crown his work by substituting numerical values for the symbols, e.g., by stating—using the relation for illustration only—that repayments on home mortgages by nonfarm households to financial institutions in any year are equal to 10 per cent of the volume of such mortgages at the beginning of the year multiplied by unity less two-hundredths of the difference between home mortgage interest rates (in per cent) in the current period and for the average of the preceding ten years, i.e.,

$$r_{hf} = a_{hf} - 0.10H \left[ 1.00 - 0.02 \left( \rho_t - \frac{1}{10} \sum_{n=t-11}^{t-1} \rho_{t-n} \right) \right].$$

The statistical problems of selecting the explanatory variables, deciding upon the form of the function, selecting the method of deriving the numerical values, and carrying through the calculations, particularly with a substantial number of terms and equations involved, are far from simple or susceptible of mechanical solutions. These problems, however, have been discussed elsewhere [25] and need not concern us here.

---

[25] See, for example, L. R. Klein, *A Textbook of Econometrics* (Evanston, 1953); L. R. Klein and A. S. Goldberger, *An Econometric Model of the United States, 1929–1952* (Amsterdam, 1955); J. Tinbergen, *Econometrics* (Philadelphia, 1951); G. Tintner, *Econometrics* (New York, 1952); S. Valavanis, *Econometrics* (New York, 1960).

If the capital market framework equations were available for a sufficiently long period, if we could identify the endogenous and exogenous independent variables most appropriate for each term, if we could decide upon the form of the functional relationship, and if we could obtain numerical values for the exogenous variables, modern computers would enable us to solve the system of simultaneous equations and thus provide us with a complete numerical model of the capital market. The difficulties roughly indicated by these "if" clauses are, however, so formidable that no serious attempt to formulate and then to numerically implement a full model of the capital market has as yet been made.[26] Most of the serious attempts at implementation have been limited to selected sectors of the capital market in which either data are relatively plentiful or the selection of independent variables seems fairly obvious, such as the market for home mortgages.[27]

Despite all these difficulties, the development of a complete econometric model of the American capital market in the postwar period is the ultimate goal of capital market analysis. No direct attack has been made on this problem here because of two overriding considerations. First, the construction and testing of such a model requires time, resources, and specialized skill in econometrics well beyond anything available within this project. Secondly, and more importantly, in order to construct a model that not only fits the data for the period from which it is calculated reasonably well but also stands up when applied to earlier and later periods—with appropriate allowances for secular and structural change—several intermediate steps must be taken that are difficult, time-consuming, and expensive in resources.

The first of these is the provision of considerably more detailed, more accurate, systematically arranged, and integrated data on gross capital market flows, asset holdings, and interest rates. This is the field to which the National Bureau's Postwar Capital Market Study

[26] Dawson's system (*American Economic Review*, May 1958, pp. 145–157) is so condensed and is regarded to such an extent by the author as illustrative rather than explanatory as not to invalidate this statement. Gurley's equations (*Liquidity and Financial Institutions in the Postwar Period*, Study Paper 14, Joint Economic Committee, Washington, 1960), although dealing with very broad fund flows, are not intended to constitute a complete economic model of the capital market.

[27] See L. Grebler and S. J. Maisel, "Determinants of Residential Construction: A Review of Present Knowledge," in *Impacts of Monetary Policy*, Commission on Money and Credit, Englewood Cliffs, 1963; and D. Fand, "The Debt-Expenditure Hypothesis and Residential Construction," *Southern Economic Journal*, July 1959.

has tried to make a contribution and to which this report is limited. The second of the intermediate steps is the intensive analysis—not limited to the postwar period—of one, possibly the basic, capital market relationship, namely, the relation between interest rate movements and fund movements. The third step is the development of a theory of finance integrated into the structure of modern general economic theory, but sufficiently specialized to serve as a guide for capital market analysis. Promising steps have been taken in this direction in recent years which have witnessed a remarkable revival of interest in the economic theory of finance—in contrast to the collection of recipes generally known as a textbook on corporate finance.[28] The results of this revival, however, represent as yet only a beginning rather than the final answer to the quest for an economic theory of finance and the capital market.

## *Actual Framework*

In the discussion of the basic problems involved in setting up a statistical framework for capital market analysis, we often have had to make concessions to the limitations of the basic data at our disposal and of the resources available within this project for the rearrangement and refinement of the basic statistics. Within these limitations it has, nevertheless, been possible to set up and implement a framework that, while still far from the ideal, provides most of the basic data needed for an analysis of the main characteristics and structural changes in the American capital market during the postwar period, even if the data are as yet insufficient to permit a close analysis of cyclical fluctuations in the capital market.

### SECTORAL BALANCE SHEETS

The core of the framework used in this report is represented by some fifty sectoral balance sheets, each containing annual data for the year-ends 1945 through 1958, which constitute Section III in Volume II of *National Balance Sheet*. These tables comprise balance sheets for the seven main sectors (nonfarm households, agriculture, unincorporated business, nonfinancial corporations, finance, state and local gov-

[28] It may suffice to point to two examples: The efforts of E. S. Shaw and J. G. Gurley culminating for the time being in *Money in a Theory of Finance* (Washington, 1960), and the report of the Radcliffe Committee and the literature which is developing around it.

ernments, and federal government), a national balance sheet (which is the sum of the seven sectoral balance sheets), and balance sheets for two dozen subsectors of the financial sector. The tables use a standard classification for assets (twenty-six items) and liabilities (thirteen items). In principle, the entries are in current values, which actually means replacement cost for reproducible tangible assets, market values or the closest approximation thereto for nonreproducible tangible assets and for corporate stock, and face value for claims and liabilities; net worth is calculated as the difference between the value of assets thus defined and that of liabilities.

The balance sheets of the financial sector, and its subsectors, may be regarded as primary since they are essentially derived from the published statements of these institutions, although some adjustments are occasionally made to conform to the standard classification of assets and liabilities or to substitute current for book values. At the other extreme, the balance sheets of the nonfarm household, farm, and nonfarm unincorporated business sectors are secondary, i.e., the entries for the different asset and liability items are not taken from financial statements of these three sectors, which are not available, but are derived indirectly from the statements of other sectors or from other statistics. The balance sheets of nonfinancial corporations, state and local governments, and the federal government occupy an intermediate position. Most of the assets and liabilities are taken from financial statements, but those for tangible assets, which are unavailable or not in acceptable form in primary statements, are derived from other statistical sources and thus are secondary. Actually, the construction of the sectoral balance sheets from the sources is a rather complicated procedure, which is described in detail in the notes to the tables.

Most of the other tables (included in Volume II of *National Balance Sheet*) can be derived from the Section III tables by rearrangement of entries. However, two additional sources of information are required in the derivation of the tables in Sections V, VI, VII, and VIII. The first of these is estimates of capital expenditures in current prices and of capital consumption allowances, which are derived from statistical sources usually entirely independent of balance-sheet data (described in detail in Appendix B of my *The National Wealth of the United States* [29]). The second additional source is the estimates

[29] Princeton for NBER, 1962.

of new issues of corporate securities and the net purchase or sales balance of corporate stock by different sectors. The derivation of these estimates is explained in the notes to the Section VIII tables.

In the tables in Section I of Volume II of *National Balance Sheet,* the sectoral balance sheets for each year from 1945 through 1958 of the tables of Section III are rearranged to produce a national balance sheet for each of the fourteen year-ends of the postwar period. These national balance sheets, which show for a given year the assets, liabilities, and net worth of the nation and of the seven main sectors, are intended to be still pictures permitting a rapid bird's-eye view and an easy comparison of the distribution of the various balance-sheet items among the main sectors.

These tables (Section IV) show for each of the thirty-odd types of assets, liabilities, and net worth the holdings for each of the seven main sectors (and, where appropriate, for the subsectors of the finance sector) for each of the year-ends 1945 through 1958. These tables thus enable us to follow the amounts of the various assets and liabilities outstanding and to study the distribution of these amounts among the different sectors.

From Sections I, III, and IV, which all deal with stocks, are derived Sections V, VII, and VIII, which show flows during each of the years 1946 through 1958. The flows are obtained for claims and liabilities by taking the first differences between the stocks at the beginning and the end of the year. This can be justified by the relatively small importance of valuation changes, including realized capital gains and losses, in most assets and liabilities of this type. This short-cut method is not permissible for items that are subject to substantial price fluctuations, i.e., tangible assets, equity securities, and net worth. For these items, true flow figures have been used, i.e., gross capital expenditures for reproducible tangible assets, net purchase or sales balances for corporate stock, and saving for changes in net worth.

The tables in Section VII are presented for the seven main sectors, the twenty subsectors of the finance sector, and the nation as a whole.

Each of these statements shows flows for the different assets and liabilities for each year from 1946 through 1958.

### NATIONAL ANNUAL FLOW-OF-FUNDS STATEMENTS

These statements (Section V), paralleling the national balance sheets in Section I, show the flows of each asset and liability distinguished for the nation as a whole and for each of the seven main sectors, thus providing a summary view of the flow of funds during a given year.

### TRANSACTION ACCOUNTS

The tables in Section VIII are derived from Section IV by differencing, except for capital expenditures and transactions in corporate stock for which true flow figures are utilized. The Section VIII tables show for a given asset or liability the flows during each of the years 1946 through 1958 for each of the seven main sectors, the nation as a whole, and the subsectors of the finance sector where applicable.

Additional basic tables were computed as an aid in analyzing the figures, but were omitted from the printed version because they can easily be derived from the tables in Volume II of *National Balance Sheet*. These supplementary tables, obtained by simple arithmetical operations from the basic set, show annual changes in flows and in balance-sheet items, in absolute and percentage terms; annual percentage distributions of each sector's balance sheets and transactions accounts; and the annual sectoral distribution, in percentages, of the several items in balance sheets, sources-and-uses-of-funds statements, and transactions accounts.

The data discussed are those now available. Unfortunately, as is so often the case in enterprises involving the processing of large masses of statistical data, the construction of the framework and the filling of the empty boxes with actual figures have practically exhausted the time and resources available for the entire project. Indeed, for reasons of economy, not even all the statistical material that has been prepared can be shown in Volume II of *National Balance Sheet,* let alone fully utilized in the text. It has been found possible, however, to include in Volume II all the basic flow and stock data in absolute figures, i.e., Sections I–VIII. Some material from other tables has been utilized in the text.

In addition to presenting the statistical raw material, it has also been found possible to present a summary discussion of some of the more obvious aspects of the American capital market during the post-war period, and a still more summary comparison of developments during this period with those in earlier periods, particularly 1901–12, 1923–29, and 1934–39. This is done in Chapter 3 for capital expenditures, a flow series basic to much of capital market analysis, and in Chapters 4 and 5 for internal and external financing and their main forms for the period as a whole and for the three cycle averages of 1946–49, 1949–54, and 1954–59. The discussion in the first part of Chapter 4 is based on national aggregates, while in the second part developments are reviewed for each of the seven main sectors.

In all cases, the approach is descriptive rather than analytical. There was no time for econometric experiments with the data or for testing specific theoretical hypotheses. It is hoped that the material, particularly the detailed data presented in Volume II of *National Balance Sheet,* will be used for these purposes later, either within the National Bureau or outside it.

# CHAPTER 3

# The National Financing Task: The Volume of Gross Capital Expenditures

IN a closed national economy, the financing task can be reduced to diverting just enough funds from current income to equal total gross capital expenditures on tangible assets which have a length of life exceeding the accounting period of one year and usually set at somewhere around two or three years. All other financial transactions among domestic units, such as the extension or repayment of credit, the issuance and retirement of securities, and purchases and sales of existing financial and tangible assets, necessarily wash out in the consolidation of the accounts on a national scale and do not call for the diversion of current income. In an open economy, the net foreign balance must be added to gross capital expenditures if the financing task is to be measured.

For individual economic units in the household, business, or government sectors—the only decision-makers—the financing task is, of course, much broader. Each economic unit must find funds not only for capital expenditures, but also for the extension of credit to other units and for the acquisition of existing tangible and financial assets. Thus, uses and sources of funds are more extensive on an individual than a national scale. While they are limited for a national economy to gross saving plus net capital imports, individual units may call, in addition to their own gross saving, on borrowing and on the sale of existing assets.

The character of a consolidated national sources-and-uses-of-funds statement, with which this chapter is concerned, is thus very different from that of a combined statement for the various sectors in the economy, and still more from a combined statement for all economic units taken separately, in which domestic borrowing and lending are preserved (to be discussed in Chapter 4). Whereas for accounting, the consolidated statement is secondary because it is derived from a combined statement, the sequence is reversed for economic analysis. In analyzing national problems, it is necessary to start with a consolidated statement in order to view the financing task of the economy as a whole, unimpeded by the multiple layers of borrowing and lending and of transactions in existing assets among domestic units that constitute a large and essential part of all financing transactions in a developed economy.

In this chapter, we shall therefore briefly review the volume and composition of capital formation in the United States during the postwar period and compare it with earlier periods, first for gross and then for net capital formation. Inquiry into the sources of finance for capital expenditures, in particular the distinction between internal sources (capital consumption allowances and current saving) and external sources (which involve recourse to the capital market), and closer examination of external financing and changes in the assets and liabilities of the main sectors of the economy are reserved for Chapter 4.

The statistics used throughout this chapter, and the following ones, are taken from the comprehensive integrated set of national and sectoral balance sheets and flow-of-funds accounts presented in Volume II of *Studies in the National Balance Sheet of the United States*. While the figures are in most cases based on data developed for the income and product accounts of the Department of Commerce or the flow-of-funds accounts of the Federal Reserve Board, substantial additions—in particular the estimates of the stock of tangible assets—and modifications were required to make the basic data fit into our integrated system of financial accounts. Some of our concepts also differ from those prevailing in official statistics, for instance, the treatment of capital expenditures of the government and of expenditures on consumer durables in a manner parallel to that of business capital expenditures; and the use of replacement cost instead of original cost depreciation. Our estimates of gross and net capital expenditures and of internal and external financing, therefore, often differ from those found in the generally used official documents.

# The National Financing Task:

## Volume and Composition of Gross Capital Formation in the Postwar Period

During the postwar period (1946–58) gross capital formation, according to the broad concept including consumer durables and durable military assets, averaged $108 billion a year; according to the standard definition excluding consumer and military durables, it was $66 billion; according to the official concept, which also omits government civilian structures, equipment, and inventories, it averaged $56 billion; and according to the narrowest definition, which includes only business-type assets (i.e., nonresidential structures, producer durables, and inventories), it averaged $39 billion. These totals and their main components will be found in Table 12 for the postwar period as a whole.

Probably the best way of visualizing the economic significance of these magnitudes is to compare them with total current output, i.e., gross national product. It is then seen that gross capital formation during the postwar period averaged almost three-tenths of GNP if the broad definition of both capital formation and gross national product is used; that it amounted to one-fifth of GNP in the standard definition of capital formation and to one-sixth of GNP in the Department of Commerce definition of capital formation; but that it equaled less than one-eighth of GNP according to the narrowest definition of capital formation. The significance of these ratios for capital market analysis is that they show the proportions of gross national product which had to be withheld from current expenditures in order to finance capital formation.

Table 13 and Chart 4 show that both the absolute volume of gross capital formation and its share in gross national product have fluctuated considerably from year to year during the postwar period, whichever definition of capital is used. They have done so in the United States for as long as we have statistics, i.e., back to the middle of the nineteenth century, and they have done so in other developed countries. Indeed, these fluctuations have come to be regarded as the chief characteristic of business cycles.

Declines in the absolute and relative volume of capital formation are evident in 1948–49, 1952, 1954, and 1958. These are three periods of recession plus 1952, in which this decline was due primarily to a reduction of inventory following the extraordinarily sharp increases during the Korean War. The sharpest increases in the volume of

TABLE 12

COMPOSITION OF GROSS CAPITAL FORMATION, 1946-58

| | Amount (billion dollars) | | Share in Total Capital Formation (per cent) | | Share in Gross National Product (per cent) | |
|---|---|---|---|---|---|---|
| | Period (1) | Annual Average (2) | Broad Concept (3) | Standard Concept (4) | Broad Concept (5) | Standard Concept (6) |
| I. Business capital formation | 507.2 | 39.0 | 36.3 | 59.5 | 10.4 | 11.6 |
| 1. Nonresidential structures | 164.2 | 12.6 | 11.7 | 19.2 | 3.4 | 3.8 |
| 2. Equipment | 258.4 | 19.9 | 18.5 | 30.3 | 5.3 | 5.9 |
| 3. Inventories | 71.8 | 5.5 | 5.1 | 8.4 | 1.5 | 1.6 |
| 4. Net foreign assets | 12.8 | 1.0 | 0.9 | 1.5 | 0.3 | 0.3 |
| II. Household capital formation | 596.9 | 45.9 | 42.7 | 24.2 | 12.2 | 4.7 |
| 1. Residential structures | 205.0 | 15.8 | 14.7 | 24.0 | 4.2 | 4.7 |
| 2. Consumer durables | 389.9 | 30.0 | 27.9 | — | 8.0 | — |
| 3. Net foreign assets | 2.0 | 0.2 | 0.1 | 0.2 | 0 | 0 |
| III. Government capital formation | 294.6 | 22.7 | 21.1 | 16.3 | 6.0 | 3.1 |
| 1. Civilian structures | 110.7 | 8.5 | 7.9 | 13.0 | 2.3 | 2.5 |
| 2. Civilian equipment | 9.4 | 0.7 | 0.7 | 1.1 | 0.2 | 0.2 |
| 3. Civilian inventories | 5.4 | 0.4 | 0.4 | 0.6 | 0.1 | 0.1 |
| 4. Monetary metals | 1.5 | 0.1 | 0.1 | 0.2 | 0 | 0 |
| 5. Net foreign assets | 11.9 | 0.9 | 0.9 | 1.4 | 0.2 | 0.3 |
| 6. Military structures | 18.1 | 1.4 | 1.3 | — | 0.4 | — |
| 7. Military equipment | 123.4 | 9.5 | 8.8 | — | 2.5 | — |
| 8. Military inventories | 14.2 | 1.1 | 1.0 | — | 0.3 | — |
| IV. 1. Total, broad concept (I + II + III) | 1,398.7 | 107.6 | 100.0 | — | 28.6 | — |
| 2. Total, standard concept [I + II (1 & 3) + III (1 - 5)] | 853.1 | 65.6 | 61.0 | 100.0 | 17.4 | 19.4 |
| 3. Total, Dept. of Commerce concept [I + II (1&3) + III(4&5)] | 727.6 | 56.0 | 52.0 | 85.3 | 14.9 | 16.7 |
| 4. Total, narrow concept (I) | 507.2 | 39.0 | 36.3 | 59.5 | 10.4 | 11.6 |

Source: All tables references below are to <u>National Balance Sheet</u>, Vol. II, unless otherwise specified.

<u>Cols. 1 and 2</u>
Line I-1: Table VIII-a-2, lines 1-5.
Line I-2: Table VIII-a-4, lines 1-5.
Line I-3: Table VIII-a-6b, lines 1-5.
Line 1-4: <u>National Wealth</u>, Table A-45, first differences of col. 3.
Line II-1: Table VIII-a-1, lines 1-5.
Line II-2: Table VIII-a-5, line 8.
Line II-3: <u>National Wealth</u>, Table A-45, first differences of col. 2.
Line III-1: Table VIII-a-1 and VIII-a-2, lines 6-7.
Line III-2: Table VIII-a-4, lines 6-7.
Line III-3: Table VIII-a-6b, lines 6-7.
Line III-4: <u>National Wealth</u>, Table A-44, first differences of col. 1.
Line III-5: <u>Ibid.</u>, Table A-45, first differences of col. 4.
Line III-6: Table VIII-a-1 and VIII-a-2, line 9.
Line III-7: Table VIII-a-4, line 9.
Line III-8: Table VIII-a-6b, line 9.

<u>Cols. 3-6</u>, numerators: Corresponding lines of col. 1.
<u>Col. 3</u>, denominator: Line IV-1, col. 1.
<u>Col. 4</u>, denominator: Line IV-2, col. 1.
<u>Col. 5</u>, denominator: Department of Commerce estimates of GNP plus depreciation at replacement cost of consumer durables (difference between Tables VIII-a-5 and VIII-a-5b, line 8) and of government civil and military capital expenditures (difference between Tables VIII-a-7 and VIII-a-7b, lines 6, 7, and 9). This adjustment is a crude approximation to the use value of consumer durable and government capital.
<u>Col. 6</u>, denominator: Dept. of Commerce estimates of GNP (<u>Survey of Current Business</u>, July 1960, Table 1).
Note: Components may not add to totals because of rounding here and elsewhere in this chapter.

capital formation were registered in 1950, 1953, 1955, and 1959 (the last of these years generally not being included in our analysis).[1] All these years—with the exception of 1953—are the initial years of cyclical recoveries. The correspondence between decreases and sharp increases in the volume of capital formation and its share in gross national product and the plan of the business cycle would be equally pronounced if adjustments were made for price changes.

When the influence of business cycles is roughly eliminated, as is done in the lower part of Table 13, by showing averages for full cycles [2] it is seen that, although the dollar volume of gross capital formation (broad concept) almost doubled between the first postwar cycle of 1946–49 and the third cycle of 1954–58, the share of gross capital formation in GNP was almost the same in all three cycles.

[1] For 1959 data, see *Survey of Current Business,* July 1960.
[2] Since business cycles do not coincide with calendar years, the cycle averages include one-half of the first and last years of the cycle, using the NBER dating. Calculations using quarterly figures (not available for our estimates of capital formation but derivable from reasonably comparable concepts) show a similar stability in the ratio of capital formation to gross national product over entire business cycles.

Closer inspection of the figures indicates a slow increase in the share of gross capital formation in GNP between the first and the third cycles, according to the broad concept of capital formation; the standard and narrow concepts, however, show a decline between Cycles I

TABLE 13

ANNUAL FLUCTUATIONS IN GROSS CAPITAL FORMATION, 1946-58

|  | Absolute Figures (billion dollars) | | | Share in Gross National Product (per cent) | | |
|---|---|---|---|---|---|---|
|  | Broad Concept (1) | Standard Concept (2) | Narrow Concept (3) | Broad Concept (4) | Standard Concept (5) | Narrow Concept (6) |
| 1946 | 64.5 | 45.7 | 34.3 | 26.9 | 21.7 | 16.3 |
| 1947 | 80.8 | 57.8 | 36.7 | 30.3 | 24.7 | 15.7 |
| 1948 | 79.3 | 54.1 | 33.1 | 27.2 | 20.9 | 12.8 |
| 1949 | 66.0 | 38.1 | 17.3 | 22.8 | 14.8 | 6.7 |
| 1950 | 100.2 | 65.2 | 45.4 | 31.6 | 22.9 | 16.0 |
| 1951 | 110.2 | 71.2 | 47.4 | 30.2 | 21.6 | 14.4 |
| 1952 | 103.7 | 55.2 | 29.2 | 26.8 | 15.9 | 8.4 |
| 1953 | 116.9 | 63.0 | 33.4 | 28.6 | 17.2 | 9.1 |
| 1954 | 111.4 | 61.2 | 32.0 | 27.2 | 16.9 | 8.8 |
| 1955 | 133.6 | 78.2 | 44.6 | 29.9 | 19.7 | 11.2 |
| 1956 | 145.7 | 90.4 | 55.4 | 30.8 | 21.6 | 13.2 |
| 1957 | 150.1 | 92.4 | 56.6 | 30.0 | 20.9 | 12.8 |
| 1958 | 136.5 | 80.8 | 41.7 | 27.3 | 18.2 | 9.4 |
| Cycle Averages | | | | | | |
| 1946-49 | 75.1 | 51.3 | 31.9 | 27.4 | 21.1 | 13.1 |
| 1949-54 | 103.9 | 60.8 | 36.0 | 28.4 | 18.6 | 11.0 |
| 1954-58 | 138.3 | 83.0 | 48.4 | 29.5 | 20.0 | 11.6 |
| Period Average | | | | | | |
| 1946-58 | 107.6 | 65.6 | 39.0 | 28.6 | 19.4 | 11.6 |

Source: Each year's total corresponds to the concepts in Table 12 as follows:
Col. 1: Table 12, col. 1, line IV-1.
Col. 2: Table 12, col. 1, line IV-2.
Col. 3: Table 12, col. 1, line IV-4.
Col. 4, numerator: Col. 1 of this table; denominator: same as for Table 12, col. 5.
Col. 5, numerator: Col. 2 of this table; denominator: same as for Table 12, col. 6.
Col. 6, numerator: Col. 3 of this table; denominator: same as for Table 12, col. 6.

and II; and there is no definite change between Cycles II and III for the narrow concept. It seems, therefore, premature to deduce from the figures for these three cycles the existence of a trend.

Stability is also fairly pronounced in the composition of gross capital formation during the postwar period, although fluctuations are larger than in total capital formation, as might be expected.

For the entire thirteen years, approximately one-third of total gross

CHART 4

GROSS CAPITAL FORMATION, 1946–58

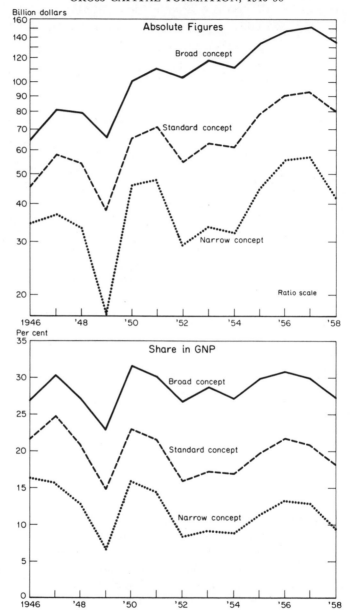

Source: Table 13.

86

TABLE 14

GROSS INVESTMENT IN CURRENT PRICES, 1946-58

| | Annual Averages (billion dollars) | | | | Distribution (per cent) | | | | | | | |
|---|---|---|---|---|---|---|---|---|---|---|---|---|
| | 1946 -49 (1) | 1949 -54 (2) | 1954 -58 (3) | 1946 -58 (4) | 1946 -49 (5) | 1949 -54 (6) | 1954 -58 (7) | 1946 -58 (8) | 1946 -49 (9) | 1949 -54 (10) | 1954 -58 (11) | 1946 -58 (12) |
| **A. By type of wealth** | | | | | BASED ON LINE A-10a | | | | BASED ON LINE A-10b | | | |
| 1. Residential structures | 9.98 | 15.74 | 20.79 | 15.77 | 13.5 | 15.1 | 15.0 | 14.7 | 14.6 | 15.2 | 15.3 | 15.1 |
| 2. Other private structures | 7.96 | 11.77 | 17.31 | 12.63 | 10.8 | 11.3 | 12.5 | 11.8 | 11.7 | 11.3 | 12.8 | 12.1 |
| 3. Government structures (civil) | 3.97 | 8.20 | 12.25 | 8.52 | 5.4 | 7.9 | 8.9 | 7.9 | 5.8 | 7.9 | 9.0 | 8.1 |
| 4. Producer durables | 16.12 | 20.18 | 25.37 | 20.60 | 21.9 | 19.3 | 18.3 | 19.2 | 23.6 | 19.4 | 18.7 | 19.7 |
| 5a. Gross inventories | 7.48 | 4.91 | 5.22 | 5.94 | 10.1 | 4.7 | 3.8 | 5.5 | | | | |
| 5b. Net inventories (value adjusted) | 2.00 | 4.38 | 2.66 | 3.14 | | | | | 2.9 | 4.2 | 2.0 | 3.0 |
| 6. Consumer durables | 21.22 | 29.85 | 37.70 | 30.00 | 28.8 | 28.6 | 27.3 | 27.9 | 31.1 | 28.8 | 27.8 | 28.7 |
| 7a. Total (incl. 5a) | 66.73 | 90.65 | 118.64 | 93.46 | 90.5 | 86.9 | 85.8 | 86.9 | | | | |
| 7b. Total (incl. 5b) | 61.25 | 90.12 | 116.08 | 90.66 | | | | | 89.7 | 86.8 | 85.5 | 86.6 |
| 8. Net foreign assets | 4.36 | 0.47 | 1.97 | 2.05 | 5.9 | 0.5 | 1.4 | 1.9 | 6.4 | 0.5 | 1.5 | 2.0 |
| 9. Military expenditures | 2.66 | 13.23 | 17.66 | 11.98 | 3.6 | 12.7 | 12.8 | 11.1 | 3.9 | 12.7 | 13.0 | 11.4 |
| 10a. Total (7a + 8 + 9)[a] | 73.75 | 104.35 | 138.27 | 107.49 | 100.0 | 100.0 | 100.0 | 100.0 | | | | |
| 10b. Total (7b + 8 + 9) | 68.27 | 103.82 | 135.71 | 104.69 | | | | | 100.0 | 100.0 | 100.0 | 100.0 |
| **B. By sector** | | | | | BASED ON LINE B-8 | | | | BASED ON LINE B-9 | | | |
| 1. Nonfarm households | 27.84 | 42.15 | 55.78 | 42.64 | 41.7 | 46.5 | 47.0 | 45.6 | 40.1 | 40.6 | 40.9 | 40.4 |
| 2. Nonfarm unincorp. business[b] | 4.70 | 5.32 | 5.78 | 5.78 | 7.0 | 5.9 | 6.1 | 6.2 | 6.8 | 5.1 | 5.3 | 5.5 |
| 3. Agriculture[b] | 6.92 | 6.84 | 7.55 | 7.31 | 10.4 | 7.5 | 6.4 | 7.8 | 10.0 | 6.6 | 5.5 | 6.9 |
| 4. Finance | 0.34 | 0.40 | 0.52 | 0.42 | 0.5 | 0.4 | 0.4 | 0.4 | 0.5 | 0.4 | 0.4 | 0.4 |
| 5. Nonfinancial corporations[b] | 22.19 | 26.34 | 34.19 | 27.64 | 33.3 | 29.1 | 28.8 | 29.6 | 32.0 | 25.4 | 25.1 | 26.2 |
| 6. State and local governments | 3.69 | 7.61 | 12.05 | 8.15 | 5.5 | 8.4 | 10.2 | 8.7 | 5.3 | 7.3 | 8.8 | 7.7 |
| 7a. Federal government, civil | 1.02 | 1.99 | 1.32 | 1.51 | 1.5 | 2.2 | 1.1 | 1.6 | | | | |
| 7b. Federal govt., civil and military | 3.68 | 15.22 | 18.98 | 13.50 | | | | | 5.3 | 14.7 | 13.9 | 12.8 |
| 8. Total, civil expenditures | 66.70 | 90.65 | 118.63 | 93.45 | 100.0 | 100.0 | 100.0 | 100.0 | | | | |
| 9. Total, civil and military expenditures[a] | 69.36 | 103.88 | 136.29 | 105.44 | | | | | 100.0 | 100.0 | 100.0 | 100.0 |

NOTES TO TABLE 14

Source: All table references below are to <u>National Balance Sheet</u>, Vol. II, unless otherwise specified.

Line A-1:   Table VIII-a-1, lines 1-5.
Line A-2:   Table VIII-a-2, lines 1-5.
Line A-3:   Table VIII-a-1, and VIII-a-2, lines 6 and 7.
Line A-4:   Table VIII-a-4, line 8.
Line A-5a:  Table VIII-a-6b, line 8.
Line A-5b:  Table VIII-a-6d, line 8.
Line A-6:   Table VIII-a-5, line 8.
Line A-7a:  Table VIII-a-7, line 8.
Line A-7b:  Table VIII-a-7d, line 8.
Line A-8:   <u>National Wealth</u>, Table A-45, first differences of col. 1.
Line A-9:   Table VIII-a-7, line 9.
Line A-10a: Sum of lines 7a, 8, and 9 of this table.
Line A-10b: Sum of lines 7b, 8, and 9 of this table.
Lines B-1 through B-9: Table VIII-a-7.

[a]Lines A-10a and B-9 differ because net foreign assets (line A-8) are not included in line B-9.

[b]The concept of inventory used here is the same as in line A-5a.

capital formation (broad concept) consisted of structures; almost three-fifths—of civil and military equipment and consumer durables; 7 per cent—of inventories; and 2 per cent—of net foreign assets. The share of structures and equipment increased between the first and second postwar cycles, while that of inventories and net foreign assets declined very sharply.[3] The latter movements represent changes from the unusually high levels of the early postwar period. Changes from the second to the third postwar cycle, on the other hand, were small in comparison. Similarly, the share of public capital formation was considerably higher in the second and third cycles than in the first cycle, reflecting the low level of military expenditures until the Korean War.

The relationships between gross capital formation according to the broad, standard, and narrow concepts is virtually the same in the second and third cycles. During the first cycle, however, the broad concept was less in excess of the standard and narrow concept, reflecting the lower level of military investment as shown in Table 13.

Turning to the narrower categories of capital formation which may be obtained from Table 14 in current prices and from Table 15 in constant (1947–49) prices, a similar stability is evident for the large components, particularly between the second and third cycles, which are less affected by special factors than the first cycle and hence may reflect a more nearly normal midcentury situation. The shares of residential structures, other private structures, and consumer durables

[3] See Tables 12 and 14.

TABLE 15

GROSS INVESTMENT IN CONSTANT PRICES,[a] 1946-58

| | Annual Averages (billion dollars) | | | | Distribution (per cent) | | | | | | | |
|---|---|---|---|---|---|---|---|---|---|---|---|---|
| | 1946 -49 (1) | 1949 -54 (2) | 1954 -58 (3) | 1946 -58 (4) | 1946 -49 (5) | 1949 -54 (6) | 1954 -58 (7) | 1946 -58 (8) | 1946 -49 (9) | 1949 -54 (10) | 1954 -58 (11) | 1946 -58 (12) |
| A. By type of wealth | | | | | BASED ON LINE A-10 | | | | BASED ON LINE B-9 | | | |
| 1. Residential structures | 10.31 | 13.69 | 16.24 | 13.53 | 14.7 | 15.0 | 14.9 | 14.8 | 15.7 | 15.1 | 15.1 | 15.1 |
| 2. Other private structures | 8.30 | 10.00 | 12.57 | 10.41 | 11.9 | 11.0 | 11.5 | 11.4 | 12.6 | 11.0 | 11.7 | 11.6 |
| 3. Government structures (civil) | 4.00 | 7.27 | 9.79 | 7.29 | 5.7 | 8.0 | 9.0 | 8.0 | 6.1 | 8.0 | 9.1 | 8.1 |
| 4. Producer durables | 16.64 | 17.39 | 19.03 | 17.51 | 23.8 | 19.1 | 17.5 | 19.2 | 25.3 | 19.1 | 17.7 | 19.6 |
| 5. Inventories | 1.90 | 3.74 | 2.09 | 2.75 | 2.7 | 4.1 | 1.9 | 3.0 | 2.9 | 4.1 | 1.9 | 3.1 |
| 6. Consumer durables | 21.80 | 27.67 | 34.56 | 28.30 | 31.2 | 30.4 | 31.7 | 31.0 | 33.1 | 30.5 | 32.1 | 31.6 |
| 7. Total | 62.95 | 79.76 | 94.28 | 79.79 | 90.1 | 87.7 | 86.5 | 87.5 | 95.7 | 87.8 | 87.5 | 89.1 |
| 8. Net foreign assets | 4.12 | 0.11 | 1.34 | 1.66 | 5.9 | 0.1 | 1.2 | 1.8 | | | | |
| 9. Military expenditures | 2.83 | 11.10 | 13.41 | 9.73 | 4.0 | 12.2 | 12.3 | 10.7 | 4.3 | 12.2 | 12.5 | 10.9 |
| 10. Total[b] | 69.90 | 90.97 | 109.03 | 91.18 | 100.0 | 100.0 | 100.0 | 100.0 | 100.0 | 100.0 | 100.0 | 100.0 |
| B. By sector | | | | | BASED ON LINE B-8 | | | | BASED ON LINE B-9 | | | |
| 1. Nonfarm households | 28.68 | 38.18 | 48.33 | 38.85 | 45.6 | 47.9 | 51.3 | 48.7 | 43.6 | 42.0 | 44.9 | 43.4 |
| 2. Nonfarm unincorp. business | 3.95 | 4.39 | 5.24 | 4.53 | 6.3 | 5.5 | 5.6 | 5.7 | 6.0 | 4.8 | 4.9 | 5.1 |
| 3. Agriculture | 5.71 | 6.60 | 5.74 | 6.09 | 9.1 | 8.3 | 6.1 | 7.6 | 8.7 | 7.3 | 5.3 | 6.8 |
| 4. Finance | 0.36 | 0.34 | 0.38 | 0.36 | 0.6 | 0.4 | 0.4 | 0.5 | 0.5 | 0.4 | 0.4 | 0.4 |
| 5. Nonfinancial corporations | 19.61 | 21.63 | 23.88 | 21.65 | 31.1 | 27.1 | 25.3 | 27.1 | 29.8 | 23.8 | 22.2 | 24.2 |
| 6. State and local governments | 3.77 | 6.79 | 9.68 | 7.01 | 6.0 | 8.5 | 10.3 | 8.8 | 5.7 | 7.5 | 9.0 | 7.8 |
| 7a. Federal government, civil | 0.88 | 1.84 | 1.04 | 1.30 | 1.4 | 2.3 | 1.1 | 1.6 | | | | |
| 7b. Federal govt., civil and military | 3.70 | 12.94 | 14.46 | 11.03 | | | | | 5.6 | 14.2 | 13.4 | 12.3 |
| 8. Total, civil expenditures | 62.96 | 79.77 | 94.29 | 79.79 | 100.0 | 100.0 | 100.0 | 100.0 | | | | |
| 9. Total, civil and military expenditures[b] | 65.78 | 90.87 | 107.71 | 89.52 | | | | | 100.0 | 100.0 | 100.0 | 100.0 |

[a]1947-49 prices.

[b]Lines A-10 and B-9 differ because net foreign assets (line A-8) are not included in line B-9.

NOTES TO TABLE 15

Source: All table references below are to <u>National Balance Sheet</u>, Vol. II, unless otherwise specified.

Line A-1: Table VIII-a-1a, lines 1-5.
Line A-2: Table VIII-a-2a, lines 1-5.
Line A-3: Table VIII-a-1a and VIII-a-2a, lines 6 and 7.
Line A-4: Table VIII-a-4a, line 8.
Line A-5: Table VIII-a-6c, line 8.
Line A-6: Table VIII-a-5a, line 8.
Line A-7: Table VIII-a-7a, line 8.
Line A-8: <u>National Wealth</u>, Table A-45, first differences of col. 1 (bottom).
Line A-9: Table VIII-a-7a, line 9.
Line A-10: Sum of lines 7, 8, and 9 of this table.
Line B-1 through B-9: Table VIII-a-7a.

were fairly stable. The share of producer durables, on the other hand, and that of inventories and net foreign assets were considerably lower in the second and third cycles than in the first cycle. In this case, it is the high share in the first cycle that may be regarded as out of line, at least in the case of inventories and net foreign assets, as it reflected special conditions prevailing immediately after the war, namely, rapid refilling of civilian inventories and extraordinarily large foreign assistance by the federal government. In contrast, the share of military expenditures in total gross capital formation was much higher in the second and third than in the first cycle, a result of a change in the international situation.

With the exception of the share of the federal government, the distribution of gross capital formation among the main sectors during the postwar period has also been fairly stable, particularly between the second and third cycles. The share of the central government sector increased substantially, due exclusively to a sharp rise in the expenditures on durable military assets.

## Comparison with Gross Capital Formation Before World War I

It is necessary now to inquire whether and how the volume and composition of gross capital formation during the postwar period differed from that observed before World War II. Since figures entirely comparable to our own estimates are not available before 1946, we must use slightly different statistics. Fortunately, the only long series that can be used, that of Simon Kuznets, comes very close to our own standard concept.[4]

It is then found that the ratio of domestic gross capital formation

[4] See Simon Kuznets, *Capital in the American Economy: Its Formation and Financing,* Princeton for NBER, 1961.

to gross national product, both expressed in current prices, did not fluctuate much between the 1870's and the 1920's if decadal averages are used to eliminate cyclical movements. The ratio, as Table 16 and Chart 5 show, is in all cases about one-fifth, using Kuznets' concept of

TABLE 16

TRENDS IN SHARE OF GROSS CAPITAL FORMATION IN GROSS NATIONAL PRODUCT,
1869-1958, CURRENT PRICES
(per cent)

| | | Gross Capital Formation (1) | Military Assets (2) | Net Foreign Assets (3) | Consumer Durables (4) | Total Including Military (5) | Total Excluding Military (6) |
|---|---|---|---|---|---|---|---|
| 1. | 1869–78 | 20.1 | | -1.3 | 6.9 | 25.7 | 25.7 |
| 2. | 1879–88 | 20.1 | | -0.4 | 6.6 | 26.3 | 26.3 |
| 3. | 1889–98 | 22.7 | | 0.1 | 6.5 | 29.3 | 29.3 |
| 4. | 1899–1908 | 22.4 | | 1.0 | 6.4 | 29.8 | 29.8 |
| 5. | 1909–18 | 19.5 | | 2.4 | 6.7 | 28.6 | 28.6 |
| 6. | 1919–28 | 19.7 | 0.5 | 1.6 | 8.6 | 30.4 | 29.9 |
| 7. | 1929–38 | 14.5 | 0.5 | 0.5 | 7.8 | 23.3 | 22.8 |
| 8. | 1939–48 | 14.8 | 5.5 | 1.0 | 7.5 | 28.8 | 23.3 |
| 9. | 1949–55 | 21.4 | 2.3 | -0.2 | 9.9 | 33.4 | 31.1 |
| 10. | 1949–58[a] | 18.8 | 4.0 | 0.3 | 9.1 | 32.2 | 28.2 |

Source

Numerator
Col. 1, lines 1-9:  Unpublished worksheets underlying R tables in Appendixes
   A - E   of Kuznets, Capital in the American Economy, minus the corresponding figures in col. 3 of this table.
Col. 1, line 10:  Standard concept as defined in Table 12 excluding lines I-4, II-3, and III-5 (foreign sector).
Col. 2, lines 1-9:  Unpublished worksheets underlying R tables (ibid.).
Col. 2, line 10:  Same source as Table 12, lines III-6 to III-8.
Col. 3, lines 1-9:  Unpublished worksheets underlying R tables (ibid.) and Table R-4, col. 4 (ibid.).
Col. 3, line 10:  Same source as Table 12, lines I-4, II-3, and III-5.
Col. 4, lines 1-9:  Unpublished worksheets underlying R tables (ibid.).
Col. 5, line 10:  Same source as Table 12, line II-2.
Denominator
Cols. 1-4, lines 1-9:  Unpublished worksheets underlying R tables   (ibid.) and Table R-1, col. 9 (ibid.).
Cols. 1-4, line 10:  Department of Commerce estimate of GNP.

   [a]These ratios differ slightly from those in Table 12, col. 5, because the denominator here does not include the adjustment for use value of consumer durables and government capital.

gross civilian capital formation. It is close to 30 per cent if allowance is made for consumer durable and military assets to make this series comparable to the broad concept of capital formation used for the postwar period.

The results of the comparison between this fairly stable level for the sixty years between 1869 and 1928 and the postwar period depend to

## CHART 5

### SHARE OF GROSS CAPITAL FORMATION
### IN GROSS NATIONAL PRODUCT, 1869–1958

■ Civilian assets (excluding consumer durables)
Consumer durables
Military assets

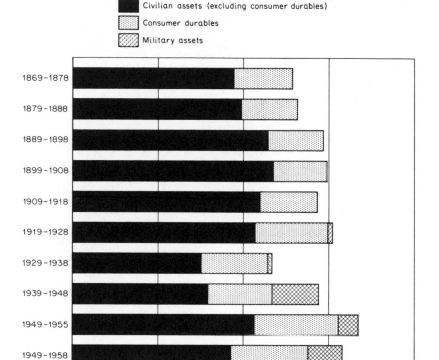

Source: Table 16.

some extent on the concept used. Under the broad concept, the average for the postwar period is virtually the same as that for the sixty years before the Great Depression. If consumer durables and military assets are excluded, the postwar average is slightly below the figure for most of the six decades before 1930.

The conclusion, therefore, is that if the broad concept of capital formation is used, no definite trend is evident in the share of gross capital formation in gross national product. The ratio has kept remarkably close to 30 per cent since about 1870 if the influence of business cycles, the war periods, and the 1930's are excluded. If the narrower definition is used, there may have been a slight decline in the gross capital formation ratio, possibly from one-fifth in the first quarter of the twentieth century to about one-seventh before the 1950's. During the 1950's the share of gross capital formation excluding consumer durables and military assets was again about one-fifth of gross national product. The changes in the proportion, however, are rather small compared to the far-reaching changes that occurred in the same period in the size and structure of the American economy and in the financing of its growth. The relation of the American economy's financing task in the broadest sense to the greatly increased gross national product, i.e., the share of total gross output that must be set aside to finance capital formation and thus to form the basis for additions to national wealth, is very similar to what it was one, two and three generations ago. Within total financing there have, of course, been significant changes. Because the shares of government and consumer durables in gross capital formation increased, the financing of these two sectors became a relatively heavier task. Consequently, the financing of nonagricultural business, and still more of agriculture, became a lighter task relative to the country's total resources as measured by its gross national product.

## Net Capital Formation

While the concept of gross capital formation is fairly clear-cut once the scope of capital assets is settled, the division of total capital expenditures into those that represent net capital formation, i.e., additions to the net stock of national wealth, and those that are needed to make good capital consumption, i.e., to keep the net stock of real wealth intact, is necessarily to some degree arbitrary because of the difficulty of calculating economically significant capital consumption allowances.

It is therefore fairly straightforward to say that gross capital formation is financed by gross saving plus net external financing, since gross capital expenditures and gross saving (internal financing is equal to current income less current expenditures) can be measured unequivocally within a system of business or national accounting.[5]

Although it may similarly be said that net capital formation is

[5] The sum of gross saving and net external financing of a unit, sector, or open national economy is, of course, not equal to gross capital formation, the difference representing the net increase or decrease in financial assets.

financed by external funds and by net saving, the estimation of the volume of net saving, and hence the financial distribution of that saving between external and internal funds, depends on the size of capital consumption allowances, the calculation of which is largely conventional. Furthermore, while net saving may be calculated informally in the same way, it has different meanings for business enterprises, on the one hand, and for households and the government, on the other. For the former, capital consumption allowances—and hence retained earnings—probably have some influence on investment and other business decisions. This influence, however, should not be overestimated. The entrepreneur in his calculations may not rely on the capital consumption allowances that appear in his books, but may make adjustments, probably implicitly rather than in exact figures, for changes in replacement cost, obsolescence, and other relevant factors. Secondly, while hardly any business keeps capital consumption allowances which it has not spent on replacement segregated in the form of liquid assets, entrepreneurs probably make some allowance in their financial planning for the expected cost of replacement, at least for the next few years. There is hardly any parallel to this in the operation of households and little in the management of government finances. Only few household and government units calculate depreciation on their tangible assets, and not many of them accumulate liquid assets in order to replace durable assets as they wear out. Certainly, no calculation or provision of this sort is made for the most important tangible asset—houses. For households and governments, therefore, net capital formation generally is not a motivationally important concept, and the separation of internal financing into capital consumption allowances and net saving is often not very meaningful.

For the entire economy, on the other hand, the distinction between gross and net capital formation is essential to measure the growth of the economy's stock of capital. We must, therefore, briefly review the volume and composition of net capital formation during the postwar period and compare it with earlier experience. In this review, the estimates of capital consumption allowances are based throughout on replacement cost and on standardized length-of-life assumptions in order to treat the different sectors of the economy and the different types of reproducible durable assets consistently, and to come as close as possible to an economically meaningful estimation of these allowances and net capital formation.

Estimates of net capital formation for the entire postwar period and for the three business cycles within it are shown in Table 17 in current prices—where depreciation allowances are based on replacement cost—and in Table 18 in constant (1947–49) prices. The two tables, parallel to Tables 14 and 15 which are on a gross basis, show separate estimates for eight main types of capital expenditures in the upper part of the tables and for each of the seven main economic sectors in the lower part.

As in the case of gross capital formation, there are considerable differences between the first cycle, on the one hand, and the second and third cycles, on the other. These differences are particularly pronounced if military assets are included because net military capital formation in the first cycle was negative to an amount equal to almost two-fifths of civilian net capital formation so that all other shares in total capital formation are much higher than in civilian net capital formation.

Even if domestic civilian net capital formation is used as the basis, substantial changes in the composition remain. The share of residential structures is considerably higher in the second and third cycles than in the first cycle. A still sharper increase is shown in the shares of nonresidential private structures and of government structures, not only from the first to the second but also from the second to the third cycle.

This increase is offset by the decline in the share of equipment, which again is not limited to the comparison between the first and second cycle but continues from the second to the third cycle. The two main reasons for this decline are that the volume of expenditures on equipment increased more rapidly immediately after World War II than construction expenditures did, and depreciation allowances on equipment were fairly low in the first few postwar years because of the low level of expenditures during the war years and the 1930's.

The share of inventories in net capital formation shows no trend if the effects of price fluctuations are eliminated (Table 18). If, on the other hand, the calculation is based on the change in book values of inventories (Table 17)—an approach which is more appropriate in an analysis of financial problems—the average share is considerably higher, reflecting the general upward movement of commodity prices during the immediate postwar period; and there is a sharp decline from the first cycle to the second and third cycles.

The significance of net capital formation can be understood best when compared to total national output, in this case appropriately

## TABLE 17

### NET INVESTMENT IN CURRENT PRICES, 1946-58

| | Annual Averages (billion dollars) | | | | Distribution (per cent) | | | | | | | |
|---|---|---|---|---|---|---|---|---|---|---|---|---|
| | 1946 -49 (1) | 1949 -54 (2) | 1954 -58 (3) | 1946 -58 (4) | 1946 -49 (5) | 1949 -54 (6) | 1954 -58 (7) | 1946 -58 (8) | 1946 -49 (9) | 1949 -54 (10) | 1954 -58 (11) | 1946 -58 (12) |
| **A. By type of wealth** | | | | | BASED ON LINE A-10a | | | | BASED ON LINE A-10b | | | |
| 1. Residential structures | 4.43 | 8.35 | 11.46 | 8.22 | 18.9 | 21.5 | 23.6 | 21.9 | 24.7 | 21.8 | 24.9 | 23.6 |
| 2. Other private structures | 2.43 | 4.58 | 7.92 | 5.11 | 10.4 | 11.8 | 16.3 | 13.6 | 13.6 | 12.0 | 17.2 | 14.7 |
| 3. Government structures (civil) | 0.51 | 3.72 | 6.45 | 3.86 | 2.2 | 9.6 | 13.3 | 10.3 | 2.8 | 9.7 | 14.0 | 11.1 |
| 4. Producer durables | 7.66 | 6.97 | 6.58 | 6.74 | 32.7 | 18.0 | 13.6 | 17.9 | 42.7 | 18.2 | 14.3 | 19.4 |
| 5a. Gross inventories | 7.48 | 4.91 | 5.22 | 5.94 | 32.0 | 12.7 | 10.8 | 15.8 | | | | |
| 5b. Net inventories (value adjusted) | 2.00 | 4.38 | 2.66 | 3.14 | | | | | 11.2 | 11.4 | 5.8 | 9.0 |
| 6. Consumer durables | 8.15 | 8.44 | 7.86 | 7.87 | 34.8 | 21.8 | 16.2 | 20.9 | 45.5 | 22.1 | 17.1 | 22.6 |
| 7a. Total (incl. 5a) | 30.66 | 36.97 | 45.49 | 37.74 | 131.0 | 95.3 | 93.7 | 100.3 | | | | |
| 7b. Total (incl. 5b) | 25.18 | 36.44 | 42.93 | 34.94 | | | | | 140.4 | 95.2 | 93.4 | 100.4 |
| 8. Net foreign assets | 4.36 | 0.47 | 1.97 | 2.05 | 18.6 | 1.2 | 4.1 | 5.5 | 24.3 | 1.2 | 4.3 | 5.9 |
| 9. Military expenditures | -11.61 | 1.35 | 1.07 | -2.18 | -49.6 | 3.5 | 2.2 | -5.8 | -64.8 | 3.5 | 2.3 | -6.3 |
| 10a. Total (7a + 8 + 9)[a] | 23.41 | 38.79 | 48.53 | 37.61 | 100.0 | 100.0 | 100.0 | 100.0 | | | | |
| 10b. Total (7b + 8 + 9) | 17.93 | 38.26 | 45.97 | 34.81 | | | | | 100.0 | 100.0 | 100.0 | 100.0 |
| **B. By sector** | | | | | BASED ON LINE B-8 | | | | BASED ON LINE B-9 | | | |
| 1. Nonfarm households | 11.32 | 16.46 | 20.32 | 16.00 | 36.9 | 44.5 | 44.7 | 42.4 | 59.5 | 43.0 | 43.6 | 45.0 |
| 2. Nonfarm unincorp. business[b] | 2.46 | 1.67 | 2.06 | 1.98 | 8.0 | 4.5 | 4.5 | 5.2 | 12.9 | 4.4 | 4.4 | 5.6 |
| 3. Agriculture[b] | 3.49 | 1.48 | 0.92 | 2.04 | 11.4 | 4.0 | 2.0 | 5.4 | 18.3 | 3.9 | 2.0 | 5.7 |
| 4. Finance | 0.09 | 0.14 | 0.17 | 0.13 | 0.3 | 0.4 | 0.4 | 0.3 | 0.5 | 0.4 | 0.4 | 0.4 |
| 5. Nonfinancial corporations[b] | 12.92 | 12.64 | 15.17 | 13.29 | 42.2 | 34.2 | 33.3 | 35.2 | 67.9 | 33.0 | 32.6 | 37.4 |
| 6. State and local governments | 0.76 | 3.75 | 6.75 | 4.03 | 2.5 | 10.1 | 14.8 | 10.7 | 4.0 | 9.8 | 14.5 | 11.3 |
| 7a. Federal government, civil | -0.39 | 0.84 | 0.10 | 0.28 | -1.3 | 2.3 | 0.2 | 0.7 | | | | |
| 7b. Federal govt., civil and military | -12.00 | 2.20 | 1.17 | -1.90 | | | | | -63.0 | 5.7 | 2.5 | -5.3 |
| 8. Total, civil expenditures | 30.65 | 36.98 | 45.49 | 37.75 | 100.0 | 100.0 | 100.0 | 100.0 | | | | |
| 9. Total, civil and military expenditures | 19.04 | 38.34 | 46.56 | 35.57 | | | | | 100.0 | 100.0 | 100.0 | 100.0 |

Source: Same as in Table 14, except that Tables VIII-a-1b through VIII-a-7b and VIII-a-7e are used instead of VIII-a-1 through VIII-a-7 and VIII-a-7d of National Balance Sheet, Vol. II.

[a] Lines A-10a and B-9 differ because net foreign assets (line A-8) are not included in line B-9.

[b] The concept of inventory used here is the same as in line A-5a.

TABLE 18

NET INVESTMENT IN CONSTANT PRICES,[a] 1946-58

| | Annual Averages (billion dollars) | | | | Distribution (per cent) | | | | | | | |
|---|---|---|---|---|---|---|---|---|---|---|---|---|
| | 1946 -49 (1) | 1949 -54 (2) | 1954 -58 (3) | 1946 -58 (4) | 1946 -49 (5) | 1949 -54 (6) | 1954 -58 (7) | 1946 -58 (8) | 1946 -49 (9) | 1949 -54 (10) | 1954 -58 (11) | 1946 -58 (12) |
| **A. By type of wealth** | | | | | BASED ON LINE A-10 | | | | | | | |
| 1. Residential structures | 4.54 | 7.28 | 8.99 | 6.99 | 26.4 | 21.9 | 24.4 | 23.7 | | | | |
| 2. Other private structures | 2.33 | 3.76 | 5.72 | 4.02 | 13.6 | 11.3 | 15.5 | 13.6 | | | | |
| 3. Government structures (civil) | 0.38 | 3.26 | 5.17 | 3.16 | 2.2 | 9.8 | 14.0 | 10.7 | | | | |
| 4. Producer durables | 7.90 | 5.98 | 4.74 | 5.84 | 46.0 | 18.0 | 12.9 | 19.8 | | | | |
| 5. Inventories | 1.90 | 3.74 | 2.09 | 2.75 | 11.1 | 11.3 | 5.7 | 9.3 | | | | |
| 6. Consumer durables | 8.38 | 8.06 | 7.85 | 7.86 | 48.8 | 24.3 | 21.3 | 26.6 | | | | |
| 7. Total | 25.43 | 32.08 | 34.56 | 30.62 | 148.0 | 96.6 | 93.7 | 103.6 | | | | |
| 8. Net foreign assets | 4.12 | 0.11 | 1.34 | 1.66 | 24.0 | 0.3 | 3.6 | 5.6 | | | | |
| 9. Military expenditures | -12.37 | 1.01 | 0.98 | -2.73 | -72.0 | 3.0 | 2.7 | -9.2 | | | | |
| 10. Total[b] | 17.18 | 33.20 | 36.88 | 29.55 | 100.0 | 100.0 | 100.0 | 100.0 | | | | |
| **B. By sector** | | | | | BASED ON LINE B-8 | | | | BASED ON LINE B-9 | | | |
| 1. Nonfarm households | 11.63 | 14.94 | 17.43 | 14.57 | 45.7 | 46.6 | 50.4 | 47.6 | 89.1 | 45.2 | 49.0 | 52.2 |
| 2. Nonfarm unincorp. business | 1.62 | 1.22 | 1.29 | 1.31 | 6.4 | 3.8 | 3.7 | 4.3 | 12.4 | 3.7 | 3.6 | 4.7 |
| 3. Agriculture | 2.16 | 1.89 | 0.39 | 1.48 | 8.5 | 5.9 | 1.1 | 4.8 | 16.5 | 5.7 | 1.1 | 5.3 |
| 4. Finance | 0.09 | 0.12 | 0.12 | 0.11 | 0.4 | 0.4 | 0.3 | 0.4 | 0.7 | 0.4 | 0.3 | 0.4 |
| 5. Nonfinancial corporations | 9.85 | 9.76 | 9.76 | 9.59 | 38.7 | 30.4 | 28.2 | 31.3 | 75.4 | 29.5 | 27.5 | 34.4 |
| 6. State and local governments | 0.70 | 3.29 | 5.42 | 3.35 | 2.8 | 10.3 | 15.7 | 10.9 | 5.4 | 9.9 | 15.3 | 12.0 |
| 7a. Federal government, civil | -0.61 | 0.85 | 0.14 | 0.21 | -2.4 | 2.7 | 0.4 | 0.7 | | | | |
| 7b. Federal govt, civil and military | -12.98 | 1.86 | 1.12 | -2.52 | | | | | -99.4 | 5.6 | 3.2 | -9.0 |
| 8. Total, civil expenditures | 25.44 | 32.07 | 34.55 | 30.62 | 100.0 | 100.0 | 100.0 | 100.0 | | | | |
| 9. Total, civil and military expenditures[b] | 13.07 | 33.08 | 35.53 | 27.89 | | | | | 100.0 | 100.0 | 100.0 | 100.0 |

Source: Same as in Table 15, except that Tables VIII-a-1c through VIII-a-7c are used instead of Tables VIII-a-1a through VIII-a-7a of National Balance Sheet, Vol. II.

[a] 1947-49 prices.

[b] Lines A-10 and B-9 differ because net foreign assets (line A-8) are not included in line B-9.

represented by net national product. The necessary figures are also shown in Table 19. For the postwar period as a whole, net capital formation was equal to about one-eighth of net national product, regardless of whether military assets are included. The movements of this ratio during the period, however, differ considerably, depending on whether the calculation is based on civilian or total capital formation. According to the former calculations, there was no significant movement in the ratio from the first to the second or from the second to the third cycle. If military assets are included, the pattern is different. The share for the second and third cycles equaled one-seventh of net national product and was higher than that for the first cycle when it stood at only 10 per cent. The difference, of course, arises because net military capital formation was heavily negative in the first period, when current expenditures on new military durables were far below the depreciation allowances calculated on the huge stock of such durables in existence at the end of World War II, while net military capital formation was positive, although only to the extent of about $1 billion a year, during the second and third cycles.

As in the case of gross capital formation, it is well to obtain some historical perspective by comparing the ratio of net capital formation to net national product observed in the postwar period with similar ratios for earlier periods. It is then found that this ratio averaged about one-seventh in the three decades ending in 1929, compared to one-eighth in the postwar period. The decline is actually somewhat larger, since the 1901–29 period includes World War I, during which net capital formation was low. If these years are excluded to make the period comparable to the postwar period, the ratio rises to one-seventh for the two periods 1901–12 and 1920–29. It therefore appears that there has been a downward shift in the ratio between the nonwar periods of the first three decades of the century and the postwar period.

No parallel to this movement was found in the ratio of gross capital formation to gross national product. The difference reflects the fact that the proportion of capital consumption allowances to gross capital formation has increased. To put it otherwise, a smaller proportion of gross capital formation now becomes an addition to the net stock of national wealth, which reflects the shorter average life of gross capital formation in the postwar period due to an increase in the share of producer and consumer durables compared to long-lived structures.

TABLE 19

TRENDS IN SHARE OF NET CAPITAL FORMATION IN NET NATIONAL PRODUCT, 1869-1958,
REPLACEMENT COST DEPRECIATION
(per cent)

| | Net Civilian Capital Formation (1) | Military Assets (2) | Net Foreign Assets (3) | Consumer Durables (4) | Total Including Military (5) | Total Excluding Military (6) |
|---|---|---|---|---|---|---|
| 1. 1869-78 | 13.1 | | -1.4 | 7.5 | 19.2 | 19.2 |
| 2. 1879-88 | 12.5 | | -0.4 | 7.2 | 19.3 | 19.3 |
| 3. 1889-98 | 13.7 | | 0.2 | 7.3 | 21.2 | 21.2 |
| 4. 1899-1908 | 13.5 | | 1.1 | 1.6 | 16.2 | 16.2 |
| 5. 1909-18 | 9.6 | | 2.7 | 0.8 | 13.1 | 13.1 |
| 6. 1919-28 | 10.0 | -0.5 | 1.8 | 1.4 | 12.7 | 13.2 |
| 7. 1929-38 | 1.8 | 0 | 0.5 | -0.3 | 2.0 | 2.0 |
| 8. 1939-48 | 3.1 | 2.8 | 1.2 | 1.9 | 9.0 | 6.2 |
| 9. 1949-55 | 8.8 | -1.2 | -0.3 | 2.7 | 10.0 | 11.2 |
| 10. 1949-58 | 10.0 | 0.3 | 0.4 | 2.5 | 13.2 | 12.9 |

Source

Numerator

Col. 1, lines 1-9: Unpublished worksheets underlying R tables in Appendixes
A - E of Kuznets, Capital in the American Economy, minus the corresponding
figures in col.3 of this table.
Col. 1, line 10: Table 16, col. 1, line 10, minus depreciation at replacement
cost of construction, producer durables, and government civil capital forma-
tion (the difference between lines 8 in Table VIII-a-7 and VIII-a-7b minus
the difference between lines 8 in Tables VIII-a-5 and VIII-a-5b of National
Balance Sheet, Vol. II).
Col. 2, lines 1-9: Unpublished worksheets underlying R tables
(Kuznets, Capital in the American Economy).
Col. 2, line 10: Table 16, col. 2, line 10, minus depreciation at replacement
cost of military capital expenditure (the difference between lines 9 in
Tables VIII-a-7 and VIII-a-7b of National Balance Sheet, Vol. II).
Col. 3: Same as Table 16, col. 3.
Col. 4, lines 1-3: Same as Table 16, col. 4, lines 1-3. (No data for re-
placement cost depreciation are available.)
Col. 4, lines 4-8: Table 16, col. 4, minus depreciation at replacement cost.
(For depreciation at replacement cost, see Goldsmith, Study of Saving,
Vol. I, Table Q-9, col. 1; Table A-28, col. 1; and Table A-29, col. 5.)
Col. 4, lines 9-10: Table 16, col. 4, line 10, minus depreciation on consumer
goods at replacement cost (the difference between lines 8 in Tables VIII-a-5
and VIII-a-5b of National Balance Sheet, Vol. II).
Denominator
Cols. 1-6, lines 1-9: Unpublished worksheets underlying R tables (Kuznets,
Capital in the American Economy) and Table R-1, col. 6 (ibid.).
Cols. 1-6, line 10: GNP figures as given in Table 16, line 10, minus depre-
ciation at replacement cost of construction, producer durables, and government capital formation (the difference between lines 10 in Tables VIII-a-7
and VIII-a-7b minus the difference between lines 8 in Tables VIII-a-5 and
VIII-a-5b of National Balance Sheet, Vol. II).

The changes in the composition of net capital formation (Table 20)
are considerably larger than those in the gross figures. This is the
result of differences in the level and changes in the ratio of capital
consumption to gross capital expenditures among different types of
capital expenditures.

Residential structures represent the most important single type of

TABLE 20

NET CAPITAL EXPENDITURES IN CONSTANT[a] PRICES, 1901-58

| | Residential Structures (1) | Nonresidential Private (2) | Nonresidential Structures Government (3) | Producer Durables (4) | Inventories (5) | Consumer Durables (6) | Total (7) | Monetary Metals (8) | Total Incl. Monetary Metals (9) |
|---|---|---|---|---|---|---|---|---|---|
| | | | I. AGGREGATES (BILLION DOLLARS) | | | | | | |
| 1901-12 | 34.0 | 33.5 | 11.5 | 17.5 | 5.0 | 11.0 | 112.5 | 1.4 | 113.9 |
| 1913-22 | 28.6 | 18.0 | 7.2 | 11.3 | 18.7 | 5.1 | 88.9 | 3.4 | 92.3 |
| 1923-29 | 61.8 | 27.4 | 16.3 | 11.4 | 7.6 | 19.5 | 144.0 | 0.4 | 144.4 |
| 1930-39 | -10.5 | -16.2 | 22.0 | -7.0 | -2.4 | 0.3 | -13.8 | 11.5 | -2.3 |
| 1940-45 | -5.0 | -10.6 | 3.1 | 12.3 | 12.3 | 3.7 | 15.8 | 3.3 | 19.1 |
| 1901-45 | 108.9 | 52.1 | 60.1 | 45.5 | 41.2 | 39.6 | 347.4 | 20.0 | 367.4 |
| 1946-58 | 92.8 | 52.2 | 39.2 | 76.0 | 35.7 | 102.1 | 398.0 | 1.0 | 399.0 |
| 1901-29 | 124.4 | 78.9 | 35.0 | 40.2 | 31.3 | 35.6 | 345.4 | 5.2 | 350.6 |
| | | | II. ANNUAL AVERAGES (BILLION DOLLARS) | | | | | | |
| 1901-12 | 2.83 | 2.79 | 0.96 | 1.46 | 0.42 | 0.92 | 9.38 | 0.12 | 9.49 |
| 1913-22 | 2.86 | 1.80 | 0.72 | 1.13 | 1.87 | 0.51 | 8.89 | 0.34 | 9.23 |
| 1923-29 | 8.83 | 3.91 | 2.33 | 1.63 | 1.09 | 2.79 | 20.58 | 0.06 | 20.63 |
| 1930-39 | -1.05 | -1.62 | 2.20 | -0.70 | -0.24 | 0.03 | -1.38 | 1.15 | -0.23 |
| 1940-45 | -0.83 | -1.77 | 0.52 | 2.05 | 2.05 | 0.62 | 2.63 | 0.55 | 3.18 |
| 1901-45 | 2.42 | 1.16 | 1.34 | 1.01 | 0.92 | 0.88 | 7.72 | 0.44 | 8.16 |
| 1946-58 | 7.14 | 4.02 | 3.02 | 5.84 | 2.75 | 7.86 | 30.62 | 0.08 | 30.69 |
| 1901-29 | 4.29 | 2.72 | 1.21 | 1.39 | 1.08 | 1.23 | 11.91 | 0.18 | 12.09 |

(continued)

TABLE 20 (concluded)

III. DISTRIBUTION (PER CENT)

| | Residential Structures (1) | Nonresidential Structures Private (2) | Nonresidential Structures Government (3) | Producer Durables (4) | Inventories (5) | Consumer Durables (6) | Total (7) | Monetary Metals (8) | Total Incl. Monetary Metals (9) |
|---|---|---|---|---|---|---|---|---|---|
| 1901–12 | 30.2 | 29.8 | 10.2 | 15.6 | 4.4 | 9.8 | 100.0 | 1.2 | 101.2 |
| 1913–22 | 32.2 | 20.2 | 8.1 | 12.7 | 21.0 | 5.7 | 100.0 | 3.8 | 103.8 |
| 1923–29 | 42.9 | 19.0 | 11.3 | 7.9 | 5.3 | 13.5 | 100.0 | 0.3 | 100.3 |
| 1930–39[b] | −76.1 | −117.4 | 159.4 | −50.7 | −17.4 | 2.2 | −100.0 | 83.3 | −16.7 |
| 1940–45 | −31.6 | −67.1 | 19.6 | 77.8 | 77.8 | 23.4 | 100.0 | 20.9 | 120.9 |
| 1901–45 | 31.3 | 15.0 | 17.3 | 13.1 | 11.9 | 11.4 | 100.0 | 5.8 | 105.8 |
| 1946–58 | 23.3 | 13.1 | 9.8 | 19.1 | 9.0 | 25.7 | 100.0 | 0.3 | 100.3 |
| 1901–29 | 36.0 | 22.8 | 10.1 | 11.6 | 9.1 | 10.3 | 100.0 | 1.5 | 101.5 |

Source

1901–45: Goldsmith, National Wealth, Table A–6 (first differences).
1946–58, col. 1: National Balance Sheet, Vol. II, Table VIII–a–1c, line 8.
1946–58, col. 3: Ibid, Table VIII–a–2c, lines 6 and 7.
1946–58, cols. 2, 4–6: Table 18.
1946–58, col. 8: Goldsmith, National Wealth, Table A–6 (first differences).

[a] 1947–49 prices.
[b] The signs have been reversed to match the sign of the numerator.

capital expenditures on the net, as well as the gross, basis; for 1901–29, they accounted on the average for more than one-third of total net capital formation against hardly one-quarter in the postwar period 1946–58. Similarly, the share of private nonresidential structures averaged only one-eighth during the postwar period against nearly one-quarter in 1901–29. Inventories and government civilian structures accounted for about the same proportion in both periods. Sharp increases are observed, on the other hand, in the share of equipment, both for producers and consumers.

From the point of view of finance, these changes in the composition of net capital formation mean that the share of relatively short-lived assets—producer durables, consumer durables, and inventories—increased from three-tenths to over one-half of total net capital formation between the first three decades of this century and the postwar period. This, in turn, implies an increased ratio of capital consumption allowances to gross capital formation and means that a smaller fraction of total gross capital formation needs to be financed by retained net earnings, net saving, or external financing. If we assume that residential structures and consumer durables must be financed by households while private nonresidential structures, producer durables, and inventories are financed by business, the share of the three main sectors in total net capital formation was about the same during the postwar period as it had been from 1901 to 1929. Households accounted for close to one-half of total net capital formation, business for slightly over two-fifths, and government for about one-tenth. These ratios are based on civilian net capital formation. If military assets are included, the government share was considerably lower in the postwar period than it had been in the first three decades of the century, and the shares of both households and business were higher in the postwar period than formerly.

# CHAPTER 4

# Internal and External Financing

---

## The National Picture for the Postwar Period

THE national aggregates of financial flows are of only limited interest because, in a country in which external flows are as small as in the United States (about 1 to 2 per cent of total sources or uses of funds [1]), gross saving is necessarily approximately equal to domestic gross capital formation, net saving is equal to net capital formation, and lending (including acquisition of equity securities) is equal to borrowing (including issuance of equity securities). The only relationships that retain significance on a national scale are the ratio of capital consumption allowances to gross capital formation, and hence the division of internal funds into capital consumption allowances and net saving; the ratio of external finance in the broadest sense (the sum of net lending or borrowing) to internal finance and to net and gross capital formation; and the structure of external financing, i.e., the division between debt and equity and between short- and long-term financing. These relations can be studied in Table 21 and Chart 6.

### THE POSTWAR PERIOD AS A WHOLE

For the postwar period as a whole, capital consumption allowances, based on replacement cost, uniform and reasonably realistic length-of-life assumptions, and straight-line depreciation, amounted to two-thirds of gross capital formation including military assets and to three-fifths excluding them (Table 22).[2] While alternative, justifiable calculations

---

[1] Raymond W. Goldsmith, *The National Wealth of the United States in the Postwar Period,* Princeton for NBER, 1962, Table B-187, p. 422.

[2] Since inventories are not subject to depreciation, it might be more appropriate to use the ratio of expenditures on structures and equipment to capital consump-

TABLE 21

COMBINED SOURCES AND USES OF FUNDS OF ALL SECTORS, 1946-58

| | Annual Averages (billion dollars) | | | | Shares (per cent) | | | |
|---|---|---|---|---|---|---|---|---|
| | 1946-49[a] (1) | 1949-54[a] (2) | 1954-58[a] (3) | 1946-58 (4) | 1946-49 (5) | 1949-54 (6) | 1954-58 (7) | 1946-58 (8) |
| **I. Uses** | | | | | | | | |
| 1. Gross capital expenditures | 69.4 | 103.9 | 136.3 | 105.4 | 65.4 | 63.4 | 63.9 | 64.3 |
| 2. Acquisition of financial assets | 36.7 | 60.2 | 76.9 | 58.6 | 34.6 | 36.7 | 36.1 | 35.7 |
| a. Short-term assets[b] | 13.2 | 28.1 | 32.7 | 24.4 | 12.4 | 17.1 | 15.3 | 14.9 |
| i. Loans | 16.7 | 25.5 | 33.1 | 25.1 | 15.7 | 15.5 | 15.5 | 15.3 |
| ii. Bills and notes | -3.5 | 2.6 | -0.4 | -0.7 | -3.3 | 1.6 | -0.2 | -0.4 |
| b. Long-term assets[b] | 21.5 | 29.2 | 40.0 | 31.0 | 20.3 | 17.8 | 18.8 | 18.9 |
| i. Loans | 17.6 | 20.8 | 28.9 | 22.6 | 16.6 | 12.7 | 13.6 | 13.8 |
| ii. Bonds | 3.9 | 8.4 | 11.1 | 8.4 | 3.7 | 5.1 | 5.2 | 5.1 |
| c. Equities[b] | 2.0 | 2.9 | 4.2 | 3.2 | 1.9 | 1.8 | 2.0 | 2.0 |
| 3. Total uses | 106.1 | 164.0 | 213.2 | 164.0 | 100.0 | 100.0 | 100.0 | 100.0 |
| **II. Sources** | | | | | | | | |
| 1. Gross saving | 74.1 | 102.6 | 137.9 | 106.6 | 69.8 | 62.6 | 64.7 | 65.0 |
| a. Depreciation | 50.3 | 65.6 | 89.7 | 69.9 | 47.4 | 40.0 | 42.1 | 42.6 |
| b. Net saving | 23.8 | 37.0 | 48.2 | 36.7 | 22.4 | 22.6 | 22.6 | 22.4 |
| 2. External sources | 32.0 | 61.5 | 75.3 | 57.4 | 30.2 | 37.5 | 35.3 | 35.0 |
| a. Short-term liabilities[b] | 10.3 | 30.6 | 33.3 | 24.9 | 9.7 | 18.7 | 15.6 | 15.2 |
| i. Loans | 14.0 | 27.5 | 33.3 | 25.3 | 13.2 | 16.8 | 15.6 | 15.4 |
| ii. Bills and notes | -3.7 | 3.1 | 0 | -0.4 | -3.5 | 1.9 | 0 | -0.2 |
| b. Long-term liabilities[b] | 19.7 | 27.9 | 37.8 | 29.3 | 18.6 | 17.0 | 17.7 | 17.9 |
| i. Loans | 15.6 | 19.5 | 26.7 | 20.9 | 14.7 | 11.9 | 12.5 | 12.7 |
| ii. Bonds | 4.1 | 8.4 | 11.1 | 8.4 | 3.9 | 5.1 | 5.2 | 5.1 |
| c. Equities[b] | 1.9 | 2.9 | 4.2 | 3.1 | 1.8 | 1.8 | 2.0 | 1.9 |
| 3. Total sources | 106.1 | 164.0 | 213.2 | 164.0 | 100.0 | 100.0 | 100.0 | 100.0 |
| 4. Inventory profits | 5.5 | 0.5 | 2.6 | 2.8 | 5.2 | 0.3 | 1.2 | 1.7 |

NOTES TO TABLE 21

Source: <u>National Balance Sheet</u>, Vol. II.

Section I
Line 1:  Table VIII-a-7, line 10.
Line 2:  Table V, line II-21.
Line 2a:  Sum of lines 2ai and 2aii.
Line 2ai:  Table V, sum of lines II-1, 2, 6, 7, 8, 10; Table VIII-b-20, line 11; and Table VIII-b-9, line 8, minus Table VIII-c-9b, line 8.
Line 2aii:  Table V, line II-13a, plus first difference of Table III-5*l*-a, col. 1.
Line 2b:  Sum of lines 2bi and 2bii.
Line 2bi:  Table V, sum of lines II-3, 4, 5, 11, 12; Table VIII-c-9b, line 8; and Table VIII-b-20, lines 9 and 10.
Line 2bii:  Table V, sum of lines II-13b, 13c, 14, and 15, minus the first difference of Table III-5*l*-a, col. 1.
Line 2c:  Table V, sum of lines II-16 and II-17.
Line 3:  Tables VII-1 through VII-7-1, lines V.

Section II
Line 1:  Tables VII, line IV-3, of all sectors.
Line 1a:  Table VIII-a-7, line 10, minus VIII-a-7b, line 10.
Line 1b:  Lines 1 minus 1a.
Line 2:  Table V, sum of lines III-14, IV-1, and IV-2.
Line 2a:  Sum of lines 2ai and 2aii.
Line 2ai:  Table V, sum of lines III-1, 2, 6, 7, 8, 10, 13, and Table VIII-c-9a, line 8.
Line 2aii:  Table VIII-b-13a, line 10, and first difference of col. 1, Table III-5*l*-a.
Line 2b:  Sum of lines 2bi and 2bii.
Line 2bi:  Table V, sum of lines III-3, 4, 5, and 11, and Table VIII-c-9b, line 8.
Line 2bii:  Table VIII-b-13b, line 9, plus Table VIII-b-13c, line 11, plus Table VIII-c-12, lines 4, 5, 6, and 7b, minus first difference of Table III-5*l*-a, col. 1.
Line 2c:  Table V, lines IV-1 and 2.
Line 3:  Same as line I-3.
Line 4:  Table VIII-a-6b, line 10, minus Table VIII-a-6d, line 10.

[a]Cycle averages.

[b]Differences between lines I-2a and II-2a, lines I-2b and II-2b, and lines I-2c and II-2c are due mainly to the fact that the rest-of-the-world sector was not introduced explicitly in all the basic tables, i.e., in <u>National Balance Sheet</u> Vol. II, Tables V and VII.

Note:  Components may not add to totals because of rounding here and elsewhere in this chapter.

of capital consumption allowances—particularly the use of declining balance instead of straight-line depreciation—would yield slightly different results, the range would probably remain between three-fifths and three-fourths including military assets and between five-ninths and six-ninths excluding them.[3]

---

tion allowances. For the postwar period as a whole, this ratio amounted to 71 per cent if military assets are included and to 64 per cent if they are excluded. (See Raymond W. Goldsmith, Robert E. Lipsey, and Morris Mendelson, *Studies in the National Balance Sheet of the United States,* Princeton for NBER, 1963, Vol. II, Tables VIII-a-6 and VIII-a-7.)

[3] Use of original (instead of replacement) cost as the basis of capital consumption allowances, for instance, would reduce the share of these allowances for the entire

CHART 6

TRENDS IN THE STRUCTURE OF FINANCING,
MAIN SECTORS COMBINED, 1901–58

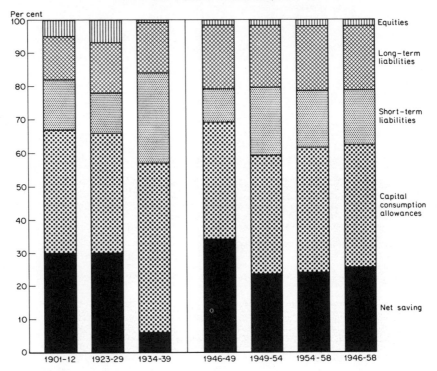

Source: Tables 23 and 22.

In the postwar period, if depreciation is considered at replacement cost, internal funds accounted for slightly less than two-thirds of total sources of funds, and external funds for slightly more than one-third. Two-thirds of internal sources of funds are accounted for by capital consumption allowances, and one-third by retained net income. Almost all external financing took the form of fixed face-value liabilities, of which slightly less than half can be classified as short-term and slightly more than half as long-term liabilities. Of the long-term liabilities, more than one-fourth were securities, while somewhat less than three-fourths were loans obtained, primarily mortgages and insurance

period 1946–58 from 66 to less than 50 per cent of capital formation. Substitution of declining balance for straight-line allowances, on the other hand, would increase their share by a few percentage points.

TABLE 22

COMBINED SOURCES AND USES OF FUNDS OF ALL SECTORS, EXCLUDING MILITARY, 1946-58

| | Annual Averages (billion dollars) | | | | Shares (per cent) | | | |
|---|---|---|---|---|---|---|---|---|
| | 1946-49[a] (1) | 1949-54[a] (2) | 1954-58[a] (3) | 1946-58 (4) | 1946-49 (5) | 1949-54 (6) | 1954-58 (7) | 1946-58 (8) |
| **I. Uses** | | | | | | | | |
| 1. Gross capital expenditures | 66.7 | 90.6 | 118.6 | 93.5 | 64.5 | 60.1 | 60.7 | 61.5 |
| 2. Acquisition of financial assets | 36.7 | 60.2 | 76.9 | 58.6 | 35.5 | 39.9 | 39.3 | 38.6 |
| a. Short-term assets[b] | 13.2 | 28.1 | 32.7 | 24.4 | 12.8 | 18.6 | 16.7 | 16.1 |
| i. Loans | 16.7 | 25.5 | 33.1 | 25.1 | 16.2 | 16.9 | 16.9 | 16.5 |
| ii. Bills and notes[b] | -3.5 | 2.6 | -0.4 | -0.7 | -3.4 | 1.7 | -0.2 | -0.5 |
| b. Long-term assets[b] | 21.5 | 29.2 | 40.0 | 31.0 | 20.8 | 19.4 | 20.5 | 20.4 |
| i. Loans | 17.6 | 20.8 | 28.9 | 22.6 | 17.0 | 13.8 | 14.8 | 14.9 |
| ii. Bonds | 3.9 | 8.4 | 11.1 | 8.4 | 3.8 | 5.6 | 5.7 | 5.5 |
| c. Equities[b] | 2.0 | 2.9 | 4.2 | 3.2 | 1.9 | 1.9 | 2.1 | 2.1 |
| 3. Total uses | 103.4 | 150.8 | 195.5 | 152.0 | 100.0 | 100.0 | 100.0 | 100.0 |
| **II. Sources** | | | | | | | | |
| 1. Gross saving | 71.4 | 89.3 | 120.2 | 94.6 | 69.1 | 59.2 | 61.5 | 62.2 |
| a. Depreciation | 36.1 | 53.7 | 73.2 | 55.7 | 34.9 | 35.6 | 37.4 | 36.6 |
| b. Net saving | 35.3 | 35.6 | 47.0 | 38.9 | 34.1 | 23.6 | 24.0 | 25.6 |
| 2. External sources | 32.0 | 61.5 | 75.3 | 57.4 | 30.9 | 40.8 | 38.5 | 37.8 |
| a. Short-term liabilities[b] | 10.3 | 30.6 | 33.3 | 24.9 | 10.0 | 20.3 | 17.0 | 16.4 |
| i. Loans | 14.0 | 27.5 | 33.3 | 25.3 | 13.5 | 18.2 | 17.0 | 16.6 |
| ii. Bills and notes | -3.7 | 3.1 | 0 | -0.4 | -3.6 | 2.1 | 0 | -0.3 |
| b. Long-term liabilities[b] | 19.7 | 27.9 | 37.8 | 29.3 | 19.1 | 18.5 | 19.3 | 19.3 |
| i. Loans | 15.6 | 19.5 | 26.7 | 20.9 | 15.1 | 12.9 | 13.7 | 13.7 |
| ii. Bonds | 4.1 | 8.4 | 11.1 | 8.4 | 4.0 | 5.6 | 5.7 | 5.5 |
| c. Equities[b] | 1.9 | 2.9 | 4.2 | 3.1 | 1.8 | 1.9 | 2.1 | 2.0 |
| 3. Total sources | 103.4 | 150.8 | 195.5 | 152.1 | 100.0 | 100.0 | 100.0 | 100.0 |
| 4. Inventory profits | 5.5 | 0.5 | 2.6 | 2.8 | 5.3 | 0.3 | 1.3 | 1.8 |

See notes to Table 21.

NOTES TO TABLE 22

Source: <u>National Balance Sheet</u>, Vol. II.

Section 1:
Line 1:  Table V, line I-7.
Lines 2, 2a-2c:  Same as source for Table 21.
Line 3: Table V, line V.
Section II
Line 1:  Table V, line IV-3.
Line 1a:  Table VIII-a-7, line 8, minus Table VIII-a-7b, line 8.
Line 1b:  Lines 1 minus 1a.
Lines 2, 2a-2c:  Same as in Table 21.
Line 3:  Same as line I-3.
Line 4:  Table VIII-a-6b, line 8, minus Table VIII-a-6d, line 8.

liabilities. Equities provided only 5 per cent of external financing, the sale of stocks in nonfinancial corporations alone accounting for 4 per cent of this total.

The implications of these figures for the relative importance of the capital market measured by the value of the external financing is misleading because net figures for entire sectors have been used as a basis of calculation. Consequently, repayments offset part of new loans made, and net purchases by some members of the sector offset net sales of financial assets by others. In many cases the volume of gross financing is more relevant for capital market analysis.

Although no comprehensive gross figures are available, the ratio of gross external financing to total gross uses of funds is obviously higher than the ratio of net external financing to total net uses, which is shown in Table 21, since such a shift would raise the volume of lending and borrowing considerably, but would affect gross capital expenditures much less, and leave capital consumption allowances and saving unchanged. While it is true that, on the basis of the combined net flow-of-funds accounts of all economic units, external financing satisfied about one-third of total needs for funds in the U.S. in the postwar period, the ratio is not well suited to measure the importance of external financing. For that purpose, figures on a gross basis and for smaller sectors are needed. Both would show higher ratios for external financing. For home mortgages, one of the few cases for which both gross and net estimates are available, the gross volume of financing during 1946–58 is two and a half times as large as the net volume (see Table 102).

### STRUCTURAL CHANGES DURING THE POSTWAR PERIOD

As in Chapter 3, structural changes during the postwar period will be studied by comparing annual averages for the three business cycles of

1946–49, 1949–54, and 1954–58. The basic data will be found in Table 21, both in absolute terms and in percentages of total funds absorbed. Examination of the figures leads to two conclusions:

1. Changes in the structure of financing, i.e., differences in the distribution of sources of funds among the three postwar cycles, are relatively small considering the sharp increase in the nominal and real values involved. The annual average volume of financing, represented by total sources of funds, rose from $106 billion in 1946–49 to $164 billion in 1949–54 and $213 billion in 1954–58. After reducing these figures to the common price basis of 1947–49 by using the GNP deflator, the average still increases from $101 billion in the first to $168 billion in the third cycle. Even in relation to gross national product, the volume of financing rose from slightly above 40 per cent in the first cycle to over 50 per cent in the second and third cycles.

2. The second and third cycles are extremely similar in the structure of financing, while the first cycle differs in several respects, although not radically.

These two conclusions are the same as those that emerged from the study of the structure of capital expenditures in the postwar period in Chapter 3.

The main difference in the structure of financing for all sectors taken together between the 1946–49 cycle, on the one hand, and the 1949–54 and 1954–58 cycles, on the other, is the lower share of internal financing in the second and third cycles. Before adjustment for inventory valuation changes, i.e., including inventory profits in internal sources of funds, the share of internal financing declines from 70 per cent in the first cycle to 63 and 65 per cent in the second and third cycles. After elimination of inventory valuation adjustments, the difference is less pronounced, but the share still declines from 65 per cent in the first to 62 and 64 per cent in the second and third cycles. However, if military capital expenditures are excluded (Table 22), the share of internal financing in total sources of funds (after exclusion of inventory profits) falls from 64 per cent in 1946–49 to about 60 per cent in the cycles of 1949–54 and 1954–58. The reduction in this case is due exclusively to the decline in the share of retained income as a source of finance. The share of capital consumption allowances in total funds is higher in the second and third cycles than in the first cycle, if only civil capital expenditures are considered, and the share of net saving within internal financing shows a substantial decline from 1946–49 to the rest of the postwar period.

The division of external funds among short- and long-term sources differed from one cycle to another. Short-term funds amounted to one-third of all external sources (including equities) in 1946–49, one-half of all external funds in 1949–54, and over two-fifths in 1954–58.[4]

Considerable shifts occurred within both short- and long-term funds. In the former, the importance of bank loans declined from about one-fifth of all short-term external financing in the first cycle to about one-fourteenth in the second cycle and one-sixteenth in the third cycle. This relative decline is possibly connected with the smaller inventory accumulation in current dollars in the second and third cycles.[5]

Among long-term funds, the share of equity securities was fairly stable, rising from 9 to 10 per cent between 1946–49 and 1954–58. Thus the sharp increase in stock prices during the second and third cycles did not lead to an increase in the share of equity financing; the absolute volume of equity financing rose by 50 per cent from each cycle to the succeeding one.

A more pronounced change in external financing occurred in bonds. They amounted to one-fifth of long-term and one-eighth of total external financing in the first cycle, and over one-fourth of long-term and about one-seventh of total external financing in both the second and third cycles. This was the result of several crosscurrents, particularly the substantial reduction in federal debt during the first cycle compared with its moderate expansion during the second cycle and no expansion in the third cycle; it is also due to a rapid growth of state and local government bond issues in the second and third cycles (Table 45).

The share of mortgages in long-term financing was about one-third in all postwar cycles. Mortgages provided with fair regularity about 6 per cent of total financing and between one-fifth and one-sixth of external financing during each of the three cycles.

The share of other long-term funds—mostly originating in insurance and pension contracts—was considerably higher during the first cycle, when they accounted for over one-third of all long-term funds, than in the third cycle, when they contributed one-fourth. The decline was concentrated in government insurance and pension funds, the abso-

---

[4] Because of insufficient identification of long-term liabilities, the proportion of long-term funds is probably slightly understated in the statistics, but the corrections would not seriously affect the relation of short- to long-term funds among the three cycles.

[5] *National Balance Sheet*, Vol. II, Table VIII-a-6b.

lute growth of which declined slightly over the period. The net flow into life insurance companies and private pension funds expanded sufficiently to maintain a constant share of one-fifth in total long-term funds during all the postwar period.[6]

## The National Picture for Prewar Periods

In view of the expansion of the American economy (both in volume and value) in the postwar period compared with the first three decades of the century, the considerable changes in the structure of the economy, and, in particular, the institutional developments in finance, the relationship between (and the structure of) internal and external financing in the postwar period might be expected to differ considerably from those of earlier periods. Table 23 shows the extent to which such expectations are borne out by the statistics. Caution is necessary in drawing inferences from the figures because of the extreme aggregation—only national totals are shown—and because of differences in the concepts and methods of derivation of the data.

The main features of the structure of financing on a national scale during the postwar period are fairly similar to those observed in the predepression periods of 1901–12 and 1923–29, although they differ considerably from those of 1934–39. In all periods except the 1930's, internal and external funds on a gross basis accounted for about the same proportion of total funds. On a net basis, the share of internal financing shows a decline between 1901–12 and 1923–29 and the postwar period. This difference reflects an increase in the ratio of capital consumption allowances to net saving between the two predepression periods and the postwar period.

Within external funds, the movements of the share of equities were erratic. The postwar ratio was considerably below the two predepression periods, but above the 1934–39 ratio. The contribution of equities to total financing, of course, shows about the same fluctuations, although it is lower in percentage points. The share of borrowing in total gross flow of funds was fairly constant in the predepression period and rose from 27–28 to 36 per cent in the postwar period. The comparable figures on a net basis also show a substantial increase, from 45 to 58 per cent.

[6] *National Balance Sheet,* Vol. II, Tables VIII-c-3, VIII-c-4, and VIII-c-5.

TABLE 23

TRENDS IN THE STRUCTURE OF FINANCING, NATIONAL AGGREGATES,[a] 1901-58

| Source | Share in Total Funds (per cent) | | | | Share in Net Funds[b] (per cent) | | | |
|---|---|---|---|---|---|---|---|---|
| | 1901-12 (1) | 1923-29 (2) | 1934-39 (3) | 1946-58[c] (4) | 1901-12 (5) | 1923-29 (6) | 1934-39 (7) | 1946-58 (8) |
| I. Internal | | | | | | | | |
|   1. Total | 67 | 66 | 57 | 62 | 47 | 47 | 12 | 39 |
|   2. Capital consumption allowances | 37 | 36 | 51 | 38 | | | | |
|   3. Net saving | 30 | 30 | 6 | 24 | 47 | 47 | 12 | 39 |
| II. External | | | | | | | | |
|   1. Total | 33 | 34 | 43 | 38 | 53 | 53 | 88 | 61 |
|   2. Borrowing | 28 | 27 | 42 | 36 | 45 | 42 | 85 | 58 |
|     a. Short-term | 15 | 12 | 26 | 17 | 24 | 19 | 53 | 27 |
|     b. Long-term | 13 | 15 | 15 | 19 | 21 | 23 | 32 | 31 |
|   3. Equities | 5 | 7 | 1 | 2 | 8 | 11 | 3 | 3 |
| III. Total | 100 | 100 | 100 | 100 | 100 | 100 | 100 | 100 |
| IV. Total (billion dollars) | 140.4 | 324.4 | 201.6 | 1,935.8 | 89.0 | 208.2 | 98.3 | 1,215.3 |

Source: Same as for Tables 36 to 42.
Note: Components may not add to total because of rounding.

[a]Where possible the classification of prewar data is according to NBER **flow-of-funds** accounts for the postwar period.
[b]Total funds minus capital consumption allowances.
[c]Depreciation of financial sector has been excluded for the sake of comparability with the pre-1946 data.

*Internal and External Financing*

*Distribution of Main Uses and Sources of Funds Among Sectors*

Tables 25 and 27, which are derived from Table 24, provide a bird's-eye view of the main characteristics of the financing process in the postwar period as a whole but, of course, only for broad sectors and for broad categories of uses and sources. A look at the distribution of the various sources and uses of funds among the main sectors (Tables 24 and 25) shows the dominating positions of households and nonfinancial business in gross capital expenditures and gross saving, of households and financial institutions in the acquisition of financial assets, and of financial institutions in the incurrence of financial liabilities.

If the agricultural sector is roughly allocated among business and household activities, households accounted during the period as a whole for about half of civilian gross capital expenditures, business for two-fifths, and government for one-tenth. If military expenditures are included, the share of the government rises to one-fifth and that of the other two main sectors is reduced (see Table 25).

Financial institutions accounted for slightly more than two-fifths of the net acqusition of financial assets, households for more than one-third, nonfinancial business for nearly one-fifth, and government for only an insignificant percentage. Considerable differences, of course, exist among the main types of financial assets. Most of the increase in the holdings of short-term claims was divided about equally among financial institutions, nonfinancial business, and households, while the increase in holdings of long-term claims was divided primarily between households and financial institutions. More than four-fifths of the increase in bonds outstanding, however, was absorbed by financial institutions. On the other hand, households absorbed nearly three-fifths of the net issues of equity securities, while financial institutions acquired about two-fifths, more by net purchases of outstanding equity securities than through the acquisition of newly issued stock.

Of the total increase in external sources, about two-fifths was incurred by financial institutions, mostly in the form of deposit and insurance liabilities; about one-third by nonfinancial business mostly as trade debt, bank loans, mortgages, and bonds and notes; and about one-fifth by households, chiefly as mortgages and consumer debt. The government during this period accounted for only 7 per cent of the

113

## TABLE 24

### SOURCES AND USES OF FUNDS, BY SECTOR, 1946-58
(billion dollars)

| | Nonfarm Households (1) | Agriculture (2) | Unincorp. Business (3) | Nonfinancial Corporations (4) | Finance (5) | State and Local Govts. (6) | Federal Government[a] (7) | Total (8) |
|---|---|---|---|---|---|---|---|---|
| **I. Uses** | | | | | | | | |
| 1. Gross capital expenditures | 554.3 | 95.1 | 75.1 | 359.3 | 5.5 | 105.9 | 175.4 | 1,370.6 |
| 2. Acquisition of financial assets | 271.9 | 7.4 | 15.3 | 117.9 | 323.5 | 17.6 | 7.4 | 761.0 |
| a. Short-term assets | 103.2 | 3.1 | 15.3 | 95.1 | 90.6 | 12.2 | -2.6 | 316.9 |
| i. Loans | 100.6 | 3.1 | 15.3 | 95.0 | 106.0 | 8.6 | -2.6 | 326.0 |
| ii. Bills and notes | 2.6 | 0 | 0 | 0.1 | -15.4 | 3.6 | 0 | -9.1 |
| b. Long-term assets | 145.4 | 4.4 | 0 | 21.0 | 216.9 | 5.5 | 10.0 | 403.2 |
| i. Loans | 134.5 | 3.3 | 0 | 20.4 | 126.3 | 1.6 | 8.2 | 294.3 |
| ii. Bonds | 10.9 | 1.1 | 0 | 0.6 | 90.6 | 3.9 | 1.8 | 108.9 |
| c. Equities | 23.2 | 0 | 0 | 1.9 | 16.0 | 0 | 0 | 41.1 |
| 3. Total uses | 826.2 | 102.5 | 90.4 | 477.3 | 329.0 | 123.5 | 182.8 | 2,131.8 |
| **II. Sources** | | | | | | | | |
| 1. Gross saving | 680.4 | 89.2 | 61.6 | 277.7 | 22.5 | 82.2 | 172.6 | 1,386.2 |
| a. Depreciation | 346.2 | 68.6 | 49.4 | 186.6 | 3.7 | 53.6 | 200.1 | 908.2 |
| b. Net saving | 334.2 | 20.6 | 12.2 | 91.1 | 18.8 | 28.6 | -27.5 | 478.0 |
| 2. External sources | 145.8 | 13.3 | 28.9 | 199.5 | 306.5 | 41.3 | 10.2 | 745.5 |
| a. Short-term liabilities | 47.2 | 6.8 | 17.5 | 90.6 | 166.8 | 1.4 | -7.0 | 323.3 |
| i. Loans | 47.2 | 6.8 | 17.5 | 90.6 | 164.3 | 1.4 | 0.7 | 328.5 |
| ii. Bills and notes | 0 | | 0 | 0 | 2.5 | 0 | -7.7 | -5.2 |
| b. Long-term liabilities | 98.6 | 6.5 | 11.4 | 78.2 | 129.6 | 39.9 | 17.2 | 381.4 |
| i. Loans | 98.6 | 6.5 | 11.4 | 32.1 | 123.2 | | | 271.8 |
| ii. Bonds | 0 | 0 | 0 | 46.1 | 6.4 | 39.9 | 17.2 | 109.6 |
| c. Equities | 0 | 0 | 0 | 30.7 | 10.1 | 0 | 0 | 40.8 |
| 3. Total sources | 826.2 | 102.5 | 90.4 | 477.3 | 329.0 | 123.5 | 182.8 | 2,131.8 |
| 4. Inventory profits | 0 | 6.5 | 5.6 | 24.3 | 0 | 0 | 0 | 36.4 |

Source: See Tables 29-35.

[a] See bottom panel of Table 34.

TABLE 25

DISTRIBUTION OF SOURCES AND USES OF FUNDS, BY SECTOR, 1946–58

(per cent)

| | Nonfarm Households (1) | Agri-culture (2) | Unincorp. Business (3) | Nonfinancial Corporations (4) | Finance (5) | State and Local Govts. (6) | Federal Government (7) | Total (8) |
|---|---|---|---|---|---|---|---|---|
| **I. Uses** | | | | | | | | |
| 1. Gross capital expenditures | 40.4 | 6.9 | 5.5 | 26.2 | 0.4 | 7.7 | 12.8 | 100.0 |
| 2. Acquisition of financial assets | 35.7 | 1.0 | 2.0 | 15.5 | 42.5 | 2.3 | 1.0 | 100.0 |
| a. Short-term assets | 32.6 | 1.0 | 4.8 | 30.0 | 28.6 | 3.8 | -0.8 | 100.0 |
| i. Loans | 30.9 | 1.0 | 4.7 | 29.1 | 32.5 | 2.6 | -0.8 | 100.0 |
| ii. Bills and notes[a] | 28.6 | 0 | 0 | 1.1 | -169.2 | 39.6 | 0 | -100.0 |
| b. Long-term assets | 36.1 | 1.1 | 0 | 5.2 | 53.8 | 1.4 | 2.5 | 100.0 |
| i. Loans | 45.7 | 1.1 | 0 | 6.9 | 42.9 | 0.5 | 2.8 | 100.0 |
| ii. Bonds | 10.0 | 1.0 | 0 | 0.6 | 83.2 | 3.6 | 1.7 | 100.0 |
| c. Equities | 56.4 | 0 | 0 | 4.6 | 38.9 | 0 | 0 | 100.0 |
| 3. Total uses | 38.8 | 4.8 | 4.2 | 22.4 | 15.4 | 5.8 | 8.6 | 100.0 |
| **II. Sources** | | | | | | | | |
| 1. Gross saving | 49.1 | 6.4 | 4.4 | 20.0 | 1.6 | 5.9 | 12.5 | 100.0 |
| a. Depreciation | 38.1 | 7.6 | 5.4 | 20.5 | 0.4 | 5.9 | 22.0 | 100.0 |
| b. Net saving | 69.9 | 4.3 | 2.6 | 19.1 | 3.9 | 6.0 | -5.8 | 100.0 |
| 2. External sources | 19.6 | 1.8 | 3.9 | 26.8 | 41.1 | 5.5 | 1.4 | 100.0 |
| a. Short-term liabilities | 14.6 | 2.1 | 5.4 | 28.0 | 51.6 | 0.4 | -2.2 | 100.0 |
| i. Loans | 14.4 | 2.1 | 5.3 | 27.6 | 50.0 | 0.4 | 0.2 | 100.0 |
| ii. Bills and notes[a] | 0 | 0 | 0 | 0 | 48.1 | 0 | -148.1 | -100.0 |
| b. Long-term liabilities | 25.9 | 1.7 | 3.0 | 20.5 | 34.0 | 10.5 | 4.5 | 100.0 |
| i. Loans | 36.3 | 2.4 | 4.2 | 11.8 | 45.3 | 0 | 0 | 100.0 |
| ii. Bonds | 0 | 0 | 0 | 42.1 | 5.8 | 36.4 | 15.7 | 100.0 |
| c. Equities | 0 | 0 | 0 | 75.2 | 24.8 | 0 | 0 | 100.0 |
| 3. Total sources | 38.8 | 4.8 | 4.2 | 22.4 | 15.4 | 5.8 | 8.6 | 100.0 |
| 4. Inventory profits | 0 | 17.9 | 15.4 | 66.8 | 0 | 0 | 0 | 100.0 |

Source: See Table 24.

[a] The signs have been reversed to match the sign of the numerator.

total increase in liabilities, and most of this represented state and local long-term debt.

Distribution is again considerably different for the various types of liabilities. Financial institutions accounted for about one-half of the total increase in short-term liabilities and one-third of the total increase in long-term liabilities, but for a smaller proportion of the net issues of stocks and bonds. Nonfinancial business was responsible for about three-fourths of net issues of equities, two-fifths of bonds, three-tenths of short-term liabilities, but only for about one-eighth of long-term nonmarketable liabilities.[7] Households accounted for well over one-third of the total increase in long-term nonmarketable debt and for one-seventh of that in short-term debt but, of course, did not participate in the issuance of marketable securities. The government was an important factor only in the case of long-term bonds, where it was responsible for about one-half of the total increase in outstandings.

Considerable interest attaches to the distribution of gross and net saving among sectors. Households accounted for one-half of gross saving, nonfinancial business for about one-fifth, and the government for nearly one-fifth including military assets but for only 8 per cent excluding them. Because of divergences in the ratio of net to gross saving, the distribution of net saving is quite different. Here the predominance of households is very marked; nonfinancial business accounted for one-fifth; and the share of the government was zero because the positive net saving of state and local government was offset by the dissaving of the federal government when military assets are included. If the calculation is limited to civilian assets, the government accounted for about 6 per cent of the national total, nonfinancial business for about one-fourth, and nonfarm households still for two-thirds.

### COMPARISON WITH PREWAR PERIOD

The distribution of total financing and its main forms among sectors during the postwar period, which has just been reviewed, does not seem very different from that during two of the three prewar periods used here for comparison. This is the general impression derived from Table 26, which shows the share of each of the seven sectors in total financing (national combined total), in external financing, and in long- and short-term debt financing. Because of some differences in concept

---

[7] This low percentage is partly due to allocation of some actually long-term liabilities to the short-term category.

TABLE 26

DISTRIBUTION OF FINANCING AMONG SECTORS, 1901-58
(per cent)

| | Nonfarm House-holds (1) | Unincor-porated Business (2) | Agricul-ture (3) | Nonfinancial Corporations (4) | Finance (5) | State and Local Govts. (6) | Federal Govt. (7) | Total (8) | Total (billion dollars) (9) |
|---|---|---|---|---|---|---|---|---|---|
| **I. TOTAL FINANCING** | | | | | | | | | |
| 1901-12 | 39.7 | 4.1 | 10.2 | 28.5 | 11.9 | 4.3 | 1.3 | 100.0 | 140.4 |
| 1923-29 | 45.2 | 3.3 | 4.1 | 26.5 | 14.1 | 6.2 | 0.5 | 100.0 | 324.4 |
| 1934-39 | 33.4 | 3.5 | 6.6 | 14.3 | 22.8 | 7.2 | 12.2 | 100.0 | 201.6[a] |
| 1946-58 | 42.7 | 4.4 | 5.0 | 23.4 | 16.8 | 6.4 | 1.4 | 100.0 | 1,935.8[a] |
| **II. EXTERNAL FINANCING** | | | | | | | | | |
| 1901-12 | 9.7 | 4.0 | 8.9 | 37.7 | 32.9 | 5.1 | 1.7 | 100.0 | 47.4 |
| 1923-29 | 23.7 | 3.0 | -1.8 | 35.3 | 39.4 | 5.9 | -5.4 | 100.0 | 110.5 |
| 1934-39 | 5.4 | -0.4 | -0.5 | 0.8 | 51.5 | 0.3 | 42.7 | 100.0 | 86.8 |
| 1946-58 | 19.6 | 3.9 | 1.8 | 26.8 | 41.1 | 5.5 | 1.4 | 100.0 | 745.5 |
| **III. SHORT-TERM DEBT FINANCING** | | | | | | | | | |
| 1901-12 | 11.1 | 7.0 | 10.2 | 14.8 | 53.3 | 0 | 3.7 | 100.0 | 21.6 |
| 1923-29 | 25.7 | 1.5 | -2.2 | 9.2 | 65.8 | 0 | 0 | 100.0 | 40.1 |
| 1934-39 | 8.2 | 2.7 | 0.8 | 0.6 | 61.5 | -0.8 | 27.0 | 100.0 | 52.6 |
| 1946-58 | 14.6 | 5.4 | 2.1 | 28.0 | 51.6 | 0.4 | -2.2 | 100.0 | 323.3 |
| **IV. LONG-TERM DEBT FINANCING** | | | | | | | | | |
| 1901-12 | 11.7 | 2.2 | 10.7 | 48.1 | 14.5 | 12.8 | 0 | 100.0 | 18.7 |
| 1923-29 | 33.2 | 5.7 | -2.3 | 38.8 | 23.7 | 13.6 | -12.5 | 100.0 | 48.0 |
| 1934-39 | 1.3 | -5.6 | -2.6 | -7.1 | 38.3 | 2.2 | 73.4 | 100.0 | 31.2 |
| 1946-58 | 25.9 | 3.0 | 1.7 | 20.5 | 34.0 | 10.5 | 4.5 | 100.0 | 381.4 |

Source: Same as for Table 23.

[a] See footnote c in Table 23.

and in methods of estimation between the postwar and earlier periods, not too much should be read into small differences in the figures.

The sectoral distribution of total financing during the postwar period was fairly similar to that observed in 1901–12 and 1923–29. During these periods, nonfarm households, nonfarm nonfinancial business, financial institutions, and state and local governments maintained reasonably stable shares and were responsible for nine-tenths of the national total of sources of funds.

Changes are more pronounced in the distribution of external financing among the sectors, but few definite long-term trends appear. The share of nonfinancial business declined from 1901–12 to 1946–58. While the decline from 1901–12 to 1923–29 was mainly due to the disappearance of external financing in agriculture in the 1920's, the further shrinkage betweeen 1923–29 and 1946–58 mostly reflects the decline in the share of external financing undertaken by nonfinancial corporations. The share of state and local governments was quite stable; that of the federal government fluctuated erratically, but was small in all three periods. Of all the movements of the share of financial institutions in total external financing, the stability between the 1920's and the postwar period is probably more interesting than the increase between 1901–12 and 1923–29.

No clear trends are visible in the sectoral distribution of short- or long-term debt financing taken separately. Probably the most significant developments are: first, the increase in the share of financial institutions in long-term debt financing, most of which occurred before or during the Great Depression; and, secondly, the increase in the share of nonfinancial corporations in short-term borrowing and the decline in their share of long-term borrowing, the latter mainly at the expense of home mortgages. The share of state and local government in long-term borrowing was approximately the same in all three periods.

### Differences Among Sectors in the Structure of Sources and Uses of Funds in the Postwar Period

The character of the capital market is reflected in and determined by the structure of the sources and uses of funds of individual economic units. Although they are too broad and therefore unduly aggregative for many analytical purposes, the seven main sectors dis-

tinguished in this study are the only groups for which complete
sources-and-uses-of-funds statements are available for the entire postwar period.[8]

The structure of uses and sources of funds for the postwar period
as a whole is shown in Tables 27 and 28 and illustrated in Chart 7
for each of the seven sectors, combining the more numerous uses and
sources into four main flows in order to facilitate a first orientation.
The presentation in Table 27 is based on gross flows, while Table 28
uses net flows, i.e., deducts capital consumption allowance from both
gross capital expenditures as a use of funds and retained earnings as
a source of funds.

Both presentations are based on a specific and extreme assumption
about the utilization of capital consumption allowances. In Table 27
it is assumed that capital consumption allowances constitute unas-
signed funds, which may finance any use, the acquisition of financial
assets or existing tangible assets, as well as current gross capital expenditures. Table 28, based on net uses, implies the opposite assumption, that capital consumption allowances are first matched against
gross capital expenditures, so that only the excess of gross capital expenditures over capital consumption allowances is regarded as a use
of funds, or the excess of capital consumption allowances over gross
capital expenditures as a source of funds. Actually, the situation generally seems to lie between the two extreme assumptions. Capital consumption allowances as part of the cash throw-off become part of the
funds of which the entrepreneur can dispose freely, but expenditures,
particularly the so-called replacement expenditures, probably are regarded as having first call on earned capital consumption allowances.
For households and governments, however, the gross basis probably
corresponds best to the actual facts, since these units are not well
aware of the existence of capital consumption allowances or of their
role as a source of replacement of worn out durable tangible assets.

The distribution of total funds raised by sectors or by other groups
in the economy according to use of funds is important in capital market analysis because certain relationships exist between forms of fund
uses and sources and forms of financing, although the link is a flexible

---

[8] Similar statements are available, or can be approximated, for several groups in
the financial and nonfinancial corporate sectors, but are unavailable for the nonfarm household, agriculture, unincorporated business, and state and local government sectors, which together account for more than half of all sources and uses of
funds.

TABLE 27

DISTRIBUTION OF GROSS SOURCES AND USES OF FUNDS, 1946-58
(per cent)

| | | SHARE IN GROSS USES | | | SHARE IN GROSS SOURCES | | | | |
| | | Financial Assets | | | Internal | | External | | |
| | | Claims | | | | | Liabilities | | |
| Sector | Gross Capital Formation (1) | Short-Term (2) | Long-Term (3) | Equities (4) | Capital Consumption Allowance (5) | Retained Income (6) | Short-Term (7) | Long-Term (8) | Equities (9) |
|---|---|---|---|---|---|---|---|---|---|
| 1. Nonfarm households | 67 | 12 | 18 | 3 | 42 | 40 | 6 | 12 | 0 |
| 2. Agriculture | 93 | 3 | 4 | 0 | 67 | 20 | 7 | 6 | 0 |
| 3. Nonfarm unincorp. business | 83 | 17 | 0 | 0 | 55 | 13 | 19 | 13 | 0 |
| 4. Nonfinan. corporations | 75 | 20 | 4 | 0 | 39 | 19 | 19 | 16 | 6 |
| 5. Finance | 2 | 28 | 66 | 5 | 1 | 6 | 51 | 39 | 3 |
| 6. State and local governments | 86 | 10 | 4 | 0 | 43 | 23 | 1 | 32 | 0 |
| 7. Federal government, civilian | 73 | -10 | 37 | 0 | 59 | 3 | -26 | 63 | 0 |
| 8. Federal government, including military | 96 | -1 | 5 | 0 | 109 | -15 | -4 | 9 | 0 |
| 9. All sectors, civilian | 61 | 16 | 20 | 2 | 37 | 26 | 16 | 19 | 2 |
| 10. All sectors, including military | 64 | 15 | 19 | 2 | 43 | 22 | 15 | 18 | 2 |

Source: See Table 24.

TABLE 28

DISTRIBUTION OF NET SOURCES AND USES OF FUNDS, 1946–58
(per cent)

| | | SHARE IN NET USES | | | SHARE IN NET SOURCES | | | |
| | | Financial Assets | | | | External | | |
| | | Claims | | | | Liabilities | | |
| Sector | Net Capital Formation (1) | Short-Term (2) | Long-Term (3) | Equities (4) | Internal (5) | Short-Term (6) | Long-Term (7) | Equities (8) |
|---|---|---|---|---|---|---|---|---|
| 1. Nonfarm households | 43 | 21 | 30 | 5 | 70 | 10 | 21 | 0 |
| 2. Agriculture | 78 | 9 | 13 | 0 | 61 | 20 | 19 | 0 |
| 3. Nonfarm unincorp. business | 63 | 37 | 0 | 0 | 30 | 43 | 28 | 0 |
| 4. Nonfinan. corporations | 59 | 33 | 7 | 1 | 31 | 31 | 27 | 11 |
| 5. Finance | 1 | 28 | 67 | 5 | 6 | 51 | 40 | 3 |
| 6. State and local governments | 75 | 17 | 8 | 0 | 41 | 2 | 57 | 0 |
| 7. Federal government, civilian | 33 | -23 | 90 | 0 | 7 | -63 | 155 | 0 |
| 8. Federal government, including military[a] | -144 | -15 | 58 | 0 | -160 | -41 | 100 | 0 |
| 9. All sectors, civilian | 39 | 25 | 32 | 3 | 40 | 26 | 30 | 3 |
| 10. All sectors, including military | 38 | 26 | 33 | 3 | 39 | 26 | 31 | 3 |

Source: See Table 24.

[a]The signs have been reversed to match the sign of the numerator.

# CHART 7

## SOURCES AND USES OF FUNDS BY SECTOR, 1946–58

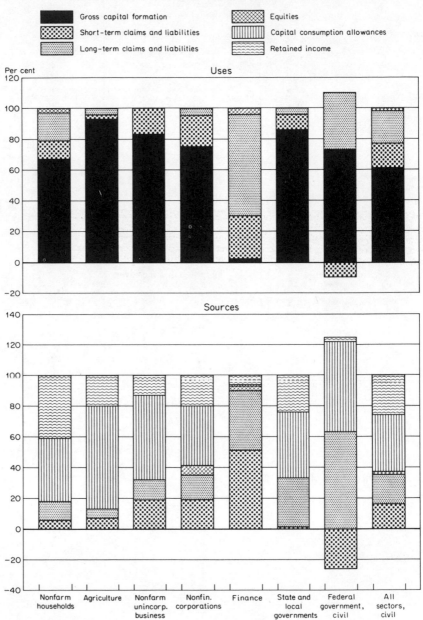

Source: Table 27.

one. Thus, gross capital expenditures, particularly expenditures on structures and equipment, are often financed internally, or if financed externally are provided by equity securities or long-term liabilities. On the other hand, funds used to finance inventory or receivables are usually provided by short-term borrowing. These relationships are of significance although, of course, permanent increases in the level of inventory and receivables which reflect the growth of the volume of business are often financed internally or by long-term external funds, and although capital expenditures on equipment and on structures are often financed temporarily or even for a fairly long time by short-term borrowing.

Similarly, the distribution of funds by sources is an important factor in the financing of assets also because certain relationships tend to be maintained between internal and external funds and between long- and short-term borrowing, given the industry, size, and age of the unit and other relevant factors.

Compared to the national ratio, the share of gross capital expenditures in total uses of funds is very high for nonfinancial business, particularly for agriculture, unincorporated business, and nonfinancial corporations (see Table 27). The ratio is also high for state and local governments and for the federal government if military assets are included. The only sector with a low ratio is finance; however, the acquisition of intangible assets by financial institutions is sufficient to offset the above average shares of gross capital expenditures by the other sectors in total uses of funds.

Considerable differences among the sectors are also evident in the distribution of financial uses of funds between claims and equities and between short- and long-term claims. Equities absorb a part of financial uses only in the households and financial institution sectors. Among claims, there are many more long- than short-term claims for households, the federal government, and financial institutions. The opposite relation prevails for nonfinancial corporations, mainly because of the large increase in trade accounts receivable during the postwar period.

The distribution of sources of funds is possibly more directly relevant to the structure of the capital market. While internal funds provide around two-thirds of all gross funds for all sectors combined, the share is much higher for nonfarm households and agriculture (see Table 27). Finance is again the only sector for which internal funds are negligible in comparison to external funds, which reflects the function of financial institutions as intermediaries.

There are great differences in the distribution of internal funds between capital consumption allowances and internal saving, a relation determined primarily by the ratio of gross saving to assets, the share of depreciable in total assets, and the length of life and age distribution of depreciable assets. For all sectors together, capital consumption allowances provided two-thirds and net saving provided one-third of total internal funds. The ratio was similar for nonfinancial corporations; for nonfarm households, the two sources were of the same size. At the other extreme, capital consumption allowances accounted for most internal funds for unincorporated business and the federal government, indicating the low level or absence of net saving.

Equities can be a source of funds only for the business sectors. Even here their share is generally small. For nonfinancial corporations—the largest business sector—equities accounted for only 6 per cent of total gross funds and for one-seventh of external funds. Short- and long-term liabilities were of about equal importance as sources of funds for all sectors together. Short-term liabilities predominate, however, in the business sectors, while long-term liabilities lead in the household and government sectors, reflecting the character of their capital expenditures.

On a net basis (Table 28) where capital consumption allowances are treated as an offset against both gross capital expenditures and internal financing, the levels of the ratios are quite different but the differences among sectors are similar. Nonfarm households and agriculture show a share of internal net financing considerably above the average, while the share of state and local governments is average and the share of financial institutions is far below average (Table 28). A comparison of the shares of gross and net internal funds of the federal government shows that they differ substantially.

The differences between the net and gross basis are pronounced in the distribution between internal and external finance. For all sectors combined, about two-fifths of all net sources are internal (net saving), compared to over three-fifths of gross sources. However, the share of retained income for households on a net basis is much larger than on a gross basis, and nonfarm business has a ratio of retained income on a net basis larger than that on a gross basis. This difference is partly explained by the ratio of capital consumption allowances to gross internal financing. In the case of households, it reflects a lower average length of life of their gross capital expenditures because of the high share of short-lived consumer durables.

## Structural Changes in Sources and Uses of Funds by Main Sectors During the Postwar Period

These changes, which were studied in the first part of this chapter by comparing differences among the three postwar cycles, ignored differences among sectors. These will now be discussed on the basis of Tables 29 to 35, which show annual averages of absolute and percentage figures of the main uses and sources of funds for the three postwar cycles for each sector. A more detailed breakdown, using all available categories of assets and liabilities, will be found in Volume II of *National Balance Sheet*.[9] No discussion is included here of the differences among subsectors of the financial sector, for which information is also available in the same source.

### NONFARM HOUSEHOLDS

Both uses and sources of funds during each of the three postwar cycles show only small variations from their shares for the whole period for the main divisions, i.e., gross capital expenditures and acquisition of financial assets among uses of funds, and internal and external financing among sources of funds. The absolute figures, of course, increase sharply, whereas in proportion to personal disposable income, the increase is much more modest (Table 29).[10]

Within financial assets, the share of long-term claims declines from the first to the second cycle and from the second to the third, and the share of short-term claims increases correspondingly. Equities account for one-tenth in the first cycle, one-eleventh in the second, and one-twelfth in the third cycle of total financial asset acquisitions.

The share of internal financing (gross saving) varied very little in all three cycles. A slow decline is, however, observable in the share of net saving at the expense of that of capital consumption allowances, the calculation of which is to some extent arbitrary.

Within external financing, the share of short-term liabilities declined slightly at the expense of long-term debt (home mortgage)

9 Tables in Section VII.

10 For personal disposable income, see *U.S. Income and Output*, Supplement to the *Survey of Current Business*, Washington, 1958, pp. 144–145; and *Survey of Current Business*, July 1960, p. 10.

TABLE 29

SOURCES AND USES OF FUNDS OF NONFARM HOUSEHOLDS, 1946-58

| | Annual Averages (billion dollars) | | | | Shares (per cent) | | | |
|---|---|---|---|---|---|---|---|---|
| | 1946-49[a] (1) | 1949-54[a] (2) | 1954-58[a] (3) | 1946-58 (4) | 1946-49 (5) | 1949-54 (6) | 1954-58 (7) | 1946-58 (8) |
| **I. Uses** | | | | | | | | |
| 1. Gross capital expenditures | 27.84 | 42.15 | 55.78 | 42.64 | 67.2 | 69.0 | 66.7 | 67.1 |
| 2. Acquisition of financial assets | 13.58 | 18.91 | 27.89 | 20.92 | 32.8 | 31.0 | 33.3 | 32.9 |
| a. Short-term claims | 3.70 | 6.85 | 11.11 | 7.94 | 8.9 | 11.2 | 13.3 | 12.5 |
| i. Loans | 2.95 | 7.02 | 10.65 | 7.74 | 7.1 | 11.5 | 12.7 | 12.2 |
| ii. Bills and notes | 0.75 | -0.17 | 0.46 | 0.20 | 1.8 | -0.3 | 0.5 | 0.3 |
| b. Long-term claims | 8.46 | 10.37 | 14.61 | 11.19 | 20.4 | 17.0 | 17.5 | 17.6 |
| i. Loans | 8.72 | 9.85 | 12.19 | 10.35 | 21.1 | 16.1 | 14.6 | 16.3 |
| ii. Bonds | -0.26 | 0.52 | 2.42 | 0.84 | -0.6 | 0.9 | 2.9 | 1.3 |
| c. Equities | 1.42 | 1.70 | 2.17 | 1.79 | 3.4 | 2.8 | 2.6 | 2.8 |
| 3. Total uses | 41.42 | 61.06 | 83.67 | 63.56 | 100.0 | 100.0 | 100.0 | 100.0 |
| **II. Sources** | | | | | | | | |
| 1. Gross saving | 33.92 | 50.07 | 68.74 | 52.34 | 81.9 | 82.0 | 82.2 | 82.4 |
| a. Depreciation | 16.52 | 25.69 | 35.46 | 26.63 | 39.9 | 42.1 | 42.4 | 41.9 |
| b. Net saving | 17.40 | 24.38 | 33.28 | 25.71 | 42.0 | 39.9 | 39.8 | 40.5 |
| 2. External sources | 7.51 | 10.99 | 14.93 | 11.22 | 18.0 | 18.0 | 17.8 | 17.7 |
| a. Short-term loans | 2.73 | 3.94 | 4.45 | 3.63 | 6.6 | 6.5 | 5.3 | 5.7 |
| b. Long-term loans | 4.78 | 7.05 | 10.48 | 7.59 | 11.5 | 11.5 | 12.5 | 11.9 |
| 3. Total sources | 41.42 | 61.06 | 83.67 | 63.56 | 100.0 | 100.0 | 100.0 | 100.0 |

[a] Cycle averages.

Source: National Balance Sheet, Vol. II.

Section I
Line 1: Table VII-1, line I-7.
Line 2: Table VII-1, line II-21.
Line 2a: Sum of lines 2ai and 2aii.
Line 2ai: Table VII-1, sum of lines II-1, 2, 10, and 20.
Line 2aii: Table VII-1, line II-13a.
Line 2b: Sum of lines 2bi and 2bii.
Line 2bi: Table VII-1, sum of lines II-3, 4, 5, 11, and 12.
Line 2bii: Table VII-1, sum of lines II-13b, 13c, 14, and 15.
Line 2c: Table VII-1, sum of lines II-16 and 17.

Section II
Line 1: Table VII-1, line IV-3.
Line 1a: Table VIII-a-7, line 1, minus Table VIII-a-7b, line 1.
Line 1b: Lines 1 minus 1a.
Line 2: Table VII-1, line III-14.
Line 2a: Table VII-1, sum of lines III-6, 7, 8, 9, and 10.
Line 2b: Table VII-1, line III-11.
Line 3: Table VII-1, line V.

financing between the second and the third cycles. As a result, 70 per cent of total external financing was in long-term form in the third cycle compared to 64 per cent in the first.

### AGRICULTURE

Since the financial assets attributed to farmers are limited to demand and savings deposits, savings bonds, insurance and pension reserves, gross capital expenditures accounted for almost all uses of funds in all three cycles (Table 30). Within gross capital expenditures, inventories accounted for about 15 per cent in the first and third cycles, but were slightly negative in the second. This difference reflects partly the price movements of agricultural products, in particular the sharp price rise during the first cycle, and partly quantity movements as in the third cycle.

Among sources, internal financing was equally predominant. External financing, however, showed slow increases from the first to the second cycle and from the second to the third, as a result exclusively of an increase in the share of borrowing on mortgages. The offsetting decline in short-term financing affected primarily nonbank borrowing.

### UNINCORPORATED BUSINESS

The notorious unreliability of the financial statistics of unincorporated nonfarm business imposes the utmost caution in the interpretation of the figures. As they stand, they show considerable variations in the structure of uses and sources of funds among the three postwar cycles (Table 31).

Among uses, the main feature is the high share of gross capital expenditures. During the first cycle a substantial proportion of these expenditures was allocated to inventories, reflecting primarily the sharp rise in prices after the war. This proportion was much smaller during the rest of the postwar period. As capital expenditures amounted to over four-fifths of the uses of funds, the accumulation of financial assets was relatively small.

Among sources, the share of internal financing increased from the first to the second cycle and declined from the second to the third. The increase is mainly accounted for by the rise in estimated capital consumption allowances. The decline is a result of the relatively high share of net saving in the first cycle and its small share during the third cycle. In view of the statistical limitations of the estimates, it is difficult to say whether this actually represents a sharp decrease in

TABLE 30

SOURCES AND USES OF FUNDS OF AGRICULTURE, 1946-58

| | Annual Averages (billion dollars) | | | | Shares (per cent) | | | |
|---|---|---|---|---|---|---|---|---|
| | 1946–49ᵃ (1) | 1949–54ᵃ (2) | 1954–58ᵃ (3) | 1946–58 (4) | 1946–49 (5) | 1949–54 (6) | 1954–58 (7) | 1946–58 (8) |
| **I. Uses** | | | | | | | | |
| 1. Gross capital expenditures | 6.92 | 6.84 | 7.55 | 7.31 | 93.1 | 93.6 | 92.6 | 92.6 |
| 2. Acquisition of financial assets | 0.51 | 0.47 | 0.60 | 0.57 | 6.9 | 6.4 | 7.4 | 7.2 |
| a. Short-term loans | 0.06 | 0.23 | 0.25 | 0.24 | 0.8 | 3.1 | 3.1 | 3.0 |
| b. Long-term assets | 0.45 | 0.24 | 0.35 | 0.33 | 6.1 | 3.3 | 4.3 | 4.2 |
| i. Loans | 0.29 | 0.20 | 0.27 | 0.25 | 3.9 | 2.7 | 3.3 | 3.2 |
| ii. Bonds | 0.16 | 0.04 | 0.08 | 0.08 | 2.2 | 0.5 | 1.0 | 1.0 |
| 3. Total uses | 7.43 | 7.31 | 8.15 | 7.88 | 100.0 | 100.0 | 100.0 | 100.0 |
| **II. Sources** | | | | | | | | |
| 1. Gross saving | 6.59 | 6.38 | 6.94 | 6.86 | 88.7 | 87.3 | 85.2 | 86.9 |
| a. Depreciation | 3.43 | 5.36 | 6.63 | 5.28 | 46.2 | 73.3 | 81.3 | 66.9 |
| b. Net saving | 3.16 | 1.02 | 0.31 | 1.58 | 42.5 | 14.0 | 3.8 | 20.0 |
| 2. External sources | 0.84 | 0.93 | 1.21 | 1.02 | 11.3 | 12.7 | 14.8 | 12.9 |
| a. Short-term loans | 0.64 | 0.41 | 0.50 | 0.52 | 8.6 | 5.6 | 6.1 | 6.6 |
| b. Long-term loans | 0.20 | 0.52 | 0.71 | 0.50 | 2.7 | 7.1 | 8.7 | 6.3 |
| 3. Total sources | 7.43 | 7.31 | 8.15 | 7.88 | 100.0 | 100.0 | 100.0 | 100.0 |
| 4. Inventory profits | 1.38 | -0.78 | 0.73 | 0.50 | 18.6 | -10.7 | 9.0 | 6.3 |

Source: National Balance Sheet, Vol. II.

Section I
Line 1: Table VII-3, line I-7.
Line 2: Table VII-3, line II-21.
Line 2a: Table VII-3, sum of lines II-1, 2, and 20.
Line 2b: Sum of lines 2bi and 2bii.
Line 2bi: Table VII-3, sum of lines II-3 and II-5.
Line 2bii: Table VII-3, line II-13.
Line 3: Table VII-3, line V.

Section II
Line 1: Table VII-3, line IV-3.
Line 1a: Table VIII-a-7, line 3, minus Table VIII-a-7b, line 3.
Line 1b: Lines 1 minus 1a.
Line 2: Table VII-3, line III-14.
Line 2a: Table VII-3, sum of lines III-6, 7, 9, and 10.
Line 2b: Table VII-3, line III-11.
Line 3: Table VII-3, line V.
Line 4: Table VIII-a-6b, line 3, minus Table VIII-a-6d, line 3.

ᵃ Cycle averages.

TABLE 31

SOURCES AND USES OF FUNDS OF NONFARM UNINCORPORATED BUSINESS, 1946–58

| | Annual Averages (billion dollars) | | | | Shares (per cent) | | | |
|---|---|---|---|---|---|---|---|---|
| | 1946–49[a] (1) | 1949–54[a] (2) | 1954–58[a] (3) | 1946–58 (4) | 1946–49 (5) | 1949–54 (6) | 1954–58 (7) | 1946–58 (8) |
| **I. Uses** | | | | | | | | |
| 1. Gross capital expenditures | 4.70 | 5.32 | 7.22 | 5.78 | 83.9 | 81.3 | 85.2 | 83.0 |
| 2. Acquisition of financial assets | 0.89 | 1.22 | 1.24 | 1.18 | 15.9 | 18.7 | 14.6 | 17.0 |
|   a. Short-term loans | 0.89 | 1.22 | 1.24 | 1.18 | 15.9 | 18.7 | 14.6 | 17.0 |
| 3. Total uses | 5.59 | 6.54 | 8.47 | 6.96 | 100.0 | 100.0 | 100.0 | 100.0 |
| **II. Sources** | | | | | | | | |
| 1. Gross saving | 3.78 | 4.82 | 5.46 | 4.74 | 67.5 | 73.7 | 64.4 | 68.1 |
|   a. Depreciation | 2.25 | 3.65 | 5.16 | 3.80 | 40.2 | 55.8 | 60.9 | 54.6 |
|   b. Net saving | 1.53 | 1.17 | 0.30 | 0.94 | 27.3 | 17.9 | 3.5 | 13.5 |
| 2. External sources | 1.81 | 1.72 | 3.01 | 2.22 | 32.3 | 26.3 | 35.6 | 31.9 |
|   a. Short-term loans | 1.10 | 0.99 | 1.86 | 1.34 | 19.6 | 15.1 | 22.0 | 19.3 |
|   b. Long-term loans | 0.71 | 0.73 | 1.15 | 0.88 | 12.7 | 11.2 | 13.6 | 12.6 |
| 3. Total sources | 5.59 | 6.54 | 8.47 | 6.96 | 100.0 | 100.0 | 100.0 | 100.0 |
| 4. Inventory profits | 0.84 | 0.23 | 0.26 | 0.43 | 15.0 | 3.5 | 3.1 | 6.2 |

[a] Cycle averages.

Source: *National Balance Sheet*, Vol. II.

Section I
Line 1: Table VII-2, line I-7.
Line 2: Table VII-2, line II-21.
Line 2a: Table VII-2, sum of lines II-1, 6, 7.
Line 3: Table VII-2, line V.

Section II
Line 1: Lines II-1 minus II-1a.
Line 1a: Table VIII-a-7, line 2, minus Table VIII-a-7b, line 2.
Line 1b: Table VII-2, line III-14.
Line 2: Table VII-2, sum of lines III-7 and III-10, and Table VIII-c-9a, line 2.
Line 2a: Table VII-2, line III-11, and Table VIII-c-9b, line 2.
Line 2b: Table VII-2, line V.
Line 3: Tables VIII-a-6b, line 2, minus Table VIII-a-6d, line 2.
Line 4: Table VIII-a-7, line IV-3.

the net investment in unincorporated business by partners and proprietors.

The share of debt financing was lower in the second cycle than in the first and third. In debt financing, the importance of bank loans declined from the first to the second cycle, reflecting a reduction of inventory investment. During the third cycle the relative share of bank loans was higher than during the second cycle, but in proportion to total debt it was smaller than in the first cycle. Other short-term financing, mainly in trade payables, showed an upward tendency in absolute and relative terms. No definite trend is visible in the share of long-term (mortgage) financing, which was around one-eighth of total sources in all three cycles.

### NONFINANCIAL CORPORATIONS

In the case of nonfinancial corporations, the structure of uses of funds is similar for Cycles II and III but different for Cycle I (Table 32).

The structure of sources of funds is considerably affected by the substantial inventory profits registered in the first cycle as a result of the sharp rise of prices after the war. If inventory profits are included, the share of internal financing in total sources is close to three-fifths of total sources in all three cycles. The share of net saving is considerably higher in the first cycle than in the second and third. On the other hand, if inventory profits are excluded, the share of net saving is the same during the first and second cycles, but varies by 4 percentage points between the second and third cycles.[11]

External funds provided an increasing share of total sources of funds during the postwar period. There is some tendency for the share of short-term financing to increase compared to long-term external financing which did not show any trend. In the distribution of the latter between mortgages and bonds, the share of bonds declined while the share of mortgages rose. The share of equity financing was equally low in all three cycles.

For an appropriate understanding of the changes in the structure of sources and uses of funds of nonfinancial corporations, it would be necessary to break down this broad group into at least three subgroups—manufacturing and mining, public utilities, and other non-

---

[11] Inventory profits may be excluded from net saving because they may be regarded as equivalent to capital consumption allowances on a replacement cost basis. Since inventory profits are realized as part of cash inflow, it is not advisable to exclude them from total internal financing or from aggregate over-all sources of funds.

TABLE 32

SOURCES AND USES OF FUNDS OF NONFINANCIAL CORPORATIONS, 1946-58

| | Annual Averages (billion dollars) | | | | Shares (per cent) | | | |
|---|---|---|---|---|---|---|---|---|
| | 1946-49[a] (1) | 1949-54[a] (2) | 1954-58[a] (3) | 1946-58 (4) | 1946-49 (5) | 1949-54 (6) | 1954-58 (7) | 1946-58 (8) |
| **I. Uses** | | | | | | | | |
| 1. Gross capital expenditures | 22.19 | 26.34 | 34.19 | 27.64 | 80.7 | 74.9 | 72.3 | 75.3 |
| 2. Acquisition of financial assets | 5.32 | 8.82 | 13.13 | 9.07 | 19.3 | 25.1 | 27.7 | 24.7 |
| a. Short-term assets | 4.43 | 7.11 | 10.41 | 7.32 | 16.1 | 20.2 | 22.0 | 19.9 |
| i. Loans | 4.78 | 6.17 | 10.75 | 7.31 | 17.4 | 17.5 | 22.7 | 19.9 |
| ii. Bills and notes | -0.35 | 0.94 | -0.34 | 0.01 | -1.3 | 2.7 | -0.7 | 0 |
| b. Long-term assets | 0.80 | 1.58 | 2.52 | 1.62 | 2.9 | 4.5 | 5.3 | 4.4 |
| i. Loans | 1.06 | 1.36 | 2.30 | 1.57 | 3.9 | 3.9 | 4.9 | 4.3 |
| ii. Bonds | -0.26 | 0.22 | 0.22 | 0.05 | -0.9 | 0.6 | 0.5 | 0.1 |
| c. Equities | 0.09 | 0.13 | 0.20 | 0.15 | 0.3 | 0.4 | 0.4 | 0.4 |
| 3. Total uses | 27.51 | 35.16 | 47.32 | 36.71 | 100.0 | 100.0 | 100.0 | 100.0 |
| **II. Sources** | | | | | | | | |
| 1. Gross saving | 17.04 | 20.68 | 26.87 | 21.36 | 61.9 | 58.8 | 56.8 | 58.2 |
| a. Depreciation | 9.27 | 13.70 | 19.02 | 14.35 | 33.7 | 39.0 | 40.2 | 39.1 |
| b. Net saving | 7.77 | 6.98 | 7.85 | 7.01 | 28.2 | 19.9 | 16.6 | 19.1 |
| 2. External sources | 10.48 | 14.48 | 20.45 | 15.35 | 38.1 | 41.2 | 43.2 | 41.8 |
| a. Short-term loans | 3.82 | 7.06 | 9.77 | 6.97 | 13.9 | 20.1 | 20.6 | 19.0 |
| b. Long-term liabilities | 4.99 | 5.10 | 7.78 | 6.01 | 18.1 | 14.5 | 16.4 | 16.4 |
| i. Loans | 2.00 | 1.86 | 3.40 | 2.47 | 7.3 | 5.3 | 7.2 | 6.7 |
| ii. Bonds | 2.99 | 3.24 | 4.38 | 3.54 | 10.9 | 9.2 | 9.3 | 9.6 |
| c. Equities | 1.67 | 2.33 | 2.90 | 2.36 | 6.1 | 6.6 | 6.1 | 6.4 |
| 3. Total sources | 27.51 | 35.16 | 47.32 | 36.71 | 100.0 | 100.0 | 100.0 | 100.0 |
| 4. Inventory profits | 3.25 | 1.08 | 1.58 | 1.87 | 11.8 | 3.1 | 3.3 | 5.1 |

[a]Cycle averages.

NOTES TO TABLE 32

Source:  <u>National Balance Sheet</u>, Vol. II.

<u>Section I</u>
Line 1:  Table VII-4, line I-7.
Line 2:  Table VII-4, line II-21.
Line 2a:  Sum of lines 2ai and 2aii.
Line 2ai:  Table VII-4, sum of lines II-1, 2, 6, 7, and Table VIII-b-20, line 4 minus line 9.
Line 2aii:  Table VII-4, line II-13a, plus first differences of Table III-5ℓ-a, cols. 4, 8, and 11.
Line 2b:  Sum of lines 2bi and 2bii.
Line 2bi:  Table VIII-b-20, line 9.
Line 2bii:  Table VII-4, sum of lines II-13b, 13c, 14, 15, minus first differences of Table III-5ℓ-a, cols. 4, 8, and 11.
Line 2c:  Table VII-4, sum of lines II-16 and II-17.
Line 3:  Table VII-4, line V.

<u>Section II</u>
Line 1:  Table VII-4, line IV-3.
Line 1a:  Table VIII-a-7, line 4, minus Table VIII-a-7b, line 4.
Line 1b:  Lines 1 minus 1a.
Line 2:  Table VII-4, lines III-14, IV-1, and IV-2.
Line 2ai:  Table VII-4, sum of lines III-7, 8, 10, and 13, and Table VIII-c-9a, line 4.
Line 2b:  Sum of lines 2bi and 2bii.
Line 2bi:  Table VII-4, line III-11, and Table VIII-c-9b, line 4.
Line 2bii:  Table VII-4, line III-12.
Line 2c:  Table VII-4, sum of lines IV-1 and IV-2.
Line 3:  Table VII-4, line V.
Line 4:  Table VIII-a-6b, line 4, minus Table VIII-a-6d, line 4.

financial business. The basic tables used in the report do not provide such a breakdown of balance sheets or sources-and-uses-of-funds statements. Such statements are, however, available for half a dozen groups within nonfinancial corporations in a separate report by Meiselman and Shapiro,[12] which forms part of the National Bureau's Postwar Capital Market Study.

From these figures, as well as from some estimates of the Department of Commerce prepared for the years 1947–56,[13] it is known that considerable differences exist in the structure of sources and uses of funds among main industrial groups, and that changes have also occurred from one cycle to another. Thus gross capital expenditures exceed nine-tenths of total uses of funds for public utilities, transportation, and railroad corporations, and three-fifths for manufacturing and mining, but account for only less than two-fifths of all uses in trade. Among sources of funds, internal financing contributes two-thirds for corporations in manufacturing, mining, and transportation other than

[12] *The Measurement of Corporate Sources and Uses of Funds,* Technical Paper 18, New York, NBER, 1964.
[13] See *Survey of Current Business,* September 1957, pp. 10 and 11. The Department of Commerce estimates cover a period longer than the Meiselman-Shapiro study, and therefore they were used here.

railroads, about seven-tenths for trade, and four-fifths for railroads, but as little as three-tenths for public utilities. Long-term debt financing accounts for nearly half of total external financing in manufacturing and mining and in public utilities, for about half in transportation corporations other than railroads, for seven-tenths in railroads, but only for one-sixth in trade corporations. Stock financing is responsible for more than one-third of external financing for public utilities, while its contribution to external financing of corporations in manufacturing and mining, transportation, and trade was small.

### STATE AND LOCAL GOVERNMENTS

At least two definite trends are observable in the uses of funds by state and local governments: an increase in the share of gross capital expenditures from the first cycle to the third and a decline in the share of funds used to acquire short-term claims (Table 33). These trends reflect the increase in financial requirements as large-scale construction programs for state and local governments got under way after the war. It may also be worth noting that the share of funds used to acquire bonds for various funds of state and local governments (excluding pension and retirement funds) increased between the first and second cycles and decreased again in the second and third.

Changes in the structure of the sources of funds were less marked. The share of internal financing rose slightly between the first and second cycles and between the second and third, and the increase is more pronounced for net saving. In fact, the share of net saving in total sources of funds was considerably higher in the second and third cycles than in the first. In relation to the total income of state and local governments, net saving represents about 10 per cent of income in the second and third cycles and about 1 per cent in the first.[14]

### FEDERAL GOVERNMENT

In the case of the federal government, differences in the structure of uses and sources of funds between the first cycle, on the one hand, and the second and third, on the other, are more pronounced than in most other sectors (Table 34). These differences are the result of revenue surpluses in the early postwar years used for debt reduction, together with a reduction in the Treasury's bank balance, and of the

[14] *U.S. Income and Output, 1958,* p. 165; and *Survey of Current Business,* July 1960, p. 19.

TABLE 33

SOURCES AND USES OF FUNDS OF STATE AND LOCAL GOVERNMENTS, 1946-58

| | Annual Averages (billion dollars) | | | | Shares (per cent) | | | |
|---|---|---|---|---|---|---|---|---|
| | 1946-49 [a] (1) | 1949-54 [a] (2) | 1954-58 [a] (3) | 1946-58 (4) | 1946-49 (5) | 1949-54 (6) | 1954-58 (7) | 1946-58 (8) |
| **I. Uses** | | | | | | | | |
| 1. Gross capital expenditures | 3.59 | 7.61 | 12.05 | 8.15 | 76.9 | 81.7 | 90.1 | 85.8 |
| 2. Acquisition of financial assets | 1.11 | 1.70 | 1.32 | 1.36 | 23.1 | 18.3 | 9.9 | 14.3 |
| a. Short-term assets | 1.05 | 1.05 | 0.84 | 0.94 | 21.9 | 11.3 | 6.3 | 9.8 |
| i. Loans | 0.78 | 0.64 | 0.50 | 0.66 | 16.2 | 6.9 | 3.7 | 6.9 |
| ii. Bills and notes | 0.27 | 0.41 | 0.34 | 0.28 | 5.6 | 4.4 | 2.5 | 2.9 |
| b. Long-term assets | 0.06 | 0.65 | 0.48 | 0.42 | 1.2 | 7.0 | 3.6 | 4.5 |
| i. Loans | 0.02 | 0.09 | 0.21 | 0.12 | 0.4 | 1.0 | 1.6 | 1.3 |
| ii. Bonds | 0.04 | 0.56 | 0.27 | 0.30 | 0.8 | 6.0 | 2.0 | 3.2 |
| 3. Total uses | 4.80 | 9.31 | 13.37 | 9.50 | 100.0 | 100.0 | 100.0 | 100.0 |
| **II. Sources** | | | | | | | | |
| 1. Gross saving | 3.08 | 6.12 | 9.08 | 6.32 | 64.2 | 65.7 | 67.9 | 66.5 |
| a. Depreciation | 2.93 | 3.87 | 5.30 | 4.12 | 61.0 | 41.6 | 39.6 | 43.4 |
| b. Net saving | 0.15 | 2.25 | 3.78 | 2.20 | 3.2 | 24.1 | 28.3 | 23.1 |
| 2. External sources | 1.72 | 3.19 | 4.29 | 3.18 | 35.8 | 34.3 | 32.1 | 33.5 |
| a. Short-term loans | 0.14 | 0.08 | 0.11 | 0.11 | 2.9 | 0.9 | 0.8 | 1.2 |
| b. Long-term bonds | 1.58 | 3.11 | 4.18 | 3.07 | 32.9 | 33.4 | 31.2 | 32.3 |
| 3. Total sources | 4.80 | 9.31 | 13.37 | 9.50 | 100.0 | 100.0 | 100.0 | 100.0 |

[a]Cycle averages.

Source: National Balance Sheet, Vol. II.

Section I
Line 1: Table VII-6, line I-7.
Line 2: Table VII-6, line II-21.
Line 2a: Sum of lines 2ai and 2aii.
Line 2ai: Table VII-6, sum of lines II-1 and II-2.
Line 2aii: Table VII-6, line II-13a.
Line 2b: Sum of lines 2bi and 2bii.
Line 2bi: Table VII-6, line II-11.
Line 2bii: Table VII-6, sum of lines II-13c, 14, and 15.

Section II
Line 1: Table VII-6, line IV-3,
Line 1a: Tables VIII-a-7, line 6, minus Table VIII-a-7b, line 6.
Line 1b: Lines II-1 minus II-1a.
Line 2: Table VII-6, line III-14.
Line 2a: Table VII-6, line III-7.
Line 2b: Table VII-6, line III-12.
Line 3: Table VII-6, line V.

TABLE 34

SOURCES AND USES OF FUNDS OF TOTAL FEDERAL GOVERNMENT, 1946-58

| | Annual Averages (billion dollars) | | | | Shares (per cent) | | | |
|---|---|---|---|---|---|---|---|---|
| | 1946-49[a] (1) | 1949-54[a] (2) | 1954-58[a] (3) | 1946-58 (4) | 1946-49 (5) | 1949-54 (6) | 1954-58 (7) | 1946-58 (8) |
| **I. Uses** | | | | | | | | |
| 1. Gross capital expenditures | 3.68 | 15.22 | 18.98 | 13.50 | 105.7 | 83.8 | 95.5 | 95.9 |
| 2. Acquisition of financial assets | -0.21 | 2.95 | 0.90 | 0.57 | -6.0 | 16.2 | 4.5 | 4.1 |
| a. Short-term loans | -1.36 | 2.49 | -0.08 | -0.20 | -39.1 | 13.7 | -0.4 | -1.4 |
| b. Long-term assets | 1.15 | 0.47 | 0.98 | 0.77 | 33.1 | 2.6 | 4.9 | 5.5 |
| i. Loans | 0.99 | 0.47 | 0.74 | 0.63 | 28.4 | 2.6 | 3.7 | 4.5 |
| ii. Bonds | 0.16 | 0 | 0.24 | 0.14 | 4.6 | 0 | 1.2 | 1.0 |
| 3. Total uses | 3.48 | 18.17 | 19.88 | 14.07 | 100.0 | 100.0 | 100.0 | 100.0 |
| **II. Sources** | | | | | | | | |
| 1. Gross saving | 8.16 | 12.90 | 18.83 | 13.28 | 234.5 | 71.0 | 94.7 | 94.4 |
| a. Depreciation | 15.68 | 13.02 | 17.81 | 15.39 | 450.6 | 71.7 | 89.6 | 109.4 |
| b. Net saving | -7.52 | -0.12 | 1.02 | -2.11 | -216.1 | -0.7 | 5.1 | -15.0 |
| 2. External sources | -4.69 | 5.28 | 1.05 | 0.79 | -134.8 | 29.1 | 5.3 | 5.6 |
| a. Short-term liabilities | -3.98 | 3.64 | -0.63 | -0.53 | -114.4 | 20.0 | -3.2 | -3.8 |
| i. Loans | -0.18 | 0.73 | -0.45 | 0.06 | -5.2 | 4.0 | -2.3 | 0.4 |
| ii. Bills and notes | -3.80 | 2.91 | -0.18 | -0.59 | -109.2 | 16.0 | -0.9 | -4.2 |
| b. Long-term bonds | -0.70 | 1.63 | 1.68 | 1.32 | -20.1 | 9.0 | 8.5 | 9.4 |
| 3. Total sources | 3.48 | 18.17 | 19.88 | 14.07 | 100.0 | 100.0 | 100.0 | 100.0 |

BREAKDOWN OF SELECTED ITEMS INTO CIVIL AND MILITARY

| | (1) | (2) | (3) | (4) |
|---|---|---|---|---|
| Gross capital expenditures | | | | |
| Civil | 1.02 | 1.99 | 1.32 | 1.51 |
| Military | 2.66 | 13.23 | 17.66 | 11.99 |
| Gross saving | | | | |
| Civil | 5.50 | -0.34 | 1.17 | 1.30 |
| Military | 2.66 | 13.24 | 17.66 | 11.98 |
| Depreciation | | | | |
| Civil | 1.41 | 1.14 | 1.22 | 1.23 |
| Military | 14.27 | 11.88 | 16.59 | 14.16 |
| Net saving | | | | |
| Civil | 4.09 | -1.48 | -0.05 | 0.07 |
| Military | -11.61 | 1.36 | 1.07 | -2.18 |

NOTES TO TABLE 34

Source: <u>National Balance Sheet</u>, Vol. II.
Section I
Line 1: Table VII-7-1, line I-7.
Line 2: Table VII-7-1, line II-21.
Line 2a: Table VII-7-1, sum of lines II-1, 2, 7, 10, 20, and Table VIII-b-20,
   line 7 minus line 10.
Line 2b: Sum of lines 2bi and 2bii.
Line 2bi: Table VII-7-1, sum of lines II-11, 12, and Table VIII-b-20, line
   10.
Line 2bii: Table VII-7-1, sum of lines II-13c and II-14.
Line 3: Table VII-7-1, line V.
Section II
Line 1: Table VII-7-1, line IV-3.
Line 1a: Table VIII-a-7, lines 7 and 9, minus Table VIII-a-7b, lines 7 and 9.
Line 1b: Lines 1 minus 1a.
Line 2: Table VII-7-1, line III-14.
Line 2a: Sum of lines 2ai and 2aii.
Line 2ai: Table VII-7-1, sum of lines III-1, 2, 7, 9, and 13.
Line 2aii: Table VIII-b-13a, line 10.
Line 2b: Sum of Table VIII-b-13b, line 9, Table VIII-b-13c, line 11, and
   Table VIII-c-12, line 7b.
Line 3: Table VII-7-1, line V.

[a]Cycle averages.

sharp increase in expenditures, primarily for military purposes, between the first and second cycles and their continuation at a high level in the third. The picture will therefore be different depending on whether outlay on durable military assets is treated as current or as capital expenditures. Thus, net saving is substantial in the first cycle and negative in the second and third if military expenditures are classified entirely as current outlay. If they are capitalized, which of course implies the inclusion of capital consumption allowances on the entire stock of military durables among current expenditures, net saving is negative to a very substantial amount in the first cycle because of the heavy depreciation allowances on the stock acquired during the war; while net saving is positive during the third cycle.

### FINANCIAL INSTITUTIONS

The over-all picture of sources and uses of funds of all financial institutions taken together, as shown in Table 35, is only of limited interest since the acquisition of financial assets completely dominates uses and the incurrence of liabilities overshadows all other sources. Among sources, however, a decrease in the share of internal funds from the first to the second and third cycles is worth noting. On the other hand, the share of equity funds in total sources increased, mainly as a result of the increasing importance of investment companies which are predominantly financed through the issuance of their own stock.

Significant structural changes thus occur within the acquisition of

TABLE 35

SOURCES AND USES OF FUNDS OF FINANCIAL INSTITUTIONS, 1946–58

| | Annual Averages (billion dollars) | | | | Shares (per cent) | | | |
|---|---|---|---|---|---|---|---|---|
| | 1946–49[a] (1) | 1949–54[a] (2) | 1954–58[a] (3) | 1946–58 (4) | 1946–49 (5) | 1949–54 (6) | 1954–58 (7) | 1946–58 (8) |
| **I. Uses** | | | | | | | | |
| 1. Gross capital expenditures | 0.34 | 0.40 | 0.52 | 0.42 | 2.1 | 1.5 | 1.6 | 1.7 |
| 2. Acquisition of financial assets | 15.50 | 26.10 | 31.82 | 24.89 | 97.9 | 98.5 | 98.4 | 98.3 |
| a. Short-term assets | 4.43 | 9.20 | 8.87 | 6.97 | 28.0 | 34.7 | 27.4 | 27.5 |
| i. Loans | 8.61 | 7.78 | 9.77 | 8.15 | 54.4 | 29.4 | 30.2 | 32.2 |
| ii. Bills and notes | −4.18 | 1.42 | −0.90 | −1.18 | −26.4 | 5.4 | −2.8 | −4.7 |
| b. Long-term assets | 10.55 | 15.83 | 21.07 | 16.68 | 66.6 | 59.8 | 65.2 | 65.9 |
| i. Loans | 6.54 | 8.80 | 13.20 | 9.71 | 41.3 | 33.2 | 40.8 | 38.4 |
| ii. Bonds | 4.01 | 7.03 | 7.87 | 6.97 | 25.3 | 26.5 | 24.3 | 27.5 |
| c. Equities | 0.52 | 1.08 | 1.87 | 1.23 | 3.3 | 4.1 | 5.8 | 4.9 |
| 3. Total uses | 15.84 | 26.49 | 32.34 | 25.30 | 100.0 | 100.0 | 100.0 | 100.0 |
| **II. Sources** | | | | | | | | |
| 1. Gross saving | 1.52 | 1.60 | 1.97 | 1.73 | 9.6 | 6.0 | 6.1 | 6.8 |
| a. Depreciation | 0.25 | 0.26 | 0.36 | 0.29 | 1.6 | 1.0 | 1.1 | 1.1 |
| b. Net saving | 1.27 | 1.34 | 1.61 | 1.44 | 8.0 | 5.0 | 5.0 | 5.7 |
| 2. External sources | 14.32 | 24.90 | 30.36 | 23.58 | 90.4 | 94.0 | 93.9 | 93.2 |
| a. Short-term liabilities | 5.88 | 14.50 | 17.26 | 12.83 | 37.1 | 54.7 | 53.4 | 50.7 |
| i. Loans | 5.73 | 14.26 | 17.07 | 12.64 | 36.2 | 53.8 | 52.8 | 50.0 |
| ii. Bills and notes | 0.15 | 0.24 | 0.19 | 0.19 | 0.9 | 0.9 | 0.6 | 0.8 |
| b. Long-term liabilities | 8.18 | 9.79 | 11.79 | 9.97 | 51.7 | 37.0 | 36.5 | 39.4 |
| i. Loans | 7.91 | 9.33 | 10.97 | 9.48 | 50.0 | 35.2 | 33.9 | 37.5 |
| ii. Bonds | 0.27 | 0.46 | 0.82 | 0.49 | 1.7 | 1.7 | 2.5 | 1.9 |
| c. Equities | 0.26 | 0.60 | 1.32 | 0.77 | 1.6 | 2.3 | 4.1 | 3.0 |
| 3. Total sources | 15.84 | 26.49 | 32.34 | 25.30 | 100.0 | 100.0 | 100.0 | 100.0 |

NOTES TO TABLE 35

Source: <u>National Balance Sheet</u>, Vol. II.

Section I
Line 1: Table VII-5, line I-7.
Line 2: Table VII-5, line II-21.
Line 2a: Sum of lines 2ai and 2aii.
Line 2ai: Table VII-5, sum of lines II-1, 2, 6, 7, 8, 10, 20, and 9, minus
    Table VIII-c-9b, line 8.
Line 2aii: Table VII-5, line 13a, plus the sum of the first differences of
    Table III-5ℓ-a, cols. 3, 7, and 10.
Line 2b: Sum of lines 2bi and 2bii.
Line 2bi: Table VII-5, sum of lines II-11, 12, and Table VIII-c-9b, line 8.
Line 2bii: Table VII-5, sum of lines II-13b, 13c, 14, and 15, minus the
    first differences of Table III-5ℓ-a, cols. 3, 7, and 10.
Line 2c: Table VII-5, sum of lines II-16 and II-17.
Line 3: Table VII-5, line V.

Section II
Line 1: Table VII-5, line IV-3.
Line 1a: Table VIII-a-7, line 5, minus Table VIII-a-7b, line 5.
Line 1b: Lines 1 minus 1a.
Line 2: Table VII-5, lines III-14, IV-1, and IV-2.
Line 2a: Sum of lines 2ai and 2aii.
Line 2ai: Table VII-5, lines III-1, 2, 7, 8, 9, 10, and 13.
Line 2aii: Table III-5ℓ-a, col. 1 (first differences).
Line 2b: Sum of lines 2bi and 2bii.
Line 2bi: Table VII-5, sum of lines III-3, 4, and 5.
Line 2bii: Table VII-5, line III-12, minus the first differences of Table
    III-5ℓ-a, col. 1.
Line 2c: Table VII-5, lines IV-1 and IV-2.
Line 3: Table VII-5, line V.

[a]Cycle averages.

financial assets and within the incurrence of liabilities. Among financial asset acquisitions, there is a marked increase in the share of common stocks from the first to the third cycle, primarily reflecting first the rapid growth of investment companies, which invest most of their assets in stocks, and secondly the increases in the total assets of non-insured pension funds and in the share of common stock in their portfolio. Bonds absorbed about one-fourth of all acquisitions of financial assets without substantial changes among the three cycles. The share of short-term claims was higher, and that of long-term claims lower, in the second than in the first cycle. This is due to the net acquisition of short-term Treasury securities in the second cycle—the only one of the three postwar cycles during which the Treasury's debt expanded —compared to net sales of such securities during the other two cycles.

Changes in external debt financing are characterized by a substantially higher share of short-term liabilities in the second and third cycles, and a correspondingly lower share of long-term liabilities, compared to the first cycle. This difference reflects the fall in the share of government pension and retirement funds from 22 per cent of total sources of financial institutions in the first cycle to 12 per cent in the second cycle and 9 per cent in the third, and a less pronounced decline in the share of life insurance company reserves from 24 per cent in the first cycle to 18 and 17 per cent in the second and third.

Fuller understanding of the structural changes in uses and sources of funds of financial institutions in the postwar period requires information similar to that in Table 35 for all the major groups of financial institutions. The figures in Table 35 are, of course, aggregates (columns 1 to 4) or weighted averages (columns 5 to 8) of the corresponding figures for the component groups. They thus reflect both structural changes in uses and sources of funds of the various component groups and changes in the shares of the component groups in the aggregate for all financial institutions.

## Long-Term Changes in the Sources of Funds of Main Sectors

As is always the case in discussing the capital market in the postwar period, some historical perspective is needed. Much of what appears new to contemporary observers and in need of explanation by specific factors turns out, on looking back over the record, to be very similar to the situation in earlier "normal" periods (defined here as periods not affected by war or an economic cataclysm like the Great Depression). Such a similarity does not of course absolve us from trying to explain the structural characteristics of the postwar capital market, but it points to long-term forces rather than to ephemeral developments as explanations.

Within the limited space and resources available here for historical comparisons, probably the best base is provided by a condensed statement of sources of funds for the two reasonably normal periods 1901–12 and 1923–29. We may also add the 1934–39 period, although in many respects it differs from both the postwar period and the two other prewar periods, since it represents from a financial viewpoint a period of near depression. To eliminate the effects of changes in the absolute level of the figures, the comments are based throughout on percentage distributions.

The outstanding impression gained from such a comparison for the two prewar periods and the postwar period is one of considerable similarity if attention is limited to the main sectors and to the main sources of funds, as in Table 23. This similarity is rather remarkable since the postwar period is approximately two and four decades removed from the two prewar periods used and since the differences not only in the size of the American economy but in many of its structural features among the three periods are pronounced.

### FINANCE

Among financial institutions, internal funds have, as Table 36 indicates, at all times constituted only a minor source of funds.[15] During the postwar period commercial and savings banks, which usually have a considerable amount of retained earnings (net saving), were much less important than in earlier periods, measured by total funds raised, in comparison to insurance companies and pension funds. Mutual life insurance organizations and pension funds show no net saving according to the method of calculation adopted here whereby virtually all assets are attributed to beneficiaries.

In the distribution of external funds, the postwar period is more similar to the 1920's than to the 1901–12 period. However, during all the periods shown in Table 36, the proportion of external sources of funds obtained as short-term liabilities exceeded long-term liabilities substantially, although the relative share of long-term funds was rising. The shift again is a result of the more rapid growth of insurance and pension organizations compared to commercial and savings banks.

The share of financing through equity securities shows an irregular movement, being much higher in the 1920's and in 1900–12 than during the postwar period. These changes reflect in part the importance of investment companies among financial institutions during the 1920's and in part the high volume of stock issues by commercial banks in the 1920's.

### NONFINANCIAL CORPORATIONS

Turning to nonfinancial corporations—which is the largest and relatively most reliably reported business sector—Table 37 and Chart 8 show that internal sources provided slightly more than half of total funds in 1901–12 and in 1923–29, about the same as during the postwar period. The division of internal sources between capital consumption allowances and retained earnings (net saving) also fails to show pronounced changes: capital consumption allowances increased relatively and the proportion of retained income declined.

The changes in the structure of external financing of nonfinancial

---

[15] Because of lack of data for the prewar periods, Table 36 does not include capital consumption allowances among internal sources. This omission, however, is of little influence for an analysis of the figures.

TABLE 36

STRUCTURAL CHANGES IN SOURCE OF FUNDS OF FINANCIAL INSTITUTIONS, 1901-58
(per cent of total funds)

| | Source | 1901-12 (1) | 1923-29 (2) | 1934-39 (3) | 1946-58 (4) |
|---|---|---|---|---|---|
| I. | Internal (net saving)[a] | 6.9 | 5.2 | 2.7 | 5.8 |
| II. | External | | | | |
| | 1. Total | 93.1 | 94.8 | 97.3 | 94.2 |
| | 2. Liabilities [b] | 85.0 | 82.2 | 96.4 | 91.1 |
| | a. Short-term[b] | 68.8 | 57.5 | 70.4 | 51.3 |
| | b. Long-term | 16.2 | 24.7 | 26.0 | 39.8 |
| | 3. Equity securities | 8.1 | 12.6 | 0.9 | 3.1 |
| III. | Total | 100.0 | 100.0 | 100.0 | 100.0 |
| IV. | Total (billion dollars) | 16.8 | 45.9 | 46.0 | 325.2 |

Source

Cols. 1-3, line I: First difference of net worth (taken from Financial
Intermediaries, Tables A-1 minus A-6, A-7, and A-18 minus A-23 and A-24,
and adjusted for capital gains) minus stock issue (line II-3) and minus
ibid., Table A-19, line 20. The adjustment for capital gains was derived
as follows. For 1923-29, the sum of: (1) first difference of ibid.,
Tables A-12 and A-13, line 16, minus Study of Saving, Vol. 1, Tables V-51
and V-52, cols. 6 and 7; (2) first difference between 1928 and 1929 in
ibid., Vol. I, Table I-6, cols. 6 and 7, less Tables V-51 and V-52, col. 2;
and (3) first difference between the end of 1926 and 1929 in ibid., Vol. I,
Tables V-60 and V-62, cols. 5 and 6, minus Tables V-51 and V-52, cols. 8
and 9. For 1934-39, the sum of: (1) the same as (1) for 1923-29; (2)
first difference of Financial Intermediaries, Table A-8, line 23, minus
Study of Saving, Vol. I, Tables V-51 and V-52, col. 2; and (3) first
difference of Financial Intermediaries, Table A-21, line 14, minus Study of
Saving, Vol. I, Table V-51, cols. 8, 9, and 11, and Table V-52, cols. 8, 9,
11, and 12.
Cols. 1-3, line II-1: Sum of lines II-2 and II-3.
Cols. 1-3, line II-2: Sum of lines II-2a and II-2b.
Cols. 1-3, line II-2a: First difference of short-term liabilities in
Financial Intermediaries, Tables A-1 minus A-6, A-7, and A-18 minus A-23
and A-24, plus A-19, line 20.
Cols. 1-3, line II-2b: First difference of long-term liabilities in ibid.,
Tables A-1 minus A-6, A-7, and A-18 minus A-23 and A-24.
Cols. 1-3, line II-3: Study of Saving, Vol. I, Tables V-17, cols. 1 and 12,
and V-19, cols. 11, 14, 15, 16, and 18.
Cols. 1-3, line IV: Sum of lines I and II-1.
Col. 4: See Table 35, col. 4.

[a]Excludes capital consumption allowances which are relatively small.
[b]Includes unclassified liabilities.

corporations are more pronounced and possibly more important for
capital market analysis. In the two predepression periods, the share
of equity securities was considerably higher than in the postwar period. This decline is so pronounced that the figures cannot be entirely misleading, despite their known statistical weakness. However,
the reasons for the decline are complicated and cannot be adequately
discussed without a breakdown of the aggregate for nonfinancial cor-

TABLE 37

STRUCTURAL CHANGES IN SOURCES OF FINANCING OF
NONFINANCIAL CORPORATIONS, 1901-58
(per cent of total funds)

| Source | | 1901-12 (1) | 1923-29 (2) | 1934-39 (3) | 1946-58 (4) |
|---|---|---|---|---|---|
| I. | Internal | | | | |
| | 1.  Total | 55.2 | 54.7 | 97.6 | 55.9 |
| | 2.  Capital consumption allowances | 37.9 | 39.8 | 124.8 | 41.2 |
| | 3.  Net saving | 17.3 | 14.9 | -27.3 | 14.8 |
| II. | External | | | | |
| | 1.  Total | 44.8[b] | 45.3 | 2.4 | 44.1 |
| | 2.  Borrowing, total | 30.8[b] | 25.9 | -6.6 | 37.3 |
| |    a.  Short-term[a] | 8.0 | 4.3 | 1.0 | 20.0 |
| |    b.  Long-term[a] | 22.5 | 21.6 | -7.6 | 17.3 |
| | 3.  Equity securities | 14.0 | 19.4 | 9.0 | 6.8 |
| III. | Total | 100.0 | 100.0 | 100.0 | 100.0 |
| IV. | Total (billion dollars) | 40.0 | 86.1 | 28.9 | 453.0 |

Source

Cols. 1-3, lines I-1, II-1, II-2, II-3, and IV:  Financial Intermediaries, p. 222.
Cols. 1-3, line I-2: Line I-1 minus line I-3.
Cols. 1-3, line I-3: Study of Saving, Vol. I, Table T-1, col. 6, minus
Table 36, line I, of this book.
Col. 4: National Balance Sheet, Vol. II, Table VII-4. Inventories at
adjusted values (lower panel) to make them comparable with the prewar saving concept.

[a]For classification of short- and long-term borrowing, see Table 32.

[b]Total does not equal sum of components because of rounding of figures in source tables.

porations into at least a half dozen subgroups, such as manufacturing, railroads, electrical power, trade, and services. Such a breakdown is not yet possible on a comparable and satisfactory basis, and time was not sufficient to build up a comparison piece by piece from scattered material on the methods of financing individual segments.[16]

The increasing share of claims in the external financing of nonfinancial corporations is due almost exclusively to the growing importance of short-term borrowing, which reflects primarily the growth in short-term liabilities to creditors other than banks (a category which in the postwar period includes a substantial amount of federal tax accruals for which there was hardly any parallel before 1929). As a result of this change, short-term and long-term liabilities were of about equal importance during the postwar period, while long-term liabili-

[16] For some attempts in this direction, see Simon Kuznets, *Capital in the American Economy: Its Formation and Financing*, Princeton for NBER, 1962, Chapters 5 and 6; and my *Financial Intermediaries*, Chapter 7.

CHART 8

STRUCTURAL CHANGES IN SOURCES OF FUNDS
OF NONFINANCIAL CORPORATIONS, 1901–58

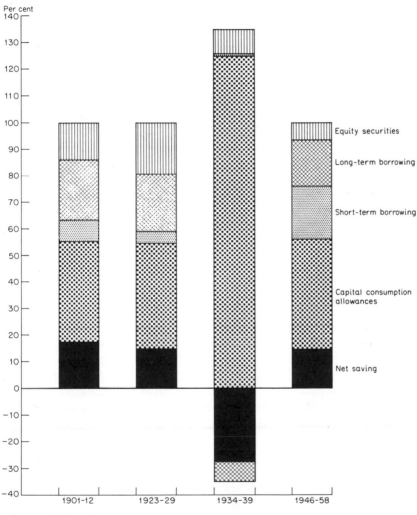

Source: Table 37.

ties had been much larger than short-term borrowing in the two pre-depression periods.

### NONFINANCIAL UNINCORPORATED BUSINESS

In the case of agriculture, the structure of financing during the post-war period can be compared usefully only with the period 1901–12

TABLE 38

STRUCTURAL CHANGES IN SOURCES OF FINANCING OF AGRICULTURE, 1901-58
(per cent of total funds)

| Source | 1901–12 (1) | 1923–29 (2) | 1934–39 (3) | 1946–58 (4) |
|---|---|---|---|---|
| I. Internal | | | | |
| 1. Total | 70.6 | 114.4 | 103.0 | 86.2 |
| 2. Capital consumption allowances | 72.6 | 106.4 | 83.4 | 71.4 |
| 3. Net saving | -1.9 | 8.0 | 19.6 | 14.7 |
| II. External[a] | | | | |
| 1. Total | 29.4 | -15.2 | -3.0 | 13.8 |
| 2. Short-term borrowing[b] | 15.4 | -6.8 | 3.0 | 7.0 |
| 3. Long-term borrowing[b] | 14.0 | -8.3 | -6.0 | 6.8 |
| III. Total | 100.0 | 100.0 | 100.0 | 100.0 |
| IV. Total (billion dollars) | 14.3 | 13.2 | 13.3 | 96.0 |

Source

Cols. 1-3, lines I-1, II-1, II-2, II-3, and IV: Financial Intermediaries, pp. 206-207.
Cols. 1-3, line I-2: Line I-1 minus line I-3.
Cols. 1-3, line I-3: Study of Saving, Vol. I, Table A-3, col. 1.
Col. 4: National Balance Sheet, Vol. II, Table VII-3. Inventories at adjusted values (lower panel) to make them comparable with the prewar saving concept.

[a]Land costs and net sales of farm land are omitted to preserve comparability with col. 4.

[b]For classification of short- and long-term borrowing, see Table 30.

because in the 1920's and the 1930's external financing was negative (Table 38).[17] The share of external financing during the postwar period, although positive, is considerably lower than in 1901–12, a period notable for a rapid expansion in cultivated area and farm output and substantial increases in the prices of agricultural production and land. In both 1901–12 and the postwar period, the distribution

[17] Table 38 does not include an additional source of financing—the net sale of farm land to nonfarm sectors—partly because the figures involved are subject to wide margins of error. It is likely, however, that this was not a negligible source of funds for agriculture in the prewar period. In the two predepression periods, their share may have approached one-tenth (*Financial Intermediaries*, p. 206), while it was probably below one-twentieth in the postwar period.

of external financing was similar, short-term and long-term funds each contributing about one-half.

The rough estimates that can be made of the sources of funds for unincorporated nonfarm business during the prewar period do not justify a discussion of changes in the structure of its financing. Such

TABLE 39

STRUCTURAL CHANGES IN SOURCES OF FINANCING OF
NONFARM UNINCORPORATED BUSINESS, 1901-58
(per cent of total funds)

| Source | 1901–12 (1) | 1923–29 (2) | 1934–39 (3) | 1946–58 (4) |
|---|---|---|---|---|
| I. Internal | | | | |
| 1. Total | 66.9 | 69.3 | 104.5 | 66.0 |
| 2. Capital consumption allowances | 52.0 | 59.4 | 73.7 | 58.3 |
| 3. Net saving | 14.9 | 9.8 | 30.9 | 7.7 |
| II. External | | | | |
| 1. Total | 33.1 | 30.7 | −4.5 | 34.0 |
| 2. Short-term borrowing[a] | 26.0 | 5.5 | 20.4 | 20.5 |
| 3. Long-term borrowing[a] | 7.2 | 25.2 | −24.9 | 13.5 |
| III. Total | 100.0 | 100.0 | 100.0 | 100.0 |
| IV. Total (billion dollars) | 5.8 | 10.8 | 7.0 | 84.8 |

Source

Cols. 1-3, line I-1: Sum of lines I-2 and I-3.
Cols. 1-3, line I-2: Study of Saving, Vol. I, sum of Table P-12, col. 5;
  Table P-13, col. 5; Table P-17, col. 7; Table R-12, col. 2; and Table R-13,
  col. 5. (Depreciation may be underestimated since it was not always possible to obtain a breakdown between the corporate and the unincorporated
  sectors.)
Cols. 1-3, line I-3: Ibid., Vol. I, Table T-1, col. 5.
Cols. 1-3, lines II-1, II-2, II-3: Ibid., Vol. III, Table W-29, first difference of liabilities.
Cols. 1-3, line III: Sum of lines I and II.
Col. 4: National Balance Sheet, Vol. II, Table VII-2. Inventories at adjusted values (lower panel) to make them comparable with the prewar concept.

[a]For classification of short- and long-term borrowing, see Table 31.

a discussion would be further complicated by the conceptual difficulty of distinguishing between retained earnings and the net contribution of capital by proprietors (Table 39).

### NONFARM HOUSEHOLDS

The sources of financing nonfarm households during the postwar period were, as Table 40 shows, very similar to those in the 1920's, but they differed substantially from those in 1901–12. In the postwar period and in the 1920's internal funds accounted for less of total financ-

TABLE 40

STRUCTURAL CHANGES IN SOURCES OF FINANCING OF NONFARM HOUSEHOLDS, 1901-58
(per cent of total funds)

| Source | 1901–12 (1) | 1923–29 (2) | 1934–39 (3) | 1946–58 (4) |
|---|---|---|---|---|
| I. Internal | | | | |
| 1. Total | 91.7 | 82.1 | 93.0 | 82.4 |
| 2. Capital consumption allowances | 37.9 | 37.9 | 63.6 | 41.9 |
| 3. Net saving | 53.9 | 44.2 | 29.4 | 40.5 |
| II. External | | | | |
| 1. Total | 8.2 | 17.9 | 7.0 | 17.7 |
| 2. Short-term borrowing[a] | 4.3 | 7.0 | 6.4 | 5.7 |
| 3. Long-term borrowing[a] | 3.9 | 10.8 | 0.6 | 11.9 |
| III. Total | 100.0 | 100.0 | 100.0 | 100.0 |
| IV. Total (billion dollars) | 55.7 | 146.6 | 67.3 | 826.2 |

Source

Cols. 1-3, lines I-1, II-1, II-2, II-3, III, and IV:  Financial
  Intermediaries, p. 193.
Cols. 1-3, line I-2:  Line I-1 minus line I-3.
Cols. 1-3, line I-3:  Study of Saving, Vol. I, Table T-8, col. 1.
Col. 4:  Table 29, col. 8.

[a]For classification of short- and long-term borrowing, see Table 29.

ing than in 1901–12. However, in the distribution of internal funds among capital consumption allowances and net saving, the postwar period, with an approximately even division among these two sources, differs not only from 1901–12 but also from the 1920's. This change reflects the increasing importance of consumer durables relative to nonfarm households' total income and tangible assets.

In the distribution of external financing, the postwar period and the 1920's are again on one side, and the 1901–12 period on the other. Long-term funds, essentially home mortgages, furnished a larger share of total external financing in the postwar period and the 1920's than in 1901–12. This increase reflects the home-building booms of the 1920's and the postwar period, during both of which borrowing terms became considerably more liberal than they had been before. Within short-term financing, the importance of commercial bank loans other than consumer credit declined considerably, which in part reflected the growth of consumer credit.

## GOVERNMENT

The share of internal funds in the financing of state and local governments is not too different in all three periods, as is evident from Table 41. Indeed, the postwar share is virtually identical with that

TABLE 41

STRUCTURAL CHANGES IN SOURCES OF FINANCING OF STATE AND LOCAL GOVERNMENTS,
1901-58
(per cent of total funds)

| Source | 1901-12 (1) | 1923-29 (2) | 1934-39 (3) | 1946-58 (4) |
|---|---|---|---|---|
| I. Internal | | | | |
| 1. Total | 60.0 | 67.8 | 97.9 | 66.5 |
| 2. Capital consumption allowances | 25.4 | 26.6 | 50.0 | 43.4 |
| 3. Net saving | 34.6 | 41.2 | 48.0 | 23.2 |
| II. External | | | | |
| 1. Total | 40.0 | 32.2 | 2.1 | 33.5 |
| 2. Short-term borrowing[a] | 0 | 0 | -2.7 | 1.2 |
| 3. Long-term borrowing[a] | 40.0 | 32.2 | 4.8 | 32.3 |
| III. Total | 100.0 | 100.0 | 100.0 | 100.0 |
| IV. Total (billion dollars) | 6.0 | 20.2 | 14.6 | 123.5 |

Source

Cols. 1-3, lines I-1, II-1, II-2, II-3, and IV: Financial Intermediaries,
p. 260.
Cols. 1-3, line I-2: Line I-1 minus line I-3.
Cols. 1-3, line I-3: Study of Saving, Vol. I, Table T-1, col. 7.
Col. 4: Table 33, col. 8.

[a]For classification of short- and long-term borrowing, see Table 33.


TABLE 42

STRUCTURAL CHANGES IN SOURCES OF FINANCING OF FEDERAL GOVERNMENT,[a]
1901-58
(per cent of total funds)

| Source | 1901-12 (1) | 1923-29 (2) | 1934-39 (3) | 1946-58 (4) |
|---|---|---|---|---|
| I. Internal | | | | |
| 1. Total | 55.6 | 458.8 | -51.4 | 62.2 |
| 2. Capital consumption allowances | 13.7 | 33.9 | 3.4 | 59.1 |
| 3. Net saving | 41.8 | 424.9 | -54.8 | 3.1 |
| II. External | | | | |
| 1. Total | 44.4 | -352.9 | 151.4 | 37.8 |
| 2. Short-term borrowing[b] | 44.4 | 0 | 58.0 | -25.7 |
| 3. Long-term borrowing[b] | 0 | -352.9 | 93.5 | 63.5 |
| III. Total | 100.0 | 100.0 | 100.0 | 100.0 |
| IV. Total (billion dollars) | 1.8 | 1.7 | 24.5 | 27.1 |

Source

Cols. 1-3, lines I-1, II-1, II-2, II-3, and IV: Financial Intermediaries,
p. 266.
Cols. 1-3, line I-2: Line I-1 minus line I-3.
Cols. 1-3, line I-3: Study of Saving, Vol. I, Table T-1, col. 8.
Col. 4: National Balance Sheet, Vol. II, Table VII-7. Sources of funds
financing civil expenditures only were included, so as to make the
saving figure comparable with the prewar concept.

[a]Including government corporations.

[b]For classification of short- and long-term borrowing, see Table 34.

of the 1920's, although it is higher than that observed during 1901–12. Here too a considerable decline is noticed in the proportion of internal financing that can be classified as net saving. External financing in all periods took the form of net issuance of tax-exempt securities, which are classified as long-term liabilities, although they are mostly issued in serial form and thus include maturities that should be regarded as short-term liabilities. However, comprehensive information is not available on the maturity distribution of tax-exempt securities that would permit a judgment on a possible shift in the proportion of short-term and long-term liabilities.

There is no point in trying to establish trends in the structure of financing of the federal government because of the sharp changes in the scope of its activities since the beginning of the century and the influence of military expenditures during the postwar period, for which there is hardly any parallel for the two predepression periods. The figures are shown in Table 42 in an arrangement identical with that of the other sectors and show the sources of funds financing civil expenditures only.

# CHAPTER 5

# The Main Sectors of the Capital Market During the Postwar Period

WITH the limited resources at our disposal, it was obviously impossible to investigate and to discuss the main segments of the American capital market in a way that would bring out all significant changes that occurred during the postwar period in the size of each of these markets; in the supply of and the demand for funds by the different economic sectors and, in particular, by the main groups of financial institutions; in the characteristics of capital market instruments and the methods of issuing them and trading in them; in absolute and relative interest or yield rates; and in the competitive relationships to other sectors of the capital market.

However, with the help of the basic statistics of flows of funds and related stocks that underlie this entire study, it is relatively easy to draw up a table for each of the main capital market instruments, showing averages of net flows for the three postwar cycles as well as an average annual net flow for the entire period from 1946 through 1958 for each of the seven main economic sectors and the thirteen subsectors of the financial sector.

These figures permit a comparison of the activity in each sector of the capital market during the three postwar cycles and of the position of the main sectors as suppliers of funds to, or as recipients of funds from, the market. An attempt is then made to explain the trends in the size and the structure of the market shown by these figures by institutional changes during the postwar periods. These explanations have been kept to fairly obvious connections except in cases where they could be based on specialized studies that form part of the Postwar Capital Market Study—home mortgages, corporate bonds and loans, and state and local government securities—or on substantial analytical work that has been done by others, such as for the market for Treasury securities.

The statistical tables unfortunately could not be extended to cover in a similar fashion the 1930's, 1920's, and the period before World War I. The preparation of data comparable to those available for the postwar period would have been too time-consuming and in many cases unfeasible. However, the data presented, although not comparable in all details, usually permit a comparison of the orders of magnitude of the structural changes in the main segments of the capital market between the postwar period as a whole, on one side, and the 1920's and the period 1900–12, on the other; the 1930's and the years of World Wars I and II are omitted because they are dominated by special factors not regarded as relevant to the American capital market of the midtwentieth century.

It bears repeating that the very brief discussion of the different capital markets presented in the following chapters is not a substitute for specialized monographs and thorough analysis; it is intended only as a first orientation and a suggestion for a more intensive study of the statistical record and of the historical, institutional, and analytical literature.

The same pattern will be followed in the discussion of each of the five main sectors of the capital market. After a brief characterization of the organization of the market and of changes in it during the postwar period, we shall discuss changes from one cycle average to the next during the postwar period and then review long-term trends since the turn of the century. No specific discussion is offered of seasonal movements since the quarterly figures in the Federal Reserve Board's flow-of-funds statistics, which are necessary for this purpose, are available only back to 1952, and since it proved impossible with the resources available to subject the quarterly figures to seasonal analysis.

The discussion will be based on tables in standard form giving information on the volume of the capital market instrument outstanding, on rates of changes in volume outstanding over each of the three postwar cycles and over longer periods, on the distribution of amounts outstanding among the main holder groups, on the importance of the instrument in the portfolio of the main holder groups (i.e., in the share of the instrument holders' total assets and in uses of funds by them), and on average interest rates for cycles and longer periods of time. The discussion will necessarily have to be highly condensed. Annual figures for all the series in the standard tables (excluding those of interest rates) and for many breakdowns by type of asset and, for financial enterprises, by subsector will be found for the postwar period in Volume II of *Studies in the National Balance Sheet of the United States*. For the prewar period, similar data can be found, although not always in exactly comparable form, in Appendix A of *Financial Intermediaries in the American Economy since 1900,* and in Volume I of *A Study of Saving in the United States*.

The five capital market instruments studied in Chapters 6 to 10— U.S. government securities, state and local government securities, residential mortgages, corporate bonds, and corporate stock—have been selected for the following reasons: they are of large absolute size; each of them accounts for a substantial fraction of total financial assets; they are fairly standardized in their legal form and the methods of issuance, trading, and redemption; and, together with short-term loans to business and consumers, they are crucial in the expansion and contraction of credit in the economy and in the formation of interest rates.

Table 43 and Chart 9 provide a bird's-eye view of the absolute size of these five capital market instruments and of their importance among all main instruments at the beginning of the postwar period and in 1958 when our statistical records terminate. For the postwar period, the five selected instruments accounted for 60 per cent of the net flow of funds of the ten main instruments, whereas their share in the total stock was about 90 per cent in 1945 and more than 80 per cent in 1958. The main reason for this discrepancy is that common stock, included among the five instruments, increased very sharply in value as a result not primarily of net sales of stock but of the sharp rise in stock prices, and that Treasury securities, although accounting for one-half of the total stock of the ten main instruments in 1945 and still more than one-fifth in 1958, showed virtually no net increase. The discrepancy is particularly pronounced for Cycle I. The five instruments accounted only for little more than two-fifths of the net flow of the ten main instruments, although their share in the stock was higher than four-fifths. In Cycles II and III they accounted for

TABLE 43

STRUCTURAL CHANGES IN MAIN CAPITAL MARKET INSTRUMENTS DURING THE POSTWAR PERIOD

| | Outstandings (billion dollars) | | Aggregate Net Flows, 1946-58 | | NET FLOWS (ANNUAL AVERAGES) | | | | | |
| --- | --- | --- | --- | --- | --- | --- | --- | --- | --- | --- |
| | | | | | Amounts (billion dollars) | | | Distribution (per cent) | | |
| | 1945 (1) | 1958 (2) | Billion Dollars (3) | Per Cent (4) | Cycle I 1946-49 (5) | Cycle II 1949-54 (6) | Cycle III 1954-58 (7) | Cycle I 1946-49 (8) | Cycle II 1949-54 (9) | Cycle III 1954-58 (10) |
| 1. U.S. Treasury securities[a] | 275.7 | 274.3 | -1.4 | -0.3 | -4.8 | 3.7 | 0 | -26 | 11 | 0 |
| 2. State and local govt. securities | 21.2 | 61.1 | 39.9 | 9.3 | 1.6 | 3.1 | 4.2 | 9 | 9 | 10 |
| 3. Nonfarm residential mortgages | 23.3 | 133.0 | 109.8 | 25.5 | 5.5 | 8.0 | 11.2 | 30 | 23 | 26 |
| 4. Corporate bonds | 27.5 | 88.8 | 61.3 | 14.2 | 3.6 | 4.2 | 6.5 | 19 | 12 | 15 |
| 5. Corporate stocks | 146.6 | 465.4 | 41.2 | 9.6 | 2.0 | 2.9 | 4.2 | 11 | 8 | 10 |
| 6. Five selected instruments | 494.3 | 1,022.6 | 250.8 | 58.3 | 7.9 | 21.9 | 26.1 | 43 | 63 | 60 |
| 7. Nonfarm nonresidential mortgages | 7.5 | 27.6 | 20.1 | 4.7 | 1.2 | 1.1 | 2.2 | 6 | 3 | 5 |
| 8. Farm mortgages | 4.8 | 11.3 | 6.5 | 1.5 | 0.2 | 0.5 | 0.7 | 1 | 1 | 2 |
| 9. Bank loans | 13.3 | 53.8 | 40.5 | 9.4 | 2.8 | 2.6 | 3.9 | 15 | 8 | 9 |
| 10. Consumer loans | 5.7 | 46.1 | 40.4 | 9.4 | 3.0 | 3.2 | 3.4 | 16 | 9 | 8 |
| 11. Trade credit | 28.1 | 100.4 | 72.2 | 16.8 | 3.5 | 5.2 | 7.5 | 19 | 15 | 17 |
| 12. Total | 553.7 | 1,261.8 | 430.5 | 100.0 | 18.6 | 34.5 | 43.8 | 100 | 100 | 100 |

Source: *National Balance Sheet*, Vol. II.
Cols. 1-2, line 1: Table IV-b-13.
Cols. 1-2, line 2: Table IV-b-14.
Cols. 1-2, line 3: Table IV-b-11a.
Cols. 1-2, line 4: Table IV-b-15.
Cols. 1-2, line 5: Tables IV-b-16 and IV-b-17.
Cols. 1-2, line 6: Sums of lines 1 through 5.
Cols. 1-2, line 7: Table IV-b-11b.
Cols. 1-2, line 8: Table IV-b-12.
Cols. 1-2, line 9: Table IV-b-9.
Cols. 1-2, line 10: Table IV-b-6.
Cols. 1-2, line 11: Table IV-b-7.
Cols. 1-2, line 12: Sums of lines 6 through 11.
Cols. 3-10: Tables VIII corresponding to the above.

[a]Domestic holdings only.

Note: Components may not add to totals because of rounding here and elsewhere in this chapter.

CHART 9

NET FLOW THROUGH MAIN CAPITAL MARKET INSTRUMENTS,
1946–58

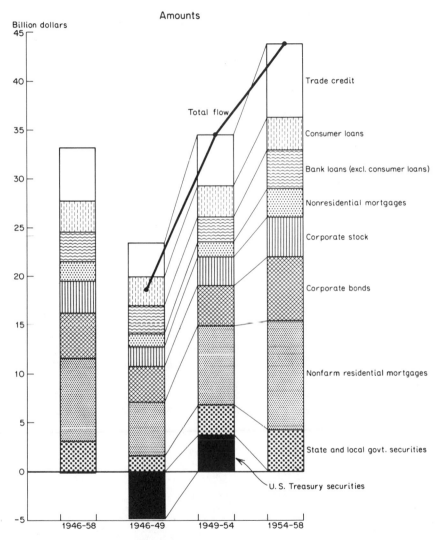

CHART 9 (CONCLUDED)
Distribution

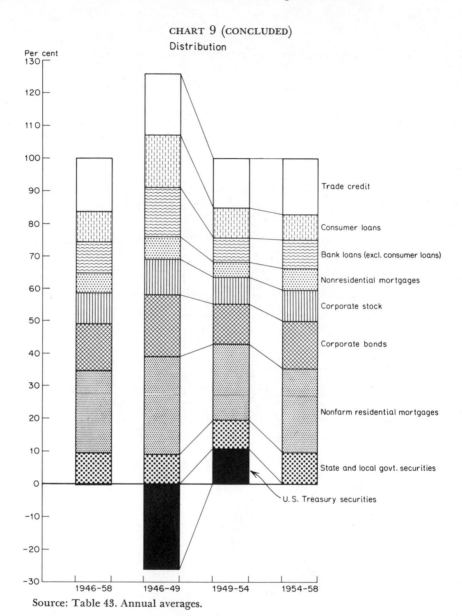

Source: Table 43. Annual averages.

more than three-fifths of total net flows, but their share in the stock was still much higher. Cycle I also differs from Cycles II and III in the distribution of the aggregate flow among individual instruments, particularly in the considerable reductions in volume of Treasury securities, and the high share of bank loans to business and of consumer credit.

In historical perspective, the share of the five instruments during the postwar period was high, as will be seen in Table 44 and Chart 10. Changes in the distribution of the flows are less pronounced. The share of the five selected instruments was not very different in 1901–12 and 1913–29 from that in the postwar period. The distribution during 1930–39, in which these instruments accounted for more than the total net flow in all ten main instruments because the remaining five instruments showed negative rather than positive flows, may be regarded as abnormal.[1]

Shorter-term variations in the net supply and absorption of the main capital market instruments can be followed in Tables 45 and 46, which provide annual data for the postwar period in absolute terms and in percentages of the year's total, and in Table 47 and Chart 11, which show annual rates of change. Among the main capital market instruments, residential and other mortgages, state and local government securities, and corporate stock exhibited considerably more stability than short-term loans and Treasury securities. Most of the main instruments conform in their annual movements to the business cycle, particularly short-term loans and corporate securities. State and local government securities and, less clearly, residential mortgages tend to move countercyclically.

We may round out this summary with a look at the changes in interest rates for the main types of financial assets for which data are provided in Table 48. Since interest rates were at an all-time low at the end of World War II and were held down during the early part of the postwar period by the policies of the Federal Reserve System, it is not astonishing that the trend of interest rates was definitely upward through most of the postwar period for all types of claims, with of course cyclical and seasonal fluctuations. In general the rise was more pronounced, in absolute and still more in relative terms, for

---

[1] The sources for these data are the same as the sources for Table 44, except for corporate stocks, which are taken from *A Study of Saving*, Vol. I, Tables V-9 and V-10.

TABLE 44

TRENDS IN VOLUME AND DISTRIBUTION OF MAIN CAPITAL MARKET INSTRUMENTS,
SELECTED YEARS, 1900-58

| | Absolute Values (billion dollars) | | | | | | Shares (per cent) | | | | | |
|---|---|---|---|---|---|---|---|---|---|---|---|---|
| | 1958 (1) | 1945 (2) | 1939 (3) | 1929 (4) | 1912 (5) | 1900 (6) | 1958 (7) | 1945 (8) | 1939 (9) | 1929 (10) | 1912 (11) | 1900 (12) |
| 1. U.S. Treasury securities | 274.3 | 275.7 | 47.0 | 16.2 | 1.2 | 1.2 | 22 | 50 | 18 | 5 | 1 | 3 |
| 2. State and local govt. securities | 61.1 | 21.2 | 19.8 | 16.9 | 4.4 | 2.0 | 5 | 4 | 7 | 5 | 5 | 5 |
| 3. Nonfarm residential mortgages | 133.0 | 23.3 | 20.8 | 24.9 | 5.0 | 3.0 | 11 | 4 | 8 | 7 | 6 | 8 |
| 4. Corporate bonds | 88.8 | 27.5 | 32.5 | 38.1 | 14.5 | 5.2 | 7 | 5 | 12 | 11 | 16 | 13 |
| 5. Corporate stock | 465.4 | 146.6 | 100.1 | 186.7 | 38.0 | 13.9 | 37 | 26 | 37 | 52 | 42 | 35 |
| 6. Five selected instruments | 1,022.6 | 494.3 | 220.2 | 282.8 | 63.1 | 25.3 | 81 | 89 | 82 | 79 | 70 | 64 |
| 7. Nonfarm nonresidential mortgages | 27.6 | 7.5 | 8.1 | 11.9 | 2.7 | 1.5 | 2 | 1 | 3 | 3 | 3 | 4 |
| 8. Farm mortgages | 11.3 | 4.8 | 6.6 | 9.6 | 4.3 | 2.3 | 1 | 1 | 2 | 3 | 5 | 6 |
| 9. Bank loans (n.e.c.) | 53.8 | 13.3 | 9.8 | 20.5 | 9.0 | 3.9 | 4 | 2 | 4 | 6 | 10 | 10 |
| 10. Consumer loans | 46.1 | 5.7 | 7.8 | 8.6 | 2.9 | 1.0 | 4 | 1 | 3 | 2 | 3 | 3 |
| 11. Trade credit | 100.4 | 28.1 | 14.7 | 25.7 | 8.1 | 5.7 | 8 | 5 | 6 | 7 | 9 | 14 |
| 12. Total | 1,261.8 | 553.7 | 267.2 | 359.1 | 90.1 | 39.7 | 100 | 100 | 100 | 100 | 100 | 100 |

Source: National Balance Sheet, Vol. II.
Cols. 1-2, lines 1-5, 7-11: Lines 8 of Tables IV-b-13, 14, 11a, 15, 16, 17, 11b, 12, 9, 6, and 7.
Cols. 3-6, lines 1-5, 7-8, 10-11: Lines 8 of Tables IV-b-13d, 14a, 11c-1, 15a, 17b, 11c-4, 12a, 6a, and 7a.
Cols. 3-6, line 9: Table Ia, line II-9.

short-term than for long-term rates. Among short-term rates, open-market rates, which had been particularly influenced by monetary policy, rose more than institutional rates (bank loans, savings deposits). Among the main types of long-term claims, the increase was fairly

CHART 10

DISTRIBUTION OF MAIN CAPITAL MARKET
INSTRUMENTS OUTSTANDING, 1900–58

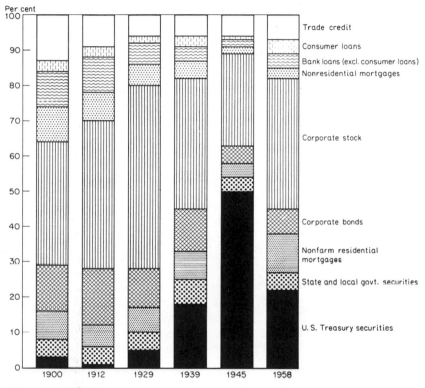

Source: Table 44.

uniform except that the yield on state and local government securities increased more than that on Treasury or corporate bonds, partly in reaction to the extraordinary low level to which the yields on state and local government securities had fallen at the end of World War II.

While the increase in short-term rates was in many cases sharper in relative terms from Cycles I to II than from Cycles II to III, re-

TABLE 45

NET SUPPLY OF MAIN CAPITAL MARKET INSTRUMENTS, 1946–58

(billion dollars)

| Year | Total (1) | U.S. Government Securities[a] (2) | State and Local Government Securities (3) | Corporate Bonds (4) | Nonfarm Residential Mortgages (5) | Corporate Stock (6) | Five Selected Instruments (7) | All Other Mortgages (8) | Bank Term Loans (9) | Short-Term Loans Commercial (10) | Short-Term Loans Consumer (11) |
|---|---|---|---|---|---|---|---|---|---|---|---|
| 1946 | 1.8[b] | -18.3 | -0.1 | 1.2 | 4.8 | 2.0 | -10.4 | 1.4 | 1.8 | 6.2 | 2.8 |
| 1947 | 28.6 | -2.9 | 1.4 | 3.3 | 5.7 | 2.1 | 9.6 | 1.5 | 1.2 | 13.0 | 3.3 |
| 1948 | 22.4 | -4.6 | 2.2 | 3.2 | 5.9 | 1.9 | 10.6 | 1.4 | 0.6 | 6.9 | 2.9 |
| 1949 | 20.6 | 4.2 | 2.4 | 3.2 | 5.3 | 2.1 | 17.2 | 1.2 | -0.9 | 0.2 | 2.9 |
| 1950 | 42.5 | -1.9 | 3.1 | 3.1 | 8.7 | 2.3 | 15.3 | 1.5 | 0.8 | 20.7 | 4.2 |
| 1951 | 33.6 | 2.5 | 2.4 | 4.5 | 7.8 | 3.1 | 20.3 | 1.7 | 1.1 | 9.2 | 1.3 |
| 1952 | 43.2 | 6.9 | 3.2 | 5.2 | 7.5 | 3.6 | 26.4 | 1.6 | 1.2 | 9.2 | 4.8 |
| 1953 | 34.0 | 7.0 | 3.6 | 4.8 | 8.2 | 2.9 | 26.5 | 1.7 | -0.2 | 2.1 | 3.9 |
| 1954 | 35.6 | 3.2 | 4.2 | 3.5 | 10.1 | 3.1 | 24.1 | 2.3 | 0 | 8.1 | 1.1 |
| 1955 | 58.0 | 0.7 | 3.5 | 5.7 | 13.4 | 3.8 | 27.1 | 2.8 | 1.4 | 20.3 | 6.4 |
| 1956 | 40.8 | -4.7 | 3.3 | 5.8 | 11.5 | 4.4 | 20.3 | 3.2 | 3.0 | 10.6 | 3.7 |
| 1957 | 39.5 | -1.6 | 4.9 | 9.9 | 9.2 | 4.6 | 27.0 | 2.8 | 1.5 | 5.4 | 2.8 |
| 1958 | 53.9 | 7.9 | 5.9 | 5.8 | 11.7 | 5.2 | 36.5 | 3.5 | 0.5 | 13.2 | 0.2 |
| Average per year | | | | | | | | | | | |
| 1946-58 | 34.9 | -0.1 | 3.1 | 4.7 | 8.4 | 3.2 | 19.3 | 2.0 | 0.9 | 9.6 | 3.1 |
| 1946-49 | 20.9 | -4.8 | 1.6 | 3.6 | 5.5 | 2.0 | 7.9 | 1.4 | 0.8 | 7.8 | 3.0 |
| 1949-54 | 36.3 | 3.7 | 3.1 | 4.2 | 8.0 | 2.9 | 21.8 | 1.6 | 0.5 | 9.1 | 3.2 |
| 1954-58 | 45.7 | 0 | 4.2 | 6.5 | 11.2 | 4.2 | 26.2 | 2.9 | 1.6 | 11.7 | 3.4 |

Source: National Balance Sheet, Vol. II.
Col. 1: Sum of columns 7, 8, 9, 10, and 11.
Cols. 2-6, 8: Tables VIII-b-13, 14, 15, 11a, 16, 17, 11b, and 12, line 8.
Col. 7: Sum of cols. 2-6.
Col. 9: Table VIII-c-9b, line 8.
Col. 10: Line 8 of Tables VIII-b-7, b-8, b-10, and b-9 minus Table VIII-c-9b.
Col. 11: Table VIII-b-6, line 8.

[a]Purchases by domestic sectors.

[b]Appears unusually small due to the large sales of U.S. government securities.

TABLE 46

DISTRIBUTION OF NET SUPPLY OF MAIN CAPITAL MARKET INSTRUMENTS, 1946–58

(per cent)

| Year | Total (1) | U.S. Government Securities (2) | State and Local Government Securities (3) | Corporate Bonds (4) | Residential Mortgages (5) | Corporate Stock (6) | Five Selected Instruments (7) | Other Mortgages (8) | Bank Term Loans (9) | Short-Term Loans Commercial (10) | Short-Term Loans Consumer (11) |
|---|---|---|---|---|---|---|---|---|---|---|---|
| 1946 | 100 | -1,017 | -6 | 67 | 267 | 111 | -578 | 78 | 100 | 344 | 156 |
| 1947 | 100 | -10 | 5 | 12 | 20 | 7 | 34 | 5 | 4 | 45 | 12 |
| 1948 | 100 | -21 | 10 | 23 | 26 | 8 | 47 | 6 | 3 | 31 | 13 |
| 1949 | 100 | 20 | 12 | 16 | 26 | 10 | 83 | 6 | -4 | 1 | 14 |
| 1950 | 100 | -4 | 7 | 7 | 20 | 5 | 35 | 4 | 2 | 49 | 10 |
| 1951 | 100 | 7 | 7 | 13 | 23 | 9 | 60 | 5 | 3 | 27 | 4 |
| 1952 | 100 | 16 | 7 | 12 | 17 | 8 | 61 | 4 | 3 | 21 | 11 |
| 1953 | 100 | 21 | 11 | 14 | 24 | 9 | 79 | 5 | -1 | 6 | 11 |
| 1954 | 100 | 9 | 12 | 10 | 28 | 9 | 68 | 6 | 0 | 23 | 3 |
| 1955 | 100 | 1 | 6 | 10 | 23 | 7 | 47 | 5 | 2 | 35 | 11 |
| 1956 | 100 | -12 | 8 | 14 | 28 | 11 | 50 | 8 | 7 | 26 | 9 |
| 1957 | 100 | -4 | 12 | 25 | 23 | 12 | 68 | 7 | 4 | 14 | 7 |
| 1958 | 100 | 15 | 11 | 11 | 22 | 10 | 69 | 6 | 1 | 24 | 0 |
| Average per year | | | | | | | | | | | |
| 1946–58 | 100 | 0 | 9 | 13 | 24 | 9 | 55 | 6 | 3 | 27 | 9 |
| 1946–49 | 100 | -23 | 8 | 17 | 26 | 10 | 38 | 7 | 4 | 38 | 14 |
| 1949–54 | 100 | 10 | 9 | 12 | 22 | 8 | 61 | 4 | 1 | 25 | 9 |
| 1954–58 | 100 | 0 | 9 | 14 | 25 | 9 | 57 | 6 | 3 | 26 | 7 |

Source: Table 45.

## TABLE 47

### RATE OF GROWTH OF SUPPLY OF MAIN CAPITAL MARKET INSTRUMENTS, 1946-58
#### (per cent)

| Year | TREASURY SECURITIES | | | State and Local Government Securities (4) | Corporate Bonds (5) | Corporate Stock | | Mortgages | | | Bank Term Loans (11) | Short-Term Bank Loans (12) | Consumer Credit (13) | Trade Credit (14) | Security Credit (15) |
| | Total (1) | Long-Term Savings Bonds (2) | Others (3) | | | Common (6) | Preferred (7) | Total Nonfarm (8) | Nonfarm Residential (9) | Farm (10) | | | | | |
|---|---|---|---|---|---|---|---|---|---|---|---|---|---|---|---|
| 1946 | -6.6 | 3.4 | -0.9 | -0.6 | 4.5 | 1.4 | 1.4 | 19.8 | 20.7 | 2.9 | 62.6 | 30.5 | 48.3 | 13.1 | -53.3 |
| 1947 | -1.1 | 4.7 | -0.9 | 6.7 | 11.6 | 1.4 | 3.2 | 19.0 | 20.1 | 3.4 | 26.9 | 24.5 | 38.8 | 19.7 | -27.5 |
| 1948 | -1.8 | 5.8 | -3.1 | 9.8 | 16.2 | 1.4 | 2.6 | 16.1 | 17.4 | 4.4 | 9.3 | 9.6 | 24.6 | 7.6 | 9.0 |
| 1949 | 1.7 | 3.1 | -5.4 | 9.5 | 8.6 | 1.5 | 2.2 | 12.2 | 13.3 | 5.5 | -13.3 | -4.1 | 20.1 | -1.9 | 24.7 |
| 1950 | -0.7 | 2.4 | -3.7 | 11.5 | 7.6 | 1.6 | 1.8 | 16.9 | 19.4 | 9.7 | 15.2 | 29.2 | 23.8 | 33.2 | 21.1 |
| 1951 | 1.0 | -0.9 | 10.6 | 8.0 | 10.3 | 1.5 | 3.9 | 13.3 | 14.5 | 9.1 | 17.7 | 15.7 | 6.2 | 8.9 | -7.4 |
| 1952 | 2.7 | 0.5 | 0.6 | 9.8 | 10.9 | 1.7 | 3.0 | 11.3 | 12.2 | 8.8 | 16.4 | 6.8 | 20.7 | 9.9 | 16.5 |
| 1953 | 2.7 | -0.2 | -6.0 | 10.0 | 9.0 | 1.2 | 2.4 | 11.2 | 12.0 | 7.0 | -1.8 | 1.9 | 14.1 | -0.2 | 16.2 |
| 1954 | 1.2 | 0.7 | 10.8 | 10.6 | 6.0 | 1.4 | 2.5 | 12.7 | 13.1 | 6.7 | 0.3 | 2.0 | 3.5 | 7.7 | 32.3 |
| 1955 | 0.2 | 0.3 | 5.5 | 8.0 | 9.3 | 1.3 | 0.4 | 14.6 | 15.4 | 9.4 | 16.3 | 18.7 | 19.6 | 16.9 | 14.2 |
| 1956 | -1.7 | -2.6 | -6.0 | 7.1 | 8.6 | 1.1 | 2.8 | 11.5 | 11.4 | 9.3 | 29.4 | 7.6 | 9.4 | 10.5 | -7.8 |
| 1957 | -0.6 | -6.7 | -2.2 | 9.7 | 13.6 | 1.2 | 2.4 | 8.4 | 8.2 | 6.0 | 11.8 | 1.4 | 6.6 | 3.7 | -4.5 |
| 1958 | 3.0 | -2.5 | 7.1 | 10.7 | 7.1 | 1.4 | 2.7 | 9.9 | 9.7 | 7.1 | 3.6 | 3.2 | 0.4 | 8.9 | 20.7 |
| Average | | | | | | | | | | | | | | | |
| 1946-49 | -2.0 | 4.2 | -2.6 | 6.3 | 10.1 | 1.4 | 2.3 | 16.7 | 17.8 | 4.0 | 18.2 | 14.3 | 32.5 | 9.3 | -17.7 |
| 1949-54 | 1.4 | 0.5 | 2.2 | 10.0 | 8.8 | 1.4 | 2.7 | 13.0 | 14.2 | 8.2 | 9.2 | 10.2 | 13.4 | 11.4 | 15.0 |
| 1954-58 | 0.2 | -2.9 | 1.0 | 8.9 | 9.6 | 1.2 | 2.1 | 11.1 | 11.1 | 7.9 | 14.9 | 7.5 | 8.8 | 9.9 | 4.9 |
| 1946-58 | 0 | 0.6 | 0.3 | 8.5 | 9.4 | 1.3 | 2.4 | 13.6 | 14.4 | 6.8 | 13.7 | 10.6 | 17.4 | 10.3 | 0.9 |

Source: National Balance Sheet, Vol. II.

Cols. 1-5, 7-10, 13-15: Lines 8 of Tables IV-b-13, 13b, 13c, 14, 15, 16, 11, 11a, 12, 6, 7, and 8, for the denominator; the corresponding Table VIII figures for the numerator.

Col. 6: Net purchase of common stock (Table VIII-b-17, line 8) as per cent of common stock outstanding (Table IV-b-17, line 8) at end of previous year.

Col. 11: Table IV-c-9b, line 8, for the denominator; Table VIII-c-9b, line 8, for the numerator.

Col. 12: Table IV-b-9, line 8, minus Table IV-c-9b, line 8, for the denominator; the corresponding Table VIII figures for the numerator.

CHART 11

RATE OF CHANGE IN SUPPLY OF MAIN CAPITAL
MARKET INSTRUMENTS, 1946–58

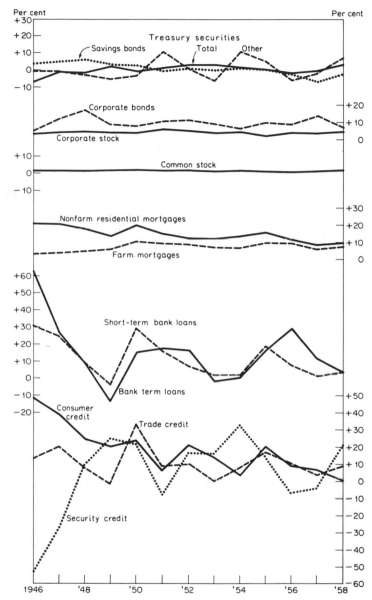

Source: Table 47.

TABLE 48

CHANGES IN INTEREST RATE STRUCTURE DURING THE POSTWAR PERIOD
(per cent)

| | Cycle Averages | | | | | 1946–58 | ABSOLUTE CHANGES In Cycle Averages | | | 1958÷ 1946 | PER CENT CHANGES In Cycle Averages | | |
|---|---|---|---|---|---|---|---|---|---|---|---|---|---|
| | 1946 (1) | 1958 (2) | Cycle I 1946–49 (3) | Cycle II 1949–54 (4) | Cycle III 1954–58 (5) | (6) | Cycles I–II (7) | Cycles II–III (8) | Cycles I–III (9) | (10) | Cycles II÷I (11) | Cycles III÷II (12) | Cycles III÷I (13) |
| **I. Short-term claims** | | | | | | | | | | | | | |
| 1. Treasury bills | 0.38 | 1.84 | 0.79 | 1.50 | 2.27 | 1.46 | 0.71 | 0.77 | 1.48 | 384 | 90 | 51 | 187 |
| 2. Treasury notes (9–12 months) | 0.82 | 2.09 | 1.00 | 1.58 | 2.44 | 1.27 | 0.58 | 0.86 | 1.44 | 155 | 58 | 54 | 144 |
| 3. Treasury certificates (3–5 years) | 1.16 | 2.90 | 1.41 | 1.95 | 2.90 | 1.74 | 0.54 | 0.95 | 1.49 | 150 | 38 | 49 | 106 |
| 4. Savings deposits, mutual savings banks | 1.57 | 3.07 | 1.66 | 2.15 | 2.78 | 1.50 | 0.49 | 0.63 | 1.12 | 96 | 30 | 29 | 67 |
| 5. Savings and loan assoc. depos. | 2.37 | 3.38 | 2.42 | 2.67 | 3.09 | 1.01 | 0.25 | 0.42 | 0.67 | 43 | 10 | 16 | 28 |
| 6. Time deposits, comm. banks | 0.84 | 2.21 | 0.88 | 1.10 | 1.70 | 1.37 | 0.22 | 0.60 | 0.82 | 163 | 25 | 55 | 93 |
| 7. Bank loans | 2.34 | 4.34 | 2.47 | 3.22 | 4.12 | 2.00 | 0.75 | 0.90 | 1.65 | 85 | 30 | 28 | 67 |
| **II. Long-term claims** | | | | | | | | | | | | | |
| 1. Treasury bonds | 2.19 | 3.43 | 2.31 | 2.58 | 3.08 | 1.24 | 0.27 | 0.50 | 0.77 | 57 | 12 | 19 | 33 |
| 2. State and local secur., avg. | 1.46 | 3.36 | 1.99 | 2.25 | 3.00 | 1.90 | 0.26 | 0.75 | 1.01 | 130 | 13 | 33 | 51 |
| 3. High-grade municipal secur. | 1.10 | 2.92 | 1.56 | 1.82 | 2.56 | 1.82 | 0.26 | 0.74 | 1.00 | 165 | 17 | 41 | 64 |
| 4. Corporate bonds, avg. | 2.74 | 4.16 | 2.93 | 3.12 | 3.67 | 1.42 | 0.19 | 0.55 | 0.74 | 52 | 6 | 18 | 25 |
| 5. Highest-grade corp. bonds | 2.53 | 3.79 | 2.68 | 2.88 | 3.41 | 1.26 | 0.20 | 0.53 | 0.73 | 50 | 7 | 18 | 27 |
| 6. New issues of high-grade corp. bonds | 2.57 | 4.19 | 2.83 | 3.11 | 3.84 | 1.62 | 0.28 | 0.73 | 1.01 | 63 | 10 | 23 | 36 |
| 7. Conventional mortgages | 4.30[a] | 5.70 | 4.44 | 4.76 | 5.28 | 1.40[a] | 0.32 | 0.52 | 0.84 | 33[a] | 7 | 11 | 19 |
| 8. FHA secondary mortgages | 4.24[a] | 5.76 | -- | 4.44 | 5.13 | 1.52[a] | -- | 0.69 | -- | 36[a] | -- | 16 | -- |
| **III. Stock** | | | | | | | | | | | | | |
| 1. Preferred stock | 3.53 | 4.45 | 3.90 | 4.07 | 4.28 | 0.92 | 0.17 | 0.21 | 0.38 | 26 | 4 | 5 | 10 |
| 2. Common stock | 3.97 | 4.05 | 5.40 | 5.82 | 4.22 | 0.08 | 0.42 | -1.60 | -1.18 | 2 | 8 | -27 | -22 |

[a] 1948 instead of 1946.

162

# The Main Sectors of the Capital Market

Source

Section I

Line 1: Rates of new issues of 3-month bills in Federal Reserve Bulletin (e.g., February 1959, p. 173).

Lines 2-3: Ibid.

Line 4, 1945-58: Balance of deposits outstanding, from National Association of Mutual Savings Banks worksheets.

Line 4, 1945-47: Interest payment on saving deposits from NAMSB worksheets.

Line 4, 1948-58: Interest payment on saving deposits, from Mutual Savings Banking Annual Report, May 1960, Table F-31. p. F-22.

Line 5: Combined Financial Statements, Members of the Federal Home Loan Bank System: annual reports of 1948 (p. 9), 1956 (p. 10), and 1958 (p. 14) were used for deposits, and annual reports of 1947 (p. 41) and 1958 (p. 50) for dividend payments.

Line 6: Annual Reports of FDIC: issues of 1945 (p. 129), 1953 (p. 107), and 1958 (p. 197) were used for time and saving deposits, and issues of 1945 (p. 128), 1954 (p. 138), and 1958 (p. 196) for interest payments.

Line 7: Federal Reserve Bulletin (e.g., February 1959, p. 173). The series is an average of interest rates prevailing in 19 large cities.

Section II

Line 1: U.S. government (taxable) long-term bonds in ibid. For 1946-51, series maturing in 15 years or over; for 1952-56, series maturing in 12 years or over; and for 1957-58, series maturing in 10 years or over.

Line 2: Average yield on state and municipal bonds Aaa, Aa, A, and Baa, in Moody's Municipal and Governments Manual, 1960, pp. A-22 to A-23. This series has been published in the FR Bulletin since 1955.

Line 3: Average yield on municipal high-grade bonds Aaa (ibid.).

Line 4: Average yield on corporate bonds outstanding Aaa, Aa, A, and Baa (Federal Reserve Bulletin for various years; primary source is Moody's Investor Service).

Line 5: Average yield on corporate bonds outstanding Aaa (ibid.).

Line 6: Average yield on new issues of high-grade corporate bonds (from unpublished figures of Banker's Trust Company, annual data only).

Line 7, 1947-56: Saul Klaman, The Postwar Residential Mortgage Market, Princeton for NBER, 1961, p. 285, Table A-4. 1946 figure was extrapolated back from 1947.

Line 7, 1957-58: FHA Research and Statistics Release, Nos. 23 and 46.

Line 8, 1946-47: N.a., figure for 1948 used instead.

Line 8, 1948-56: Secondary source: Leo Grebler, Housing Issues in Economic Stabilization Policy, NBER Occasional Paper 72, 1960, p. 117. Primary source: Jack M. Guttentag, "Some Studies of the Post-World War II Residential Construction and Mortgage Markets," unpublished Ph.D. dissertation, Columbia University, 1958, p. 70.

Line 8, 1957-58: Weekly Bond Buyer, March 6, 1961, p. 17.

Section III

Line 1: Primary source: Standard and Poor's. Secondary source as follows:

Line 1, 1946-48: 1949 Statistical Supplement to Survey of Current Business, p. 103.

Line 1, 1949-52: Business Statistics, 1953 Supplement to the Survey of Current Business, p. 101.

Line 1, 1953-54: Ibid., 1955, p. 100.

Line 1, 1955-58: Ibid., 1959, p. 103.

Line 2: Primary source: Moody's Investor Service. Secondary source: same as line III-1.

flecting the abandonment of the peg of interest rates on government securities early in Cycle II, the opposite relation obtained for long-term securities. The yield of corporate securities and home mortgages advanced by less than one-tenth from Cycles I to II. From Cycles II to III, on the other hand, yields on long-term debt advanced by between fully one-tenth (conventional home mortgages) to more than one-third (state and local government securities), with an average of about one-fifth. Only one of the main capital market instruments showed a decline in yield—common stock from Cycles II to III. The sharp increase in price-dividend and price-earnings ratios, which is reflected in this movement, is the result of a level shift in investors' evaluation of prospective corporate profits and dividends and of the possibilities of appreciation of common stock.

# CHAPTER 6

# The Market for U.S. Government Securities [1]

## Basic Characteristics of the Market

THE market for Treasury securities occupies a special, and particularly important, position in the American postwar capital market. For long-term obligations of the U.S. government are one of the main outlets for savers' funds, competing with state and local government securities, corporate bonds, mortgages, and less directly with equity securities; and short-term Treasury securities in the postwar period came to constitute one of the most important forms of holding the liquid reserves of business, financial institutions, and wealthy individuals, competing primarily with demand and time deposits in commercial banks, with certain short-term instruments such as bankers' acceptances, commercial paper, and finance company paper, and to a lesser extent with savings deposits in commercial banks, mutual savings banks, and savings and loan associations. After World War II

[1] Because of the richness and high quality of the literature on the market for Treasury securities, and the fact that the Postwar Capital Market Study includes two special studies in this field (George Hanc, *The United States Savings Bond Program in the Postwar Period*, New York, NBER Occasional Paper 81, 1962, and Morris Mendelson, "Some Aspects of the Market for Treasury Securities," in preparation), this chapter is limited in the main to a summary of the characteristics and changes in the holdings of Treasury securities during the postwar years and their comparison with earlier periods. The discussion specifically excludes subjects such as the determination of the supply of Treasury securities, the organization of the dealer market for Treasury securities, the management of the federal debt and its relations to monetary policy, and the determinants of the yield differentials among Treasury securities according to maturity and between Treasury securities and other claims—for each of which subject an extensive monographic or textbook literature exists.

Treasury securities—primarily those of maturity up to one year—became the balancing item in the portfolios not only of most financial institutions but also of many large nonfinancial corporations. This means that Treasury securities are usually not the first choice of any substantial group of private investors, but are acquired when the assets in which financial institutions or nonfinancial corporations prefer to invest their funds are not available in sufficient amounts or on satisfactory terms, and they are liquidated when the demand for these other assets is high.[2] In the case of the Federal Reserve banks, Treasury securities, although one of the main assets, are not acquired for yield or liquidity but in pursuance of the banks' monetary policy. Here, too, the acquisition or sale of Treasury securities is not primarily determined by the characteristics of these securities, such as safety and yield, but by other considerations.

Only in the postwar period did this role of Treasury securities as the balancing item in the portfolios of many investor groups become evident, although a trend in that direction could be detected after World War I. The development, of course, was caused by the sharp increase during the war in the volume of Treasury securities outstanding, both in absolute and relative terms, which is evident from Table 49.

Between the last quarter of the nineteenth century and the beginning of World War I, the volume of Treasury securities was so small as to make them a capital market instrument of at best secondary importance; their significance was further reduced because a large part of them was held permanently by national banks as a basis for note issues. The large increase in the federal debt caused by American participation in World War I brought Treasury securities, for the first time since the turn of the century on a large scale, into the portfolios of financial institutions other than national banks and into those of individuals. The basic change, however, was brought about by the massive issues of Treasury securities during World War II, as a result of which their share in the total assets of financial institutions rose considerably from 1939 to 1945 and the ratio of Treasury securities to the total of the five selected instruments shot up.

---

[2] These preferred assets are business loans and to a lesser extent consumers loans for commercial banks, mortgage loans for savings and loan associations and mutual savings banks, mortgage loans and corporate bonds for life insurance companies, consumers loans for finance companies, common stock and state and local government securities for property insurance companies, and plant and equipment, inventories and accounts receivable credit for nonfinancial corporations.

TABLE 49

POSITION OF U.S. GOVERNMENT SECURITIES IN THE NATIONAL BALANCE SHEET,
SELECTED DATES, 1900-58

| | U.S. Government Securities Outstanding (billion dollars) (1) | PERCENTAGE SHARE OF U.S. GOVERNMENT SECURITIES IN | | | | | |
|---|---|---|---|---|---|---|---|
| | | National Assets (2) | Financial Assets (3) | Claims (4) | Main Capital Market Instruments[a] Outstanding (5) | Total Assets of | |
| | | | | | | Financial Institutions (6) | Nonfarm Households (7) |
| 1900 | 1.2 | 0.8 | 1.8 | 2.8 | 5.2 | 3.9 | 0.9 |
| 1912 | 1.2 | 0.4 | 0.8 | 1.3 | 2.1 | 2.2 | 0.3 |
| 1922 | 23.6 | 3.7 | 7.3 | 10.9 | 18.8 | 9.4 | 4.0 |
| 1929 | 17.5 | 1.8 | 3.2 | 5.6 | 6.8 | 5.8 | 1.1 |
| 1939 | 55.1 | 6.4 | 11.3 | 15.9 | 26.2 | 19.5 | 2.5 |
| 1945A | 278.5 | 18.3 | 28.7 | 36.8 | 58.1 | 52.1 | 10.2 |
| 1945B | 279.0 | 18.2 | 28.5 | 35.8 | 57.9 | 51.6 | 9.6 |
| 1951 | 261.1 | 10.7 | 19.8 | 25.9 | 44.5 | 34.2 | 6.0 |
| 1958 | 288.5 | 7.7 | 13.9 | 19.4 | 28.5 | 25.0 | 3.7 |

Source: National Balance Sheet, Vol. II, unless otherwise specified.
Col. 1, 1900-45A: Table III-7f, line III-12.
Col. 1, 1945B-58: Table III-7, line III-12. Includes securities of govt. agencies.
Cols. 2-4: Tables I and Ia, lines V, II-21, III-14.
Col. 5, 1900-45A: Bonds from Tables III-4b, 5a, 6a, and 7f,
    line III-12; nonfarm residential mortgages from Table IV-b-11c-1, line 8; common
    stock from Goldsmith, Supplementary Appendixes to Financial Intermediaries Since
    1900, New York, 1958, Table F-4, line 2.
Col. 5, 1945B-58: Bonds from Table IV-c-12, lines 4, 5, 6, and 7; nonfarm residential
    mortgages from Table IV-c-11a and 11b, line 8; common stock from Table IV-b-17,
    line 11.
Col. 6: Tables I and Ia, col. 5, lines II-13 and V.
Col. 7: Tables I and Ia, col. 1, lines II-13 and V.

[a]U.S. government securities, state and local government securities, corporate
bonds, common stocks, nonfarm residential mortgages.

## Developments During the Postwar Period

The essential figures needed to follow developments in the market for Treasury securities during the postwar period are provided in Tables 50 to 52 and Chart 12. The data on the absolute values of holdings and of net flows of Treasury securities by the various sectors may be found in the basic tables in Volume II of *Studies in the National Balance Sheet* not only for the total of all Treasury securities, but also separately for short-term (less than one year) obligations, for savings bonds, and for other long-term obligations.

While the amount of Treasury securities outstanding increased by about 1 per cent between the end of 1945 and the end of 1958, three investor groups expanded their holdings substantially, both in absolute and relative terms: government insurance and pension funds, which increased their holdings by 125 per cent; state and local governments,

TABLE 50

STRUCTURAL CHANGES IN OWNERSHIP OF U.S. GOVERNMENT SECURITIES DURING THE POSTWAR PERIOD

| | Outstandings (billion dollars) | | Aggregate Net Flows, 1946-58 (billion dollars) | NET FLOWS (ANNUAL AVERAGES) | | | | | |
| | | | | Amounts (billion dollars) | | | Distribution (per cent) | | |
| | 1945 (1) | 1958 (2) | (3) | Cycle I 1946-49 (4) | Cycle II 1949-54 (5) | Cycle III 1954-58 (6) | Cycle I 1946-49 (7) | Cycle II 1949-54 (8) | Cycle III 1954-58 (9) |
|---|---|---|---|---|---|---|---|---|---|
| 1. Nonfarm households | 59.69 | 58.57 | -1.12 | 0.61 | -0.33 | -0.01 | 13.1 | -7.6 | -2.8 |
| 2. Agriculture | 4.15 | 5.21 | 1.06 | 0.16 | 0.04 | 0.08 | 3.4 | 0.9 | 22.2 |
| 3. Nonfinancial corporations | 20.72 | 17.62 | -3.10 | -0.76 | 0.88 | -0.61 | -16.3 | 20.4 | -169.4 |
| 4. Finance | 181.65 | 176.01 | -5.64 | -5.20 | 2.33 | -0.21 | -111.8 | 53.9 | -58.3 |
| a. Federal Reserve banks and Treasury monetary funds | 24.29 | 26.44 | 2.15 | -0.90 | 0.86 | -0.02 | -19.4 | 19.9 | -5.6 |
| b. Government insurance and pension funds | 24.05 | 54.05 | 30.00 | 3.29 | 2.49 | 1.53 | 70.8 | 57.6 | 425.0 |
| c. Commercial banks | 90.61 | 66.18 | -24.43 | -5.96 | 0.28 | -1.00 | -128.2 | 6.5 | -277.8 |
| d. Mutual savings banks | 10.68 | 7.26 | -3.42 | 0.08 | -0.50 | -0.39 | 1.7 | -11.6 | -108.3 |
| e. Savings and loan associations | 2.42 | 3.82 | 1.40 | -0.25 | 0.10 | 0.38 | -5.4 | 2.3 | 105.6 |
| f. Investment companies | 0.23 | 0.49 | 0.26 | -0.02 | 0.01 | 0.06 | -0.4 | 0.2 | 16.7 |
| g. Credit unions | 0.18 | 0.13 | -0.05 | -0.01 | 0 | 0 | -0.2 | 0 | 0 |
| h. Life insurance | 20.58 | 7.18 | -13.40 | -1.70 | -1.31 | -0.59 | -36.6 | -30.3 | -163.9 |
| i. Fire and casualty insurance | 3.22 | 5.40 | 2.18 | .48 | 0.27 | -0.16 | 10.3 | 6.2 | -44.4 |
| j. Noninsured pension plans | 1.47 | 2.45 | 0.98 | .15 | 0.11 | -0.04 | 3.2 | 2.5 | -11.1 |
| k. Other private insurance | 0.52 | 0.80 | 0.28 | 0 | 0.02 | 0.04 | 0 | 0.5 | 11.1 |
| l. Other finance | 3.40 | 1.81 | -1.59 | -.36 | 0 | -0.02 | -7.7 | 0 | -5.6 |
| 5. State and local governments | 4.99 | 11.08 | 6.09 | .23 | 0.77 | 0.56 | 4.9 | 17.8 | 155.6 |
| 6. Federal government | 4.52 | 5.82 | 1.30 | .15 | -0.02 | 0.18 | 3.2 | -0.5 | 50.0 |
| 7. Rest-of-world assets | 2.57 | 7.61 | 5.04 | .16 | 0.65 | 0.37 | 3.4 | 15.0 | 102.8 |
| 8. Total | 278.29 | 281.92 | 3.63 | -4.65 | 4.32 | 0.36 | -100.0[a] | 100.0 | 100.0 |

Source: National Balance Sheet, Vol. II. Cols. 1-2 from Table IV-b-13; cols. 3-9 from Table VIII-b-13.
Note: Components may not add to totals because of rounding here and elsewhere in this chapter.

[a]The signs have been reversed to match the sign of the numerator.

TABLE 51

DISTRIBUTION OF HOLDINGS OF U.S. GOVERNMENT SECURITIES, BY SECTOR, 1945-58

(per cent)

| | 1945 | 1946 | 1947 | 1948 | 1949 | 1950 | 1951 | 1952 | 1953 | 1954 | 1955 | 1956 | 1957 | 1958 |
|---|---|---|---|---|---|---|---|---|---|---|---|---|---|---|
| 1. Nonfarm households | 21.4 | 22.8 | 23.7 | 24.0 | 24.0 | 23.9 | 23.1 | 22.5 | 22.0 | 21.1 | 21.6 | 22.4 | 22.1 | 20.8 |
| 2. Agriculture | 1.5 | 1.6 | 1.7 | 1.8 | 1.8 | 1.8 | 1.8 | 1.7 | 1.7 | 1.8 | 1.8 | 1.8 | 1.9 | 1.8 |
| 3. Nonfinancial corporations | 7.4 | 5.8 | 5.4 | 5.8 | 6.4 | 7.6 | 7.8 | 7.3 | 7.7 | 6.8 | 8.1 | 6.6 | 6.4 | 6.2 |
| 4. Finance | 65.3 | 65.3 | 64.2 | 63.1 | 62.4 | 60.8 | 61.3 | 61.8 | 61.5 | 62.6 | 60.2 | 60.4 | 60.4 | 62.4 |
| a. Federal Reserve banks and Treasury monetary funds | 8.7 | 9.0 | 8.8 | 9.2 | 7.4 | 8.1 | 9.2 | 9.3 | 9.4 | 9.0 | 8.9 | 9.1 | 8.9 | 9.4 |
| b. Govt. insurance and pension funds | 8.6 | 10.7 | 12.3 | 13.7 | 14.3 | 14.5 | 15.8 | 16.8 | 17.3 | 17.6 | 18.3 | 19.4 | 20.0 | 19.2 |
| c. Commercial banks | 32.6 | 28.8 | 26.9 | 24.8 | 26.1 | 24.2 | 23.7 | 23.7 | 23.1 | 24.8 | 22.0 | 21.2 | 21.3 | 23.5 |
| d. Mutual savings banks | 3.8 | 4.5 | 4.7 | 4.5 | 4.4 | 4.2 | 3.8 | 3.5 | 3.3 | 3.1 | 3.0 | 2.9 | 2.8 | 2.6 |
| e. Savings and loan associations | 0.9 | 0.8 | 0.7 | 0.6 | 0.6 | 0.6 | 0.6 | 0.7 | 0.7 | 0.7 | 0.8 | 1.0 | 1.2 | 1.4 |
| f. Investment companies | 0.1 | 0.1 | 0.1 | 0.1 | 0.1 | 0.1 | 0.1 | 0.1 | 0.1 | 0.1 | 0.1 | 0.1 | 0.1 | 0.2 |
| g. Credit unions | 0.1 | 0.1 | 0.1 | 0.1 | 0.1 | 0 | 0.1 | 0.1 | 0.1 | 0.1 | 0 | 0.1 | 0 | 0 |
| h. Life insurance | 7.4 | 8.3 | 7.8 | 6.6 | 5.9 | 5.2 | 4.2 | 3.8 | 3.6 | 3.3 | 3.1 | 2.7 | 2.6 | 2.5 |
| i. Fire and casualty insurance | 1.2 | 1.3 | 1.6 | 1.8 | 1.9 | 2.1 | 2.1 | 2.2 | 2.2 | 2.2 | 2.1 | 2.1 | 2.0 | 1.9 |
| j. Noninsured pension plans | 0.5 | 0.6 | 0.7 | 0.8 | 0.8 | 0.9 | 0.9 | 0.9 | 0.9 | 0.9 | 1.0 | 1.0 | 0.9 | 0.9 |
| k. Other private insurance | 0.2 | 0.2 | 0.2 | 0.2 | 0.2 | 0.2 | 0.2 | 0.2 | 0.2 | 0.2 | 0.3 | 0.3 | 0.3 | 0.3 |
| l. Other finance | 1.2 | 0.9 | 0.5 | 0.7 | 0.6 | 0.6 | 0.5 | 0.6 | 0.6 | 0.7 | 0.5 | 0.5 | 0.6 | 0.6 |
| 5. State and local governments | 1.8 | 1.7 | 2.0 | 2.1 | 2.1 | 2.2 | 2.4 | 2.7 | 3.1 | 3.6 | 3.7 | 4.0 | 4.3 | 3.9 |
| 6. Federal government | 1.6 | 1.9 | 2.0 | 2.1 | 2.1 | 2.0 | 1.9 | 1.9 | 1.8 | 1.9 | 1.9 | 2.0 | 2.2 | 2.1 |
| 7. Rest-of-world assets | 0.9 | 0.8 | 1.0 | 1.1 | 1.1 | 1.7 | 1.7 | 2.0 | 2.1 | 2.3 | 2.7 | 2.8 | 2.8 | 2.7 |
| 8. Total | 100.0 | 100.0 | 100.0 | 100.0 | 100.0 | 100.0 | 100.0 | 100.0 | 100.0 | 100.0 | 100.0 | 100.0 | 100.0 | 100.0 |
| 9. Total (billion dollars) | 278.29 | 259.52 | 257.24 | 252.77 | 257.12 | 256.68 | 259.14 | 267.08 | 274.70 | 278.37 | 280.21 | 275.00 | 273.99 | 281.92 |

Source: National Balance Sheet, Vol. II, Table IV-b-13.

TABLE 52

DISTRIBUTION OF FLOW OF FUNDS, U.S. GOVERNMENT SECURITIES, BY SECTOR, 1946-58
(per cent)

| | 1946[a] | 1947[a] | 1948[a] | 1949 | 1950[a] | 1951 | 1952 | 1953 | 1954 | 1955 | 1956[a] | 1957[a] | 1958 |
|---|---|---|---|---|---|---|---|---|---|---|---|---|---|
| 1.Nonfarm households | -2.6 | 79.8 | -5.1 | 22.3 | -75.0 | -58.9 | 2.9 | 2.5 | -41.7 | 95.7 | 25.2 | -63.0 | -25.6 |
| 2.Agriculture | 0.3 | 7.5 | 4.9 | 2.8 | -6.8 | 0.8 | -1.0 | 1.3 | 6.5 | 10.9 | -2.5 | 3.3 | 1.1 |
| 3.Nonfinancial corporations | -30.4 | -52.6 | 17.9 | 44.1 | 652.3 | 37.8 | -10.1 | 20.7 | -62.4 | 216.8 | -104.1 | -44.2 | 2.4 |
| 4.Finance | -64.4 | -191.7 | -128.9 | 26.2 | -1,027.3 | 111.0 | 80.3 | 50.5 | 143.1 | -310.3 | -45.8 | -51.9 | 131.4 |
| a.Federal Reserve banks and Treasury monetary funds | -4.9 | -34.6 | 17.2 | -102.3 | 431.8 | 122.8 | 11.3 | 16.0 | -27.0 | -8.2 | 5.0 | -42.0 | 27.5 |
| b.Govt. insurance and pension funds | 20.0 | 164.5 | 70.2 | 50.3 | 93.2 | 146.3 | 49.4 | 35.3 | 39.2 | 130.4 | 51.0 | 59.1 | -7.8 |
| c.Commercial banks | -84.3 | -243.9 | -147.6 | 100.7 | -1,129.5 | -20.7 | 22.7 | 1.4 | 151.2 | -401.6 | -68.9 | -17.1 | 100.1 |
| d.Mutual savings banks | 5.9 | 8.8 | -11.2 | -1.1 | -127.3 | -42.7 | -5.0 | -3.1 | -11.7 | -15.8 | -11.1 | -23.2 | -3.7 |
| e.Savings and loan associations | -2.2 | -11.8 | -6.3 | 0 | 6.8 | 4.5 | 2.4 | 1.7 | 2.7 | 17.4 | 10.0 | 21.5 | 8.2 |
| f.Investment companies | -0.3 | 0.4 | -1.1 | 0.9 | 4.5 | 0 | -0.1 | 0 | 0 | 7.6 | 0.5 | -0.6 | 1.8 |
| g.Credit unions | 0 | 0 | -0.4 | -0.5 | -4.5 | 0.8 | 0 | -0.1 | 0 | 0 | 0.2 | | |
| h.Life insurance | 5.6 | -70.6 | -73.2 | -33.6 | -415.9 | -99.6 | -9.6 | -5.5 | -20.7 | -26.6 | -23.1 | -29.3 | 1.9 |
| i.Fire and casualty insurance | 1.0 | 25.9 | 11.0 | 11.7 | 79.5 | 5.3 | 4.3 | 2.8 | 3.0 | -7.6 | -7.5 | -11.6 | -0.8 |
| j.Noninsured pension plans | 1.0 | 7.0 | 2.9 | 3.4 | 47.7 | 4.9 | 0 | 2.1 | 0.3 | 16.3 | -4.5 | -14.9 | 0.4 |
| k.Other private insurance | 0.1 | 0.4 | 0 | 0 | 2.3 | 0.8 | 0.4 | 0.1 | 1.1 | 3.8 | 0.7 | -0.6 | 0.8 |
| l.Other finance | -6.2 | -37.7 | 9.6 | -3.4 | -15.9 | -11.4 | 4.7 | -0.1 | 4.9 | -26.1 | 2.0 | 6.6 | 3.0 |
| 5.State and local governments | -3.3 | 28.9 | 7.2 | 0.5 | 81.8 | 15.0 | 13.6 | 17.2 | 39.2 | 22.3 | 15.9 | 40.9 | -8.8 |
| 6.Federal government | 2.9 | 1.8 | 2.2 | 1.8 | -54.5 | -3.7 | 1.3 | 0.3 | 3.5 | 1.1 | 5.7 | 24.3 | -1.1 |
| 7.Rest-of-world assets | -2.5 | 26.3 | 1.8 | 2.3 | 329.5 | -2.0 | 13.0 | 7.5 | 11.7 | 63.6 | 5.7 | -9.4 | 0.6 |
| 8.Total | -100.0 | -100.0 | -100.0 | 100.0 | -100.0 | 100.0 | 100.0 | 100.0 | 100.0 | 100.0 | -100.0 | -100.0 | 100.0 |
| | | | | | | | | | | | | | |
| 9.Total (billion dollars) | -18.77 | -2.28 | -4.47 | 4.35 | -0.44 | 2.46 | 7.94 | 7.62 | 3.67 | 1.84 | -4.41 | -1.81 | 7.93 |

Source: National Balance Sheet, Vol. II, Table VIII-b-13.

[a]The signs have been reversed to match the sign of the numerator.

## CHART 12

### MARKET FOR U.S. GOVERNMENT SECURITIES: SUPPLY AND ABSORPTION BY SECTOR, 1946–58

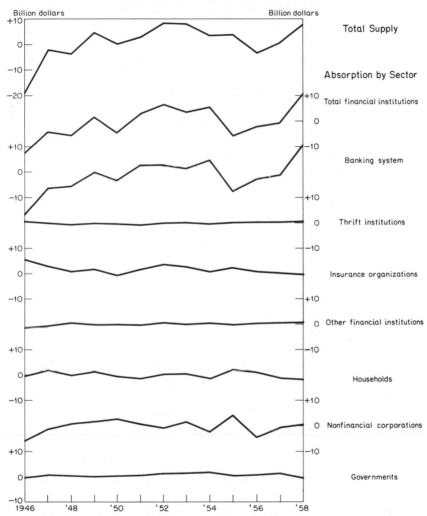

Source: *National Balance Sheet,* Vol. II, Tables VIII-b-13 and VIII-c-12.

which expanded theirs by 122 per cent; and foreigners (mostly monetary authorities), who tripled their holdings (see Table 50).

The Federal Reserve banks, although making net purchases of fully $2 billion, increased their holdings by only 9 per cent. Among domestic private financial institutions, only two groups added appreciably to their holdings: fire and casualty insurance companies, which increased their holdings almost 70 per cent, and savings and loan associations, which increased theirs by 60 per cent. All these purchases were almost offset by the massive net sales of commercial banks, totaling 27 per cent of their holdings at the end of 1945, and of life insurance companies, which liquidated 65 per cent of their holdings at the beginning of the period. Substantial sales, absolutely or relatively, were also made by mutual savings banks and nonfinancial corporations. The holdings of nonfarm households were virtually the same at the end of the period as at the beginning.

Turning to net flows during each of the three business cycles, the differences among investor groups were most pronounced in Cycle I when large liquidation of Treasury securities by banks and life insurance companies were absorbed almost exclusively by the U.S. government, either by retirement of securities or by acquisitions on behalf of its pension and insurance funds. The net sale or purchase balances of the different groups were smaller in Cycle II and still smaller in Cycle III. Government insurance and pension funds continued to be the main net buyers of Treasury securities, while life insurance companies and mutual savings banks were the main sellers, joined in Cycle III by commercial banks and nonfinancial corporations.

Closer study of developments in the market for U.S. government securities during the postwar period requires at least annual data, though quarterly figures are preferable,[3] and is best based on the share of Treasury securities in the total assets of the different holder groups and in the total users of funds rather than on the absolute figures. The basic data will be found in Tables 50 to 54. In following developments in the market for Treasury securities, it is also necessary to consider the level of interest rates on U.S. government securities, particularly the yield differential compared to other investments, primarily corporate bonds, commercial loans, mortgages, state and local government securities, and in the case of individual holders, the rates of savings bank deposits and savings and loan shares. The course of

---

[3] Such figures are available beginning with 1952 in the Federal Reserve Board's flow-of-funds statistics.

TABLE 53

SHARE OF U.S. GOVERNMENT SECURITIES IN TOTAL ASSETS OF MAIN SECTORS AND SUBSECTORS, 1945-58

(per cent)

| | 1945 | 1946 | 1947 | 1948 | 1949 | 1950 | 1951 | 1952 | 1953 | 1954 | 1955 | 1956 | 1957 | 1958 |
|---|---|---|---|---|---|---|---|---|---|---|---|---|---|---|
| 1. Nonfarm households | 9.6 | 8.7 | 8.1 | 7.6 | 7.5 | 6.7 | 6.0 | 5.7 | 5.5 | 4.9 | 4.6 | 4.4 | 4.2 | 3.7 |
| 2. Agriculture | 4.0 | 3.6 | 3.3 | 3.3 | 3.4 | 3.0 | 2.7 | 2.7 | 2.8 | 2.9 | 3.0 | 2.8 | 2.7 | 2.5 |
| 3. Nonfinancial corporations | 8.3 | 5.2 | 4.1 | 4.0 | 4.4 | 4.4 | 4.2 | 3.8 | 4.0 | 3.3 | 3.6 | 2.7 | 2.4 | 2.3 |
| 4. Finance | 51.6 | 48.0 | 43.9 | 40.5 | 39.4 | 35.9 | 34.2 | 33.2 | 32.3 | 31.2 | 28.1 | 26.4 | 25.2 | 25.0 |
| a. Federal Reserve banks and Treasury monetary funds | 34.8 | 33.2 | 30.0 | 29.5 | 25.2 | 27.8 | 30.7 | 30.8 | 32.6 | 32.0 | 31.2 | 31.2 | 29.8 | 33.4 |
| b. Govt. insurance and pension funds | 93.1 | 94.3 | 94.5 | 94.1 | 93.6 | 91.6 | 91.3 | 91.2 | 90.5 | 88.7 | 87.9 | 86.4 | 84.3 | 81.8 |
| c. Commercial banks | 56.5 | 49.8 | 44.4 | 40.3 | 42.1 | 36.4 | 34.0 | 33.3 | 32.6 | 33.8 | 28.9 | 26.6 | 25.8 | 27.4 |
| d. Mutual savings banks | 62.7 | 62.8 | 60.6 | 55.4 | 52.4 | 47.9 | 41.5 | 37.0 | 33.5 | 29.6 | 26.8 | 23.7 | 21.3 | 19.1 |
| e. Savings and loan associations | 27.6 | 19.6 | 14.8 | 11.2 | 9.9 | 8.8 | 8.3 | 7.9 | 7.1 | 6.4 | 6.2 | 6.4 | 6.5 | 6.9 |
| f. Investment companies | 6.3 | 5.1 | 5.4 | 3.9 | 4.1 | 3.7 | 3.0 | 2.4 | 2.3 | 1.6 | 2.3 | 2.3 | 2.4 | 2.4 |
| g. Credit unions | 40.9 | 36.0 | 30.5 | 22.9 | 16.9 | 12.0 | 11.7 | 9.2 | 6.8 | 5.7 | 4.7 | 4.3 | 3.4 | 3.0 |
| h. Life insurance | 45.9 | 44.6 | 38.4 | 30.0 | 25.3 | 20.7 | 16.0 | 13.8 | 12.4 | 10.6 | 9.4 | 7.8 | 6.8 | 6.6 |
| i. Fire and casualty insurance | 42.1 | 41.9 | 43.4 | 43.5 | 42.0 | 40.4 | 37.8 | 36.2 | 34.4 | 30.7 | 27.4 | 25.0 | 23.8 | 21.1 |
| j. Noninsured pension plans | 54.8 | 50.7 | 46.5 | 42.7 | 39.7 | 36.9 | 31.1 | 25.4 | 22.6 | 18.1 | 16.7 | 13.4 | 10.8 | 8.8 |
| k. Other private insurance | 28.4 | 27.1 | 25.9 | 24.8 | 23.4 | 22.5 | 22.0 | 21.5 | 20.6 | 20.4 | 21.0 | 20.7 | 20.2 | 20.5 |
| l. Other finance | 46.8 | 41.0 | 29.7 | 34.3 | 28.4 | 24.0 | 19.8 | 23.7 | 22.2 | 19.8 | 14.3 | 15.2 | 15.1 | 15.3 |
| 5. State and local governments | 7.1 | 5.2 | 5.1 | 5.1 | 5.1 | 4.9 | 4.8 | 5.3 | 6.0 | 6.6 | 6.4 | 6.2 | 6.2 | 5.5 |
| 6. Federal government | 5.7 | 8.1 | 7.3 | 6.8 | 6.8 | 5.6 | 5.0 | 4.9 | 4.8 | 5.0 | 4.7 | 4.9 | 5.2 | 5.0 |
| 7. Total | 18.0 | 15.6 | 13.8 | 12.7 | 12.7 | 11.2 | 10.4 | 10.2 | 10.1 | 9.5 | 8.8 | 8.1 | 7.7 | 7.3 |

Source: National Balance Sheet, Vol. II, Tables III-1, III-3, III-4, III-5, III-5a, 5b, 5c, 5d, 5e, 5f, 5g, 5h, 5i, 5j, 5k, 5m, III-6, III-7 (line II-13); line 8 from Table I, line II-13.

TABLE 54

SHARE OF NET PURCHASES OF TREASURY SECURITIES IN TOTAL USES OF FUNDS OF MAIN SECTORS AND SUBSECTORS, 1946-58

(per cent)

| | 1946 | 1947 | 1948 | 1949 | 1950 | 1951 | 1952 | 1953 | 1954 | 1955 | 1956 | 1957 | 1958 |
|---|---|---|---|---|---|---|---|---|---|---|---|---|---|
| 1.Nonfarm households | -1.3 | 4.4 | -0.5 | 2.3 | -0.6 | -2.4 | 0.4 | 0.3 | -2.2 | 2.1 | 1.3 | -1.3 | -2.4 |
| 2.Agriculture | 0.7 | 1.8 | 3.2 | 3.1 | -0.2 | 0.2 | -3.2 | 2.9 | 3.4 | 3.5 | -1.5 | 0.6 | 0.7 |
| 3.Nonfinancial corporations | -25.5 | -3.6 | 2.8 | 11.0 | 6.2 | 2.3 | -2.4 | 5.1 | -6.9 | 7.1 | -9.1 | -1.7 | 0.5 |
| 4.Finance | -755.6 | -18.7 | -33.4 | 9.3 | -17.8 | 9.5 | 19.6 | 15.5 | 17.9 | -15.6 | -6.7 | -3.2 | 27.6 |
| a.Federal Reserve banks and Treasury monetary funds | -146.0 | -16.0 | 20.1 | 106.0 | -1,266.7 | 108.6 | 35.3 | -196.8 | 58.9 | -10.1 | 24.4 | -74.5 | -103.8 |
| b.Govt. insurance and pension funds | 102.7 | 96.6 | 90.5 | 86.2 | 31.3 | 88.5 | 90.1 | 79.6 | 53.5 | 74.1 | 62.8 | 37.5 | -50.4 |
| c.Commercial banks | 151.2 | -95.0 | 1,885.7 | 140.4 | -43.5 | -4.8 | 19.5 | 2.4 | 58.7 | -86.9 | -43.5 | -5.8 | 50.3 |
| d.Mutual savings banks | 64.0 | 19.8 | -50.0 | -4.9 | -60.9 | -106.1 | -22.6 | -12.6 | -20.1 | -14.4 | -24.1 | -22.8 | -11.1 |
| e.Savings and loan associations | -27.2 | -17.6 | -20.1 | 0 | 1.3 | 4.6 | 5.6 | 3.2 | 2.0 | 5.3 | 8.5 | 7.5 | 9.4 |
| f.Investment companies | -41.7 | 4.8 | -31.2 | 15.4 | 7.1 | 0 | -1.9 | 0 | 0 | 16.5 | 2.8 | 1.9 | 10.5 |
| g.Credit unions | 0 | 0 | -18.2 | -15.4 | -11.8 | 10.0 | 0 | -2.6 | 0 | 0 | 1.9 | -1.9 | 0 |
| h.Life insurance | 28.4 | -44.6 | -87.2 | -36.9 | -42.2 | -57.9 | -15.4 | -8.1 | -14.0 | -8.7 | -17.7 | -9.8 | 2.7 |
| i.Fire and casualty insurance | 31.7 | 49.6 | 43.4 | 45.9 | 36.1 | 13.3 | 25.6 | 14.3 | 9.5 | -13.9 | -53.2 | -21.6 | -5.5 |
| j.Noninsured pension plans | 31.0 | 25.3 | 20.3 | 20.2 | 22.2 | 8.5 | -0.2 | 8.3 | 0.4 | 14.6 | -7.8 | -9.5 | 1.1 |
| k.Other private insurance | 7.4 | 7.3 | 0 | 3.5 | 6.1 | 12.2 | 15.5 | 8.1 | 17.6 | 30.0 | 15.0 | -33.3 | 25.3 |
| l.Other finance | 65.0 | 104.9 | 72.9 | -25.9 | -9.7 | -2,800.0 | 92.5 | -2.4 | 10.5 | -240.0 | -225.0 | 18.2 | 14.5 |
| 5.State and local governments | -26.6 | 14.3 | 6.0 | 0.3 | 4.6 | 4.4 | 10.9 | 11.8 | 11.8 | 3.4 | 5.6 | 4.9 | -4.4 |
| 6.Federal government | -2.7 | 0.7 | 1.8 | 3.7 | -2.8 | -1.1 | 4.3 | 0.5 | 18.1 | 0.3 | 45.5 | 29.1 | -3.9 |
| 7.Total | -31.3 | -2.3 | -4.1 | 4.8 | -1.1 | 1.5 | 4.6 | 4.7 | 2.1 | 0.3 | -2.4 | -0.8 | 3.9 |

Source: National Balance Sheet, Vol. II, Tables VII-1, VII-3, VII-4, VII-5, VII-5a, 5b, 5c, 5d, 5e, 5f, 5g, 5h, 5i, 5j, 5k, 5m, VII-6, and VII-7 (line II-13); line 7 from Table V, line II-13.

these differentials over the postwar period may be followed in Table 57.

The picture is fairly simple for the holdings of Treasury securities by nonfarm and farm households. Not only was the total held approximately the same at the beginning and at the end of the period, but annual fluctuations were also small, with the exception of 1958 when net sales of nonfarm households amounted to about $2 billion or 3 per cent of holdings.[4] Throughout the period the bulk of all the holdings of households was in savings bonds, a legacy from the intensive sales drives of World War II.[5] These holdings rose over the period from $44.5 to $48.25 billion,[6] but this increase was less than interest accruing to holders and added to the maturity value of the bonds on which the statistics are based. Hence, on a cash basis, redemptions of savings bonds at or before maturity slightly exceeded cash payments for newly acquired savings bonds. There is no comprehensive information on the extent to which the changes in savings bonds outstanding were the result of net liquidations by old holders and net purchases by new holders, or of the shifts that may have occurred among groups of individual holders of savings bonds, although there is some evidence that most of the holdings are owned by individuals in the lower and middle income groups.[7]

There is no clear relation between the net acquisitions or liquidations of savings bonds and the business cycle change. Net acquisitions prevailed throughout Cycle I from 1946 to 1949 and proceeded at an average level of $1.5 billion per year.[8] These acquisitions may be explained by investors' inertia—a considerable proportion of acquisitions of savings bonds resulted from payroll deduction plans—and by the relatively favorable yield on savings bonds compared to savings deposits and savings and loan shares. Since the beginning of 1951, net sales predominated, particularly if the calculation is made on a cash rather than on an accrual basis, and net redemptions considerably increased in the three closing years of the period. These liquidations were probably influenced by the declining relative yield on sav-

---

[4] A much larger increase—over $5 billion—occurred in 1959, partly as a result of substantial purchases of the new 5 per cent notes which offered an unprecedentedly high yield for this type of security.

[5] The market for U.S. savings bonds is described in detail by Hanc in *U.S. Savings Bond Program*.

[6] *National Balance Sheet*, Vol. II, Table IV-b-13b, lines 1 and 3.

[7] Hanc, *U.S. Savings Bond Program*, Chapter 3.

[8] *National Balance Sheet*, Vol. II, Table VIII-b-13b, lines 1 and 3.

ings bonds, although their absolute yield if held to maturity was raised in steps from 2.9 to 3.75 per cent.[9] Since the absolute level of holdings of savings bonds was fairly stable while the total assets of nonfarm and farm households increased considerably, the share of savings bonds in individuals' total assets declined year after year, from about 6 per cent at the end of World War II to not much over 2½ per cent in 1958.

Households are also credited with substantial amounts of other U.S. long-term securities and with small amounts of short-term securities. Together these totaled slightly more than $19 billion in 1945 and nearly $16 billion in 1958, and constituted between one-fourth and two-fifths of individuals' holdings of savings bonds throughout the postwar period.[10] The movements in the net flow of these Treasury securities differ considerably from those of savings bonds, indicating that they are probably held by different groups of owners. Holdings of Treasury securities other than savings bonds by individuals declined during 1946–49 by about $3.7 billion from their initial level of somewhat over $19 billion, but then showed only relatively small changes. A definite shift, however, appears to have occurred from long- to short-term securities and the statistics also indicate larger fluctuations in the holdings of short- than of long-term Treasury securities. Great caution is, however, necessary in interpreting these figures because they are derived as residuals between the total amounts of Treasury securities outstanding and the reported or estimated holdings of other types of Treasury securities for each investor group, and therefore are subject to substantial errors of estimation of level and annual changes.[11] This movement and the participation of individuals in the issue of the 5 per cent notes in 1959 clearly indicate the effect of narrowing the interest rate differential (until it disappeared almost completely) between long-term Treasury securities and the highest-grade corporate issues. It only shows, however, that sharp shocklike shifts (what the Radcliffe report calls a "change in gear") in the absolute level of interest rates or in differentials may considerably affect the

[9] Hanc, *U.S. Savings Bond Program*, p. 18.

[10] *National Balance Sheet*, Vol. II, Tables IV-b-13a, IV-b-13b, and IV-b-13c.

[11] The most spectacular change in the holdings of long-term Treasury securities other than savings bonds by individuals occurred in 1959, after the end of the period covered in this report, partly in the form of the acquisition of substantial amounts of 5 per cent Treasury notes in the fall of 1959 (Hanc, *U.S. Savings Bond Program*, p. 63). A considerable part of the net purchases of 1959 was offset by net sales in 1960 and 1961 (*Federal Reserve Bulletin*, August 1962, p. 1026).

direction of the flow of funds of individuals, not that such a correlation habitually exists between more gradual interest changes and the distribution of the individuals' saving.

The absolute volume of holdings of Treasury securities by nonfinancial corporations did not change much over the postwar period as a whole (see Table 50). These holdings, however, were subject to considerable annual (and also seasonal) fluctuations, and some changes occurred in the type of Treasury securities held by nonfinancial corporations. Short-term issues, nevertheless, accounted at all times for more than three-fourths of total holdings. The volume of holdings at the end of 1945 obviously represented to a considerable degree the temporary investment of funds for which no use could be found in the holders' regular business. As a result, the holdings of Treasury securities by nonfinancial corporations were reduced by almost $7 billion, or nearly one-third, in the two years 1946–47. During the remainder of the period, sharp increases occurred in 1949–50, 1955, and, after the end of the period, in 1959. Considerable decreases took place in 1954, 1956, and 1960. Some of these movements confirmed the expectation that holdings of Treasury securities, as a form of liquid assets, are increased in recessions and decreased during recoveries and booms. Some of the movements, however, do not conform to this pattern, particularly the decrease in 1954 and the increases in 1955 and 1959. The movements in 1954–55 may possibly be connected with an advance in the dates of corporate income tax payments.[12] In comparison with total assets, Treasury securities lost almost continuously in importance, declining from over 8 per cent at the end of 1945 to slightly over 2 per cent in 1958, most of the decline occurring in 1946–47 and in 1956–57.

The market for Treasury securities is primarily influenced, of course, by the changes in the holdings of financial institutions. Here, at least seven groups must be distinguished whose behavior in their portfolio of Treasury securities during the postwar period showed considerable differences—the Federal Reserve banks, commercial banks, fire and casualty insurance companies and private pension funds, life insurance

---

[12] A more adequate analysis of the participation of nonfinancial corporations in the market for Treasury securities would require the use of quarterly rather than annual data, the breakdown of all nonfinancial corporations into a number of more homogeneous industrial and size groups, and the correlation of changes in the holdings of Treasury securities with shifts in other liquid assets of nonfinancial corporations. Although the material for such a study is available, there was neither a need here to investigate the problem in such detail nor the time to do so.

companies and mutual savings banks, and government insurance funds. Closer inspection shows that there are almost as many patterns of flows of Treasury securities as there are types of institutions—and that further diversity exists within groups, each reflecting the special situation of the different types of institutions.

Changes in the holdings of Treasury securities by the Federal Reserve System, although small compared to similar transactions by several other financial institutions, are of particular importance because of their effect on bank reserves and hence on the volume of credit. They are, of course, determined by considerations of monetary policy rather than by interest rate differentials. For the period as a whole, the Federal Reserve banks increased their holdings of Treasury securities by about $2 billion, or 9 per cent, but holdings ranged between $19 and $26 billion, annual changes being moderate except for a sharp reduction in 1949 and substantial increases in 1950–51.

Government insurance and pension funds used approximately three-fourths of the total net funds available to them during the postwar period to acquire Treasury securities, and actually showed a ratio of more than one-half in ten of the thirteen years of the period (see Tables 53 and 54). The proportion was considerably lower—around one-third of total net uses of funds—only twice (1950 and 1957); and there was only one year (1958) in which the holdings of Treasury securities were actually reduced, partly reflecting an unusually small increase of total net funds available due to the recession.

Four other groups of financial institutions also were net investors in Treasury securities. The share of Treasury securities in total net uses of funds, however, was considerable only for one of them, property insurance companies, the share averaging about one-sixth.[13] Net investment in Treasury securities accounted for a considerable part of all net uses of funds in 1946–50 and for a smaller but still positive share in 1951–54. In 1955–58, on the other hand, the holdings of Treasury securities were reduced in absolute amounts, thus acting as a source rather than a use of funds. This configuration—the gradual decline of the share of Treasury securities as a net outlet for funds—is also found, among the larger groups of financial institutions, for noninsured pension funds.

For some other groups, among which life insurance companies and mutual savings banks are the most important, Treasury securities con-

---

[13] See *National Balance Sheet*, Vol. II, Table VII-5i.

stituted during the postwar period a predominant source of funds, rather than an outlet. Life insurance companies financed more than one-fifth of their total net uses of funds through net sales of Treasury securities. The corresponding share was about one-sixth for mutual savings banks. Treasury securities were relatively most important as a source of funds in the early years of the period, particularly from 1948 to 1951.

Commercial banks show a different pattern, which is explained by their primary interest in short-term business loans. For the postwar period as a whole, net sales of Treasury securities provided almost one-third of all net uses of funds. Sales were heaviest in the years 1946–48, 1950, 1955–56, and 1959 when demands for commercial loans were high. In the recession years 1949, 1954, and 1958, purchases of Treasury securities absorbed more than one-half of the total net uses of funds.

During the postwar period, and particularly from 1948 on, as a whole foreigners constituted an important group of buyers of Treasury securities. Their net purchases amounted to $5 billion, mostly in short-term securities, and represented the third largest sectoral purchase balance following state and local governments and, by a large distance, federal pension funds. These purchases were made mostly by foreign monetary authorities and therefore were only in part motivated by commercial considerations. They averaged almost $0.5 billion per year, after net sales of $0.5 billion in 1946 when the dollar shortage was very pronounced, but reached over $1.0 billion within the period only twice (1950 and 1955).[14]

### Historical Background

In the case of U.S. government securities, it is not necessary to go back beyond World War I. (The basic data for a historical review will be found in Tables 55 and 56 and Charts 13 and 14.) For the two benchmark dates of 1900 and 1912, the total value of U.S. government securities outstanding was extremely small and a large portion of the total was held by national banks as cover for their notes. In 1900, shortly after the public sale of Treasury securities in connection

---

[14] The net purchase balance rose to an all-time high with about $3.0 billion in 1959 (*Flow of Funds/Saving Accounts, 1946–1960*, Federal Reserve Board, Supplement 5, p. 40).

TABLE 55

DISTRIBUTION OF U.S. GOVERNMENT SECURITIES AMONG DOMESTIC HOLDER GROUPS, 1900–58

(per cent)

| | 1958 (1) | 1945A (2) | 1945B (3) | 1939 (4) | 1929 (5) | 1912 (6) | 1900 (7) |
|---|---|---|---|---|---|---|---|
| 1. Households | 23.3 | 23.2 | 25.2 | 20.0 | 31.2 | 33.3 | 46.5 |
| 2. Nonfinancial corporations | 6.4 | 7.5 | 6.4 | 3.8 | 19.5 | 0 | 0 |
| 3. State and local governments | 4.0 | 1.8 | 1.6 | 0.5 | 1.6 | 0 | 0 |
| 4. Federal government[a] | 2.1 | 1.6 | 1.6 | 4.3 | 0.3 | 0 | 0 |
|   a. Govt. lending agencies | 1.5 | 0.5 | 0.6 | 1.7 | 0 | | |
| 5. Financial institutions, total[b] | 64.2 | 65.9 | 65.2 | 71.3 | 47.3 | 66.7 | 53.5 |
|   a. Monetary authorities[b] | 9.6 | 8.8 | 8.8 | 5.3 | 3.2 | | |
|   b. Commercial banks | 24.1 | 32.9 | 33.0 | 34.7 | 28.9 | 64.8 | 41.6 |
|   c. Mutual savings banks | 2.6 | 3.9 | 3.9 | 6.6 | 3.3 | 1.0 | 8.2 |
|   d. Savings and loan associations | 1.4 | 0.9 | 0.9 | 0.2 | 0.1 | 0 | |
|   e. Credit unions | 0 | 0.1 | 0.1 | 0 | 0 | | |
|   f. Life insurance | 2.6 | 7.5 | 7.5 | 11.5 | 2.1 | 0.1 | 0.5 |
|   g. Noninsured pension plans | 0.9 | 0.5 | 0.5 | 0.3 | 0.3 | | |
|   h. Fire and casualty insurance | 2.0 | 1.2 | 1.2 | 2.5 | 2.9 | 0.6 | 3.1 |
|   i. Other private insurance | 0.3 | 0.2 | 0.1 | 0.2 | 0 | 0.2 | 0.1 |
|   j. Govt. insurance and pension funds | 19.7 | 8.7 | 8.8 | 9.7 | 4.8 | | |
|   k. Investment companies[c] | 0.2 | 0.1 | 0 | 0 | 0.2 | | |
|   l. Brokers and dealers | 0.3 | 0.8 | 0.2 | 0.1 | 0.6 | 0 | 0 |
|   m. Other finance | 0.4 | 0.5 | 0 | 0.1 | 0.8 | 0 | 0 |
| 6. Total | 100.0 | 100.0 | 100.0 | 100.0 | 100.0 | 100.0 | 100.0 |
| 7. Total (billion dollars) | 274.3 | 275.7 | 274.4 | 47.0 | 16.2 | 1.2 | 1.2 |

Source: National Balance Sheet, Vol. II; cols. 1–2 from Table IV-b-13 and Table III-7c, III-5m-1; cols. 3–7 from Table IV-b-13d.

Note: A blank space indicates that the given type of financial institution did not exist in that year (see my Financial Intermediaries, Chart 3, p. 61).

For notes and further explanations, see Table 56.

TABLE 56

SHARE OF U.S. GOVERNMENT SECURITIES IN TOTAL ASSETS OF DOMESTIC HOLDER GROUPS, 1900-58
(per cent)

| | 1958 (1) | 1954A (2) | 1945B (3) | 1939 (4) | 1929 (5) | 1912 (6) | 1900 (7) |
|---|---|---|---|---|---|---|---|
| 1. Households | 3.5 | 8.8 | 9.3 | 2.2 | 1.0 | 0.3 | 0.7 |
| 2. Nonfinancial corporations | 2.3 | 8.3 | 7.5 | 1.2 | 1.4 | 0 | 0 |
| 3. State and local governments | 5.5 | 7.1 | 6.2 | 0.5 | 0.6 | 0 | 0 |
| 4. Federal government [a] | 5.0 | 5.7 | 6.0 | 8.1 | 0.6 | 0 | 0 |
|   a. Govt. lending agencies | 13.5 | 8.2 | 4.7 | 8.2 | 1.1 | | |
| 5. Financial institutions, total [b] | 25.0 | 51.6 | 52.1 | 19.5 | 5.8 | 2.2 | 3.9 |
|   a. Monetary authorities [b] | 33.4 | 34.8 | 53.8 | 13.1 | 9.4 | | |
|   b. Commercial banks | 27.4 | 56.5 | 56.5 | 24.6 | 7.1 | 3.5 | 5.2 |
|   c. Mutual savings banks | 19.1 | 62.7 | 62.8 | 26.2 | 5.4 | 0.3 | 4.2 |
|   d. Saving and loan associations | 6.9 | 27.6 | 28.1 | 1.9 | 0.3 | 0 | 0 |
|   e. Credit unions | 3.0 | 40.9 | 48.3 | 3.1 | 0 | 0 | |
|   f. Life insurance | 6.6 | 45.9 | 45.9 | 18.5 | 1.9 | 0 | 0.3 |
|   g. Noninsured pension plans | 8.8 | 54.8 | 45.0 | 15.0 | 10.0 | | |
|   h. Fire and casualty insurance | 21.1 | 42.1 | 42.1 | 24.0 | 9.8 | 0.7 | 7.9 |
|   i. Other private insurance | 20.5 | 28.4 | 22.6 | 5.8 | 0.4 | 1.2 | 4.0 |
|   j. Govt. insurance and pension funds | 81.8 | 93.1 | 94.0 | 73.5 | 52.3 | | |
|   k. Investment companies | 2.4 | 6.3 | 4.6 | 1.1 | 0.9 | | |
|   l. Brokers and dealers [c] | 11.4 | 43.3 | 26.0 | 3.3 | 1.3 | | |
|   m. Other finance | 19.7 | 54.4 | 0 | 0 | 0 | 0 | 0 |
| 6. Total | 7.3 | 18.0 | 18.1 | 5.4 | 1.7 | 0.4 | 0.8 |

Source: National Balance Sheet, Vol. II, unless otherwise specified.
Line 1: Tables I and Ia, sum of nonfarm households and agriculture.
Lines 2-5: Tables I and Ia.
Line 4a: Table III-7c and Financial Intermediaries, Table A-24.
Lines 5a-5k, cols. 1-2: Tables III-5a through III-5k.
Lines 5a-5k, cols. 3-7: Numerators from Table IV-b-13d; denominators from *Financial Intermediaries*, Tables A-2 through A-5, A-19, A-20, A-8, A-10, A-12, A-13, A-9, A-14, A-11 and A-21.

NOTES TO TABLE 56 (concluded)

Line 5*l*:     Table III-5m-1,  and Goldsmith, Study of Saving, Vol. III, Table W-37.
Line 5m:     Table III-5m minus Table III-5m-1.
Line 6:     Tables I and Ia.

a Includes government corporations and credit agencies, and postal savings system.

b Columns 3-7 include federal reserve banks only.  Columns 1-2 also include Treasury monetary funds.

c Columns 3-7 include unincorporated brokers and dealers only.  Columns 1-2 include both incorporated and unincorporated.
See note to Table 55.

with the Spanish-American War, there were still appreciable holdings by mutual savings banks and property insurance companies, totaling somewhat more than one-tenth of the federal debt. These holdings had virtually disappeared by 1912. Similarly, holdings of households, estimated as a residual, declined from nearly one-half of the total in 1900 to one-third in 1912.

At the benchmark date of 1922,[15] when the value of Treasury securities outstanding ($23 billion) was already slightly below the peak, households held about one-half of the total, as a result of the intensive sales campaigns during and immediately after World War I. Holdings of nonfinancial corporations also were still substantial, accounting for 15 per cent of the outstanding federal debt. Financial institutions therefore held about one-third of all Treasury securities, most of which were in the hands of commercial banks, with mutual savings banks and life insurance companies following at a distance.

During the 1920's when the total amount of Treasury securities outstanding was reduced by about one-third, as well as during the 1930's when it almost trebled, Treasury securities gravitated toward the portfolios of financial institutions. How rapidly this process operated is indicated by the fact that financial institutions held almost one-half of all Treasury securities outstanding in 1929, compared to only one-third in 1922, and by 1939 held almost three-fourths of the total.

Among financial institutions, commercial banks remained by far the most important holders, absorbing in 1939 more than one-third of the total federal debt. Life insurance companies and government insurance and pension funds also were important holders, each accounting for about one-tenth of all Treasury securities outstanding. Individuals' holdings had been reduced to one-fifth of the total federal debt by about 1939, and the holdings of nonfinancial business had become relatively negligible.

[15] *National Balance Sheet,* Vol. II, Table IV-b-13d.

Up to World War II—with the possible exception of a few years during and after World War I—Treasury securities represented a substantial part of total assets only of financial institutions. Even here they acquired this position only during the 1930's, their share rising

CHART 13

DISTRIBUTION OF U.S. GOVERNMENT SECURITIES
AMONG MAIN DOMESTIC HOLDER GROUPS, 1900–58

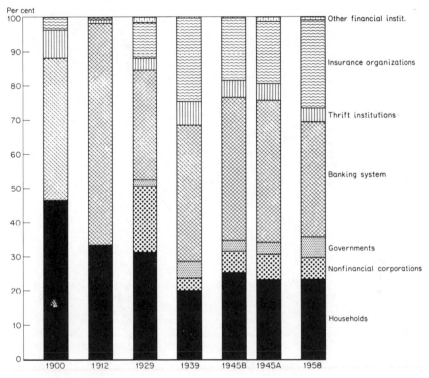

Source: Table 55.

—after a decline from 9 per cent in 1922 [16]—from 6 per cent in 1929 to 19.5 per cent in 1939. Apart from government insurance and pension funds, most of whose assets were always invested in Treasury securities, the obligations of the federal government represented the largest single asset only for commercial banks, mutual savings banks, and property insurance companies (for all of which they accounted

[16] *Ibid.*, and *Study of Saving*, Vol. III, Table W-11.

# CHART 14

## SHARE OF U.S. GOVERNMENT SECURITIES IN TOTAL ASSETS OF MAIN DOMESTIC HOLDER GROUPS, 1900–58

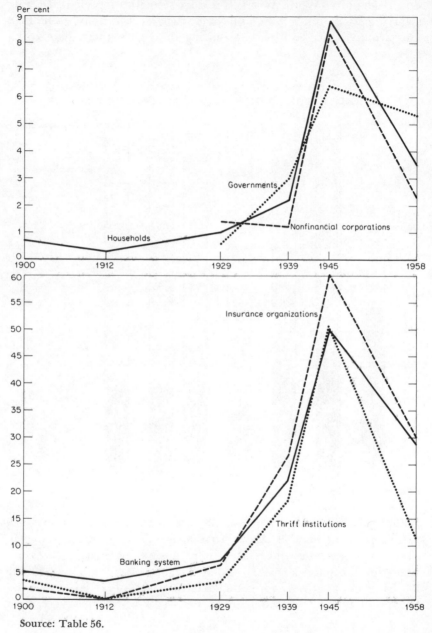

Source: Table 56.

TABLE 57

INTEREST RATE DIFFERENTIALS BETWEEN SELECTED FINANCIAL INSTRUMENTS AND LONG-TERM TREASURY SECURITIES, 1929, 1939, AND 1946-58

| | Absolute Differentials | | | | | Relative Differentials | | | | |
|---|---|---|---|---|---|---|---|---|---|---|
| | High-Grade Municipal Bonds (1) | High-Grade Corporate Bonds (2) | Conventional Home Mortgages (3) | Total Savings Deposits (4) | Common Stock (5) | High-Grade Municipal Bonds (6) | High-Grade Corporate Bonds (7) | Conventional Home Mortgages (8) | Total Savings Deposits (9) | Common Stock (10) |
| 1929 | 0.67 | 1.13 | (2.40) | 0.47 | -0.10 | 19 | 31 | (67) | 13 | -3 |
| 1939 | 0.40 | 0.65 | (2.60) | -0.36 | 1.84 | 17 | 28 | (110) | -15 | 78 |
| 1946 | -1.09 | 0.34 | 2.11 | -0.94 | 1.78 | -50 | 16 | 96 | -43 | 81 |
| 1947 | -.80 | 0.36 | 2.12 | -0.96 | 2.88 | -36 | 16 | 94 | -43 | 128 |
| 1948 | -.57 | 0.38 | 2.06 | -1.09 | 3.34 | -23 | 16 | 84 | -45 | 137 |
| 1949 | -.66 | 0.35 | 2.30 | -0.87 | 4.32 | -29 | 15 | 100 | -38 | 187 |
| 1950 | -.76 | 0.30 | 2.26 | -0.82 | 3.95 | -33 | 13 | 97 | -35 | 170 |
| 1951 | -.96 | 0.29 | 2.07 | -0.97 | 3.55 | -37 | 11 | 81 | -38 | 138 |
| 1952 | -.88 | 0.28 | 2.13 | -0.88 | 2.82 | -33 | 10 | 79 | -33 | 105 |
| 1953 | -.62 | 0.27 | 2.00 | -1.01 | 2.56 | -21 | 9 | 68 | -34 | 87 |
| 1954 | -.49 | 0.37 | 2.49 | -0.51 | 2.25 | -19 | 15 | 98 | -20 | 89 |
| 1955 | -.62 | 0.26 | 2.12 | -0.67 | 1.26 | -22 | 9 | 76 | -24 | 45 |
| 1956 | -.55 | 0.31 | 1.91 | -0.74 | 1.02 | -18 | 10 | 63 | -24 | 33 |
| 1957 | -.37 | 0.42 | 2.41 | -0.81 | 0.86 | -11 | 12 | 69 | -23 | 25 |
| 1958 | -.51 | 0.36 | 2.27 | -0.65 | 0.62 | -15 | 10 | 66 | -19 | 18 |

Source

Treasury securities: Federal Reserve Bulletin, May 1940, p. 389.
1929, 1939, cols. 1-2: Ibid.
1929, 1939, col. 3: Extrapolated.
1929, 1939, col. 4: Computed from figures Study of Saving, Vol. I, as weighted averages of the three following financial institutions: commercial banks (deposit and interest payments) from Tables L-6, col. 6, and L-23, col. 7; mutual savings banks (deposits and interest payments) from Tables L-28, col. 2, and L-38, col. 4; and savings and loan associations (deposits and interest payments) from Table J-11, cols. 1 and 3.
1929, 1939, col. 5: 1940 Supplement to the Survey of Current Business, p. 76. Primary source is Moody's Investor Service figures for 200 stocks.
1946-58, all cols.: See sources to Table 48.

for about one-fourth of the total assets in 1939), and for life insurance and noninsured pension plans (among which their share was around one-sixth). The role of the U.S. government obligations was relatively negligible not only for nonfinancial corporations, for which it hardly exceeded 1 per cent, but also for nonfarm households, for which it amounted to 2 per cent, and for state and local governments, for which it was only ½ per cent.

# CHAPTER 7

# The Market for State and Local Government Securities [1]

---

## Character of the Market

THE market for state and local government securities is one of the best-defined sectors of the capital market, identified chiefly by the exemption of these securities from federal income tax. As a result of this privilege, high-grade state and local government securities sell at a lower yield than U.S. government or corporate securities of the same maturity or comparable quality. This makes state and local government securities unattractive to those investors whose income is tax exempt (such as government insurance and trust funds, private pension funds, nonprofit institutions, credit unions, and mutual investment companies) or whose income is subject to only relatively low rates of tax (such as mutual savings banks, savings and loan associations, life insurance companies, and individuals with low incomes). On the other hand, these securities have a special attraction for financial institutions subject to the full corporate income tax, primarily commercial banks and property insurance companies, and for individuals in the higher income tax brackets. This attraction, however,

---

[1] The very brief description of the institutional aspects of the market for state and local government securities is based on Roland I. Robinson's *Postwar Market for State and Local Government Securities* (Princeton for NBER, 1960). The statistics used here, however, sometimes differ slightly from Robinson's. Because of the availability of Robinson's study, this summary does not deal with the relation of the level and movements of the yield on state and local government securities to the level and change in relevant tax rates.

depends on the relative yield difference between state and local government securities and otherwise equivalent other securities.

The demand for state and local government securities thus essentially depends on the funds available for investment by the three above-mentioned groups (funds which may come from current savings or from the liquidation of other assets), on interest rate differentials, and on income tax rates. The supply of tax-exempt securities, on the other hand, is mainly determined by the difference between the capital expenditures of the state and local government and their gross savings (current income minus current expenditure, excluding capital consumption allowances).

The character of the market for these securities is also influenced by a number of additional economic and institutional factors:

1. Regular issues of state and local government securities (so-called "full faith and credit obligations") are offered in serial form, among which final maturities of twenty, twenty-five, and thirty years predominate. Revenue bonds, however, are usually issued as term securities with a maturity of thirty to forty years.[2] The serial form increases the range of potential buyers to include both investors primarily interested in short-term securities, such as commercial banks, and those preferring long-term bonds, such as property insurance companies and individuals.

2. The demand for these securities is further encouraged by tailoring the securities to the special needs, primarily determined by tax considerations, of important groups of investors. These needs are responsible for some issues, usually very early or late maturities, with abnormally high coupon rates which enable the buyers to take advantage of certain tax provisions on capital gains or losses.

3. The market for state and local government securities is entirely over the counter and in the hands of specialists, either separate departments of commercial banks and investment banking houses or firms which limit their activities to these securities.

4. Most new issues of state and local government securities are sold through competitive bidding. One of the results of this method seems to be that the cost of selling small issues is not significantly higher than that of large issues.

5. Considerable support for the market is provided by the issuance in serial form. Each year a large amount of outstanding securities is

[2] Robinson, *Postwar Market,* p. 46.

retired and these retirements provide substantial funds available for reinvestment in state and local government securities. Retirements averaged less than $1 billion in 1947–51, but rose to an average of over $2 billion in 1954–58 as the retirements from the heavy postwar issues began to make their weight felt (see Table 59).

6. Secondary transactions in state and local government securities are relatively small compared to new offerings, and their volume has tended to move inversely to that of new offerings.

7. Revenue obligations, issued mostly for financing highways, constitute a fairly definite submarket of growing importance. At the end of the fiscal year 1958, about 36 per cent of total state and local government long-term debt consisted of revenue obligations, compared to only 11 per cent ten years earlier.[3] Slightly more than one-fourth of all new issues of state and government securities during the postwar period were revenue obligations, the proportion rising from about one-fifth in 1946–51 to almost one-third in 1952–58.[4] Because revenue obligations are not backed by the "full faith and credit" of the issuing state and local authorities, they generally sell at a yield of ½ to 1½ per cent above regular state and local government issues. It is unfortunately not possible to separate the holdings of revenue bonds in the portfolios of the main holder groups, but it is thought that they are held to a larger extent by individuals than by financial institutions compared to full faith and credit obligations.[5]

8. Another still smaller submarket is constituted by the bonds of public housing authorities, which have been offered since 1951. Since the U.S. Treasury guarantees the deficits of these authorities, the bonds are regarded as equivalent to federal government obligations. Public Housing Authority bonds have accounted for 5 per cent of all state and local government securities issued during the period 1951–58.[6]

---

[3] The 1958 figure is from *Summary of Governmental Finances in 1958* (U.S. Bureau of the Census, Government Division, p. 18); earlier figures are from Robinson, *Postwar Market*, p. 203.

[4] *Ibid.*, p. 204, and *Federal Reserve Bulletin*, August 1959, p. 1015.

[5] In mid-1956 insured commercial banks held only about 11 per cent of all revenue obligations compared to 28 per cent in full faith and credit obligations (*Assets, Liabilities and Capital Accounts, Commercial and Mutual Savings Banks*, Federal Deposit Insurance Corporation, Report No. 45, June 30, 1956, p. 62, and *Summary of Governmental Finances in 1956*, p. 33).

[6] *Federal Reserve Bulletin*, August 1959, p. 1015; *Thirteenth Annual Report*, Housing and Home Finance Agency, 1959, p. 207.

9. State and local government securities have been subject to relatively wide price fluctuation considering their high quality. These fluctuations have been wider than those in either high-grade corporate bonds or in Treasury securities of comparable maturity.

10. Within the market for state and local government securities, the yield differentials associated with difference in quality have declined over the postwar period. While the narrowing has not been pronounced in absolute terms, it has been quite considerable relative to the rising level of yield rates.

11. During the postwar period, approximately two-fifths of all state and local government securities have been issued for productive purposes, i.e., highways, water supply, sewerage, other enterprises, bridges, tunnels, ports and airports, and industrial buildings. About one-third has been issued for welfare purposes, primarily schools and secondarily housing and hospitals. Issues to provide funds for aid to veterans have amounted to less than 10 per cent of the total, mostly during the early part of the postwar period. Refunding issues have been almost negligible.[7]

12. The differential between the yield on state and local government securities and taxable securities of comparable quality and maturity, which can be regarded as a measure of the capitalized value of the tax-exemption preference, has fluctuated widely during the postwar period, although there has been only one substantial change in tax rates, the increase occurring around 1950. Table 58 shows, as a basis for analysis, first the differential between the yield on an average of state and local government securities and the yields on long-term Treasury bonds and on an average of corporate bonds of the first four rating groups, and secondly the differential between the yield on high-grade (Aaa) state and local government securities and the yields on long-term Treasury securities and on corporate bonds.

Closer study suggests that the main factor in the movement of the differentials was the relative supply of state and local government securities as measured by the ratio of net issues of these securities to the net issuance of all main capital market instruments. This positive relationship was fairly pronounced, although not entirely regular. In years in which the share of state and local government securities in the total value of capital market issues was high or rising, the differential also was at a high level or showed an increase. Similarly, low

---

[7] Robinson, *Postwar Market*, p. 40.

TABLE 58

YIELD DIFFERENTIALS OF TAX-EXEMPT SECURITIES, 1946-58
(per cent of yield of security compared)

| | Averages of State and Local Government Bonds[a] Compared with | | Highest-Grade State and Local Government Bonds[b] Compared with | |
|---|---|---|---|---|
| | Long-Term Treasury Bonds (1) | Average Corporate Bonds Outstanding (2) | Long-Term Treasury Bonds (3) | Highest-Grade Corporate Bonds Outstanding (4) |
| 1946 | -33 | -47 | -50 | -57 |
| 1947 | -18 | -36 | -36 | -44 |
| 1948 | -5 | -24 | -23 | -34 |
| 1949 | -7 | -27 | -29 | -38 |
| 1950 | -16 | -32 | -33 | -40 |
| 1951 | -23 | -36 | -37 | -44 |
| 1952 | -17 | -30 | -33 | -39 |
| 1953 | -4 | -18 | -21 | -28 |
| 1954 | -3 | -22 | -19 | -30 |
| 1955 | -8 | -21 | -22 | -29 |
| 1956 | -4 | -18 | -18 | -26 |
| 1957 | 3 | -15 | -11 | -20 |
| 1958 | -2 | -19 | -15 | -23 |
| 1946-49 | -14 | -32 | -32 | -42 |
| 1949-54 | -13 | -28 | -29 | -37 |
| 1954-58 | -3 | -18 | -17 | -25 |

Source:  See notes to Table 48.

[a]Aaa, Aa, and Baa bond.

[b]Aaa bonds.

levels or decreases in the new issue ratio were associated with low or declining differentials.

Possibly the most interesting feature is the level of the differential between high-grade state and local government bonds and high-grade corporate bonds, which was about 40 per cent during Cycles I and II and about 25 per cent in Cycle III. All of these values are below the rates of either the corporate income tax (52 per cent during the second half of the period) or the marginal rates applicable to wealthy individuals. Thus, the tax-exemption privilege was sold in the market at considerably less than its value to most holders of state and local government securities. Since 1953 the market value of the tax-exemption privilege actually has been about one-half of the corporate tax rate, and at about the first bracket rate of the personal income tax (20 per cent). As a consequence, the federal government has lost more of potential tax revenue than would have been needed to compensate state and local governments for the relatively slight saving in interest costs which accrued to them as a result of the lower yield of tax-exempt securities. The reasons for this low valuation of the tax-exemption privilege by the market are complicated. Possibly the most important factor was the increasing level of new issues of state and local government securities, which made it necessary to tap layers of buyers for whom the tax-exemption privilege was of relatively little value because of their tax status or because of basic predilection for equity securities. This seems to have been the case particularly for some financial institutions, such as mutual savings banks and property insurance companies, and for some of the individual purchasers of tax-exempt securities.

## Developments During the Postwar Period

There is no point in commenting separately on each of Tables 59 to 64. It will suffice to summarize the main features of the market for state and local government securities during the postwar period which are disclosed by the tables and by Chart 15.

TABLE 59

CAPITAL EXPENDITURES AND SECURITY ISSUES OF
STATE AND LOCAL GOVERNMENTS, 1946-58
(billion dollars)

| | | | Net Acquisition of Financial Assets (3) | Security Issues | | |
| | Gross Saving (1) | Gross Capital Expenditures (2) | | Net (4) | New Long-Term Issues (5) | Retirements (6) |
|---|---|---|---|---|---|---|
| 1946 | 2.31 | 2.02 | .29 | -.13 | 1.16 | 1.29 |
| 1947 | 3.04 | 3.07 | -.03 | 1.41 | 2.32 | .91 |
| 1948 | 3.01 | 4.11 | -1.10 | 2.21 | 2.69 | .48 |
| 1949 | 4.07 | 5.76 | -1.69 | 2.35 | 2.91 | .56 |
| 1950 | 4.57 | 6.45 | -1.88 | 3.11 | 3.53 | .42 |
| 1951 | 5.97 | 7.14 | -1.17 | 2.41 | 3.19 | .78 |
| 1952 | 6.65 | 8.17 | -1.52 | 3.18 | 4.40 | 1.22 |
| 1953 | 7.44 | 8.60 | -1.16 | 3.58 | 5.56 | 1.98 |
| 1954 | 7.87 | 9.64 | -1.77 | 4.18 | 6.97 | 2.79 |
| 1955 | 8.26 | 10.94 | -2.68 | 3.48 | 5.98 | 2.50 |
| 1956 | 9.18 | 11.52 | -2.34 | 3.32 | 5.45 | 2.13 |
| 1957 | 10.10 | 13.36 | -3.26 | 4.87 | 6.96 | 2.09 |
| 1958 | 9.73 | 15.13 | -5.40 | 5.92 | 7.45 | 1.53 |
| 1946-49 | 3.08 | 3.69 | -0.60 | 1.58 | 2.35 | 0.77 |
| 1949-54 | 6.12 | 7.61 | -1.49 | 3.11 | 4.32 | 1.22 |
| 1954-58 | 9.08 | 12.05 | -2.97 | 4.18 | 6.40 | 2.22 |

Source: <u>National Balance Sheet</u>, Vol. II, unless otherwise specified.
Cols. 1-3: Table VII-6, lines IV-3, I-7, and II-21 minus III-14.
Col. 4: Table VIII-c-12, line 6.
Col. 5: <u>Federal Reserve Bulletin</u>, various issues (e.g., 1955, p. 684; 1957, p. 446; and 1961, p. 1450).
Col. 6: Col. 5 minus col. 4.

TABLE 60

DISTRIBUTION OF HOLDINGS OF STATE AND LOCAL SECURITIES, 1945-58

(per cent)

| | 1945 | 1946 | 1947 | 1948 | 1949 | 1950 | 1951 | 1952 | 1953 | 1954 | 1955 | 1956 | 1957 | 1958 |
|---|---|---|---|---|---|---|---|---|---|---|---|---|---|---|
| 1.Nonfarm households | 56.3 | 55.9 | 54.2 | 53.4 | 51.0 | 47.0 | 44.5 | 43.7 | 43.9 | 41.2 | 41.7 | 42.3 | 42.4 | 40.6 |
| 2.Nonfinancial corporations | 1.5 | 1.5 | 1.6 | 1.7 | 1.7 | 1.8 | 1.8 | 1.8 | 1.9 | 2.4 | 2.6 | 2.7 | 2.7 | 2.7 |
| 3.Finance | 33.0 | 34.0 | 36.3 | 37.5 | 39.8 | 43.3 | 45.2 | 45.4 | 46.7 | 50.2 | 49.9 | 49.3 | 49.2 | 51.1 |
| a.Govt. insurance and pension funds | 5.6 | 5.2 | 5.3 | 5.4 | 5.7 | 5.8 | 5.6 | 5.4 | 5.5 | 5.7 | 6.0 | 6.4 | 6.7 | 6.8 |
| b.Commercial banks | 18.8 | 20.9 | 23.5 | 23.0 | 24.3 | 27.0 | 28.3 | 28.5 | 27.5 | 29.0 | 27.1 | 25.7 | 25.2 | 27.0 |
| c.Mutual savings banks | 0.4 | 0.3 | 0.3 | 0.3 | 0.3 | 0.3 | 0.5 | 0.9 | 1.0 | 1.4 | 1.4 | 1.3 | 1.2 | 1.2 |
| d.Life insurance | 3.4 | 2.9 | 2.7 | 3.5 | 3.9 | 3.8 | 3.6 | 3.2 | 3.3 | 4.3 | 4.3 | 4.5 | 4.3 | 4.4 |
| e.Fire and casualty insurance | 1.1 | 1.1 | 1.4 | 2.1 | 2.8 | 3.5 | 4.5 | 5.2 | 6.7 | 7.8 | 8.9 | 9.6 | 9.9 | 10.1 |
| f.Other private insurance | 1.7 | 1.8 | 1.7 | 1.6 | 1.4 | 1.2 | 1.1 | 1.0 | 0.9 | 0.9 | 0.9 | 0.9 | 0.8 | 0.7 |
| g.Other finance | 1.9 | 1.8 | 1.3 | 1.6 | 1.4 | 1.7 | 1.7 | 1.1 | 1.7 | 1.2 | 1.2 | 0.9 | 1.1 | 1.0 |
| 4.State and local governments | 6.8 | 6.3 | 5.7 | 5.1 | 5.7 | 6.1 | 6.1 | 5.8 | 5.5 | 5.1 | 4.8 | 4.6 | 4.3 | 4.0 |
| 5.Federal government | 2.4 | 2.3 | 2.2 | 2.3 | 1.8 | 1.9 | 2.5 | 3.2 | 2.1 | 1.1 | 1.0 | 1.1 | 1.4 | 1.6 |
| 6.Total | 100.0 | 100.0 | 100.0 | 100.0 | 100.0 | 100.0 | 100.0 | 100.0 | 100.0 | 100.0 | 100.0 | 100.0 | 100.0 | 100.0 |
| 7.Total (billion dollars) | 21.17 | 21.04 | 22.45 | 24.66 | 27.01 | 30.12 | 32.53 | 35.71 | 39.29 | 43.47 | 46.95 | 50.27 | 55.14 | 61.06 |

Source: National Balance Sheet, Vol. II, Table IV-b-14.
Note: Components may not add to totals because of rounding here and elsewhere in this chapter.

TABLE 61

STRUCTURAL CHANGES IN OWNERSHIP OF STATE AND LOCAL GOVERNMENT SECURITIES DURING THE POSTWAR PERIOD

| | Outstandings (billion dollars) | | Aggregate Net Flows, 1946-58 (billion dollars) | NET FLOWS (ANNUAL AVERAGES) | | | | | |
| | | | | Amounts (billion dollars) | | | Distribution (per cent) | | |
| | 1945 (1) | 1958 (2) | (3) | Cycle I 1946-49 (4) | Cycle II 1949-54 (5) | Cycle III 1954-58 (6) | Cycle I 1946-49 (7) | Cycle II 1949-54 (8) | Cycle III 1954-58 (9) |
|---|---|---|---|---|---|---|---|---|---|
| 1. Nonfarm households | 11.92 | 24.79 | 12.87 | 0.54 | 0.82 | 1.63 | 34.2 | 26.4 | 39.0 |
| 2. Nonfinancial corporations | 0.32 | 1.63 | 1.31 | 0.04 | 0.09 | 0.17 | 2.5 | 2.9 | 4.1 |
| 3. State and local governments | 1.45 | 2.44 | 0.99 | 0.01 | 0.16 | 0.06 | 0.6 | 5.1 | 1.4 |
| 4. Federal government | 0.50 | 0.97 | 0.47 | 0.01 | 0.02 | 0.06 | 0.6 | 0.6 | 1.4 |
| 5. Financial instit., total | 6.98 | 31.23 | 24.25 | 0.97 | 2.02 | 2.27 | 61.4 | 65.0 | 54.3 |
| a. Commercial banks | 3.97 | 16.50 | 12.53 | 0.64 | 1.12 | 0.88 | 40.5 | 36.0 | 21.1 |
| b. Mutual savings banks | 0.09 | 0.73 | 0.64 | 0 | 0.09 | 0.05 | 0 | 2.9 | 1.2 |
| c. Life insurance | 0.72 | 2.68 | 1.96 | 0.10 | 0.12 | 0.24 | 6.3 | 3.9 | 5.7 |
| d. Fire and casualty insurance | 0.24 | 6.15 | 5.91 | 0.13 | 0.47 | 0.70 | 8.2 | 15.1 | 16.7 |
| e. Fraternal orders | 0.37 | 0.43 | 0.06 | 0 | 0 | 0.01 | 0 | 0 | 0.2 |
| f. Other finance | 0.40 | 0.60 | 0.20 | 0 | 0.04 | 0 | 0 | 1.3 | 0 |
| g. Government insurance and pension funds | 1.19 | 4.14 | 2.95 | 0.10 | 0.18 | 0.39 | 6.3 | 5.8 | 9.3 |
| 6. Total | 21.17 | 61.06 | 39.89 | 1.58 | 3.11 | 4.18 | 100.0 | 100.0 | 100.0 |

Source: National Balance Sheet, Vol. II. Cols. 1-2 from Table IV-b-14; cols. 3-9 from Table VIII-b-14.

TABLE 62

DISTRIBUTION OF FLOW OF FUNDS, STATE AND LOCAL GOVERNMENT SECURITIES, 1946–58
(per cent)

| | 1946[a] | 1947 | 1948 | 1949 | 1950 | 1951 | 1952 | 1953 | 1954 | 1955 | 1956 | 1957 | 1958 |
|---|---|---|---|---|---|---|---|---|---|---|---|---|---|
| 1. Nonfarm households | -123.1 | 29.1 | 44.8 | 26.0 | 12.2 | 12.9 | 36.4 | 45.0 | 15.8 | 48.3 | 50.6 | 43.5 | 24.0 |
| 2. Nonfinancial corporations | 0 | 2.8 | 2.3 | 2.1 | 2.3 | 2.1 | 1.9 | 2.5 | 7.9 | 5.2 | 3.3 | 3.1 | 2.2 |
| 3. Finance | +138.5 | 70.2 | 49.8 | 63.4 | 73.6 | 69.2 | 48.3 | 59.2 | 83.5 | 45.1 | 41.6 | 47.8 | 69.4 |
| a. Govt. insurance and pension funds | -76.9 | 7.1 | 6.8 | 8.9 | 6.1 | 2.9 | 4.1 | 6.7 | 7.4 | 9.8 | 12.0 | 9.2 | 7.8 |
| b. Commercial banks | +330.8 | 62.4 | 17.2 | 37.9 | 50.5 | 45.0 | 31.0 | 17.6 | 42.3 | 3.2 | 6.0 | 20.9 | 43.6 |
| c. Mutual savings banks | -23.1 | 0 | 0.5 | 0.9 | 0 | 2.5 | 5.3 | 2.5 | 4.5 | 1.1 | 0.9 | 0.2 | 0.8 |
| d. Life insurance | -84.6 | 0 | 11.8 | 7.7 | 3.2 | 0.8 | -0.6 | 4.2 | 13.2 | 5.5 | 6.9 | 2.3 | 5.1 |
| e. Fire and casualty insurance | 0 | 5.7 | 9.5 | 9.4 | 10.0 | 16.2 | 13.2 | 20.9 | 18.7 | 22.7 | 19.0 | 12.7 | 12.0 |
| f. Other private insurance | +7.7 | 0.7 | 0 | -0.4 | -0.3 | -0.4 | 0 | 0.3 | 0.5 | 1.4 | 0 | -0.4 | 0.2 |
| g. Other finance | -15.4 | -5.7 | 4.1 | -0.9 | 4.2 | 2.1 | -4.7 | 7.0 | -3.1 | 1.4 | -3.3 | 2.9 | 0 |
| 4. State and local governments | -100.0 | -3.5 | 0 | 11.9 | 9.6 | 5.0 | 3.4 | 2.5 | 0.7 | 1.4 | 2.1 | 1.4 | 0.8 |
| 5. Federal government | -15.4 | 1.4 | 3.2 | -3.4 | 2.3 | 10.8 | 10.0 | -9.2 | -7.9 | 0 | 2.4 | 4.1 | 3.5 |
| 6. Total | -100.0 | 100.0 | 100.0 | 100.0 | 100.0 | 100.0 | 100.0 | 100.0 | 100.0 | 100.0 | 100.0 | 100.0 | 100.0 |
| 7. Total (billion dollars) | -.13 | 1.41 | 2.21 | 2.35 | 3.11 | 2.40 | 3.19 | 3.58 | 4.18 | 3.48 | 3.32 | 4.87 | 5.92 |

Source: National Balance Sheet, Vol. II, Table VIII-b-14.

[a]The signs have been reversed to match the sign of the numerator.

TABLE 63

SHARE OF STATE AND LOCAL SECURITIES IN ASSETS OF EACH SECTOR, 1945–58

(per cent)

| | 1945 | 1946 | 1947 | 1948 | 1949 | 1950 | 1951 | 1952 | 1953 | 1954 | 1955 | 1956 | 1957 | 1958 |
|---|---|---|---|---|---|---|---|---|---|---|---|---|---|---|
| 1. Nonfarm households | 1.9 | 1.7 | 1.6 | 1.6 | 1.7 | 1.5 | 1.5 | 1.5 | 1.6 | 1.5 | 1.5 | 1.5 | 1.6 | 1.5 |
| 2. Nonfinancial corporations | 0.1 | 0.1 | 0.1 | 0.1 | 0.1 | 0.1 | 0.1 | 0.1 | 0.1 | 0.2 | 0.2 | 0.2 | 0.2 | 0.2 |
| 3. Finance | 2.0 | 2.0 | 2.2 | 2.4 | 2.6 | 3.0 | 3.2 | 3.3 | 3.5 | 3.9 | 3.9 | 3.9 | 4.1 | 4.4 |
| a. Govt. insurance and pension funds | 4.6 | 3.7 | 3.6 | 3.6 | 3.9 | 4.3 | 4.0 | 3.9 | 4.2 | 4.5 | 4.8 | 5.2 | 5.7 | 6.3 |
| b. Commercial banks | 2.5 | 2.9 | 3.4 | 3.6 | 4.1 | 4.8 | 5.1 | 5.4 | 5.6 | 6.2 | 6.0 | 5.9 | 6.2 | 6.8 |
| c. Mutual savings banks | 0.5 | 0.3 | 0.3 | 0.3 | 0.4 | 0.4 | 0.6 | 1.3 | 1.5 | 2.0 | 2.0 | 2.0 | 1.9 | 1.9 |
| d. Life insurance | 1.6 | 1.3 | 1.2 | 1.6 | 1.7 | 1.8 | 1.7 | 1.5 | 1.6 | 2.2 | 2.2 | 2.3 | 2.3 | 2.5 |
| e. Fire and casualty insurance | 3.1 | 3.0 | 3.5 | 5.1 | 6.3 | 8.0 | 10.0 | 11.6 | 15.0 | 17.0 | 19.2 | 21.3 | 23.7 | 24.0 |
| f. Other private insurance | 19.9 | 19.2 | 18.7 | 17.8 | 16.5 | 15.2 | 14.1 | 13.0 | 12.4 | 12.3 | 12.8 | 12.1 | 11.6 | 10.9 |
| g. Other finance | 5.5 | 7.0 | 6.5 | 7.4 | 6.4 | 7.6 | 8.4 | 5.7 | 8.7 | 5.6 | 6.0 | 4.8 | 5.8 | 5.1 |
| 4. State and local governments | 2.1 | 1.6 | 1.3 | 1.2 | 1.5 | 1.6 | 1.6 | 1.5 | 1.5 | 1.5 | 1.4 | 1.3 | 1.3 | 1.2 |
| 5. Federal government | 0.6 | 0.8 | 0.7 | 0.7 | 0.6 | 0.6 | 0.8 | 1.1 | 0.8 | 0.5 | 0.4 | 0.5 | 0.7 | 0.8 |
| 6. Total | 1.4 | 1.3 | 1.2 | 1.3 | 1.3 | 1.3 | 1.3 | 1.4 | 1.5 | 1.5 | 1.5 | 1.5 | 1.6 | 1.6 |

Source: National Balance Sheet, Vol. II, Tables III-1; III-4, III-5, 5b, 5c, 5d, 5h, 5i, 5k, 5m, III-6, III-7; line 6 from Table I.

TABLE 64

SHARE OF NET PURCHASES OF STATE AND LOCAL GOVERNMENT SECURITIES
IN TOTAL NET USES OF FUNDS OF SECTORS, 1946-58
(per cent)

| | 1946 | 1947 | 1948 | 1949 | 1950 | 1951 | 1952 | 1953 | 1954 | 1955 | 1956 | 1957 | 1958 |
|---|---|---|---|---|---|---|---|---|---|---|---|---|---|
| 1. Nonfarm households | -.4 | 1.0 | 2.3 | 1.4 | 0.7 | 0.5 | 1.8 | 2.3 | 1.0 | 2.0 | 1.9 | 2.5 | 1.7 |
| 2. Nonfinancial corporations | 0 | 0.1 | 0.2 | 0.3 | 0.2 | 0.1 | 0.2 | 0.3 | 1.0 | 0.3 | 0.2 | 0.3 | 0.4 |
| 3. Finance | 11.2 | 4.2 | 6.4 | 12.2 | 9.0 | 5.8 | 4.7 | 8.5 | 11.9 | 4.3 | 4.6 | 8.0 | 10.9 |
| a. Govt. insurance and pension funds | -2.7 | 2.6 | 4.3 | 8.3 | 14.5 | 1.7 | 3.0 | 7.1 | 11.5 | 10.5 | 11.2 | 15.8 | 37.4 |
| b. Commercial banks | -4.1 | 15.0 | -108.6 | 28.5 | 13.7 | 10.1 | 10.7 | 14.0 | 18.7 | 1.3 | 2.9 | 19.0 | 16.3 |
| c. Mutual savings banks | -1.7 | 0 | 1.0 | 2.0 | 0 | 6.1 | 9.6 | 4.7 | 8.9 | 2.0 | 1.5 | 0.5 | 1.9 |
| d. Life insurance | -3.0 | 0 | 6.9 | 4.5 | 2.3 | 0.5 | -0.4 | 2.9 | 10.2 | 3.4 | 4.0 | 2.0 | 5.4 |
| e. Fire and casualty insurance | 0 | 6.7 | 18.6 | 19.8 | 32.0 | 39.8 | 31.6 | 51.0 | 67.2 | 78.2 | 101.6 | 63.9 | 64.5 |
| f. Other private insurance | 8.3 | 10.5 | 0 | -4.3 | -6.8 | -5.4 | -2.8 | 4.3 | 11.3 | 19.8 | -1.7 | 45.5 | 1.7 |
| g. Other finance | 1.1 | 9.8 | 15.3 | -3.4 | 18.1 | 500.0 | -37.5 | 61.0 | -7.6 | 25.0 | 275.0 | 21.2 | 0 |
| 4. State and local governments | -5.6 | -1.1 | 0 | 4.3 | 3.9 | 1.4 | 1.1 | 0.8 | 0.2 | 0.4 | 0.6 | 0.5 | 0.3 |
| 5. Federal government | 0.1 | .3 | 1.3 | -3.7 | 0.8 | 3.2 | 9.7 | -8.4 | 45.8 | 0 | 14.5 | 13.2 | 9.1 |
| 6. Total | -0.2 | 1.1 | 2.0 | 2.7 | 1.9 | 1.5 | 2.1 | 2.4 | 2.7 | 1.7 | 1.7 | 2.5 | 2.9 |

Source: National Balance Sheet, Vol. II, Table VII-1, VII-4, VII-5, 5b, 5c, 5d, 5h, 5i, 5k, 5m, VII-6, and VII-7; line 6 from Table V.

## CHART 15

### MARKET FOR STATE AND LOCAL GOVERNMENT SECURITIES: SUPPLY AND ABSORPTION BY SECTOR, 1946–58

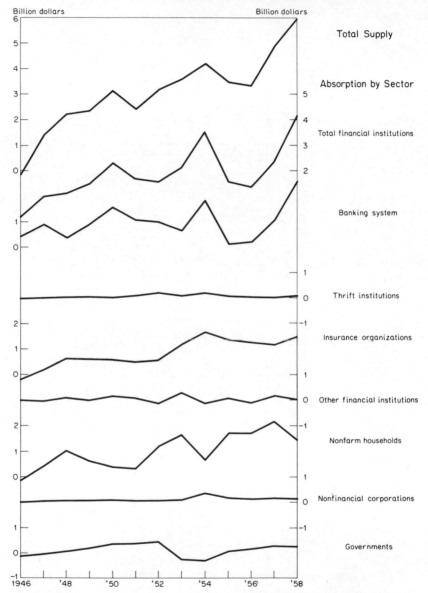

Source: *National Balance Sheet,* Vol. II, Tables VIII-c-12 and VIII-b-14.

1. A definite, although not rigid, relationship existed between new and net issues of state and local government securities, on the one hand, and the capital expenditures of state and local government, on the other (Table 59). Net new issues and total offerings of these securities amounted to about two-fifths and close to three-fifths, respectively, of the year's capital expenditures for the entire postwar period and for the first two cycles as well.

2. The increase in the volume of net issues of state and local government securities was considerably larger in Cycle II than in Cycle I and larger again, although by a smaller margin, in Cycle III than in Cycle II. The share of these securities in the net issuance of the five main types of capital market instruments taken together varied between one-fifth and one-seventh. However, their share in the ten capital market instruments was stable at almost one-tenth of the total for all three cycles (Table 43). Thus, if all ten capital market instruments are considered, the relative position of state and local government securities in the capital market was unchanged during the postwar period.

3. In absolute terms, net issues of state and local government securities were at their highest level in 1950, 1954, and 1958, i.e., in recession years or in the early stage of recovery (1950). They were low or declining in 1955–56 at the top of the business upswing. In relation to the total of the ten types of capital market instruments, net issues of state and local government securities were highest in 1948–49, 1953–54, and 1957–58 (Table 46). Here, the cyclically inverted relationship of net issues of state and local government securities to other important capital market instruments is even clearer.

4. While the amount of state and local government securities outstanding tripled from $20 to $60 billion between 1945 and 1958 (Table 61), the holdings of the main investor groups increased at different rates so that the distribution of holdings changed appreciably (Table 60). Nonfarm households held 56 per cent of the total outstanding at the beginning of the postwar period, but about 41 per cent at the end, most of the relative decline occurring in holdings outside of personal trust funds. Governmental holdings (excluding those in government insurance and pension funds) also declined from almost 10 per cent in 1945 to not much over 5 per cent in 1958. As a result, the share of financial institutions in total state and local government securities outstanding rose from one-third to one-half. Most of the increase was contributed by two groups: commercial banks, whose share

rose from less than 20 to more than 27 per cent, and fire and casualty insurance companies, whose share shot up from 1 to 10 per cent.

5. These differences in the rate of growth of holdings of various investor groups are clearly reflected in the changes in the distribution of net flows (i.e., net purchases and sales). Of total net purchases of $40 billion, households absorbed only approximately 30 per cent, compared to their share in holdings of over one-half at the beginning of the postwar period; governments absorbed 4 per cent, and nonfinancial corporations 3 per cent. This left more than 60 per cent of the net supply of state and local government securities to be absorbed by financial institutions, commercial banks alone taking more than 30 per cent and fire and casualty insurance companies 15 per cent (Table 61).

6. Compared to these differences, differences in the distribution among the main holder groups from one of the three postwar cycles to another were moderate. Thus, the share of all financial institutions together in the net supply of state and local government securities in the three cycles varied from 61 to 65 to 54 per cent. Variations were, of course, more pronounced for individual groups of financial institutions. Thus, the share of commercial banks declined from approximately two-fifths of the total in the first two cycles to only one-fifth in the third cycle, while that of fire and casualty insurance companies rose from one-twelfth in the first cycle to about one-sixth in the second and third cycles.

7. Further important differences exist in the annual distribution of net flows (Table 62). The share of absorption by financial institutions was highest in 1950–51, in 1954, and in 1958, i.e., during or close to recessions, and was lowest in 1948, 1952–53, and 1955–57 at the top of the upswings. The countercyclical behavior was most pronounced for commercial banks. The share of fire and casualty insurance companies, on the other hand, moved irregularly upward.

8. The reason for some of these changes in the net flows of funds in the market for state and local government securities are better observed in Table 63, which shows the share of these securities in total assets, and in Table 64, which provides the same information on the basis of total uses of funds.

9. For households, the proportion of state and local government securities in their total assets was low throughout the postwar period, varying only between 1.5 and 1.9 per cent. Similarly, the share of

these in total uses of funds was rather moderate. The relevant figures, however, are not those for all households together, but those for households with high income who are the buyers of state and local government securities. Unfortunately, figures are lacking to make the comparison separately for these households on an annual basis.

10. Among commercial banks, the share of state and local government securities in total assets showed a marked upward trend from 2½ per cent in 1945 to 7 per cent in 1958. In addition, Table 64 shows that there were countercyclical variations, increasing the share in 1949–50, 1953–54, and 1957–58, because state and local government securities become an attractive and important outlet for funds when the demand for commercial loans falls off, as happens during periods of recession. When the demand for commercial loans is strong, only a small proportion of the total increase in assets is invested in state and local government securities. Thus commercial banks used less than 5 per cent of total net funds for the increase of their portfolio of state and local government securities in 1955 and 1956, and only 10 per cent or less in 1951–52, compared to a period average of 16 per cent and ratios as high as 19 per cent in 1954 and 1957 and 28 per cent in 1949.

11. In the case of fire and casualty insurance companies, the rapid increase in the holdings of state and local government securities during the postwar period, which brought their share in total assets up from 3 to 24 per cent and absorbed about a third of the total uses of their funds, was primarily a substitution for Treasury securities, the holdings of which were sharply reduced in relative terms. The share of all government securities, remained close to one-half of total assets with only minor variations during the postwar period (see Tables 53 and 54).

12. State and local government securities became of growing importance for mutual savings banks, increasing their share in total assets from less than ½ per cent in the early postwar period to 2 per cent in 1954 and accounting for 5–9 per cent of total uses of funds during the years 1951–54. Since most mutual savings banks were subject to only very light income taxation, the reasons for this increase are not evident. (A large proportion of the securities in question may have been acquired by the minority of savings banks with capital accounts in excess of 12 per cent of deposits, for whom the tax-exemption privilege is of great value.)

## *Historical Background*

In the case of state and local government securities, it is particularly instructive to take a longer view and to look, even if only superficially, at the market before 1945.

The main difference between the market for these securities in the postwar period and that before 1940 is that the exemption from the federal income tax was of no value before World War I and was worth much less between the wars than it has been since World War II. This change is dramatically reflected both in the differences of the distribution of holdings of state and local government securities among the main sectors in the postwar period and earlier (Table 65 and Chart 16), and in the share of these securities in the assets of different holder groups (Table 66 and Chart 17).

Before World War I, when interest differentials may be regarded as the main influence, individuals held between one-fourth and one-third of all state and local government securities outstanding, financial institutions approximately two-fifths, and state and local governments (mostly in sinking and trust funds) more than one-fourth. The holdings of the latter group undoubtedly were not primarily determined by interest rate considerations, but rather were the result of inertia, lack of financial experience on the part of state and local government treasurers, and the desire to reserve funds for the use of one's own state or locality. Among financial institutions, mutual savings banks were by far the most important holders, but their share in the total of state and local government securities outstanding declined from almost 30 per cent in 1900 to less than 20 per cent before World War I. Commercial banks were also substantial holders of state and local government securities, accounting for about one-tenth of the total amount outstanding.

At the benchmark dates of 1929 and 1939, the share of the groups that could benefit substantially from tax exemption was considerably higher than in 1900 and 1912. Individuals now held more than two-fifths of the total amount outstanding, and it may be assumed that these holdings were increasingly concentrated in the hands of the individuals in higher income groups. Some evidence of such a trend is indicated by the increase in the share of state and local governments held by personal trust funds from less than one-tenth in 1900–12 to

TABLE 65

DISTRIBUTION OF STATE AND LOCAL GOVERNMENT SECURITIES
AMONG HOLDER GROUPS, 1900–58
(per cent)

| | 1958 (1) | 1945A (2) | 1945B (3) | 1939 (4) | 1929 (5) | 1912 (6) | 1900 (7) |
|---|---|---|---|---|---|---|---|
| 1. Nonfarm households | 40.6 | 56.3 | 43.6 | 41.9 | 45.3 | 32.8 | 25.9 |
| 2. Nonfinancial corporations | 2.7 | 1.5 | 1.7 | 1.9 | 3.8 | 2.3 | 2.5 |
| 3. State and local governments | 4.0 | 6.8 | 10.3 | 14.0 | 21.5 | 26.0 | 27.5 |
| 4. Federal government | 1.6 | 2.4 | 3.0 | 1.5 | 0 | 0 | 0 |
| 5. Financial institutions, total | 51.1 | 33.0 | 41.3 | 40.7 | 29.4 | 39.0 | 44.1 |
| a. Commercial banks | 27.0 | 18.8 | 25.0 | 17.7 | 12.2 | 11.9 | 9.0 |
| b. Mutual savings banks | 1.2 | 0.4 | 0.6 | 3.1 | 5.4 | 17.8 | 28.8 |
| c. Savings and loan associations | 0 | 0 | 0.2 | 0.1 | 0.2 | 0.1 | 0 |
| d. Life insurance | 4.4 | 3.4 | 4.5 | 8.9 | 3.4 | 4.1 | 3.5 |
| e. Fire and casualty insurance | 10.1 | 1.1 | 1.7 | 1.6 | 2.5 | 2.7 | 1.9 |
| f. Other private insurance | 0.7 | 1.7 | 2.3 | 2.7 | 2.9 | 2.2 | 0.6 |
| g. Government insurance and pension funds | 6.8 | 5.6 | 6.9 | 6.6 | 2.7 | 0.3 | 0.2 |
| h. Other finance | 1.0 | 1.9 | 0 | 0 | 0 | 0 | 0 |
| 6. Total | 100.0 | 100.0 | 100.0 | 100.0 | 100.0 | 100.0 | 100.0 |
| 7. Total (billion dollars) | 61.1 | 21.2 | 15.9 | 19.8 | 16.9 | 4.4 | 2.0 |

Source: National Balance Sheet, Vol. II; cols. 1–2 from Table IV-b-14; cols. 3–7 from Table IV-b-14a.

about one-fifth in 1929 and 1939.[8] The share of commercial banks in total state and local government securities outstanding increased slowly, while that of mutual savings banks fell rapidly, particularly between World War I and the 1920's.

CHART 16

DISTRIBUTION OF STATE AND LOCAL GOVERNMENT SECURITIES
AMONG MAIN HOLDER GROUPS, 1900–58

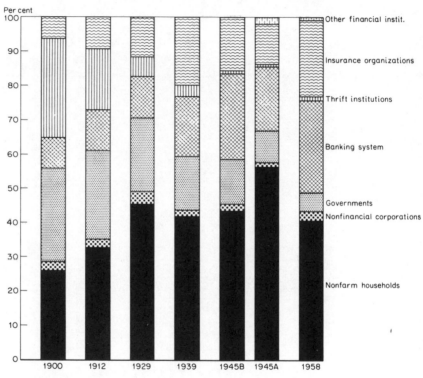

Source: Table 65.

The effects of tax exemptions on the distribution of state and local government securities outstanding are also reflected in the share of these securities in the portfolios of different investor groups. The share is higher for the two dates after tax exemption became valuable for households, personal trust funds, and commercial banks, while it is lower for state and local governments, government insurance and

[8] *Study of Saving,* Vol. III, Tables W-9, W-10, W-12, and W-14.

TABLE 66

SHARE OF STATE AND LOCAL GOVERNMENT SECURITIES IN TOTAL
ASSETS OF HOLDER GROUPS, 1900–58
(per cent)

| | 1958 (1) | 1945A (2) | 1945B (3) | 1939 (4) | 1929 (5) | 1912 (6) | 1900 (7) |
|---|---|---|---|---|---|---|---|
| 1. Nonfarm households | 1.5 | 1.9 | 1.1 | 2.2 | 1.7 | 1.2 | 0.8 |
| 2. Nonfinancial corporations | 0.2 | 0.1 | 0.1 | 0.2 | 0.3 | 0.2 | 0.1 |
| 3. State and local governments | 1.2 | 2.1 | 2.3 | 5.4 | 8.7 | 8.6 | 10.2 |
| 4. Federal government | 0.8 | 0.6 | 0.6 | 1.2 | 0 | 0 | 0 |
| 5. Financial institutions, total | 4.4 | 2.0 | 1.9 | 4.7 | 3.7 | 4.9 | 5.3 |
| a. Commercial banks | 6.8 | 2.5 | 2.5 | 5.3 | 3.1 | 2.4 | 1.8 |
| b. Mutual savings banks | 1.9 | 0.5 | 0.5 | 5.2 | 9.2 | 19.6 | 23.9 |
| c. Savings and loan associations | 0 | 0 | 0.4 | 0.2 | 0.4 | 0.3 | 0 |
| d. Life insurance | 2.5 | 1.6 | 1.6 | 6.0 | 3.3 | 4.2 | 4.1 |
| e. Fire and casualty insurance | 24.0 | 3.1 | 3.5 | 6.5 | 9.1 | 11.9 | 8.1 |
| f. Other private insurance | 10.9 | 19.9 | 21.8 | 43.2 | 56.7 | 58.5 | 52.0 |
| Fraternal orders | 14.9 | 21.7 | 22.6 | 44.2 | 57.2 | 58.5 | 52.0 |
| g. Government insurance and pension funds | 6.3 | 4.6 | 4.3 | 21.1 | 31.2 | 88.2 | 100.0 |
| h. Other finance | 5.1 | 5.5 | 0 | 0 | 0 | 0 | 0 |
| 6. Total | 1.6 | 1.4 | 1.0 | 2.3 | 1.7 | 1.4 | 1.3 |

Source: *National Balance Sheet*, Vol. II, unless otherwise specified.
Lines 1–5, 6: Tables I and Ia.
Lines 5a–5h, cols. 1–2: Tables III–5b throughIII–5m.
Lines 5a–5h, cols. 3–7: Numerators from Table IV–b–14a; denominators from *Financial Intermediaries*, Tables A–3, A–4, A–5, A–19, A–8, A–12, A–13, A– 9, A–14, and A–11.

CHART 17

SHARE OF STATE AND LOCAL GOVERNMENT SECURITIES
IN TOTAL ASSETS OF MAIN HOLDER GROUPS, 1900–58

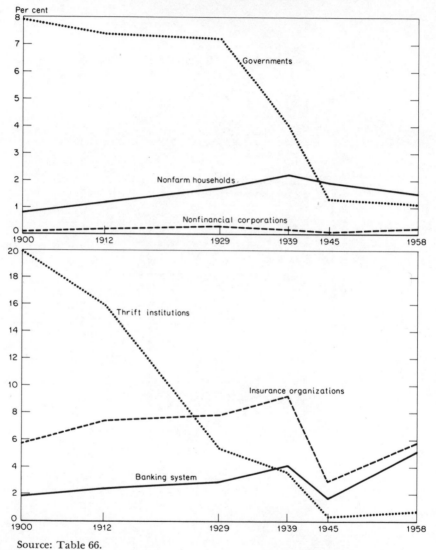

Source: Table 66.

pension funds, mutual savings banks, and (after 1929) fraternal orders —all holders not able to profit to a substantial extent from the tax-exemption privilege. One group for which the share of state and local government securities in total assets seems to move contrary to the presumed effects of tax exemption is property insurance companies. The increase between 1929 and 1939 of the proportion which state and local government securities constitute of the portfolio of life insurance companies, who benefit very little from tax exemption, seems to reflect the shortage of other outlets and the utilization of favorable investment opportunities in state and local government securities available during the Great Depression.

The structural changes in the market for state and local government securities before 1945 thus corroborate the effects of tax exemptions that have been observed for the postwar period. The decline in the share of these securities in the total assets of all holder groups between 1939 and 1945 is, of course, primarily a reflection of the decline in the total supply of these securities, together with a large increase in total assets caused by deficit financing by the federal government and repressed inflation during the war period. The joint effect of these forces can be seen in the decline in the ratio which state and local government securities constitute of total national assets, from 2.3 per cent in 1939 to 1.0 per cent in 1945, which followed a fairly regular increase from 1.3 to 2.3 per cent in the preceding forty years.

# CHAPTER 8

# The Market for Corporate Bonds

## *Character of the Market*

CORPORATE bonds constitute one of the major sectors of the American capital market. The total amount outstanding during the postwar period was larger than that of tax-exempt securities or preferred stock, although smaller than Treasury securities, residential mortgages, or common stock. The corporate bond market is characterized by the great variety of securities it covers, differing in maturity, callability, security, and convertibility, as well as in the variety of issuers, holders, and methods of distribution. Hence, general statements about corporate bonds are more difficult to make than for Treasury or state and local government securities.

1. While corporate bonds are issued for many purposes, their proceeds are used most commonly to defray fixed capital expenditures, then for the retirement of maturing or called bond issues, the repayment of other debt, and the financing of inventories and receivables, particularly bond issues of trade corporations and finance companies. The fluctuations in the volume of net corporate bond issues are therefore related primarily to those in business expenditures on structures and equipment.

The volume of offerings of corporate bonds and of the net change in corporate bonds outstanding depends partly on corporate expenditures on fixed capital, but the relationship is not a very close or invariable one. For the postwar period as a whole, aggregate offerings of bonds and notes by nonfinancial corporations (i.e., all corporations less those classified by the Securities and Exchange Commission as "financial and real estate") averaged one-fourth of their expenditures on fixed capital, while the net increase in bonds and notes outstanding was about one-sixth of fixed capital expenditures. The link between these two ratios is that the average net increase in bonded debt was three-fifths of new bond offerings; these ratios were very similar in Cycles II and III (Table 67).

2. Three main methods of bringing together the issuers and the buyers of corporate bonds were used on a large scale throughout the postwar period: negotiated public offerings, competitive public offerings, and direct placements. Public offering of corporate bonds acquired by investment bankers from the issuers as a result of competitive bidding was the prevalent method of distributing public utility (excluding telephone) bonds. The bonds of industrial, telephone, and railroad corporations, on the other hand, were distributed either by public offerings of issues acquired as a result of negotiations between the investment bankers and the issuers, or by direct placement, in which a small group of institutional investors acquires the securities directly from the issuer. Life insurance companies and, to a lesser extent, pension funds acquired most of the directly placed bonds. Public offerings were absorbed mostly by other institutional investors, although insurance companies and pension funds were important buyers also.

3. The distribution of corporate bond offerings among the main groups of issuers can be followed in Table 68, while Table 71 shows the share of directly placed bonds and notes for the same groups. Of total bond offerings of about $90 billion,[1] approximately 30 per cent each were issued by manufacturing companies and by electric and gas utilities. Communications, primarily the Bell system, accounted for 11 per cent and railroads for 6 per cent. The last fourth of corporate bond offerings was divided among finance companies, real estate corporations, and trade and miscellaneous corporations. The distribution of bond offerings among the main industries did not significantly differ from one cycle to the other (Table 68). Yet, as shown in Table 71, between 1949–54 and 1954–58 the share of privately placed bonds issued by the major industries, such as manufacturing, public utilities, and financial and real estate corporations, declined; as a result, the share of total bonds issued and privately placed was only 44 per cent in Cycle III compared to 52 per cent in Cycle II.

[1] *25th Annual Report,* SEC, p. 222.

TABLE 67

CORPORATE BOND ISSUES IN RELATION TO CAPITAL EXPENDITURE, 1946–58
(billion dollars)

| | Gross Issues | | | Net Issues | | | Gross Capital Expenditures of Nonfinancial Corporations | | |
| | Total (1) | Privately Placed (2) | Total Nonfinancial (3) | Total (4) | Nonfinancial Corp. (5) | Finance Companies (6) | Total (7) | Durable (8) | Inventory[a] (9) |
|---|---|---|---|---|---|---|---|---|---|
| 1946 | 4.72 | 1.86 | n.a. | 1.14 | .88 | .26 | 23.44 | 12.22 | 11.22 |
| 1947 | 5.02 | 2.15 | n.a. | 3.12 | 2.84 | .28 | 24.17 | 17.02 | 7.15 |
| 1948 | 5.94 | 3.01 | 5.50 | 4.81 | 4.23 | .58 | 23.74 | 19.53 | 4.21 |
| 1949 | 4.87 | 2.45 | 4.39 | 3.42 | 2.90 | .52 | 13.89 | 17.46 | -3.57 |
| 1950 | 4.81 | 2.56 | 4.28 | 2.03 | 1.61 | .42 | 28.75 | 18.98 | 9.77 |
| 1951 | 5.68 | 3.33 | 5.40 | 3.87 | 3.30 | .57 | 32.43 | 22.68 | 9.75 |
| 1952 | 7.34 | 3.96 | 6.99 | 5.26 | 4.72 | .54 | 24.77 | 23.52 | 1.25 |
| 1953 | 6.65 | 3.23 | 5.30 | 4.93 | 3.35 | 1.58 | 27.25 | 25.45 | 1.80 |
| 1954 | 7.83 | 3.48 | 7.14 | 3.73 | 3.54 | .19 | 23.13 | 24.73 | -1.60 |
| 1955 | 7.57 | 3.30 | 6.19 | 4.40 | 2.77 | 1.63 | 34.16 | 27.50 | 6.66 |
| 1956 | 7.93 | 3.78 | 6.59 | 4.86 | 3.67 | 1.19 | 40.73 | 33.15 | 7.58 |
| 1957 | 9.64 | 3.84 | 8.29 | 7.48 | 6.35 | 1.13 | 37.77 | 35.03 | 2.74 |
| 1958 | 9.67 | 3.32 | 8.91 | 5.93 | 5.92 | .01 | 25.10 | 29.54 | -4.44 |
| Annual averages | | | | | | | | | |
| 1946–49 | 5.25 | 2.44 | n.a. | 3.40 | 2.99 | .42 | 22.19 | 17.13 | 5.06 |
| 1949–54 | 6.17 | 3.21 | 5.55 | 3.93 | 3.24 | .69 | 26.34 | 22.35 | 4.00 |
| 1954–58 | 8.47 | 3.58 | 7.27[b] | 5.39 | 4.38 | 1.01 | 34.19 | 30.70 | 3.49 |
| 1946–58 | 6.74 | 3.10 | 6.27[b] | 4.23 | 3.54 | .68 | 27.64 | 23.60 | 4.04 |

Source

Col. 1: SEC mimeographed release, April 1, 1959, and April 1, 1961, "Net Change in Corporate Securities Outstanding,"
all industries.
Col. 2: SEC 25th Annual Report, p. 226.
Col. 3: Ibid., total excluding financial and real estate.
Col. 4: Sum of cols. 5 and 6.
Cols. 5–6: National Balance Sheet, Vol. II, Table VIII-c–12.
Col. 7: Sum of cols. 8 and 9.
Cols. 8–9: Ibid., Table VII-4.

[a]Inventory at book value.
[b]Annual average for 1948–58.

4. The cost of distribution was considerably lower for direct placements, in which the investment banking machinery is not involved, than for public offerings. In the latter case, the cost depended mainly on the size and the quality of the issue. In comparison to earlier periods and to other types of securities, the costs of distribution of corporate bonds were low, generally amounting to only 1 to 2 per cent

TABLE 68

DISTRIBUTION OF BOND OFFERINGS BY INDUSTRY DURING THE POSTWAR PERIOD[a]
(per cent)

|  | 1949-54 (1) | 1954-58 (2) | 1948-58 (3) |
|---|---|---|---|
| Manufacturing | 32 | 30 | 31 |
| Commercial and miscellaneous[b] | 7 | 7 | 7 |
| Electricity, gas, and water | 31 | 28 | 29 |
| Communication | 9 | 12 | 11 |
| Other transportation | 4 | 4 | 4 |
| Railroads | 7 | 5 | 6 |
| Financial and real estate (excluding investment companies) | 10 | 14 | 12 |
| All industries | | | |
| Per cent | 100 | 100 | 100 |
| Billion dollars per year | 6.31 | 8.49 | 7.16 |

Source: <u>Statistical Bulletin</u>, SEC. 1948-50: December 1951, p. 5; 1951-52: December 1953, p. 7; 1953-54: December 1955, p. 4; 1955-56: December 1957, p. 7; and 1957-58: December 1959, p.7.

[a]No industrial breakdown before 1948.

[b]The SEC included mining in this group prior to December 1953 and therefore mining was added to commercial and miscellaneous after 1953. (See <u>Statistical Bulletin</u>, SEC, December 1954, p. 4.) In this table this classification was continued through 1958 for the sake of comparability.

for medium-size or large offerings of high-grade securities; they were, however, considerably higher for small issues (see Table 69). In the case of direct placements, the small costs varied less with size or quality of the issue, but these differences were instead reflected in the interest rate and in indenture provisions.[2]

5. Most publicly offered corporate bonds have the form of issues with only one final maturity, commonly between fifteen and thirty years. A slight tendency toward lengthening final maturities was observed at least for industrial bonds; the average maturity rose from about eighteen years in the earlier part of the period to twenty-one

[2] For data, see *Cost of Flotation of Corporate Securities, 1951–1955*, SEC, Washington, 1957, and *Privately Placed Securities—Cost of Flotation*, SEC, Washington, 1952.

years in 1956–58. Public utility bonds usually had longer final maturities, averaging close to twenty-five years for direct placements and negotiated public offerings, and thirty years for issues sold by competitive bidding.[3] In most issues, particularly those placed directly, a substantial part of the principal is refunded before maturity through

TABLE 69

COST OF FLOTATION OF CORPORATE SECURITIES DURING THE POSTWAR PERIOD
(per cent of total proceeds)

| Size of Issue (million dollars) | Publicly Offered Securities, 1951, 1953, 1955 | | | Directly Placed Securities, 1947, 1949, 1950, Bonds, Notes, and Debentures (4) |
|---|---|---|---|---|
| | Bonds, Notes, and Debentures (1) | Preferred Stock (2) | Common Stock (3) | |
| Under 0.5 | | | 27.2 | 1.1 |
| 0.5 to 1 | 11.5 | 12.6 | 21.8 | 0.8 |
| 1 to 2 | 8.2 | 8.1 | 13.6 | 0.5[a] |
| 2 to 5 | 3.8 | 4.9 | 10.0 | 0.4[b] |
| 5 to 10 | 1.8 | 3.7 | 6.2 | 0.3 |
| 10 to 20 | 1.5 | 2.9 | 4.7 | 0.2[c] |
| 20 to 50 | 1.3 | 3.2 | 5.4 | } 0.2[d] |
| 50 and over | 1.2 | 2.5 | | |
| All sizes[e] | 1.5 | 4.3 | 10.3 | 0.5 |

Source

Cols. 1-3: *Cost of Flotation of Corporate Securities, 1951-1955*, SEC, p. 37.

Col. 4: *Privately Placed Securities--Cost of Flotation*, SEC, p. 23.

[a] Size of issue $1 to $3 million.

[b] Size of issue $3 to $5 million.

[c] Size of issue $10 to $25 million.

[d] Size of issue $25 million and over.

[e] Median values.

sinking-fund operations. The only important types of corporate bonds sold in serial form are railroad equipment trust certificates, but they constituted only about 4 per cent of total corporate bond gross issues during 1948–58.[4]

[3] A. B. Cohan, *Private Placements and Public Offerings: Market Shares Since 1935*, Chapel Hill, 1961, p. 29.

[4] For all corporate and railroad bonds issues, see *Statistical Bulletin*, SEC, March issues (e.g., March 1961, p. 8).

Railroad equipment trust certificates were computed as the difference between all bonds issued by railroads and railroad bonds excluding railroad equipment trust certificates (see Cohan, *Private Placements*, p. 8).

6. The size of corporate bond issues varied over a very wide range. On the average, private placements were considerably smaller than public offerings. For public utility bonds, the size of issues acquired by bankers through competitive bidding was usually higher than that of issues obtained through direct negotiation with the issuer. In 1958, for instance, the average size of directly placed issues of more than $1 million was about $6 million, and more than three-fourths of them fell between $1 and $5 million. On the other hand, only 6 per cent of the publicly offered issues were in the $1 to $5 million class, while 37 per cent exceeded $25 million, and the average size was $25 million. For industrial bonds (IFS category), the average size of privately placed issues was $8 million compared with an average size of $69 million for public offering.[5]

7. A considerable proportion of all corporate bonds is callable at the option of the issuer, beginning a few years after issuance and usually at small and declining premiums above issue price. This occurs because many institutional buyers, particularly life insurance companies, with long-term contracts embodying assumptions about average yield rates want to be protected against calls before maturity, which occur only when rates on new issues are low. There was a tendency to restrict callability as the capital market tightened during the latter half of the 1950's.

8. Virtually all transactions in corporate bonds occur in the over-the-counter market, the only exceptions being convertible bonds which resemble common stock. The volume of transactions in corporate bonds after issuance, however, is small. During the only period for which statistics are available, a few months in late 1949, the volume of over-the-counter and exchange transactions was equivalent only to an annual turnover rate of about 10 per cent of corporate bonds outstanding.[6] If this ratio applies to the whole period, the volume of secondary transactions in corporate bonds is below that of new offerings, in contrast to the situation in the markets for corporate stock or for government securities.

9. The yields of corporate bonds differ according to the size of the issue and the issuer, the type of security pledged, the industry of the issuer, the maturity of the bond and its quality rating, and possibly other factors.

[5] *Ibid.*, pp. 27 and 44–45.
[6] The figures on corporate bond sales are from Irwin Friend, *The Over-the-Counter Securities Markets,* New York, 1958, p. 119.

## Developments During the Postwar Period

Between the end of 1945 and the end of 1958 the volume of corporate bonds more than tripled, rising from $27 to $89 billion, an average increase of 9.5 per cent per year (Table 70 and Chart 18).[7] Cyclical variations were considerable, but intercyclical changes point toward an upward trend. The volume of new bond offerings, of course, was considerably higher because some of the new issues were used to retire outstanding issues. The ratio between net increase in bonds outstanding and bond offerings, however, was about two-thirds in all three cycles.[8]

### THE ROLE OF CORPORATE BONDS IN FINANCING
### NONFINANCIAL CORPORATIONS

Corporate bonds provided approximately one-tenth of total financing, over one-fifth of external financing, and over one-fourth of debt financing of nonfinancial corporations (Table 32). These ratios would be slightly higher if term loans by banks, particularly those with maturity of more than five years, were included. The relative importance of corporate bonds as a means of financing was fairly stable between the three cycles, particularly if bonds are related to total net sources of funds.

The share of bonds in total internal or debt financing, of course, varied considerably among industries and among corporations of different size or other characteristics. Bonds, for instance, were a much more important means of financing for electric and gas utilities than for industrial corporations, and for large than for small companies. Thus, for the period 1947–56 long-term debt provided about 14 per cent of the total funds of manufacturing and mining corporations, but supplied 34 per cent of the total funds of public utilities. On the other hand, trade corporations raised 6 per cent of their total funds through the issuance of long-term debt.[9] (The source does not permit separation of corporate bonds from other long-term liabilities of more than one year's maturity.) The share of corporate bonds in external financing amounted to somewhat less than two-fifths in manufactur-

---

[7] When figures for all corporate bonds are used, they include a relatively small amount of foreign government bonds.

[8] See Table 67, cols. 1 and 4.

[9] Figures from *Survey of Current Business*, various issues, e.g., September 1957, pp. 10–11.

TABLE 70

STRUCTURAL CHANGES IN OWNERSHIP OF CORPORATE BONDS DURING THE POSTWAR PERIOD

| | Outstandings (billion dollars) | | Aggregate Net Flows, 1946-58 (billion dollars) | NET FLOWS (ANNUAL AVERAGES) | | | | | |
| --- | --- | --- | --- | --- | --- | --- | --- | --- | --- |
| | | | | Amounts (billion dollars) | | | Distribution (per cent) | | |
| | 1945 (1) | 1958 (2) | (3) | Cycle I 1946-49 (4) | Cycle II 1949-54 (5) | Cycle III 1954-58 (6) | Cycle I 1946-49 (7) | Cycle II 1949-54 (8) | Cycle III 1954-58 (9) |
| 1. Nonfarm households | 9.29 | 11.12 | 1.83 | -0.66 | -0.15 | 1.27 | -18.4 | -3.6 | 19.5 |
| 2. Nonfinancial corporations | 0.18 | 2.68 | 2.50 | 0.12 | 0.19 | 0.33 | 3.4 | 4.5 | 5.1 |
| 3. Financial institutions, total | 17.70 | 74.30 | 56.60 | 4.05 | 4.10 | 4.93 | 113.1 | 97.9 | 75.6 |
| a. Government insurance and pension funds | 0.14 | 5.31 | 5.17 | 0.05 | 0.29 | 0.75 | 1.4 | 6.9 | 11.5 |
| b. Commercial banks | 2.96 | 3.52 | 0.56 | 0.04 | 0.02 | 0.04 | 1.1 | 0.5 | 0.6 |
| c. Mutual savings banks | 1.02 | 4.11 | 3.09 | 0.32 | 0.16 | 0.23 | 8.9 | 3.8 | 3.5 |
| d. Investment companies | 0.22 | 1.22 | 1.00 | 0 | 0.06 | 0.16 | 0 | 1.4 | 2.5 |
| e. Life insurance | 11.30 | 44.37 | 33.07 | 3.15 | 2.54 | 2.21 | 88.0 | 60.6 | 33.9 |
| f. Fire and casualty insurance | 0.46 | 1.48 | 1.02 | 0.09 | 0.09 | 0.06 | 2.5 | 2.1 | 0.9 |
| g. Noninsured pension plans | 0.78 | 12.44 | 11.66 | 0.32 | 0.84 | 1.40 | 8.9 | 20.0 | 21.5 |
| h. Other private insurance | 0.50 | 1.24 | 0.74 | 0.06 | 0.06 | 0.04 | 1.7 | 1.4 | 0.6 |
| i. Other finance | 0.32 | 0.61 | 0.29 | 0.03 | 0.03 | 0.04 | 0.8 | 0.7 | 0.6 |
| 4. State and local governments | 0.29 | 0.67 | 0.38 | 0.07 | 0.05 | 0 | 2.0 | 1.2 | 0 |
| 5. Total | 27.46 | 88.77 | 61.31 | 3.58 | 4.19 | 6.52 | 100.0 | 100.0 | 100.0 |

Source: National Balance Sheet, Vol. II; cols. 1-2 from Table IV-b-15; cols. 3-9 from Table VIII-b-15.
Note: Components may not add to totals because of rounding here and elsewhere in this chapter.

CHART 18

MARKET FOR CORPORATE BONDS: SUPPLY AND ABSORPTION
BY SECTOR, 1946–58

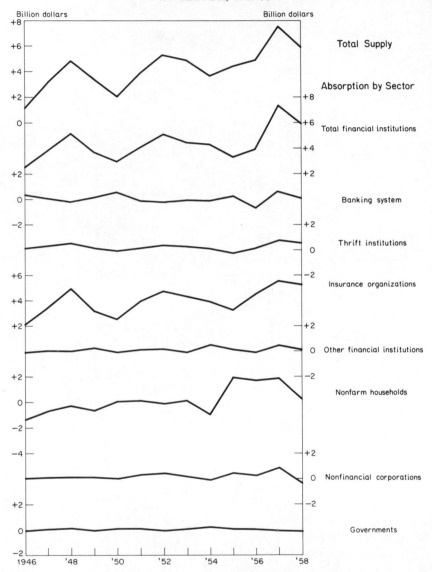

Source: *National Balance Sheet,* Vol. II, Tables VIII-b-15 and VIII-c-12.

ing and mining corporations, about one-half in public utilities, and 70 per cent in railroads, but less than 20 per cent in trade.

The difference in the share of corporate bonds in total and external financing are due to numerous factors: the character of the uses of funds, particularly the share of fixed capital expenditures against inventories and receivables; the character of the industry, particularly the stability of earnings and the influence of regulatory agencies. The main determinant appears to be the volume of fixed capital expendi-

TABLE 71

SHARE OF PRIVATELY PLACED CORPORATE SECURITIES[a]
IN TOTAL BOND OFFERINGS BY INDUSTRY, 1948-58
(per cent)

|  | 1949-54 | 1954-58 | 1948-58 |
|---|---|---|---|
| Manufacturing | 71 | 56 | 64 |
| Commercial and miscellaneous[b] | 88 | 68 | 77 |
| Electricity, gas, and water | 36 | 28 | 31 |
| Communication | 11 | 12 | 11 |
| Other transportation | 84 | 92 | 89 |
| Railroads | 4 | 3 | 3 |
| Financial and real estate | 77 | 63 | 71 |
| All industries | 52 | 44 | 48 |

Source: For numerator, 25th Annual Report, SEC, p. 226; for denominator, see source to Table 68.

[a]The numerators include a small amount of corporate stocks privately placed. The source does not provide a breakdown by industry between privately placed bonds and stocks.

[b]Includes extractive industry (see note b in Table 68).

tures, although corporate bond issues usually are considerably smaller than fixed capital expenditures. For all nonfinancial corporations together, corporate bonds provided about one-sixth of fixed capital expenditures during the postwar period, and changes in the ratio from cycle to cycle were moderate.

CHANGES IN METHOD OF MARKETING CORPORATE BONDS

The proportion of corporate bonds placed directly averaged about 45 per cent for the entire postwar period. It was highest at slightly above 50 per cent in Cycle II, the ratio for Cycle I being 47 per cent, and for Cycle III 44 per cent.[10] As can be seen from Table 71, most industrial subdivisions followed the main pattern, but the level of the share of private placements varied widely among industries. Of the two most important issuer groups, electric utilities had an average

[10] Cohan, *Private Placements,* pp. 6–8.

ratio of direct placements of about 30 per cent since many regulatory agencies prescribe offerings through competitive bidding, while bond offerings of manufacturing had an average ratio of almost two-thirds.

### CHANGE IN DISTRIBUTION OF HOLDINGS

The outstanding characteristic of the distribution of net purchases of corporate bonds during the postwar period is the dominance of financial institutions (see Table 70 for cycle averages and Tables 72 and 73 for annual data). While financial institutions absorbed only about three-fourths of the total increase in Cycle III, their purchases were virtually as large as or even larger than the entire increase in supply in Cycles I and II. In Cycle I the increase in holdings of financial institutions was higher than the rise in total corporate bonds outstanding so that all other holders together showed a net sales balance, even though the total supply of corporate bonds increased by about 50 per cent from 1945 to 1949. The share of financial institutions in the net issuance of corporate bonds, while remaining high throughout the postwar period, declined from cycle to cycle.

Among financial institutions, the insurance sector was the predominant buyer of corporate bonds, and here again private life insurance companies were the decisive factor. For the entire postwar period the increase in the holdings by life insurance companies amounted to slightly more than one-half of the total increase in corporate bonds outstanding. The addition of private and government pension and social insurance funds brings the share to four-fifths of the total, and to almost nine-tenths of the absorption of corporate bonds for all financial institutions. In comparison to the insurance sector, the net purchases of other financial institutions were relatively small. Mutual savings banks absorbed about 5 per cent of the total increase in corporate bonds outstanding during the postwar period. Net purchases by commercial banks were virtually nil, but consideration must be given to the fact that at least part of their term loans are very similar in character to directly placed corporate bonds, such as were purchased in large amounts by insurance organizations. If term loans with a maturity of more than five years are included, the share of commercial banks in the net issuance of corporate bonds would rise to about one-tenth of the total, which is still much lower than the purchases of life insurance companies and private pension plans.

The predominance of life insurance companies is most pronounced during Cycle I; their share remained high during Cycle II, but

## TABLE 72

### DISTRIBUTION OF DOMESTIC HOLDINGS OF CORPORATE BONDS, 1945-58
#### (per cent)

| | 1945 | 1946 | 1947 | 1948 | 1949 | 1950 | 1951 | 1952 | 1953 | 1954 | 1955 | 1956 | 1957 | 1958 |
|---|---|---|---|---|---|---|---|---|---|---|---|---|---|---|
| 1. Nonfarm households | 33.8 | 27.6 | 22.6 | 18.7 | 15.6 | 14.6 | 13.4 | 11.8 | 11.0 | 8.8 | 10.9 | 12.3 | 13.1 | 12.5 |
| 2. Nonfinancial corporations | 0.7 | 0.8 | 1.1 | 1.3 | 1.5 | 1.5 | 2.0 | 2.6 | 2.7 | 2.4 | 2.8 | 2.9 | 3.5 | 3.0 |
| 3. Finance | 64.5 | 70.6 | 75.3 | 78.7 | 81.6 | 82.6 | 83.3 | 84.6 | 85.2 | 87.4 | 85.0 | 83.6 | 82.4 | 83.7 |
| a. Govt. insurance and pension funds | 0.5 | 0.5 | 0.5 | 0.6 | 0.9 | 1.2 | 1.6 | 2.0 | 2.6 | 3.2 | 3.8 | 4.4 | 5.0 | 6.0 |
| b. Commercial banks | 10.8 | 11.5 | 10.5 | 8.5 | 8.2 | 9.0 | 7.9 | 6.7 | 5.9 | 5.3 | 5.2 | 4.0 | 4.2 | 4.0 |
| c. Mutual savings banks | 3.7 | 4.1 | 4.7 | 5.4 | 5.3 | 4.8 | 4.6 | 4.8 | 4.9 | 4.8 | 4.0 | 3.9 | 4.3 | 4.6 |
| d. Investment companies | 0.8 | 0.7 | 0.6 | 0.5 | 0.5 | 0.6 | 0.6 | 0.8 | 0.7 | 0.9 | 1.1 | 1.2 | 1.2 | 1.4 |
| e. Life insurance | 41.2 | 45.7 | 50.4 | 54.7 | 56.7 | 56.9 | 57.2 | 57.4 | 57.3 | 57.5 | 55.2 | 53.8 | 50.6 | 50.0 |
| f. Fire and casualty insurance | 1.7 | 1.6 | 1.6 | 1.9 | 1.9 | 1.9 | 1.8 | 2.0 | 2.0 | 1.9 | 1.8 | 1.7 | 1.7 | 1.7 |
| g. Noninsured pension plans | 2.8 | 3.6 | 4.2 | 4.6 | 5.0 | 5.7 | 7.0 | 8.3 | 9.5 | 10.9 | 11.3 | 12.6 | 13.2 | 14.0 |
| h. Other private insurance | 1.8 | 2.0 | 1.9 | 1.8 | 1.8 | 1.8 | 1.8 | 1.7 | 1.7 | 1.7 | 1.6 | 1.5 | 1.4 | 1.4 |
| i. Other finance | 1.2 | 0.8 | 0.8 | 0.7 | 1.1 | 0.8 | 0.8 | 0.8 | 0.6 | 1.1 | 1.0 | 0.6 | 0.9 | 0.7 |
| 4. State and local governments | 1.1 | 1.0 | 1.1 | 1.4 | 1.2 | 1.3 | 1.4 | 1.1 | 1.1 | 1.4 | 1.3 | 1.2 | 1.0 | 0.8 |
| 5. Total | 100.0 | 100.0 | 100.0 | 100.0 | 100.0 | 100.0 | 100.0 | 100.0 | 100.0 | 100.0 | 100.0 | 100.0 | 100.0 | 100.0 |
| 6. Total (billion dollars) | 27.46 | 28.69 | 32.01 | 37.21 | 40.42 | 43.49 | 47.99 | 53.23 | 58.04 | 61.50 | 67.24 | 73.02 | 82.92 | 88.77 |

Source: National Balance Sheet, Vol. II, Table IV-b-15.

TABLE 73

DISTRIBUTION OF DOMESTIC FLOW OF FUNDS, CORPORATE BONDS, 1946-58

(per cent)

| | 1946 | 1947 | 1948 | 1949 | 1950 | 1951 | 1952 | 1953 | 1954 | 1955 | 1956 | 1957 | 1958 |
|---|---|---|---|---|---|---|---|---|---|---|---|---|---|
| 1. Nonfarm households | -111.4 | -20.8 | -5.4 | -19.6 | 1.0 | 1.6 | -2.9 | 2.5 | -28.0 | 33.3 | 28.7 | 18.7 | 4.8 |
| 2. Nonfinancial corporations | 3.3 | 3.6 | 2.7 | 4.4 | 1.0 | 6.7 | 7.8 | 3.7 | -2.0 | 7.1 | 4.0 | 8.4 | -4.4 |
| 3. Finance | 207.3 | 116.0 | 99.4 | 115.6 | 96.1 | 89.6 | 96.4 | 92.7 | 124.3 | 58.9 | 67.1 | 73.9 | 101.7 |
| a. Government insurance and pension funds | 0 | 0.3 | 1.2 | 4.7 | 4.9 | 5.3 | 6.5 | 8.3 | 14.2 | 10.3 | 10.9 | 9.7 | 19.7 |
| b. Commercial banks | 28.5 | 1.8 | -3.8 | 4.7 | 18.9 | -2.9 | -4.2 | -2.5 | -4.0 | 4.2 | -11.1 | 6.1 | 0.5 |
| c. Mutual savings banks | 13.8 | 9.6 | 9.6 | 4.4 | -2.6 | 2.9 | 7.1 | 6.0 | 2.6 | -4.5 | 2.2 | 7.5 | 9.4 |
| d. Investment companies | -1.6 | -0.6 | 0.2 | 0.6 | 1.3 | 1.1 | 1.9 | 0.2 | 4.0 | 3.1 | 1.9 | 1.4 | 4.1 |
| e. Life insurance | 147.2 | 91.0 | 81.3 | 80.1 | 59.6 | 60.2 | 59.2 | 56.3 | 60.7 | 30.5 | 37.2 | 27.0 | 41.4 |
| f. Fire and casualty insurance | 0 | 1.8 | 3.3 | 2.8 | 1.6 | 1.1 | 3.1 | 2.5 | 0.9 | -0.2 | 0.5 | 1.8 | 1.5 |
| g. Noninsured pension plans | 21.1 | 9.3 | 6.7 | 10.6 | 14.3 | 19.6 | 20.2 | 22.2 | 35.0 | 15.9 | 27.5 | 17.5 | 25.8 |
| h. Other private insurance | 4.9 | 1.8 | 1.2 | 1.9 | 1.6 | 1.3 | 1.3 | 1.5 | 1.7 | 0.3 | 1.0 | 0.3 | 1.4 |
| i. Other finance | -6.5 | 0.9 | -0.2 | 5.9 | -3.6 | 0.9 | -1.3 | -1.9 | 9.2 | -0.7 | -3.1 | 2.7 | -2.1 |
| 4. State and local governments | 0.8 | 1.2 | 3.3 | -0.3 | 2.0 | 2.2 | -1.3 | 1.0 | 5.8 | 0.7 | 0.2 | -1.0 | -2.1 |
| 5. Total | 100.0 | 100.0 | 100.0 | 100.0 | 100.0 | 100.0 | 100.0 | 100.0 | 100.0 | 100.0 | 100.0 | 100.0 | 100.0 |
| 6. Total (billion dollars) | 1.23 | 3.32 | 5.20 | 3.21 | 3.07 | 4.50 | 5.24 | 4.81 | 3.46 | 5.74 | 5.78 | 9.90 | 5.85 |

Source: National Balance Sheet, Vol. II, Table VIII-b-15.

dropped markedly in Cycle III. Life insurance companies' purchases in Cycle III were also considerably below those in Cycles I and II in absolute figures. On the other hand, the contribution of private pension plans was more important in Cycle III than in Cycles I or II. In Cycle III the absolute volume of their net purchases equaled two-thirds of those of life insurance companies. The importance of state and local government insurance and pension funds increased rapidly during the postwar period until in Cycle III they had become the third most important buyers of corporate bonds. Insurance organizations were net buyers of corporate bonds in practically every year, as were on a smaller scale mutual savings banks, fire and casualty insurance companies, and investment companies. Commercial banks, on the other hand, shifted from net buying to selling in several years of upswing (1948, 1951, 1952, 1953, 1956), and also occasionally in recession years (1954).

CORPORATE BONDS IN THE ASSET STRUCTURE OF HOLDER GROUPS

A better understanding of some of the reasons for the changes in volume and distribution of the net flow of funds through corporate bonds can be obtained from Table 74, which shows holdings of corporate bonds as a percentage of total assets of the main investor groups, and Table 75, in which the net purchases of corporate bonds are expressed as percentages of the total net uses of funds by these sectors. It will be seen from these tables that, in relation to total uses, corporate bonds absorbed a larger amount of funds in the last year of cyclical upswings (1948, 1952, 1953, and 1957) than in the following years of recession or early upswing. The years 1948, 1953, and 1957 were periods of relatively high interest rates on corporate bonds and it is reasonable to assume that these interest rate differentials—in the case of financial institutions, particularly the difference between the more volatile yield on corporate bonds and the more sluggish interest rates on mortgages—were an important factor in the high share of corporate bonds in total uses of funds. There were, on the other hand, no great differences among cycles in the percentage of total funds invested in corporate bonds, the share being close to 3 per cent in all three cycles for all sectors of the economy taken together. In the case of all financial institutions, the proportion of total funds allocated to the net purchase of corporate bonds varied as a result of the considerable differences in the share of corporate bonds in the total supply of funds by different types of financial institutions. Corporate

TABLE 74

SHARE OF CORPORATE BONDS IN ASSETS OF EACH SECTOR, 1945-58

(per cent)

| | 1945 | 1946 | 1947 | 1948 | 1949 | 1950 | 1951 | 1952 | 1953 | 1954 | 1955 | 1956 | 1957 | 1958 |
|---|---|---|---|---|---|---|---|---|---|---|---|---|---|---|
| 1. Nonfarm households | 1.5 | 1.2 | 1.0 | 0.9 | 0.8 | 0.7 | 0.6 | 0.6 | 0.6 | 0.5 | 0.6 | 0.6 | 0.7 | 0.7 |
| 2. Nonfinancial corporations | 0.1 | 0.1 | 0.1 | 0.1 | 0.2 | 0.1 | 0.3 | 0.3 | 0.3 | 0.3 | 0.3 | 0.3 | 0.4 | 0.4 |
| 3. Finance | 5.0 | 5.7 | 6.4 | 7.4 | 8.1 | 8.3 | 8.6 | 9.0 | 9.5 | 9.6 | 9.5 | 9.7 | 10.4 | 10.6 |
| a. Government insurance and pension funds | 0.5 | 0.5 | 0.4 | 0.6 | 0.9 | 1.3 | 1.7 | 2.2 | 2.8 | 3.6 | 4.4 | 5.2 | 6.4 | 8.0 |
| b. Commercial banks | 1.8 | 2.2 | 2.2 | 2.0 | 2.1 | 2.3 | 2.1 | 1.9 | 1.8 | 1.6 | 1.7 | 1.3 | 1.5 | 1.5 |
| c. Mutual savings banks | 6.0 | 6.3 | 7.6 | 9.7 | 9.9 | 9.1 | 9.3 | 10.1 | 10.4 | 10.0 | 8.5 | 8.4 | 10.0 | 10.8 |
| d. Investment companies | 6.1 | 5.6 | 5.1 | 5.2 | 4.8 | 4.7 | 4.5 | 5.2 | 5.0 | 4.7 | 5.0 | 5.5 | 6.8 | 6.0 |
| e. Life insurance | 25.2 | 27.1 | 31.0 | 36.4 | 37.9 | 38.2 | 39.8 | 41.2 | 41.9 | 41.4 | 40.5 | 40.4 | 40.9 | 40.8 |
| f. Fire and casualty insurance | 6.0 | 5.7 | 5.6 | 6.7 | 6.5 | 6.3 | 6.1 | 6.5 | 6.6 | 5.9 | 5.4 | 5.3 | 6.1 | 5.8 |
| g. Noninsured pension plans | 29.1 | 32.0 | 34.6 | 37.4 | 38.9 | 39.9 | 43.1 | 46.4 | 48.0 | 46.8 | 43.9 | 45.9 | 49.1 | 44.7 |
| h. Other private insurance | 27.2 | 28.5 | 30.1 | 31.2 | 31.9 | 32.4 | 32.7 | 32.9 | 33.3 | 32.8 | 31.0 | 31.3 | 31.8 | 31.8 |
| i. Other finance | 4.4 | 4.4 | 5.8 | 5.0 | 7.8 | 5.2 | 5.8 | 6.4 | 4.8 | 7.3 | 6.7 | 4.8 | 7.0 | 5.2 |
| 4. State and local governments | 0.4 | 0.4 | 0.3 | 0.5 | 0.5 | 0.5 | 0.5 | 0.4 | 0.5 | 0.6 | 0.5 | 0.5 | 0.4 | 0.3 |
| 5. Total | 1.8 | 1.7 | 1.7 | 1.9 | 2.0 | 1.9 | 2.0 | 2.1 | 2.2 | 2.2 | 2.2 | 2.2 | 2.4 | 2.4 |

Source: National Balance Sheet, Vol.II, Tables III-1, III-4, III-5, 5-b, 5c, 5d, 5f, 5h, 5i, 5j, 5k, 5m, III-6; line 5 from Table I.

TABLE 75

SHARE OF NET PURCHASES OF CORPORATE BONDS IN TOTAL NET USES OF FUNDS OF SECTORS, 1946-58
(per cent)

| | 1946 | 1947 | 1948 | 1949 | 1950 | 1951 | 1952 | 1953 | 1954 | 1955 | 1956 | 1957 | 1958 |
|---|---|---|---|---|---|---|---|---|---|---|---|---|---|
| 1. Nonfarm households | -3.6 | -1.7 | -0.7 | -1.5 | 0.1 | 0.1 | -0.2 | 0.2 | -1.4 | 2.2 | 1.9 | 2.2 | 0.3 |
| 2. Nonfinancial corporations | 0.2 | 0.4 | 0.5 | 0.8 | 0.1 | 0.7 | 1.3 | 0.6 | -0.2 | 0.7 | 0.5 | 1.7 | -0.7 |
| 3. Finance | 159.4 | 16.5 | 30.0 | 30.4 | 11.6 | 14.0 | 15.5 | 17.8 | 14.7 | 9.3 | 12.8 | 25.2 | 15.8 |
| a. Govt. insurance and pension funds | 0 | 0.3 | 1.7 | 5.9 | 11.5 | 5.9 | 7.8 | 11.8 | 18.2 | 18.2 | 17.6 | 33.7 | 93.5 |
| b. Commercial banks | -3.3 | 1.0 | 57.1 | 4.8 | 5.1 | -1.2 | -2.4 | -2.7 | -1.5 | 2.8 | 9.2 | 11.2 | 0.2 |
| c. Mutual savings banks | 9.9 | 31.7 | 50.0 | 13.7 | -8.7 | 13.1 | 20.9 | 15.2 | 4.2 | -12.9 | 6.4 | 40.2 | 21.0 |
| d. Investment companies | -16.7 | -9.5 | 6.2 | 7.7 | 14.3 | 20.0 | 19.2 | 2.4 | 31.8 | 21.2 | 15.5 | 14.7 | 18.0 |
| e. Life insurance | 48.9 | 83.7 | 112.8 | 64.9 | 42.2 | 64.1 | 62.8 | 52.3 | 38.8 | 31.2 | 37.3 | 49.3 | 43.8 |
| f. Fire and casualty insurance | 0 | 5.0 | 15.0 | 8.1 | 5.2 | 5.1 | 12.0 | 8.2 | 2.6 | -1.0 | 4.8 | 18.6 | 8.2 |
| g. Noninsured pension plans | 45.4 | 47.8 | 54.3 | 48.0 | 45.3 | 60.7 | 66.4 | 54.8 | 59.6 | 43.9 | 61.0 | 60.0 | 49.2 |
| h. Other private insurance | 53.7 | 54.0 | 56.3 | 44.0 | 38.6 | 37.4 | 37.6 | 39.8 | 26.7 | 7.6 | 37.0 | 84.8 | 34.4 |
| i. Other finance | 4.4 | -3.7 | -1.7 | 32.8 | -15.3 | 400.0 | 17.5 | -22.0 | 18.7 | -20.0 | 450.0 | 40.9 | -7.2 |
| 4. State and local governments | 0.4 | 0.9 | 3.2 | -0.2 | 0.8 | 1.2 | -0.7 | 0.4 | 1.6 | 0.3 | 0.1 | -0.7 | -0.8 |
| 5. Total | 2.1 | 2.7 | 4.6 | 3.6 | 1.9 | 2.7 | 3.5 | 3.2 | 2.2 | 2.7 | 2.9 | 5.0 | 2.9 |

Source: National Balance Sheet, Vol. II, Tables VII--, VII-4, VII-5, 5b, 5c, 5d, 5f, 5h, 5i, 5j, 5k, 5m, VII-6; line 5 from Table V.

223

bonds were very important for life insurance companies and private pension funds. The share of corporate bonds in total net uses of private noninsured pension funds averaged over one-half for the entire period. For other financial institutions, the net acquisition of corporate bonds was important but more erratic. In the case of mutual savings banks, net purchases of corporate bonds averaged 15 per cent of total uses for the entire period, but ranged from negative values in two early years of upswing (1950, 1955) to more than 30 per cent in three later years of cyclical rise (1947, 1948, 1957). Fire and casualty insurance companies invested relatively most heavily in corporate bonds in the middle or later years of upswings (1948, 1952, 1957) and least heavily in recessions and in early upswing years (1946–47, 1949–50, 1954–56), but did not show a net sales balance in corporate bonds during any year except 1955. Commercial and mutual savings banks showed a more erratic behavior. Mutual savings banks allocated a considerable proportion of total net uses of funds to corporate bonds in the later phases of upswings (1947–48, 1952–53, 1957), but on balance sold corporate bonds in only two years (1950, 1955). Commercial banks reduced their holdings of corporate bonds in about as many years as they increased them. In relation to total net uses, the purchases were substantial only in three years (1957, 1950, 1949), while sales occurred mostly in the later phases of cyclical upswings, being particularly large in relation to total net uses of funds in 1948 [11] and 1956.

## Historical Background

A comparison of the market for corporate bonds in the postwar period with that in the preceding half century, particularly from 1900 to 1929, shows that the main structural changes occurred in the distribution of the bonds among the main investor groups, in the methods of marketing them, and in the distribution of the issuance of the bonds among the main industries. Changes in the characteristics of corporate bonds (such as maturity, security, and callability), in the role of corporate bonds as a source of finance, and in the cyclical behavior of new issues, retirements, and interest rates have been less pronounced.

1. The change in the distribution of corporate bonds outstanding between the postwar and the predepression periods is characterized

---

[11] Both net uses of funds and net bond purchases were negative in 1948 (i.e., they represented net sales of assets) and hence the ratio was positive (Table 75).

by a far-reaching shift toward institutional holdings accompanied by a substantial reduction of individuals' holdings.[12] As Table 76 and Chart 19 show, individuals accounted for nearly two-thirds of all corporate bonds outstanding at the three benchmark dates of 1900, 1912, and 1929. Hence individuals also may be assumed to have absorbed about two-thirds of all new issues of corporate bonds during these thirty years. Even as late as 1939, individuals still held more than one-half of all corporate bonds outstanding, although the absolute amounts were considerably lower than ten years earlier, while the holdings by financial institutions had increased. This situation is in sharp contrast to the rapid decline during the postwar period of individuals' holdings.

The distribution of holdings of corporate bonds among financial institutions also shows considerable differences between the predepression and the postwar periods. In 1900, 1912, and 1929 commercial banks held more corporate bonds than life insurance companies, although there was a slight tendency for the latter to increase relative to the former. During the postwar period on the other hand, the holdings of life insurance companies rose from almost four to twelve times those of commercial banks. As a result, the holdings of commercial banks declined between 1945 and 1958 from about one-sixth to one-twentieth of institutional holdings of all financial institutions.[13] Mutual savings banks and fire and casualty insurance companies also were more important among financial institutions as holders of corporate bonds during the predepression than during the postwar period, but the difference was less pronounced than for commercial banks. The outstanding change, however, occurred in the role of life insurance organizations. While they had held only about one-eighth of total amounts outstanding and one-third of total institutional holdings of corporate bonds in 1900, 1912, and 1929, their share in the postwar period rose to two-fifths of total outstandings in 1945 and to one-half in 1958, and they accounted for three-fifths of institutional holdings of corporate bonds.

[12] Actually a residual, the difference between estimated total bonds outstanding and reported or estimated institutional holdings.

[13] The decline in the share of holdings would be partly offset if allowance were made for the holdings by commercial banks of term loans, particularly loans of more than five years' maturity which expanded considerably during the postwar period. Even if these loans are included (*Federal Reserve Bulletin*, April 1959, p. 358), commercial banks in 1958 held only a little over one-tenth of all bonds and term loans of more than five years.

TABLE 76

DISTRIBUTION OF CORPORATE BONDS AMONG HOLDER GROUPS, 1900–58

(per cent)

| | 1958 (1) | 1945A (2) | 1945B (3) | 1939 (4) | 1929 (5) | 1912 (6) | 1900 (7) |
|---|---|---|---|---|---|---|---|
| 1. Nonfarm households | 12.5 | 33.8 | 37.7 | 51.8 | 63.2 | 65.3 | 64.5 |
| 2. Nonfinancial corporations | 3.0 | 0.7 | 0 | 1.4 | 0 | 0 | 0 |
| 3. State and local governments | 0.8 | 1.1 | 0 | 0 | 0 | 0 | 0 |
| 4. Federal government | 0 | 0 | 0 | 2.6 | 0 | 0 | 0 |
| 5. Financial institutions, total | 83.7 | 64.5 | 62.3 | 45.2 | 35.3 | 34.7 | 35.5 |
| a. Commercial banks | 4.0 | 10.8 | 11.0 | 10.5 | 12.4 | 13.9 | 13.1 |
| b. Mutual savings banks | 4.6 | 3.7 | 3.6 | 4.2 | 5.3 | 6.7 | 8.6 |
| c. Investment companies | 1.4 | 0.8 | 0.9 | 0.4 | 0.3 | | |
| d. Life insurance | 50.0 | 41.2 | 38.9 | 25.5 | 12.2 | 11.0 | 10.6 |
| e. Noninsured pension plans | 14.1 | 2.8 | 4.0 | 1.8 | 0.8 | | |
| f. Fire and casualty insurance | 1.7 | 1.7 | 1.5 | 2.0 | 3.3 | 2.4 | 2.2 |
| g. Other private insurance | 1.4 | 1.8 | 1.8 | 0.5 | 0.2 | 0.1 | 0 |
| h. Government insurance and pension funds | 6.0 | 0.5 | 0.5 | 0.2 | 0 | | |
| i. Brokers and dealers[a] | 0.7 | 1.2 | 0.2 | 0.2 | 0.7 | 0.7 | 1.0 |
| 6. Total | 100.0 | 100.0 | 100.0 | 100.0 | 100.0 | 100.0 | 100.0 |
| 7. Total (billion dollars) | 88.8 | 27.5 | 25.9 | 32.5 | 38.1 | 14.5 | 5.2 |

Source: National Balance Sheet, Vol. II, Table IV-b-15 and IV-b-15a.
See note to Table 55.

[a]Cols. 1-2 include both incorporated and unincorporated brokers and dealers. Cols. 3-7 include unincorporated only.

These changes in the distribution of holdings reflect partly the changed position of corporate bonds among the assets of different investor groups, which can be followed in Table 77 and Chart 20, and partly differences in the rate of growth of total assets of different

CHART 19

DISTRIBUTION OF CORPORATE BONDS AMONG MAIN
HOLDER GROUPS, 1900–58

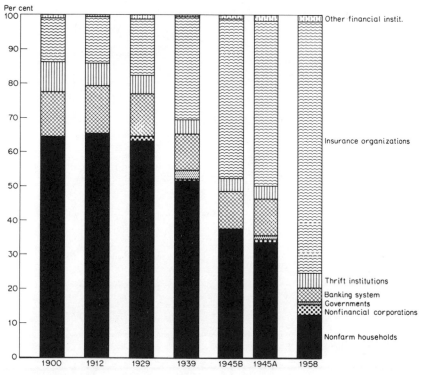

Source: Table 76.

investor groups. The share of corporate bonds in individual's total assets declined considerably from the predepression to the postwar period. There was no great difference in the relative importance of corporate bonds in 1958 and in the predepression period for all financial institutions together—particularly if allowance is made for longer bank term loans, but very substantial differences appear if attention is turned to individual institutions.

TABLE 77

SHARE OF CORPORATE BONDS IN TOTAL ASSETS OF HOLDER GROUPS, 1900-58

(per cent)

|  | 1958 (1) | 1945A (2) | 1945B (3) | 1939 (4) | 1929 (5) | 1912 (6) | 1900 (7) |
|---|---|---|---|---|---|---|---|
| 1. Nonfarm households | 0.7 | 1.5 | 1.5 | 4.5 | 5.4 | 7.9 | 5.4 |
| 2. Nonfinancial corporations | 0.4 | 0.1 | 0 | 0.1 | 0.2 | 0 | 0 |
| 3. State and local governments | 0.3 | 0.4 | 0 | 0 | 0 | 0 | 0 |
| 4. Federal government | 0 | 0 | 0 | 3.4 | 0.2 | 0 | 0 |
| 5. Financial institutions, total | 10.6 | 5.0 | 4.7 | 8.5 | 10.2 | 14.1 | 10.8 |
| a. Commercial banks | 1.5 | 1.8 | 1.8 | 5.2 | 7.1 | 9.3 | 6.7 |
| b. Mutual savings banks | 10.8 | 6.0 | 5.5 | 11.6 | 20.4 | 24.1 | 18.3 |
| c. Investment companies | 6.0 | 6.1 | 8.6 | 8.0 | 4.4 |  |  |
| d. Life insurance | 40.8 | 25.2 | 22.5 | 28.3 | 26.7 | 36.1 | 31.4 |
| e. Noninsured pension plans | 44.7 | 29.1 | 36.0 | 55.0 | 60.0 |  |  |
| f. Fire and casualty insurance | 5.8 | 6.0 | 4.9 | 13.6 | 27.0 | 35.0 | 22.9 |
| g. Other private insurance | 31.8 | 27.2 | 26.7 | 12.1 | 8.6 | 7.3 | 4.0 |
| h. Government insurance and pension funds | 8.0 | 0.5 | 0.5 | 0.9 | 1.2 |  |  |
| i. Brokers and dealers[a] | 5.7 | 5.9 | 2.0 | 3.3 | 3.3 | 10.0 | 9.1 |
| 6. Total | 2.4 | 1.8 | 1.7 | 3.8 | 3.9 | 4.7 | 3.3 |

Source: *National Balance Sheet*, Vol. II, unless otherwise specified.

Lines 1-5: Tables I and Ia.

Lines 5a-5h, cols. 1-2: Tables III-5a through III-5*l* and Table III-5m-1.

Lines 5a-5h, cols. 3-7: Numerators from Table IV-b-15a; denominators from *Financial Intermediaries*, Tables A-3, A-4, A-5, A-21, A-8, A-10, A-12, A-13, A-9, A-14, and A-11.

Line 5i: *A Study of Saving*, Vol. III, Table W-37.

Line 6: Tables I and Ia.

[a]Cols. 1-2 include both incorporated and unincorporated brokers and dealers. Cols. 3-7 include unincorporated only.

See note to Table 55.

## Market for Corporate Bonds

CHART 20

SHARE OF CORPORATE BONDS IN TOTAL ASSETS
OF MAIN HOLDER GROUPS, 1900–58

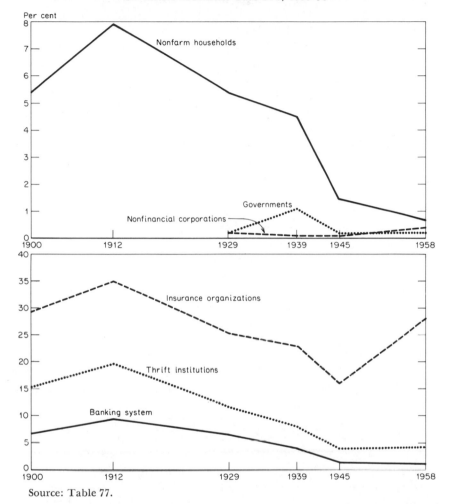

Source: Table 77.

In the case of commercial banks, the decline in their share in total corporate bonds outstanding was due largely to a reduction in the proportion of their total assets invested in corporate bonds. Inclusion of term loans would, however, considerably reduce the difference, for a substitution of term loans for corporate bonds occurred rather than a reduction in the share of all long-term advances to corporate business in the assets of commercial banks. The increasing importance of life insurance companies as holders of corporate bonds, on the other hand, is due mostly to the rapid growth of total assets of these institutions and only secondarily to the increased allocation of funds to corporate bonds. The 1958 share was considerably higher than the shares of 1929 and 1945, but was not much above the proportion before World War I. Mutual savings banks, fire and casualty insurance companies, and investment companies showed a considerably lower share of corporate bonds in total assets in the postwar than in the predepression or prewar period. On the other hand, corporate bonds were much less important in the portfolios of "other private insurance" in the predepression period than after World War II. In a few investor groups corporate bonds, while still representing only a relatively small proportion of total assets, were essentially introduced after World War II, particularly state and local governments and their pension and insurance funds.

The second major difference between the postwar and prewar periods is the much greater importance of railroad bonds compared to public utility, and particularly to industrial bonds, in the prewar period. The decline in the share of railroad issues, however, was already evident during the prewar period, foreshadowing their precipitous decline in 1958 (see Table 78). The share of railroads in net new corporate bond issues showed the same movement in still more pronounced form falling from almost one-half in 1900–12 to about one-fifth in 1913–29, and almost to zero in the postwar period.[14]

2. The combination of the shift from railroad to public utility and industrial bonds and from scattered individual to relatively concentrated institutional holdings resulted in considerable differences in the methods used in offering and marketing corporate bonds. Before 1929, public offering by groups of investment bankers on the basis of direct negotiation with the issuers was predominant. Direct placements were virtually unknown and competitive bidding rare except for railroad equipment trust certificates. This difference was accompanied by considerably higher costs of offerings before the 1930's, reflecting the much smaller average amount per sale and the reliance on retail bond salesmen. Thus publicly offered larger corporate bond issues ($5 million or over) in the postwar period carried an invest-

---

[14] *A Study of Saving,* Vol. I, Table V-15, and David Meiselman and Eli Shapiro, *The Measurement of Corporate Sources and Uses of Funds,* Technical Paper 18, New York, NBER, 1964, Table C-23.

ment banking compensation of less than 1 per cent [15] compared to a spread of 3 to 5 per cent for similar offerings in the 1920's. The predominantly retail market of the first three decades of the century thus contrasts sharply with the wholesale market for corporate bonds of the postwar period.

TABLE 78

DISTRIBUTION OF NONFINANCIAL CORPORATE BONDS OUTSTANDING BY INDUSTRY, 1900-58

|   |   | 1900 (1) | 1912 (2) | 1929 (3) | 1939 (4) | 1945 (5) | 1950 (6) | 1958 (7) |
|---|---|---|---|---|---|---|---|---|
|   |   | BILLIONS DOLLARS | | | | | | |
| 1. | Railroads | 5.2 | 9.8 | 12.3 | 11.9 | 10.2 | 10.2 | 10.2 |
| 2. | Public utilities[a] | 1.3 | 5.0 | 11.5 | 11.7 | 10.3 | 17.4 | 33.9 |
| 3. | Industrial and other[b] | 0.4 | 2.6 | 6.2 | 4.0 | 3.0 | 8.1 | 25.0 |
| 4. | Total | 6.9 | 17.4 | 30.0 | 27.6 | 23.5 | 35.7 | 69.1 |
| 5. | Real estate | 0 | 0.1 | 6.2 | 3.0 | 1.9 | 0 | 0 |
|   |   | PER CENT | | | | | | |
| 6. | Railroads | 75 | 56 | 41 | 43 | 43 | 28 | 15 |
| 7. | Public utilities[a] | 19 | 29 | 38 | 42 | 44 | 49 | 49 |
| 8. | Industrial and other[b] | 6 | 15 | 21 | 14 | 13 | 23 | 36 |
| 9. | Total | 100 | 100 | 100 | 100 | 100 | 100 | 100 |

Source

Cols. 1-6: W. B. Hickman, <u>Trends and Cycles in Corporate Bond Financing</u>, New York, NBER Occasional Paper 37, 1952, p. 33.
Col. 7: Extrapolation of col. 6 on the basis of SEC mimeographed releases of April 1, 1959, and April 1, 1961, "Net Change in Corporate Securities Outstanding."
Line 5: <u>Study of Saving</u>, Vol. I, Table R-40.

[a] Consists of the following two components: electricity, gas, and water; and communications.

[b] Consists of manufacturing, extractive, commercial, and miscellaneous, and other transportation.

3. We close with a brief look backward at what may be regarded as the most important point, the share of corporate bonds in financing corporations of different type. Unfortunately the material permits only very approximative statements and limits them to all nonfinancial corporations taken together and a few of their major subgroups.

For all nonfinancial corporations, the importance of corporate bonds as a source of funds appears to have been much the same in the predepression period as it was in the postwar period. The sources underlying Table 37 show this share to have declined from 20 per cent in

[15] *Cost of Flotation of Corporate Securities, 1951–1955*, SEC, Washington, 1957, p. 38.

1901–12 and 14 per cent in 1923–29 to 10 per cent in 1945–58. The difference would be reduced, possibly by about 2 per cent, if allowance were made for term loans of more than five years by commercial banks.

While this similarity in the role of corporate bonds in providing funds may hide important differences in size or other characteristics among industries and among corporations, this does not seem to be the case in the only direction in which at least rough comparisons can be made between the predepression and the postwar periods, that is, the share of corporate bonds in total sources of funds of railroads, electric light and power companies, and industrial and manufacturing corporations, which together account for the bulk of corporate bonds issued.

Among manufacturing and mining corporations, bonds accounted for 12 per cent of internal financing plus net sales of securities in 1900–14 and 5 per cent in 1919–29 against a share of 10 per cent in 1946–53.[16] The difference is even smaller for electric light and power utilities. In this industry bonds supplied about 40 per cent of all net funds for 1881–1937,[17] compared to a share of about 32 per cent in 1950–55 for electric and gas corporations,[18] so that there is hardly any difference if allowance is made for bank term loans. In the case of railroads, on the other hand, the role of corporate bonds declined considerably. Here bonds predominated among sources of funds until World War I and still accounted for more than one-third in 1914–30,[19] but their contribution to total net funds was very small in the postwar period.

Hence, corporate bonds (including bank term loans of over five years' inactivity) played about the same role, notwithstanding many changes in detail, in total and in external financing of corporations in the postwar period as during the generation before the Great Depression; but great changes occurred in the distribution of corporate bonds among issuers, the share of industrials increasing at the ex-

---

16 Daniel Creamer, Sergei Dobrovolsky, and Israel Borenstein, *Capital in Manufacturing and Mining*, Princeton for NBER, 1960, pp. 121, 331–332. Figures for long-term external financing other than bonds and for short-term financing are not given in the source and are not easily obtainable elsewhere.

17 Melville J. Ulmer, *Capital in Transportation, Communications, and Public Utilities*, Princeton for NBER, 1960, p. 151.

18 Meiselman and Shapiro, *Measurement of Corporate Sources and Uses of Funds*, Table 9.

19 Ulmer, *Capital in Transportation*, p. 150.

pense of railroads; in the distribution among investor groups, financial institutions, particularly insurance organizations, almost entirely supplanting individual holders; and in market techniques, direct placement and competitive bidding acquiring equal importance with negotiated public offerings. Another important change, which has not been documented here, is the increasing flexibility of corporate bonds as instruments of financing. This is evidenced in a wider range of maturity, security, and callability provisions and an increasing ease of modifying original bond indenture provisions, all contributing to adapting corporate bonds to the specific needs of individual borrower and lender groups.

# CHAPTER 9

# The Market for Corporate Stock

THE market for corporate stock, particularly that for common stock issues, is of crucial importance for the American capital market and for the entire economy. Since equities in unincorporated business are not marketable, common stock, apart from some instruments which resemble common stock in certain respects (such as some convertible bonds, preferred stocks, and some junior mortgages), is the only instrument through which a large number of investors can participate in the external equity financing of enterprises they do not operate, or in supplying what has been called "venture" capital. Careful analysis of the market for common stock and the flow of funds through common stock is also necessary because the statistics are less satisfactory and more open to misunderstanding than those for most other sectors of the capital market.[1]

With few exceptions, this chapter will deal only with common stock. Preferred stock was relatively important in an earlier period of corporate finance and, while still not negligible in a few industries, it now represents only a small percentage of the market value of all stocks. It is, however, more important when measured by the amount of corporate stock issued in the postwar period. The tables, therefore, provide information for all corporate stock as well as for common stock alone, so that the data for preferred stock can be obtained by subtraction.

## Character of the Market

The market for common stock in the postwar period is characterized by two outstanding features: first, the small amount of new common

[1] Background data on stock prices, yields, and trading will be found in Table 93.

stock issues compared to the issuance of other capital market instruments, to the volume of internal and external finance of corporations, to the value of common stock outstanding, and to the total assets of most investor groups; and second, the large amount of trading in common stock, with a resulting shift in the portfolios of the different investor groups that were substantial and of considerable importance for the smooth functioning of the capital market.

Measured by the value of capital market instruments outstanding and by the volume of trading, the market for common stock in the postwar period constituted the largest sector of the American capital market. It is marked by extreme variety in the size, quality, trading, and price behavior of different types of common stock and in the character of issuers and holders.

1. There are now outstanding in the United States approximately one million different issues of stock, but the overwhelming majority is issued by small and medium-sized closely held corporations, the stock of which is not handled by the capital market machinery when first issued and does not become the object of trading after issuance. Only a small number of issues, probably not more than 50,000, can be regarded as constituting the market for common stock, but these issues account for probably more than four-fifths of the total value of all common stock.

2. The market for common stock is partly an exchange and partly an over-the-counter market involving direct transactions over the telephone among brokers and dealers or between brokers and dealers and their customers. Only about 3,000 common stock issues are listed on exchanges, half of them on the New York Stock Exchange. This small number of issues, however, is responsible for more than three-fifths of the value of all common stock and an even higher proportion of marketable common stock. The New York Stock Exchange alone accounts for roughly nine-tenths of the value of all common stock listed on exchanges, and for more than one-half of all common stock outstanding in the United States. The stock of financial institutions—commercial banks, fire and casualty insurance companies, and investment companies—is, however, predominantly traded in the over-the-counter market.[2]

---

[2] *25th Annual Report of the Securities and Exchange Commission,* Washington, 1959, pp. 62–69.

3. In the absence of current statistical information, it is estimated that approximately one-third of all stock trading takes place in the over-the-counter market, while fully two-thirds takes place on the floor of stock exchanges, mostly the New York Stock Exchange.[3] A substantial fraction, possibly around one-fourth, of over-the-counter trading is in stocks listed on exchanges.

4. The (full lot) turnover ratio—a measure of trading intensity of stocks listed on the New York Stock Exchange—averaged 16 per cent a year during the postwar period, compared to a ratio of about 95 per cent in the 1920's.[4] The turnover ratio in the over-the-counter market is probably lower. The differences in this ratio among individual stocks and groups of them are, however, very large.

5. There are four main methods of selling new issues of common stock, apart from placement with small groups of investors which is prevalent for small and medium-sized corporations, particularly new ones.[5]

I. Direct placement with a small number of investors, usually financial institutions:
   A. Without intermediary
   B. With the help of an intermediary ("finder") who usually receives a small fee.
II. Offering to the general public:
   A. Without underwriting, including offerings made with the technical assistance of an investment banker or other organization which does not assume any risk but undertakes the operation on what is called a "best effort" basis.
   B. With underwriting:
      1. As a result of competitive bidding among several investment bankers or groups of them, a technique prescribed for some regulated industries, particularly electric power and light companies.
      2. As a result of direct negotiation between the issuer and an investment banker of his choice.
III. Offering to stockholders under pre-emptive rights:
   A. With underwriting
   B. Without underwriting

[3] Irwin Friend, *The Over-the-Counter Securities Market*, New York, 1958, p. 116.
[4] *New York Stock Exchange Fact Book, 1960*, New York, 1960, p. 42.
[5] This classification also applies broadly to corporate bonds.

IV. Issuance in accordance with the exercise of conversion rights or warrants attached to other securities, usually preferred stock or debentures of the same issuer.

Offering to the general public was the most common form of placement. Offerings to stockholders under rights appear to have accounted for only about one-fifth of all registered common stock offerings.[6]

Direct placement with financial institutions was rare in the case of common stock, in contrast to corporate bonds and preferred stock; for 1946–58 it accounted for less than 1 per cent of total net issues of common stock but for more than 20 per cent of preferred stock.[7]

6. The cost of issuance of common stock depends primarily upon the method of distribution used, the size of the issues, and the size, industry, age, and record of the issues. The cost is relatively low for offerings to stockholders, particularly if they are not underwritten. For issues offered to the general public, costs decrease rapidly with increasing size. These relationships can be followed in Table 79. For issues of the same size, costs are considerably lower for public utility than for industrial and other issues, particularly for mining issues. The average cost of issuing stocks of public utility companies amounts to from one-half to two-thirds of the mean for the size class; it is close to this average for stock issues of manufacturing corporations, but the issues of mining corporations cost between 50 and 200 per cent more than the average for their size class. In the case of open-end investment companies, cost of issuance bears little relation to the size of issue or other characteristics of issue and issuer, amounting fairly uniformly to 7–9 per cent for companies using the investment banking mechanism for distribution.[8]

7. The redistribution of outstanding stock takes place either through the ordinary mechanism of exchange or over-the-counter trading, or, when large blocks are involved, through formal secondary distributions on the floor of an exchange or using the selling or-

---

[6] No comprehensive statistics for the entire period exist. The figure in the text refers to the share of offerings to security holders of common stock issues registered with the Securities and Exchange Commission during the fiscal years 1954 to 1960 (see *24th Annual Report*, SEC, p. 204).

[7] SEC unpublished data.

[8] A study of mutual funds published after the manuscript was completed shows that, out of 214 companies, 123 had a sales load of 8.0 to 8.9 per cent, thirty-six had a load of 7.0 to 7.9 per cent, thirty-four had no load, and nine had a load of less than 7 per cent. (*A Study of Mutual Funds*, Washington, 1962, pp. 469–470.)

ganizations of investment bankers and dealers. Block distributions through the New York Stock Exchange aggregated about $3 billion during the postwar period, an amount equal to about one-eighth of all new issues of marketable common stock.[9]

TABLE 79

COST OF FLOTATION OF REGISTERED CORPORATE STOCK  ISSUES OFFERED
TO THE GENERAL PUBLIC, 1951, 1953, AND 1955
(per cent of proceeds)

| Size of Issue (million dollars) | All Industries (1) | Manu- facturing (2) | Electric, Gas, and Water (3) | Communi- cations (4) | Mining (5) | Other In- dustries (6) |
|---|---|---|---|---|---|---|
| COMMON STOCK | | | | | | |
| Under  0.5 | 27.2 | 19.7 | | | 33.4 | 14.8 |
| 0.5  to  1 | 21.8 | 13.7 | 12.2 | 8.2 | 33.0 | 21.4 |
| 1  to  2 | 13.6 | 12.8 | 6.5 | 6.0 | 22.2 | 11.5 |
| 2  to  5 | 10.0 | 8.6 | 5.4 | 5.8 | 17.7 | 12.9 |
| 5  to 10 | 6.2 | 6.4 | 4.5 | 6.7 | 12.3 | 14.3 |
| 10  to 20 | 4.7 | 4.9 | 3.0 | 5.1 | 11.5 | 6.6 |
| 20  to 50 | 5.4 | 5.5 | 4.2 | | 15.6 | |
| 50 and over | | | | | | |
| All sizes[a] | 10.3 | 10.1 | 4.6 | 6.1 | 20.0 | 12.3 |
| PREFERRED STOCK | | | | | | |
| Under  0.5 | | | | | | |
| 0.5  to  1 | 12.6 | 18.4 | 10.7 | 7.4 | | 11.6 |
| 1  to  2 | 8.1 | 11.2 | 6.1 | 6.4 | | 12.7 |
| 2  to  5 | 4.9 | 5.1 | 3.8 | 5.4 | | 7.3 |
| 5  to 10 | 3.7 | 4.0 | 3.4 | 4.9 | | 3.6 |
| 10  to 20 | 2.9 | 2.6 | 2.8 | 4.2 | | 2.8 |
| 20  to 50 | 3.2 | 3.6 | 3.1 | | | |
| 50 and over | 2.5 | 2.5 | | | | |
| All sizes[a] | 4.3 | 5.2 | 3.1 | 6.5 | | 6.8 |

Source:  Cost of Flotation of Corporate Securities, 1951-1955, SEC, Washington, 1957, pp. 39-40.

[a]Median values.

8. Credit is used to a substantial extent in financing stock trading, particularly trading by professionals. Credit to the public to purchase or carry stocks is provided primarily by brokers and dealers, and secondarily by direct loans of commercial banks to customers. Brokers and dealers, in turn, obtain their external financing partly from domestic commercial banks, partly from foreign banks, and partly from miscellaneous lenders.[10] The total volume of credit on common stock,

[9] *27th Annual Report*, SEC, Washington, 1961, p. 221.
[10] See Jules I. Bogen and Herman E. Krooss, *Security Credit,* Englewood Cliffs, 1960, p. 22.

however, is moderate compared with the value of common stock out-standing. On the average during the postwar period, borrowing on stocks listed on the New York Stock Exchange amounted to only 2 per cent of their value. Credit is also used, and is relatively more important, in financing investment bankers when they offer new stock issues to the public, but in these cases it is usually required only for very short periods.

TABLE 80

DISTRIBUTION OF STOCK TRADING ON NEW YORK STOCK EXCHANGE, 1952–60
(total volume = 100)

| Date | Public Individuals[a] (1) | N.Y. Stock Exchange Members (2) | Institutions and Intermediaries | | | | |
|------|-----|-----|-----|-----|-----|-----|-----|
| | | | Total (3) | Commercial Banks[b] (4) | Brokers and Dealers[c] (5) | Investment Companies[d] (6) | Other (7) |
| Sept. 1952 | 57.0 | 18.4 | 24.6 | 7.1 | 4.6 | 3.9 | 9.0 |
| March 1953 | 61.4 | 19.3 | 19.3 | 6.2 | 4.7 | 2.4 | 6.0 |
| March 1954 | 56.4 | 20.1 | 23.5 | 7.5 | 4.3 | 2.7 | 8.9 |
| Dec.  1954 | 62.3 | 20.2 | 17.5 | 5.3 | 3.9 | 1.3 | 6.9 |
| June  1955 | 59.2 | 21.3 | 19.5 | 6.5 | 3.9 | 1.7 | 7.4 |
| March 1956 | 58.9 | 21.0 | 20.1 | 6.8 | 3.7 | 2.2 | 7.4 |
| Oct.  1957 | 54.3 | 22.4 | 23.3 | 8.7 | 3.4 | 2.2 | 9.0 |
| Sept. 1958 | 55.8 | 21.3 | 22.9 | 6.2 | 3.7 | 13.1 | |
| June  1959 | 53.5 | 23.7 | 22.8 | 8.8 | 3.1 | 10.9 | |
| Sept. 1960 | 52.6 | 23.1 | 24.3 | 9.7 | 2.7 | 4.3 | 7.6 |
| Average | 57.1 | 21.1 | 21.8 | 7.3 | 3.8 | 2.6 | 7.8 |

Source: Cols. 1–2 from Tenth Public Transaction Study, New York Stock Exchange, 1960, Part I, p. 3; cols. 3–7 from Ibid., Part II, p. 8.

[a]Public individuals are defined in the source to include only customers who have an account with N.Y. Stock Exchange member firms.

[b]Including trust departments.

[c]Excluding members of New York Stock Exchange.

[d]Open-end investment companies only, called "mutual funds" in the source.

9. The objectives of transactions in common stock are difficult to determine. According to estimates of the New York Stock Exchange, based on sample inquiries, about one-eighth of all transactions in common stock by the public—accounting, according to Table 80, for slightly more than half of the total transactions on the New York Stock Exchange—are made for trading purposes, i.e., are intended to be liquidated within thirty days; about one-fourth are regarded as short-term investments, intended for one to six months; while about five-eighths are classified as long-term investments.[11] Transactions by

[11] *Tenth Public Transaction Study,* New York Stock Exchange, 1960, Part I, p. 4.

members, presumably mostly for trading purposes, account for fully one-fifth of trading on the New York Stock Exchange. Transactions by financial institutions, probably to a substantial extent for long-term investments, are responsible for another full fifth.

## *Developments During the Postwar Period*

### VOLUME OF COMMON STOCK ISSUES

Net issues of corporate stock from 1946 through 1958 amounted to $41 billion, $36 billion of which represented common stock (Tables 81 and 82 and Chart 21). These figures include both marketable and nonmarketable issues. The statistics of the Securities and Exchange Commission and those in *National Balance Sheet* [12] show that marketable common stock issues amounted to $21 billion excluding investment companies and $28 billion including them. The difference of $8 billion represents nonmarketable issues, primarily those of small and medium-sized corporations sold without the use of the investment banking machinery.

Thus the amount contributed by common stock toward the financing of corporate business and hence of the economy is not negligible. The amounts raised through issuance of common stock in the postwar period, however, were small compared to the funds raised by the main fixed value capital market instruments (see Table 43). For the entire postwar period the volume of common stock issues, even including nonmarketable securities, was below the net sales of state and local government securities. It was only three-fifths as large as the net sales of corporate bonds; it amounted to one-third of the increase in residential mortgage debt; and it was smaller than the funds made available through the increase in consumer loans and through bank loans to business. As a result, common stock constituted only 14 per cent of the funds raised through the five main capital market instruments, only 8 per cent of the ten instruments listed in Table 43, and 5 per cent of all external financing in the economy (Table 21).

Still more pronounced is the low rate of growth of the total supply of common stock, i.e., the ratio of the amount of a year's net issues to the average value outstanding during the year. The growth

[12] Raymond W. Goldsmith, Robert E. Lipsey, and Morris Mendelson, *Studies in the National Balance Sheet of the United States,* Princeton for NBER, 1963, Vol. II, Table IV-b-17a.

TABLE 81

STRUCTURAL CHANGES IN OWNERSHIP OF CORPORATE STOCK DURING POSTWAR PERIOD

| | Outstandings (billion dollars) | | Aggregate Net Flows 1946-58 (billion dollars) | NET FLOWS (ANNUAL AVERAGES) | | | | | |
| --- | --- | --- | --- | --- | --- | --- | --- | --- | --- |
| | | | | Amounts (billion dollars) | | | Distribution (per cent) | | |
| | 1945 (1) | 1958 (2) | (3) | Cycle I 1946-49 (4) | Cycle II 1949-54 (5) | Cycle III 1954-58 (6) | Cycle I 1946-49 (7) | Cycle II 1949-54 (8) | Cycle III 1954-58 (9) |
| 1. Nonfarm households | 111.62 | 342.99 | 23.22 | 1.42 | 1.70 | 2.17 | 69.6 | 58.4 | 51.2 |
| 2. Nonfinancial corporations | 27.67 | 75.00 | 1.89 | 0.09 | 0.13 | 0.20 | 4.4 | 4.5 | 4.7 |
| 3. Financial institutions, total | 7.36 | 43.46 | 16.09 | 0.53 | 1.09 | 1.87 | 26.0 | 37.1 | 44.1 |
| a. Government insurance and pension funds | 0.04 | 0.50 | 0.46 | 0.01 | 0.02 | 0.06 | 0.5 | 0.7 | 1.4 |
| b. Commercial banks | 0.22 | 0.19 | -0.03 | -0.02 | 0 | 0.01 | -1.0 | 0 | 0.2 |
| c. Mutual savings banks | 0.14 | 0.86 | 0.72 | 0 | 0.07 | 0.08 | 0 | 2.4 | 1.9 |
| d. Investment companies | 2.90 | 18.08 | 4.87 | 0.15 | 0.27 | 0.63 | 7.4 | 9.3 | 14.9 |
| e. Life insurance | 1.00 | 4.11 | 1.75 | 0.15 | 0.17 | 0.07 | 7.4 | 5.8 | 1.7 |
| f. Fire and casualty insurance | 2.40 | 8.34 | 1.74 | 0.10 | 0.16 | 0.14 | 4.9 | 5.5 | 3.3 |
| g. Noninsured pension plans | 0.29 | 10.80 | 6.62 | 0.11 | 0.39 | 0.92 | 5.4 | 13.4 | 21.7 |
| h. Other private insurance | 0.05 | 0.12 | 0.06 | 0.01 | 0 | 0 | 0.5 | 0 | 0 |
| i. Other finance | 0.32 | 0.46 | -0.10 | 0.01 | 0 | -0.04 | 0.5 | 0 | -0.9 |
| 4. Total | 146.65 | 465.45 | 41.20 | 2.04 | 2.91 | 4.24 | 100.0 | 100.0 | 100.0 |
| Memorandum | | | | | | | | | |
| 5. Total domestic outstandings and net issues | 148.40 | 470.65 | 40.72 | 1.93 | 2.94 | 4.22 | 100.0 | 100.0 | 100.0 |
| 6. Rest-of-world assets and net purchases of domestic issues | 3.01 | 8.30 | 0.42 | -0.11 | 0.05 | 0.14 | -5.7 | 1.7 | 3.3 |

Source: *National Balance Sheet*, Vol. II. Cols. 1-2 from Tables IV-b-16 and IV-b-17; cols. 3-9 from Tables VIII-b-16 and VIII-b-17.

Note: Components may not add to totals because of rounding here and elsewhere in this chapter.

TABLE 82

STRUCTURAL CHANGES IN OWNERSHIP OF COMMON STOCK DURING THE POSTWAR PERIOD

| | Outstandings (billion dollars) | | Aggregate Net Flows, 1946-58 (billion dollars) | NET FLOWS (ANNUAL AVERAGES) | | | | | |
| --- | --- | --- | --- | --- | --- | --- | --- | --- | --- |
| | | | | Amounts (billion dollars) | | | Distribution (per cent) | | |
| | 1945 | 1958 | | Cycle I 1946-49 | Cycle II 1949-54 | Cycle III 1954-58 | Cycle I 1946-49 | Cycle II 1949-54 | Cycle III 1954-58 |
| | (1) | (2) | (3) | (4) | (5) | (6) | (7) | (8) | (9) |
| 1. Nonfarm households | 103.47 | 332.62 | 21.00 | 1.22 | 1.56 | 1.94 | 72.2 | 62.4 | 49.9 |
| 2. Nonfinancial corporations | 24.20 | 75.45 | 1.81 | 0.08 | 0.12 | 0.19 | 4.7 | 4.8 | 4.9 |
| 3. Financial institutions, total | 5.53 | 39.10 | 13.56 | 0.39 | 0.82 | 1.75 | 23.1 | 32.8 | 45.0 |
| a. Government insurance and pension funds | 0.02 | 0.25 | 0.23 | 0 | 0.01 | 0.03 | 0 | 0.4 | 0.8 |
| b. Commercial banks | 0.22 | 0.19 | -0.03 | -0.02 | 0 | 0.01 | -1.2 | 0 | 0.3 |
| c. Mutual savings banks | 0.14 | 0.86 | 0.72 | 0 | 0.07 | 0.08 | 0 | 2.8 | 2.1 |
| d. Investment companies | 2.65 | 17.15 | 4.19 | 0.14 | 0.22 | 0.56 | 8.3 | 8.8 | 14.4 |
| e. Life insurance | 1.81 | 2.55 | 1.01 | 0.06 | 0.08 | 0.09 | 3.6 | 3.2 | 2.3 |
| f. Fire and casualty insurance | 0.18 | 7.51 | 1.50 | 0.10 | 0.10 | 0.15 | 5.9 | 4.0 | 3.9 |
| g. Noninsured pension plans | 0.20 | 10.07 | 5.98 | 0.08 | 0.33 | 0.86 | 4.7 | 13.2 | 22.1 |
| h. Other private insurance | 0.01 | 0.08 | 0.06 | 0 | 0 | 0 | 0.6 | 0 | -1.0 |
| i. Other finance | 0.30 | 0.44 | -0.10 | 0.01 | 0 | -0.04 | | | |
| 4. Total | 133.20 | 447.17 | 36.37 | 1.69 | 2.50 | 3.89 | 100.0 | 100.0 | 100.0 |
| Memorandum | | | | | | | | | |
| 5. Total domestic outstandings and net issues | 134.67 | 452.04 | 35.84 | 1.60 | 2.52 | 3.87 | 100.0 | 100.0 | 100.0 |
| 6. Rest-of-world assets and net purchases of domestic issues | 2.73 | 7.97 | 0.37 | -0.10 | 0.04 | 0.13 | -6.2 | 1.6 | 3.4 |

Source: National Balance Sheet, Vol. II. Cols 1-2 from Table IV-b-17; cols. 3-9 from Table VIII-b-17.

CHART 21

ISSUANCE AND ABSORPTION OF COMMON STOCK, 1946–58

I. Issuance

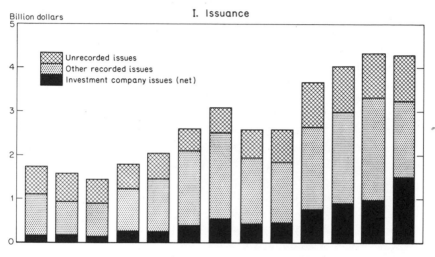

II. Absorption by Financial Intermediaries

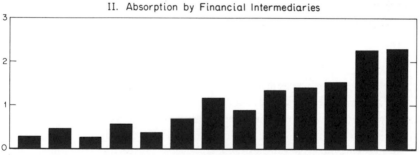

III. Noninstitutional Absorption

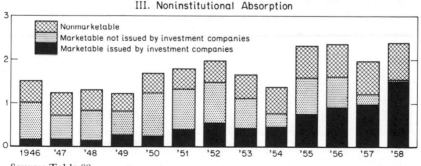

Source: Table 88.

rate of the supply of common stock is below that for all other main capital market instruments, except U.S. government securities. While the average rate of growth lay between 7 and 17 per cent per year for the main types of long- and short-term debt excluding U.S. government obligations, the average amount of new common stock issues during the postwar period was less than 1½ per cent of the value of common stock outstanding, and the ratio did not differ substantially from cycle to cycle (Table 47).

In contrast to the low share of common stock in total new issues of capital market instruments and to the slow rate of growth in supply, the share of common stock in the current value of financial assets increased during the postwar period because of the sharp rise in stock prices (Table 43). Thus the share of corporate stock in the total financial assets of all sectors increased from about 15 per cent in 1945 to 22 per cent in 1958.[13] The share of corporate stock advanced equally sharply—from 30 to 46 per cent—in comparison to the aggregate value of the five main capital market instruments.

New issues of common stock showed a considerable upward trend throughout the postwar period (see Table 82). This increase, however, was smaller than the expansion in the rate at which other main capital market instruments, other than U.S. government securities, were absorbed by investors. As a result, the share of common stock in the net issuance of the five main capital market instruments declined from fully one-fifth in Cycle I to one-ninth in Cycle II and about one-sixth in Cycle III. The share, however, remained at less than one-tenth in comparison to the ten main instruments.

The distribution of new common stock by industry is known only for marketable issues (Table 83). Of the $25 billion of new issues of common stock, almost three-tenths were accounted for by net issues of investment companies (here marketable issues include only cash issues). On a gross basis, which is relevant for the investment banking industry, their share was even higher because of the substantial redemptions of investment companies which have hardly any parallel among other industries. On that basis, investment companies accounted for $11 billion out of $28 billion of gross sales of marketable common stock, or about two-fifths of the total (Table 83).

Among the common stock issues of corporations other than investment companies, manufacturing and electric and gas utilities led with a share of nearly one-third each. The communications industry ac-

[13] *Ibid.*, Table I, 1945, 1958.

counted for about one-tenth of net common stock issues, represented largely by those of the Bell System. Commercial issuers were responsible for another one-tenth, leaving the remaining one-sixth for the common stock issues of real estate and finance corporations other than investment companies. As can be seen from Table 83, the share of common stock issues for some industries did not change substantially from cycle to cycle, but the proportion of issues of investment companies to other corporate stock companies increased considerably, particularly between Cycles I and II.

The distribution of marketable securities according to the method of distribution has been tabulated only for 1951, 1953, and 1955.[14] For these three years, slightly more than two-thirds of all marketable common stock issues excluding those of investment companies were offered to stockholders under rights (if investment company offerings are included, the proportion declines to 42 per cent on a gross and to about 50 per cent on a net basis), nearly two-thirds of which was in turn underwritten by investment bankers. Of the common stocks offered to the general public (excluding investment company issues), all but 7 per cent were underwritten. Thus investment bankers offered, usually with an underwriting contract, slightly more than 70 per cent of marketable noninvestment company common stock. Inclusion of investment company issues, which are not underwritten although most of them are distributed by investment bankers, reduces this share to slightly over 50 per cent on a net and to nearly 45 per cent on a gross sales basis.

A considerable part of all common stock issues originates, not through the simultaneous offering by the issuer and an investment banker, but through the conversion of other securities into common stock or through the exercise of options on common stock in accordance with arrangements made earlier. For the postwar years 1948–58, common stock issues resulting from conversion aggregated approximately $6 billion,[15] consisting primarily of common stock of the American Telephone and Telegraph Company issued in exchange for the company's convertible debentures. This was equal to one-fifth of all common stock and to nearly one-third of marketable issues, excluding

[14] *Volume and Nature of Corporate Security Offerings,* Securities and Exchange Commission (Supplemental Report to *Cost of Flotation of Corporate Securities*), Washington, July 1957, pp. 14, 15.

[15] SEC unpublished data, and *National Balance Sheet,* Vol. II, Table IV-17-a, line 5.

TABLE 83

DISTRIBUTION OF STOCK OFFERINGS BY INDUSTRY, 1946-58
(per cent)

| | Common Stock | | | | Preferred Stock | | | |
|---|---|---|---|---|---|---|---|---|
| | 1946-49 (1) | 1949-54 (2) | 1954-58 (3) | 1948-58 (4) | 1946-49 (5) | 1949-54 (6) | 1954-58 (7) | 1948-58 (8) |
| Manufacturing | n.a. | 25 | 35 | 31 | n.a. | 30 | 23 | 27 |
| Commercial and miscellaneous[a] | n.a. | 10 | 10 | 10 | n.a. | 7 | 5 | 6 |
| Electricity, gas, and water | n.a. | 44 | 22 | 32 | n.a. | 53 | 59 | 55 |
| Communication | n.a. | 5 | 12 | 9 | n.a. | 3 | 5 | 4 |
| Other transportation | n.a. | 1 | 1 | 1 | n.a. | 1 | 1 | 1 |
| Railroads | n.a. | 0 | 0 | 0 | n.a. | 0 | 0 | 0 |
| Financial[b] and real estate | n.a. | 15 | 20 | 17 | n.a. | 6 | 7 | 7 |
| All industries (per cent) | 100 | 100 | 100 | 100 | 100 | 100 | 100 | 100 |
| All industries (billion dollars)[g] | 0.74 | 1.14 | 2.07 | 1.42[c] | 0.68 | 0.63 | 0.59 | 0.59[d] |
| Investment companies[e] | | | | | | | | |
| Per cent | 43 | 59 | 65 | 65 | -- | -- | -- | -- |
| Billion dollars[g] | .32 | .67 | 1.35 | .93[f] | -- | -- | -- | -- |

Source: SEC Statistical Bulletin, March issues for 1947 to 1959 (e.g., March 1959, p. 8) and SEC worksheets "Domestic Corporate Securities Issued and Retired." For investment companies, see also Irwin Friend, Individual Saving, New York, 1954, pp. 235 and 237, line 2.

[a]Includes mining.

[b]Excluding investment companies.

[c]1946-58 = 1.33.

[d]1946-58 = 0.65.

[e]Includes very small amounts of preferred stock. Does not include capital gains and dividends reinvested in additional shares.

[f]1946-58 = 0.84. The comparable figure for net issues is 0.54.

[g]Annual averages.

in both cases investment company securities. Since the volume of conversions into common stock depends largely on a rise in stock prices, it was probably small in Cycle I. In Cycles II and III, however, the share of conversions in the total issue of marketable common stock other than investment company issues approximated one-fourth.

### THE ROLE OF COMMON STOCK IN FINANCING NONFINANCIAL CORPORATIONS [16]

For the period from 1946 through 1958 stocks provided 6 per cent of the total funds absorbed by all nonfinancial corporations and the ratio was approximately the same for all three cycles (Table 32). The share of common stocks alone was 5 per cent. In relation to total external financing, common stocks contributed about one-eighth, again without substantial changes among the three cycles. Common stocks supplied less than three-fifths as large a volume of funds as corporate bonds did, and an even smaller proportion if bank term loans of five years' maturity or longer are included with bonds.

While common stocks thus were not a primary means of financing for all nonfinancial corporations taken together, very great differences are known to exist among individual corporations and groups of them. The available statistics unfortunately are not sufficiently comprehensive or detailed to identify the types of corporations for which the

[16] As is common practice, financing through equity securities is limited here to new corporate stock issues sold for cash. It is sometimes argued, however, that the retention of earnings is to be regarded as another form of equity financing since it also increases net worth. The similarity to equity financing through cash issuance of stock is held to be particularly pronounced in the case of undistributed earnings evidenced by stock dividends. The argument for statistical combination of these two forms of increasing net worth does not appear to be persuasive since no external financing is involved. Nevertheless, it may be well to realize that in the postwar period internal equity financing through retention of earnings was much larger than external equity financing through issuance of stock, and that the retained earnings evidenced by stock dividends alone were equal to about 40 per cent of the volume of external financing through new stock issues. The figures for the period as a whole and the three cycles are given below (annual averages in billion dollars). It is evident that, as the postwar period progressed, stock issues sold for cash increased compared to either total earnings or to that part evidenced by stock dividends.

|  | *1946–58* | *1946–49* | *1949–54* | *1954–58* |
|---|---|---|---|---|
| 1. Retained earnings | 10.4 | 12.0 | 9.9 | 10.2 |
| 2. Stock dividends | 1.3 | .8 | 1.2 | 2.0 |
| 3. Stock issues | 3.1 | 1.9 | 2.9 | 4.2 |

Lines 1 and 2 are from *Statistics of Income;* line 3 is from *National Balance Sheet,* Vol. II, Tables VIII-d-1 and VIII-d-2.

issuance of marketable common stock constituted an essential part of total or external financing, let alone to measure the share of common stock issues in the total and external financing of these corporations. We can follow with reasonable accuracy only the contribution of common stock to the financing of corporations in the main industrial sectors treated as broad aggregates and their role in the financing of large corporations.

For the entire period from 1947 through 1956, all stocks (common and preferred) contributed 2 per cent toward the aggregate financing of manufacturing and mining corporations, 24 per cent to that of power and light and communications corporations, but virtually nothing to the funds secured by corporations in transportation and trade. The share of stock in the external financing of these groups was similarly varied. It amounted to only 5 per cent for manufacturing and mining corporations, but to 38 per cent among electric and gas utilities, and was, of course, negligible again for transportation and trade. Compared, finally, with the total of issuance of securities and long-term debt, stocks accounted for 12 per cent in the case of manufacturing and mining and 43 per cent in public utilities.[17] The low level of the ratios in most industries, other than the electric and gas utilities and the telephone industry, is partly explained by the scarcity of public stock issues by smaller and medium-sized corporations.

Among large corporations (Federal Reserve Board sample of 293–300 corporations), the share of stock financing was considerably more important. For the period 1946–55, these corporations raised more than $10 billion through stock issues. This is equal to three-fifths of the total of all marketable stock issues other than those of investment companies, an indication of the high degree of concentration of stock issues, since the same corporations accounted for less than one-third of total assets of nonfinancial corporations and for not much more than two-fifths of their fixed assets (book values). For these large corporations, stock issues were equal to 40 per cent of long-term external financing, 27 per cent of all external financing, and 9 per cent of all financing, internal and external. The relatively high ratios of stock in financing are, however, partly due to the character of the sample in which large public utilities, including the Bell System, are heavily represented.[18]

---

[17] *Survey of Current Business*, September 1957, pp. 10–11.

[18] Of this group of large corporations' stock issues, almost half is accounted for by the Bell System alone, while the other half is divided about equally between

### NET ACQUISITION OF COMMON STOCK BY INVESTOR GROUPS

Because of the decisive influence of price fluctuations on the value and distribution of the holdings of common stock, it is best to base an analysis of the market on net flows, i.e., the difference between the cost of purchases and the proceeds from sales of common stock by the various investor groups, rather than on changes in the value of holdings of the different investor groups. These net flows are shown for common stock on an annual basis [19] and for cycle averages in Table 82. Similar figures for all corporate stock, which also permit the derivation of net flows for preferred stock, will be found in Table 81.[20] The annual movements are illustrated in Chart 22 for all corporate stock together. The sectoral composition of these flows is shown in Tables 86 and 87 for all and for common stock. The distribution of holdings among sectors, in terms of market values, finally, can be followed on an annual basis in Table 84 for all stock and in Table 85 for common stock alone.

For the entire period, identified financial institutions, which include all major ones except the personal trust departments of commercial banks, had a net purchase balance of common stock of $14 billion. This was equivalent to about two-fifths of total net issues of common stock. If investment company new issues are excluded, since only a small part of their net issue are acquired by other financial institutions, the net purchase balance of financial institutions rises to almost one-half of total new issues of common stock. This, of course, does not mean that almost one-half of all new issues were actually acquired by financial institutions. In fact, considerably less than this per cent of the new issues of common stock made during the postwar period found their way into the portfolios of financial institutions, as it is likely that financial institutions bought considerably more outstanding common stocks than they sold. Since the data on which these calculations are based do not separate the net acquisition of newly issued from the net purchases of already outstanding common stock issues, the amount of new issues actually acquired by financial institutions is unknown.

Although the ratio of financial institutions' net purchases to total

---

electric utilities and manufacturing and mining corporations (see *Federal Reserve Bulletin:* 1948, p. 631; 1950, p. 642; 1952, p. 641; 1954, p. 820; 1956, p. 588).

[19] In *National Balance Sheet,* Vol. II, Table VIII-b-17.

[20] And in *ibid.,* Table VIII-b-16.

CHART 22

MARKET FOR CORPORATE STOCK: SUPPLY AND ABSORPTION
BY SECTOR, 1946–58

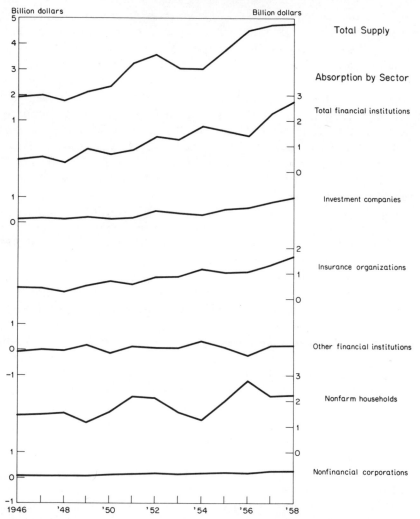

TABLE 84

DISTRIBUTION OF HOLDINGS OF CORPORATE STOCK,[a] 1945-58

(per cent)

| | 1945 | 1946 | 1947 | 1948 | 1949 | 1950 | 1951 | 1952 | 1953 | 1954 | 1955 | 1956 | 1957 | 1958 |
|---|---|---|---|---|---|---|---|---|---|---|---|---|---|---|
| 1. Nonfarm households | 76.1 | 75.5 | 75.3 | 75.1 | 74.6 | 75.0 | 74.9 | 74.5 | 74.0 | 73.9 | 74.1 | 74.2 | 73.7 | 73.7 |
| 2. Nonfinancial corporations | 18.9 | 18.9 | 18.9 | 18.9 | 18.8 | 18.6 | 18.3 | 18.1 | 17.9 | 17.6 | 17.5 | 17.3 | 17.2 | 17.0 |
| 3. Finance | 5.0 | 5.6 | 5.9 | 6.0 | 6.6 | 6.5 | 6.8 | 7.5 | 8.1 | 8.4 | 8.4 | 8.5 | 9.1 | 9.3 |
| a. Government insurance and pension funds | 0 | 0 | 0 | 0 | 0 | 0 | 0 | 0.1 | 0.1 | 0.1 | 0.1 | 0.1 | 0.1 | 0.1 |
| b. Commercial banks | 0.2 | 0.1 | 0.1 | 0.1 | 0.1 | 0.1 | 0.1 | 0.1 | 0.1 | 0.1 | 0 | 0 | 0.1 | 0 |
| c. Mutual savings banks | 0.1 | 0.1 | 0.1 | 0.1 | 0.1 | 0.1 | 0.1 | 0.2 | 0.2 | 0.2 | 0.2 | 0.2 | 0.2 | 0.2 |
| d. Investment companies | 2.0 | 2.1 | 2.1 | 2.1 | 2.4 | 2.4 | 2.7 | 3.0 | 3.2 | 3.4 | 3.5 | 3.5 | 3.6 | 3.9 |
| e. Life insurance | 0.7 | 0.9 | 1.1 | 1.1 | 1.2 | 1.2 | 1.1 | 1.1 | 1.2 | 1.1 | 1.0 | 0.9 | 1.0 | 0.9 |
| f. Fire and casualty insurance | 1.6 | 1.8 | 1.8 | 1.8 | 2.0 | 1.9 | 1.9 | 2.0 | 2.0 | 2.0 | 1.9 | 1.9 | 1.9 | 1.8 |
| g. Noninsured pension plans | 0.2 | 0.3 | 0.4 | 0.4 | 0.5 | 0.5 | 0.7 | 0.9 | 1.1 | 1.3 | 1.6 | 1.7 | 2.0 | 2.3 |
| h. Other private insurance | 0 | 0.1 | 0.1 | 0.1 | 0.1 | 0.1 | 0 | 0 | 0 | 0 | 0 | 0 | 0 | 0 |
| i. Other finance | 0.2 | 0.2 | 0.2 | 0.2 | 0.3 | 0.2 | 0.2 | 0.2 | 0.2 | 0.2 | 0.2 | 0.1 | 0.2 | 0.1 |
| 4. Total | 100.0 | 100.0 | 100.0 | 100.0 | 100.0 | 100.0 | 100.0 | 100.0 | 100.0 | 100.0 | 100.0 | 100.0 | 100.0 | 100.0 |
| 5. Total (billion dollars) | 146.65 | 132.99 | 131.08 | 131.97 | 147.28 | 178.86 | 203.17 | 219.47 | 217.94 | 298.57 | 364.33 | 381.55 | 347.49 | 465.45 |
| **Memorandum** | | | | | | | | | | | | | | |
| 6. Total domestic outstandings (billion dollars) | 148.40 | 134.23 | 132.17 | 132.93 | 148.70 | 180.80 | 205.61 | 222.26 | 220.87 | 302.19 | 368.70 | 386.34 | 351.73 | 470.65 |
| 7. Total domestic outstandings | 100.0 | 100.0 | 100.0 | 100.0 | 100.0 | 100.0 | 100.0 | 100.0 | 100.0 | 100.0 | 100.0 | 100.0 | 100.0 | 100.0 |
| 8. Rest-of-world assets | 2.0 | 2.0 | 1.9 | 1.7 | 1.7 | 1.6 | 1.7 | 1.7 | 1.7 | 1.7 | 1.8 | 1.8 | 1.7 | 1.8 |

Source: National Balance Sheet, Vol. II, Tables IV-b-16 and IV-b-17.

[a] Common and preferred stock.

## TABLE 85

### DISTRIBUTION OF HOLDINGS OF COMMON STOCK, 1945-58
(per cent)

| | 1945 | 1946 | 1947 | 1948 | 1949 | 1950 | 1951 | 1952 | 1953 | 1954 | 1955 | 1956 | 1957 | 1958 |
|---|---|---|---|---|---|---|---|---|---|---|---|---|---|---|
| 1. Nonfarm households | 77.7 | 77.3 | 77.1 | 76.9 | 76.3 | 76.5 | 76.2 | 75.7 | 75.4 | 75.0 | 75.0 | 75.0 | 74.6 | 74.4 |
| 2. Nonfinancial corporations | 18.2 | 18.2 | 18.2 | 18.2 | 18.3 | 18.1 | 17.9 | 17.8 | 17.6 | 17.4 | 17.3 | 17.2 | 17.0 | 16.9 |
| 3. Finance | 4.2 | 4.5 | 4.7 | 4.9 | 5.5 | 5.4 | 5.8 | 6.5 | 7.0 | 7.5 | 7.7 | 7.8 | 8.4 | 8.7 |
| a. Government insurance and pension funds | 0 | 0 | 0 | 0 | 0 | 0 | 0 | 0 | 0 | 0 | 0 | 0 | 0.1 | 0.1 |
| b. Commercial banks | 0.2 | 0.2 | 0.1 | 0.1 | 0.1 | 0.1 | 0.1 | 0.1 | 0.1 | 0.1 | 0 | 0 | 0.1 | 0 |
| c. Mutual savings banks | 0.1 | 0.1 | 0.1 | 0.1 | 0.1 | 0.1 | 0.1 | 0.2 | 0.2 | 0.2 | 0.2 | 0.2 | 0.2 | 0.2 |
| d. Investment companies | 2.0 | 2.1 | 2.2 | 2.2 | 2.4 | 2.5 | 2.8 | 3.1 | 3.2 | 3.5 | 3.5 | 3.5 | 3.6 | 3.8 |
| e. Life insurance companies | 0.1 | 0.2 | 0.3 | 0.3 | 0.3 | 0.4 | 0.4 | 0.5 | 0.5 | 0.5 | 0.5 | 0.5 | 0.6 | 0.6 |
| f. Fire and casualty insurance | 1.4 | 1.4 | 1.5 | 1.5 | 1.7 | 1.7 | 1.7 | 1.7 | 1.8 | 1.8 | 1.7 | 1.8 | 1.8 | 1.7 |
| g. Noninsured pension plans | 0.2 | 0.2 | 0.3 | 0.3 | 0.4 | 0.4 | 0.5 | 0.8 | 1.0 | 1.2 | 1.5 | 1.6 | 1.9 | 2.3 |
| h. Other private insurance | 0 | 0 | 0 | 0 | 0 | 0 | 0 | 0 | 0 | 0 | 0 | 0 | 0 | 0 |
| i. Other finance | 0.2 | 0.2 | 0.2 | 0.2 | 0.3 | 0.2 | 0.2 | 0.2 | 0.2 | 0.2 | 0.2 | 0.1 | 0.2 | 0.1 |
| 4. Total | 100.0 | 100.0 | 100.0 | 100.0 | 100.0 | 100.0 | 100.0 | 100.0 | 100.0 | 100.0 | 100.0 | 100.0 | 100.0 | 100.0 |
| 5. Total (billion dollars) | 133.20 | 119.35 | 117.01 | 117.54 | 132.53 | 163.85 | 187.58 | 203.41 | 201.50 | 281.72 | 347.41 | 364.16 | 329.69 | 447.17 |
| **Memorandum** | | | | | | | | | | | | | | |
| 6. Total domestic outstandings (billion dollars) | 134.67 | 120.31 | 117.83 | 118.25 | 133.70 | 165.54 | 189.75 | 205.93 | 204.15 | 285.04 | 351.47 | 368.63 | 333.61 | 452.04 |
| 7. Total domestic outstandings | 100.0 | 100.0 | 100.0 | 100.0 | 100.0 | 100.0 | 100.0 | 100.0 | 100.0 | 100.0 | 100.0 | 100.0 | 100.0 | 100.0 |
| 8. Rest-of-world assets | 2.0 | 2.0 | 1.9 | 1.7 | 1.7 | 1.6 | 1.7 | 1.7 | 1.7 | 1.7 | 1.8 | 1.8 | 1.7 | 1.8 |

Source: National Balance Sheet, Vol. II, Table IV-b-17.

## TABLE 86

### DISTRIBUTION OF FLOW OF FUNDS, CORPORATE STOCK, 1946-58
### (per cent)

| | 1946 | 1947 | 1948 | 1949 | 1950 | 1951 | 1952 | 1953 | 1954 | 1955 | 1956 | 1957 | 1958 |
|---|---|---|---|---|---|---|---|---|---|---|---|---|---|
| 1. Nonfarm households | 71.4 | 69.0 | 77.8 | 54.0 | 65.7 | 69.1 | 58.0 | 53.1 | 39.2 | 52.5 | 63.5 | 47.2 | 42.6 |
| 2. Nonfinancial corporations | 5.0 | 4.2 | 4.6 | 4.3 | 4.7 | 3.9 | 4.7 | 4.5 | 4.8 | 5.3 | 4.4 | 4.7 | 4.5 |
| 3. Finance | 23.6 | 26.8 | 17.5 | 41.7 | 29.6 | 27.0 | 37.3 | 42.5 | 56.1 | 42.2 | 32.1 | 48.1 | 52.9 |
| a. Government insurance and pension funds | 0 | 0 | 1.0 | 0 | 0.9 | 0.7 | 0.6 | 1.4 | 1.3 | 1.6 | 0.9 | 1.7 | 2.3 |
| b. Commercial banks | -1.5 | -1.4 | 0 | -0.5 | 0 | -0.3 | 0.3 | 0 | 0 | 0.3 | 0 | 0.4 | 0.2 |
| c. Mutual savings banks | 0.5 | 0 | 0.5 | 0 | 0.9 | 1.6 | 3.0 | 3.1 | 4.5 | 2.4 | 0.9 | 1.5 | 1.7 |
| d. Investment companies | 7.0 | 7.5 | 6.2 | 9.5 | 5.6 | 5.9 | 11.9 | 12.3 | 9.6 | 13.5 | 13.3 | 17.0 | 18.8 |
| e. Life insurance | 13.6 | 7.0 | 2.1 | 10.9 | 13.7 | 1.6 | 4.4 | 3.1 | 8.6 | 1.8 | 0 | 0.9 | 1.2 |
| f. Fire and casualty insurance | 2.5 | 6.1 | 5.2 | 5.7 | 5.2 | 4.9 | 5.0 | 6.5 | 4.8 | 4.5 | 3.0 | 2.6 | 2.5 |
| g. Noninsured pension plans | 4.0 | 5.6 | 5.2 | 6.6 | 9.4 | 10.7 | 12.7 | 17.8 | 21.7 | 18.7 | 20.2 | 23.3 | 25.2 |
| h. Other private insurance | 1.0 | 0.5 | 0 | 0.5 | 0.4 | -0.3 | 0.3 | 0 | 0.3 | 0 | -0.2 | 0 | 0.2 |
| i. Other finance | -3.5 | 1.4 | -2.6 | 9.0 | -6.4 | 2.3 | -0.8 | -1.7 | 5.4 | -0.5 | -6.0 | 0.6 | 0.8 |
| 4. Total | 100.0 | 100.0 | 100.0 | 100.0 | 100.0 | 100.0 | 100.0 | 100.0 | 100.0 | 100.0 | 100.0 | 100.0 | 100.0 |
| 5. Total (billion dollars) | 1.99 | 2.13 | 1.94 | 2.11 | 2.33 | 3.07 | 3.62 | 2.92 | 3.14 | 3.79 | 4.36 | 4.64 | 5.16 |
| **Memorandum** | | | | | | | | | | | | | |
| 6. Total domestic net issues (billion dollars) | 1.93 | 2.00 | 1.78 | 2.11 | 2.31 | 3.21 | 3.56 | 3.03 | 3.02 | 3.75 | 4.51 | 4.74 | 4.77 |
| 7. Total domestic net issues | 100.0 | 100.0 | 100.0 | 100.0 | 100.0 | 100.0 | 100.0 | 100.0 | 100.0 | 100.0 | 100.0 | 100.0 | 100.0 |
| 8. Rest-of-world net purchases | -3.1 | -7.5 | -7.9 | -0.9 | 0 | 3.7 | 0 | 2.0 | 4.6 | 3.5 | 5.8 | 3.0 | -1.3 |

Source: National Balance Sheet, Vol. II, Tables VIII-b-16 and VIII-b-17.

TABLE 87

DISTRIBUTION OF FLOW OF FUNDS, COMMON STOCK, 1946–58
(per cent)

| | 1946 | 1947 | 1948 | 1949 | 1950 | 1951 | 1952 | 1953 | 1954 | 1955 | 1956 | 1957 | 1958 |
|---|---|---|---|---|---|---|---|---|---|---|---|---|---|
| 1. Nonfarm households | 78.9 | 68.2 | 77.8 | 63.1 | 76.8 | 67.1 | 57.8 | 59.8 | 45.4 | 57.3 | 55.8 | 41.6 | 46.2 |
| 2. Nonfinancial corporations | 5.0 | 4.7 | 5.1 | 5.0 | 4.8 | 4.8 | 5.1 | 5.1 | 5.1 | 5.1 | 4.9 | 5.0 | 4.9 |
| 3. Finance | 16.1 | 27.1 | 17.1 | 31.8 | 18.4 | 28.1 | 37.1 | 35.0 | 49.5 | 37.6 | 39.3 | 53.4 | 48.9 |
| a. Government insurance and pension funds | 0 | 0 | 0.6 | 0 | 0.5 | 0.4 | 0.3 | 0.8 | 0.7 | 0.8 | 0.5 | 0.9 | 1.3 |
| b. Commercial banks | -1.7 | -1.8 | 0 | -0.6 | | -0.4 | 0.3 | 0 | 0 | 0.3 | 0 | 0.5 | 0.2 |
| c. Mutual savings banks | 0.6 | 0 | 0.6 | 0 | 1.0 | 2.0 | 3.5 | 3.5 | 5.1 | 2.4 | 1.0 | 1.7 | 1.9 |
| d. Investment companies | 8.3 | 8.8 | 6.3 | 11.2 | 4.8 | 5.6 | 15.2 | 7.5 | 8.1 | 10.8 | 12.9 | 21.3 | 14.1 |
| e. Life insurance | 6.7 | 5.3 | 0.6 | 1.7 | 6.3 | 4.0 | 2.2 | 2.0 | 2.6 | 1.6 | 4.9 | 1.7 | 0.4 |
| f. Fire and casualty insurance | 2.2 | 7.6 | 7.0 | 3.4 | 4.3 | 4.4 | 3.2 | 5.5 | 3.7 | 4.6 | 5.4 | 2.4 | 3.0 |
| g. Noninsured pension plans | 2.8 | 4.7 | 5.1 | 6.1 | 7.7 | 9.6 | 13.0 | 17.7 | 23.1 | 17.7 | 21.1 | 24.6 | 26.7 |
| h. Other private insurance | 0.6 | 0.6 | 0 | 0 | 0.5 | | 0.3 | 0 | 0.4 | 0 | 0 | 0 | 0.2 |
| i. Other finance | -3.3 | 1.8 | -3.2 | 10.1 | -6.8 | 2.4 | -1.0 | -2.0 | 5.9 | -0.5 | -6.4 | 0.5 | 1.1 |
| 4. Total | 100.0 | 100.0 | 100.0 | 100.0 | 100.0 | 100.0 | 100.0 | 100.0 | 100.0 | 100.0 | 100.0 | 100.0 | 100.0 |
| 5. Total (billion dollars) | 1.80 | 1.70 | 1.58 | 1.79 | 2.07 | 2.49 | 3.15 | 2.54 | 2.73 | 3.72 | 3.89 | 4.23 | 4.68 |
| Memorandum | | | | | | | | | | | | | |
| 6. Total domestic net issues (billion dollars) | 1.74 | 1.58 | 1.44 | 1.79 | 2.05 | 2.61 | 3.09 | 2.64 | 2.59 | 3.67 | 4.03 | 4.33 | 4.28 |
| 7. Total domestic net issues | 100.0 | 100.0 | 100.0 | 100.0 | 100.0 | 100.0 | 100.0 | 100.0 | 100.0 | 100.0 | 100.0 | 100.0 | 100.0 |
| 8. Rest-of-world net purchases | -3.4 | -8.1 | -8.3 | -1.1 | 0 | 3.8 | 0 | 1.9 | 4.6 | 3.3 | 6.2 | 3.2 | -1.6 |

Source: National Balance Sheet, Vol. II, Table VIII-b-17.

issues of common stock other than investment company issues (nearly one-half) may appear high, it is much lower than the comparable ratios for the other main capital market instruments. Thus financial institutions' net purchases are estimated at 95 per cent of the net issuance of corporate bonds and about 90 per cent of the increase in total residential mortgage debt.

Net purchases of common stock were concentrated in two groups of financial institutions—private pension plans and investment companies—which accounted for more than two-fifths and for about one-third, respectively, of all net institutional purchase of common stock (Table 82). For all other groups of financial institutions, net purchases were moderate in comparison to the size of the market. Thus the net purchases of life insurance and fire and casualty insurance companies each amounted to only a little over $1 billion in thirteen years, i.e., about one-thirteenth and one-ninth of total institutional net purchases and 3 and 5 per cent, respectively, of new offerings of common stock other than investment company securities.

The share of the net purchases of common stock by institutions, however, increased very markedly over the postwar period: it was less than one-fourth of net new common stock issues in Cycle I, rose to one-third in Cycle II, and advanced to over two-fifths in Cycle III. Since financial institutions do not commonly acquire substantial amounts of nonmarketable stock issues or of investment company stocks, a comparison which excludes these two types of issues is more relevant. It then appears that institutional net purchases of common stock were equal to more than two-fifths of total new issues in Cycle I, to one-half in Cycle II, and to about four-fifths in Cycle III.

The predominance of financial institutions as net buyers of marketable common stock other than investment company securities is still more dramatically illustrated by the fact that net noninstitutional absorption of such securities averaged $0.6 billion over the postwar period and it increased from Cycle I to Cycle II but decreased from Cycle II to Cycle III.[21] Noninstitutional investors, apart from their acquisition of considerable amounts of new investment company shares and of nonmarketable stock, thus hardly had any excess of purchases of common stock—newly issued during the postwar period or already outstanding—over sales. If, as is likely, they acquired substantial amounts of new marketable noninvestment-company issues,

[21] This figure includes converted bonds and would be smaller excluding them.

they must on balance have sold almost equally large amounts of outstanding seasoned marketable common stocks to institutions.

On an annual basis, the absorption by the general public of marketable noninvestment-company securities fluctuated substantially. These fluctuations were generally in accordance with the business cycle, showing particularly low values in recession years as can be seen in Table 88. Net purchases varied only between $0.6 and $1.0 billion per year from 1947 through 1952. They fell to $0.3 billion in 1954, but rose sharply to $0.8 billion in 1955 and $0.7 billion in 1956. After declining to $0.2 billion in 1957, the balance became small in 1958, i.e., $0.04 billion.

The statistics are unfortunately insufficient to break down the residual (new issues of marketable securities less institutional net purchases) into groups of noninstitutional investors. It is known, however, that the $7 billion of net new issues of investment-company common stock was purchased mainly by individual U.S. investors, and here again largely by investors of moderate means. Most of the unrecorded issues of small and medium-sized corporations, aggregating $9.5 billion, probably were bought by the same groups of investors, although by active entrepreneurs rather than by salaried employees. Fragmentary information is also available on the net purchases of some groups other than U.S. individuals that are included in the residual of $8 billion of marketable noninvestment-company common stock. The residual, for instance, includes foreign investors who are estimated to have made net purchases of American common stock of about $0.4 billion during the postwar period. Also included are nonfinancial corporations, but their estimated net purchases of $1.8 billion may include substantial amounts of unrecorded or foreign securities. Thus, domestic private investors (still including nonprofit institutions) showed net purchases of marketable noninvestment-company securities of between $7.5 billion and $5.5 billion over the entire period, depending upon the proportion of the estimated net purchases of nonfinancial corporations regarded as marketable domestic issues. This balance is further reduced by the net purchases of nonprofit institutions which are not known, but may have been on the order of $1 to $2 billion for the entire postwar period. One may thus conclude that from 1946 to 1958 individuals (excluding foreigners) made net purchases of marketable common stock other than investment-company securities of between $3.5 (lower limit) and $6.5 billion (upper limit).

Although little is known definitely about net purchases and sales

TABLE 88

ISSUANCE AND ABSORPTION OF COMMON STOCK, 1946-58
(billion dollars)

| Year | Recorded Net Issues | | | Unrecorded Net Issues (4) | Net Purchases by Financial Institutions (5) | NONINSTITUTIONAL PURCHASES | | |
|---|---|---|---|---|---|---|---|---|
| | | | | | | All Issues (6) | Marketable Issues | |
| | Total (1) | Investment Companies (2) | Other (3) | | | | All (7) | Excl. Invest. Companies (8) |
| 1946 | 1.10 | 0.16 | 0.94 | 0.64 | 0.29 | 1.51 | 1.01 | 0.85 |
| 1947 | 0.94 | 0.17 | 0.77 | 0.64 | 0.46 | 1.24 | 0.72 | 0.55 |
| 1948 | 0.90 | 0.14 | 0.76 | 0.54 | 0.27 | 1.31 | 0.83 | 0.69 |
| 1949 | 1.24 | 0.26 | 0.98 | 0.55 | 0.57 | 1.22 | 0.82 | 0.56 |
| 1950 | 1.46 | 0.25 | 1.21 | 0.59 | 0.38 | 1.69 | 1.24 | 0.99 |
| 1951 | 2.10 | 0.40 | 1.70 | 0.51 | 0.70 | 1.79 | 1.33 | 0.93 |
| 1952 | 2.52 | 0.55 | 1.97 | 0.57 | 1.17 | 1.98 | 1.49 | 0.94 |
| 1953 | 1.99 | 0.43 | 1.56 | 0.65 | 0.89 | 1.65 | 1.12 | 0.69 |
| 1954 | 1.84 | 0.46 | 1.38 | 0.75 | 1.35 | 1.38 | 0.77 | 0.31 |
| 1955 | 2.64 | 0.76 | 1.88 | 1.03 | 1.40 | 2.32 | 1.59 | 0.83 |
| 1956 | 2.99 | 0.91 | 2.08 | 1.04 | 1.53 | 2.36 | 1.60 | 0.69 |
| 1957 | 3.31 | 0.98 | 2.33 | 1.02 | 2.26 | 1.97 | 1.21 | 0.23 |
| 1958 | 3.24 | 1.50 | 1.74 | 1.04 | 2.29 | 2.39 | 1.54 | 0.04 |
| Average | | | | | | | | |
| 1946-49 | 1.00 | 0.17 | 0.83 | 0.59 | 0.39 | 1.30 | 0.82 | 0.65 |
| 1949-54 | 1.92 | 0.40 | 1.52 | 0.59 | 0.82 | 1.68 | 1.20 | 0.80 |
| 1954-58 | 2.87 | 0.91 | 1.96 | 1.00 | 1.75 | 2.13 | 1.39 | 0.48 |
| 1946-58 | 2.02 | 0.54 | 1.49 | 0.74 | 1.04 | 1.75 | 1.17 | 0.63 |

Source: National Balance Sheet, Vol. II.

Col. 1: Table IV-b-17a, line 10, minus col. 4 of this table.
Col. 2: Table VIII-d-1, line 5f.
Col. 3: Col. 1 minus col. 2 of this table.
Col. 4: Table IV-b-17a, sum of lines 5, 7, 8, and 9, minus line 6.
Col. 5: Table VIII-b-17, line 5.
Col. 6: Table VIII-b-17, line 8, minus col. 5 of this table.
Col. 7: Col. 6 minus Table IV-b-17a, line 9.
Col. 8: Col. 7 minus col. 2 of this table.

of common stock, and hence shifts of holdings, among groups of individual U.S. investors, there are some indications that investors of moderate means and in the younger-age groups made net acquisitions while large and older investors had either no net purchase balance or a net sales balance. One of these indicators is a considerable increase in the number of individuals who own common stock, from six to twelve million from 1952 to 1959.[22] The average holdings as of 1958 of these additional six million shareholders were undoubtedly quite small and their aggregate holdings represented only a small fraction —around 5 per cent—of total stocks outstanding.

A second, and regularly available, indicator is the purchase or sales balance in odd lots on the New York Stock Exchange which suggests a shift from larger to smaller holdings. From 1946 through 1958, the aggregate odd lot purchase balance amounted to about $3 billion,[23] i.e., about 1 per cent[24] of the value of all listed stock.

Another indication arguing against far-reaching changes in the distribution of share ownership, and hence against large-scale net sales from large to small shareholders, is the similarity in the distribution, measured by the Lorenz curves, of dividends reported on individual tax returns at the beginning and end of the postwar period. The top 600,000 shareholders in 1946—estimated to account for over 10 per cent —reported 83 per cent of all dividend receipts declared in that year. In 1956 the 600,000 top dividend recipients accounted for 80 per cent of all recorded dividends, while the number then corresponding to one-tenth of the estimated number of shareholders—1,200,000—reported 90 per cent of all dividends declared in individuals' tax returns. It took only 168,000 additional tax returns in 1958[25] to reach the 1946 ratio (83 per cent) of the top 600,000 shareholders reporting dividend income on personal income tax returns.

Although some net sales from wealthy and older investors to younger and lower income and wealth groups is likely, the shift in-

[22] *New York Stock Exchange Fact Book, 1960,* p. 27.

[23] *Ibid.,* pp. 44–45.

[24] *25th Annual Report,* SEC, p. 63.

[25] The figures in the text refer to the dividends of top shareholders as a percentage of all dividends declared on individual tax returns (*Statistics of Income: Individual Income Tax Returns,* 1946, p. 152; 1956, p. 37; 1958, p. 44). The estimate of top shareowners was taken from *Shareownership in America, 1959,* New York Stock Exchange, p. 6, and Lewis H. Kimmel, *Shareownership in the United States,* Washington, 1952, p. 90. The 1946 figure is a rough estimate. The New York Stock Exchange figures for top shareowners were used in order to adjust for the low estimate of the number of shareholders as reported in the *Statistics of Income.*

volved is probably moderate compared with the total value of total stock outstanding and is not likely to change the degree of concentration of ownership of common stock substantially. Both in 1958 and in 1945, a very large proportion of all common stock was in the hands of a relatively small proportion of families.[26]

More definite conclusions about net flows among individual stockholder groups are not yet possible, since even now there is no direct, reliable, and comprehensive information on the net balance of stock transactions by groups of individual investors; such information is, of course, virtually absent for earlier parts of the period. Estimates of the distribution of the value of stockholdings at different dates within the period are only of limited significance in inferring the net currents of net purchases and sales among groups of individuals because of the possibility of systematic differences in the price experience of different investor groups.

### THE POSITION OF COMMON STOCK IN THE PORTFOLIOS OF INVESTOR GROUPS

Between 1945 and 1958 the ratio of the value of common stock to the value of national assets (the combined footing of the balance sheets of all economic units, private and governmental) increased from 9 to 12 per cent. This rise, of course, was due exclusively to the sharp increase in the price of common stock, since the rate of growth of common stock (defined as the ratio of net flow to the average value of the stock) was smaller than that of almost all other main tangible and financial assets. The advance was even more pronounced in relation to all financial assets: from 14 per cent in 1945 to 21 per cent in 1958. Table 89 shows the movements of the share of all corporate stock in the total assets of various investor groups for each year of the period. Table 90 provides the same information for common stock. The increase is found to have been considerably more pronounced for financial institutions than for households, where it reflected exclusively the effect of rising stock prices.

The near quadrupling of the share of common stocks among the assets of financial institutions from 1.6 to 5.6 per cent, on the other hand, was the combined result of net purchases and the rise in stock prices. The rise in the share was most pronounced for trusteed pen-

---

[26] Cf. Robert J. Lampman, *The Share of Top Wealth-Holders in National Wealth, 1922–56,* Princeton for NBER, 1962, Chapter 6.

## TABLE 89

### SHARE OF CORPORATE STOCK IN ASSETS OF EACH SECTOR, 1945-58
(per cent)

| | 1945 | 1946 | 1947 | 1948 | 1949 | 1950 | 1951 | 1952 | 1953 | 1954 | 1955 | 1956 | 1957 | 1958 |
|---|---|---|---|---|---|---|---|---|---|---|---|---|---|---|
| 1. Nonfarm households | 17.9 | 14.8 | 13.1 | 12.4 | 13.4 | 14.6 | 15.3 | 15.5 | 14.7 | 18.4 | 20.4 | 20.0 | 17.7 | 21.4 |
| 2. Nonfinancial corporations | 11.0 | 8.8 | 7.4 | 6.8 | 7.4 | 7.6 | 7.7 | 7.8 | 7.4 | 9.3 | 10.2 | 9.7 | 8.2 | 10.3 |
| 3. Finance | 2.1 | 2.1 | 2.0 | 2.0 | 2.4 | 2.7 | 3.0 | 3.3 | 3.4 | 4.5 | 5.1 | 5.1 | 4.8 | 6.2 |
| a. Government insurance and pension funds | 0.2 | 0.1 | 0.1 | 0.2 | 0.2 | 0.2 | 0.2 | 0.2 | 0.3 | 0.4 | 0.4 | 0.5 | 0.6 | 0.8 |
| b. Commercial banks | 0.1 | 0.1 | 0.1 | 0.1 | 0.2 | 0.1 | 0.1 | 0.1 | 0.1 | 0.1 | 0.1 | 0.1 | 0.1 | 0.1 |
| c. Mutual savings banks | 0.8 | 0.8 | 0.8 | 0.8 | 0.7 | 0.8 | 1.0 | 1.3 | 1.6 | 1.9 | 2.1 | 2.1 | 2.2 | 2.3 |
| d. Investment companies | 79.9 | 79.1 | 78.0 | 78.0 | 80.1 | 81.1 | 83.4 | 84.8 | 84.7 | 88.2 | 88.2 | 87.8 | 86.2 | 88.4 |
| e. Life insurance | 2.2 | 2.6 | 2.7 | 2.6 | 2.8 | 3.2 | 3.2 | 3.3 | 3.2 | 3.8 | 4.0 | 3.6 | 3.3 | 3.8 |
| f. Fire and casualty insurance | 31.4 | 28.7 | 25.6 | 23.4 | 24.8 | 26.0 | 26.7 | 26.9 | 25.5 | 29.7 | 31.6 | 31.8 | 29.0 | 32.5 |
| g. Noninsured pension plans | 10.8 | 11.3 | 12.2 | 12.7 | 13.7 | 15.1 | 17.8 | 20.6 | 21.4 | 27.8 | 32.6 | 32.9 | 31.6 | 38.8 |
| h. Other private insurance | 2.6 | 3.3 | 3.5 | 3.3 | 3.4 | 3.8 | 3.4 | 3.3 | 3.1 | 3.3 | 3.1 | 3.0 | 2.7 | 3.2 |
| i. Other finance | 4.4 | 4.2 | 5.4 | 4.4 | 6.7 | 4.4 | 5.5 | 5.8 | 4.7 | 6.7 | 6.6 | 4.3 | 6.3 | 3.9 |
| 4. Total | 9.6 | 8.1 | 7.1 | 6.7 | 7.3 | 8.0 | 8.3 | 8.5 | 8.2 | 10.4 | 11.7 | 11.5 | 10.0 | 12.5 |

Source: *National Balance Sheet*, Vol. II, Tables III-1, III-4, III-5, 5b, 5c, 5d, 5f, 5h, 5i, 5j, 5k, 5m; line 4 from Table I.

TABLE 90

SHARE OF COMMON STOCK IN ASSETS OF EACH SECTOR, 1945–58
(per cent)

| | 1945 | 1946 | 1947 | 1948 | 1949 | 1950 | 1951 | 1952 | 1953 | 1954 | 1955 | 1956 | 1957 | 1958 |
|---|---|---|---|---|---|---|---|---|---|---|---|---|---|---|
| 1. Nonfarm households | 16.6 | 13.6 | 12.0 | 11.3 | 12.3 | 13.6 | 14.4 | 14.6 | 13.9 | 17.6 | 19.7 | 19.3 | 16.9 | 20.8 |
| 2. Nonfinancial corporations | 9.6 | 7.6 | 6.4 | 5.8 | 6.4 | 6.8 | 7.0 | 7.1 | 6.7 | 8.7 | 9.6 | 9.2 | 7.8 | 9.9 |
| 3. Finance | 1.6 | 1.5 | 1.5 | 1.5 | 1.8 | 2.0 | 2.4 | 2.7 | 2.7 | 3.8 | 4.5 | 4.5 | 4.2 | 5.6 |
| a. Government insurance and pension funds | 0.1 | 0.1 | 0.1 | 0.1 | 0.1 | 0.1 | 0.1 | 0.1 | 0.2 | 0.2 | 0.2 | 0.2 | 0.3 | 0.4 |
| b. Commercial banks | 0.1 | 0.1 | 0.1 | 0.1 | 0.1 | 0.1 | 0.1 | 0.1 | 0.1 | 0.1 | 0.1 | 0.1 | 0.1 | 0.1 |
| c. Mutual savings banks | 0.8 | 0.8 | 0.8 | 0.8 | 0.7 | 0.8 | 1.0 | 1.3 | 1.6 | 1.9 | 2.1 | 2.1 | 2.2 | 2.3 |
| d. Investment companies | 73.0 | 72.3 | 71.0 | 70.5 | 74.0 | 75.5 | 78.2 | 81.1 | 79.1 | 83.5 | 83.7 | 83.0 | 81.9 | 83.9 |
| e. Life insurance | 0.4 | 0.6 | 0.7 | 0.7 | 0.8 | 1.0 | 1.2 | 1.3 | 1.3 | 1.8 | 2.1 | 2.0 | 1.8 | 2.3 |
| f. Fire and casualty insurance | 23.7 | 21.3 | 19.1 | 17.7 | 19.3 | 20.8 | 21.7 | 21.9 | 20.6 | 25.2 | 27.5 | 28.2 | 25.4 | 29.3 |
| g. Noninsured pension plans | 7.3 | 7.5 | 8.3 | 3.7 | 9.7 | 10.8 | 13.3 | 16.3 | 17.2 | 24.1 | 29.2 | 29.7 | 28.5 | 36.2 |
| h. Other private insurance | 0.5 | 0.8 | 1.0 | 0.9 | 1.0 | 1.3 | 1.3 | 1.4 | 1.4 | 1.7 | 1.8 | 1.8 | 1.6 | 2.1 |
| i. Other finance | 4.1 | 4.0 | 5.2 | 4.2 | 6.4 | 4.3 | 5.2 | 5.5 | 4.4 | 6.4 | 6.3 | 4.1 | 6.1 | 3.7 |
| 4. Total | 8.7 | 7.2 | 6.4 | 6.0 | 6.6 | 7.3 | 7.7 | 7.9 | 7.5 | 9.9 | 11.2 | 11.0 | 9.5 | 12.0 |

Source: National Balance Sheet, Vol. II, Tables III-1, III-4, III-5, 5b, 5c, 5d, 5f, 5h, 5i, 5j, 5k, 5m; line 4 from Table I.

sion funds. It was also substantial relative to the initial level, although still small relative to total assets, for life insurance companies, government insurance funds, fraternal orders, and mutual savings banks. The increase was small for investment companies and fire and casualty insurance companies, two groups which always have kept a large proportion of their assets in common stock.

More relevant is the share of net purchases of stock in total uses of funds which can be followed in Table 91 (all corporate stock) and in Table 92 (common stock) for each year and for each major investor group. For nonfarm households, net purchases of common stock—including investment company and unrecorded issues—averaged $2\frac{1}{2}$ per cent of total uses of funds a year; if limited to marketable common stock, they are reduced to 1.6 per cent. If investment company issues are also excluded, the ratio is further lowered to 0.8 per cent. Few differences are found in the movements of this ratio between cycles, or from year to year in response to the business cycle situation; nor is there clear evidence of the effects of stock price movements.

Another way to visualize the relative importance of common stocks is to compare net purchases with individuals' saving.[27] For the period 1946–58, aggregate net purchases of common stock of all types represented 3.1 per cent of total nonfarm households' saving; net purchases of marketable common stock alone were equivalent to 2.0 per cent of individuals' savings. Exclusion of investment company stock reduces the share to 1.0 per cent. Net purchases of common stock, of whichever scope, thus constituted only a minor outlet for current saving for all individuals taken together.[28] The situation is quite different if the comparison is limited to saving through financial assets. In this case, the ratios are 17 per cent of aggregate financial saving for all common stock, 11 per cent for marketable common stock, and 5 per cent for marketable common stock other than investment company securities. Common stocks were undoubtedly a more important outlet for the saving of some groups of individuals, particularly middle- and upper-income and younger- and middle-aged groups. There is, unfortunately, no material that would enable us to measure these differences reliably.

In the case of financial institutions, the share of net purchases of

[27] *National Balance Sheet,* Vol. II, Table VII-1.
[28] This statement would not be correct if savings were defined to include realized or both realized and unrealized net capital gains. These gains, however, are excluded from all statistics of current saving.

TABLE 91

SHARE OF NET PURCHASES OF CORPORATE STOCK IN TOTAL
NET USES OF FUNDS OF SECTORS, 1946–58
(per cent)

| | 1946 | 1947 | 1948 | 1949 | 1950 | 1951 | 1952 | 1953 | 1954 | 1955 | 1956 | 1957 | 1958 |
|---|---|---|---|---|---|---|---|---|---|---|---|---|---|
| 1. Nonfarm households | 3.7 | 3.5 | 3.6 | 2.7 | 2.8 | 3.6 | 3.2 | 2.2 | 1.8 | 2.3 | 3.2 | 2.6 | 2.6 |
| 2. Nonfinancial corporations | 0.4 | 0.3 | 0.3 | 0.5 | 0.2 | 0.3 | 0.5 | 0.4 | 0.5 | 0.4 | 0.4 | 0.5 | 0.6 |
| 3. Finance | 29.4 | 2.4 | 2.0 | 7.1 | 2.7 | 2.9 | 4.2 | 4.9 | 6.0 | 4.4 | 4.7 | 7.7 | 7.2 |
| a. Government insurance and pension funds | 0 | 0 | 0.6 | 0 | 1.5 | 0.5 | 0.5 | 1.2 | 1.5 | 1.9 | 1.1 | 2.8 | 9.8 |
| b. Commercial banks | 0.3 | -0.5 | 0 | -0.3 | 0 | -0.1 | 0.1 | 0 | 0 | 0.1 | 0 | 0.4 | 0.1 |
| c. Mutual savings banks | 0.6 | 0 | 1.0 | 0 | 2.2 | 5.1 | 6.2 | 4.7 | 6.5 | 4.5 | 2.0 | 3.8 | 3.4 |
| d. Investment companies | 116.7 | 76.2 | 75.0 | 76.9 | 46.4 | 72.0 | 82.7 | 85.7 | 68.2 | 60.0 | 81.7 | 83.2 | 72.9 |
| e. Life insurance | 7.3 | 4.2 | 1.1 | 5.8 | 7.4 | 1.2 | 3.2 | 1.7 | 5.0 | 1.2 | 0 | 0.7 | 1.1 |
| f. Fire and casualty insurance | 8.3 | 10.9 | 8.8 | 10.8 | 12.4 | 15.3 | 13.5 | 12.9 | 12.9 | 16.8 | 21.0 | 12.4 | 11.8 |
| g. Noninsured pension plans | 13.7 | 17.1 | 15.3 | 20.2 | 22.3 | 22.5 | 28.5 | 26.6 | 33.2 | 34.4 | 33.6 | 37.5 | 42.5 |
| h. Other private insurance | 16.7 | 5.6 | 1.0 | 6.4 | 8.3 | -2.7 | 3.3 | 0 | 6.3 | -0.4 | 0.6 | 0 | 3.3 |
| i. Other finance | 3.9 | -3.7 | -8.5 | 32.8 | -20.8 | 700.0 | -7.5 | -12.2 | 9.9 | -10.0 | 650.0 | 4.5 | 2.4 |
| 4. Total | 3.4 | 1.7 | 1.7 | 2.4 | 1.4 | 1.9 | 2.4 | 1.9 | 2.0 | 1.8 | 2.2 | 2.4 | 2.6 |

Source: National Balance Sheet, Vol. II, Tables VII-1, VII-4, VII-5, 5b, 5c, 5d, 5f, 5h, 5i, 5j, 5k, 5m; line 4 from Table V.

TABLE 92

SHARE OF NET PURCHASES OF COMMON STOCK IN TOTAL
NET USES OF FUNDS OF SECTORS, 1946-58
(per cent)

| | 1946 | 1947 | 1948 | 1949 | 1950 | 1951 | 1952 | 1953 | 1954 | 1955 | 1956 | 1957 | 1958 |
|---|---|---|---|---|---|---|---|---|---|---|---|---|---|
| 1. Nonfarm households | 3.7 | 2.8 | 2.9 | 2.7 | 2.9 | 2.8 | 2.8 | 2.2 | 1.8 | 2.5 | 2.5 | 2.1 | 2.5 |
| 2. Nonfinancial corporations | 0.4 | 0.2 | 0.3 | 0.5 | 0.2 | 0.3 | 0.5 | 0.4 | 0.4 | 0.3 | 0.4 | 0.4 | 0.6 |
| 3. Finance | 18.1 | 1.9 | 1.6 | 4.7 | 1.5 | 2.4 | 3.6 | 3.6 | 4.6 | 3.8 | 5.1 | 7.8 | 6.1 |
| a. Government insurance and pension funds | 0 | 0 | 0.3 | 0 | 0.8 | 0.2 | 0.2 | 0.6 | 0.7 | 0.9 | 0.6 | 1.4 | 4.9 |
| b. Commercial banks | 0.3 | -0.5 | 0 | -0.3 | 0 | -0.1 | 0.1 | 0 | 0 | 0.1 | 0 | 0.4 | 0.1 |
| c. Mutual savings banks | 0.6 | 0 | 1.0 | 0 | 2.2 | 5.1 | 6.2 | 4.7 | 6.5 | 4.5 | 2.0 | 3.8 | 3.4 |
| d. Investment companies | 125.0 | 71.4 | 62.5 | 76.9 | 35.7 | 56.0 | 92.3 | 45.2 | 50.0 | 47.1 | 70.4 | 94.7 | 49.6 |
| e. Life insurance | 3.2 | 2.5 | 0.3 | 0.8 | 3.0 | 2.4 | 1.4 | 1.0 | 1.3 | 1.1 | 3.3 | 1.3 | 0.4 |
| f. Fire and casualty insurance | 6.7 | 10.9 | 9.7 | 5.4 | 9.3 | 11.2 | 7.5 | 9.5 | 8.6 | 16.8 | 33.9 | 10.3 | 12.7 |
| g. Noninsured pension plans | 8.6 | 12.1 | 11.6 | 15.5 | 16.7 | 16.4 | 24.9 | 23.4 | 30.4 | 32.0 | 31.3 | 36.1 | 40.9 |
| h. Other private insurance | 5.6 | 4.0 | 1.0 | 2.8 | 4.5 | 2.7 | 3.3 | 1.1 | 6.3 | 1.7 | 2.3 | 9.1 | 2.5 |
| i. Other finance | 3.3 | -3.7 | -8.5 | 31.0 | -19.4 | 600.0 | -7.5 | -12.2 | 9.4 | -10.0 | 625.0 | 3.0 | 3.0 |
| 4. Total | 3.1 | 1.4 | 1.4 | 2.0 | 1.3 | 1.5 | 2.1 | 1.7 | 1.7 | 1.8 | 2.0 | 2.2 | 2.3 |

Source: National Balance Sheet, Vol. II, Tables VII-1, VII-4, VII-5, 5b, 5c, 5d, 5f, 5h, 5i, 5j, 5k, 5m; line 4 from Table V.

common stock in total uses of funds shows a considerable increase over the period, if the exceptional value of 1946 is ignored (see Table 92). The increase is most spectacular in trusteed pension funds. A substantial but very irregular increase can also be observed in the case of mutual savings banks. In addition to the trend among these two groups, there appears a tendency to increase the share of common stocks in total uses of funds beginning with 1956. This probably reflects a change in the basic investment policies of many financial institutions, namely the increasing acceptance of common stock (at least those of large seasoned companies) as a substantial element in the portfolio. For most institutions, however, this change in policy was still in its initial stages at the end of the period under study. Liberalization of investment regulations for financial institutions in several states, particularly New York, was another factor.

## Historical Background

The main differences in the characteristics of the market for common stock between the postwar period and the forty years preceding World War II are summarized in the following paragraphs. The comparison is primarily between the postwar period, on the one hand, and the 1920's and the interval between the turn of the century and World War I, on the other. Because of the nature of the statistics, most of the quantitative data refer to common and preferred stock combined.

1. While the volume of corporate stock outstanding and of the trading in common stock increased greatly, the basic structure of the market, particularly the division between the exchange and the over-the-counter market, remained basically the same before World War II and the postwar period. There is, however, some evidence that the relative importance of the over-the-counter market was smaller in earlier periods.[29]

2. Common stocks accounted for at least four-fifths of the total value of all corporate stock throughout the prewar period and their share rose to between 85 and 90 per cent in the 1920's. The market for preferred stocks thus was relatively more important in earlier periods.[30]

[29] See Friend, *The Over-the-Counter Securities Market,* p. 109.
[30] Raymond W. Goldsmith, *Supplementary Appendixes to Financial Intermediaries Since 1900,* New York, NBER, 1958, p. F-29.

TABLE 93

STOCK PRICES AND YIELDS, 1946–58

| | Prices (1957–59 = 100) | | Price Changes (per cent) | | | | | Corporation Profits (billion dollars) | Corporation Dividends (billion dollars) | Stock Trading | |
| | Beginning of Year (1) | Average (2) | Year to Year (3) | Average (4) | Earning-Price Ratio (per cent) (5) | Dividend Yield (per cent) (6) | (7) | (8) | Shares (millions) (9) | Value (billion dollars) (10) |
|---|---|---|---|---|---|---|---|---|---|---|
| 1946 | 41.0 | 40.1 | | | 5.7 | 3.97 | 13.4 | 5.8 | 63.0 | 1.6 |
| 1947 | 35.6 | 35.1 | −13 | −12 | 10.7 | 5.13 | 18.2 | 6.5 | 39.5 | 1.0 |
| 1948 | 34.7 | 35.6 | −3 | −1 | 14.5 | 5.78 | 20.5 | 7.2 | 45.0 | 1.1 |
| 1949 | 34.4 | 34.3 | −1 | −4 | 15.1 | 6.63 | 16.0 | 7.5 | 39.8 | .9 |
| 1950 | 37.6 | 41.4 | 9 | 21 | 15.1 | 6.27 | 22.8 | 9.2 | 71.4 | 1.8 |
| 1951 | 45.9 | 49.6 | 22 | 20 | 10.8 | 6.12 | 19.7 | 9.0 | 65.5 | 1.8 |
| 1952 | 51.8 | 52.3 | 13 | 5 | 9.6 | 5.50 | 17.2 | 9.0 | 52.2 | 1.4 |
| 1953 | 54.8 | 51.9 | 6 | −1 | 10.3 | 5.49 | 18.1 | 9.2 | 52.8 | 1.4 |
| 1954 | 52.6 | 61.7 | −4 | 19 | 8.9 | 4.78 | 16.8 | 9.8 | 82.8 | 2.3 |
| 1955 | 72.2 | 81.8 | 37 | 33 | 8.7 | 4.06 | 23.0 | 11.2 | 101.0 | 3.2 |
| 1956 | 88.4 | 92.6 | 22 | 13 | 7.1 | 4.07 | 23.5 | 12.1 | 90.3 | 2.9 |
| 1957 | 91.5 | 89.8 | 4 | −3 | 7.8 | 4.33 | 22.3 | 12.6 | 89.2 | 2.7 |
| 1958 | 82.0 | 93.2 | −10 | −4 | 6.0 | 4.05 | 19.1 | 12.4 | 108.9 | 3.2 |
| *Averages* | | | | | | | | | | |
| 1946–49 | 36.0 | 36.0 | | | 11.9 | 5.40 | 17.8 | 6.8 | 45.3 | 1.1 |
| 1949–54 | 46.7 | 48.6 | 7 | 8 | 11.6 | 5.82 | 18.8 | 9.0 | 60.6 | 1.6 |
| 1954–58 | 79.8 | 85.4 | 13 | 13 | 7.8 | 4.22 | 21.7 | 11.8 | 94.1 | 2.9 |
| 1946–58 | 55.6 | 58.4 | | | 10.0 | 5.09 | 19.3 | 9.3 | 69.3 | 1.9 |

Source

Cols. 1–2: Securities and Exchange Commission Stock Price Index (Nov. 1, 1960). Index refers to weekly closing prices of 300 common stock issues listed on the N. Y. Stock Exchange; prices weighted by number of outstanding shares, pp. 26–29.
Cols. 3–4: Derived from cols. 1 and 2.
Col. 5: Standard and Poor's Trade and Securities Statistics. Security price index record, 1962 ed., p. 114.
Col. 6: Business Statistics, 1959 Edition, p. 103. Figures refer to 200 stocks.
Cols. 7–8: Economic Report of the President, January, 1961, p. 192. Figures taken from tax returns refer to all corporations.
Cols. 9–10: Business Statistics, 1959 Edition, p. 105. Figures refer to all registered exchanges.

3. There was a radical shift in the distribution of corporate stock by industry which can be followed in Table 94: a sharp decline in the share of railroad stocks and a less pronounced fall in that of the stock of commercial banks, offset by increases in the shares of manufacturing companies, investment companies, and to a lesser extent public utilities. These differences, however, arise primarily in comparing the postwar period with the decade before World War I, and are much less pronounced in comparing the postwar period with the 1920's and 1930's.

TABLE 94

DISTRIBUTION OF MARKET VALUE OF CORPORATE STOCK BY
MAJOR INDUSTRIES, 1900–58
(per cent)

|   |   | 1900 (1) | 1912 (2) | 1922 (3) | 1929 (4) | 1933 (5) | 1939 (6) | 1945 (7) | 1958 (8) |
|---|---|---|---|---|---|---|---|---|---|
| 1. | Railroads | 39 | 26 | 10 | 6 | 5 | 4 | 4 | 2 |
| 2. | Public utilities | 7 | 7 | 5 | 11 | 10 | 12 | 9 | 12 |
| 3. | Commercial banks | 18 | 14 | 14 | 9 | 4 | 6 | 6 | 5 |
| 4. | Investment companies |  |  | 0 | 1 | 1 | 1 | 2 | 5 |
| 5. | Other | 36 | 53 | 71 | 73 | 80 | 77 | 79 | 76 |
| 6. | Total | 100 | 100 | 100 | 100 | 100 | 100 | 100 | 100 |
| 7. | Total (billion dollars) | 14 | 37 | 68 | 178 | 74 | 95 | 147 | 458 |

Source: Col. 1–7 from Goldsmith, <u>Supplementary Appendixes</u>, pp. F-18 and F-29; col. 8, rough estimates.

4. Excluding the late 1920's, the relation of the value of corporate stock to total national assets varied little, notwithstanding very pronounced changes in the size of the national economy, the price level, and the financial structure. The value of corporate stock was equal to less than one-tenth of total national assets in 1900, and about one-eighth in the periods immediately before World War I and World War II. As a result of the war (the substantial increase of U.S. government bond holdings), the share of corporate stock in total assets declined to one-tenth of all assets. During the 1950's the increase in the price of stocks raised their share in national assets, so that in 1958 they amounted to one-eighth of national assets (see Table 96).

5. Whether the role of corporate stock in financing corporations changed is probably the most important problem, but also the most difficult to answer. Using the only comprehensive although rough estimates available (see Table 37), it appears that the postwar share of stock in financing nonfinancial corporations of 7 per cent of total net sources was considerably lower than the figures for the period before

1929: 14 per cent for 1901–12, 11 per cent for 1913–22, 19 per cent for 1922–29, and 9 per cent even for 1934–39. In proportion to external financing, the postwar ratio of 15 per cent was as much below the predepression rates of 31 per cent for 1901–12, and 43 per cent for 1923–29. Finally, the postwar ratio of stock financing to long-term debt financing was also considerably below the predepression rates, particularly those for 1923–29 when common stock financing almost equaled long-term debt financing in size. For all nonfinancial corporations taken together, stock financing thus lost considerably in importance, although less for common stock alone than for total stock financing. This reduction is partly the result of the shift of stock issues toward industries using less external financing, particularly manufacturing. This shift, however, does not explain the decline of common stock in external financing. Here the provision of the tax law, which permits the deduction of debt interest but not of dividends from taxable corporate income, may have provided an incentive for corporate management to shift external financing as far as possible to debt issues.

The changes in the role of stock in internal and external financing can be followed only for a few main industries. In the electric light and power industry, for example, stock issues provided between one-third and one-half of total financing in the prewar period [31] against about one-seventh in 1950–55.[32] In manufacturing and mining, the postwar share of stock financing of 6 per cent in 1946–53 (the denominator here excludes short-term debt) is well below the predepression ratio of one-fifth for 1919–29 and one-seventh for 1900–14.[33] There thus was a genuine decline, not explained by a change in the share of different industries in total financing, in the proportion of stock issues in total or in external financing. Hence the demand for stock financing increased less than the total financial requirements of corporate business.

6. Notwithstanding the well-known increase in the institutional holdings of common stock during the postwar period, the changes in the division of total stock outstanding among institutions and individual investors have not been striking as Table 95 and Chart 23

[31] Melville J. Ulmer, *Capital in Transportation, Communications, and Public Utilities,* Princeton for NBER, 1960, p. 151.

[32] David Meiselman and Eli Shapiro, *The Measurement of Corporate Sources and Uses of Funds,* Technical Paper 18, New York, NBER, 1964, Table 9.

[33] David Creamer, Sergei Dobrovolsky, and Israel Borenstein, *Capital in Manufacturing and Mining,* Princeton for NBER, 1960, pp. 121 and 331.

TABLE 95

DISTRIBUTION OF CORPORATE STOCK AMONG HOLDER GROUPS, 1900-53

(per cent)

| | 1958 (1) | 1945A (2) | 1945B (3) | 1939 (4) | 1929 (5) | 1912 (6) | 1900 (7) |
|---|---|---|---|---|---|---|---|
| 1. Nonfarm households | 73.7 | 76.1 | 76.8 | 73.1 | 74.1 | 79.3 | 77.0 |
| 2. Nonfinancial corporations | 17.0 | 18.9 | 18.7 | 21.9 | 22.7 | 18.8 | 20.3 |
| 3. Federal government | 0 | 0 | 0.2 | 0.6 | 0 | 0 | 0 |
| 4. Financial institutions, total | 9.3 | 5.0 | 4.3 | 4.4 | 3.3 | 1.9 | 2.7 |
| a. Commercial banks | 0 | 0.2 | 0.2 | 0.6 | 0.6 | 0.7 | 0.7 |
| b. Mutual savings banks | 0.2 | 0.1 | 0.1 | 0.1 | 0 | 0.1 | 0.3 |
| c. Investment companies | 3.9 | 2.0 | 1.3 | 1.2 | 1.2 | | |
| d. Life insurance companies | 0.9 | 0.7 | 0.7 | 0.6 | 0.2 | 0.2 | 0.4 |
| e. Noninsured pension plans | 2.3 | 0.2 | 0.2 | 0.6 | 0.1 | | |
| f. Fire and casualty insurance | 1.8 | 1.6 | 1.6 | 1.5 | 0.8 | 0.6 | 0.9 |
| g. Other private insurance | 0 | 0 | 0 | 0 | 0 | 0 | 0 |
| h. Government insurance and pension funds | 0.1 | 0 | 0 | 0 | 0 | | |
| i. Finance companies | 0 | 0 | 0.2 | 0 | 0 | | |
| j. Brokers and dealers[a] | 0.1 | 0.2 | 0.1 | 0.1 | 0.3 | 0.3 | 0.4 |
| 5. Total | 100.0 | 100.0 | 100.0 | 100.0 | 100.0 | 100.0 | 100.0 |
| 6. Total (billion dollars) | 465.4 | 146.6 | 150.8 | 100.1 | 186.7 | 38.0 | 13.9 |

Source: *National Balance Sheet*, Vol. II; cols. 1-2 from Table IV-b-16 and IV-b-17; cols. 3-7 from Table IV-b-17b.

Note: The sum of components may not add up to total because of rounding.

[a]Cols. 1 and 2 include both incorporated and unincorporated brokers and dealers. Cols. 3-7 include un-incorporated only.

See note to Table 55.

show. The share of individual investors of three-fourths is still the same as it was, with only minor fluctuations, in the half century before 1945. The postwar share of financial institutions was higher than in any earlier period.

CHART 23

DISTRIBUTION OF CORPORATE STOCK AMONG MAIN
HOLDER GROUPS, 1900–58

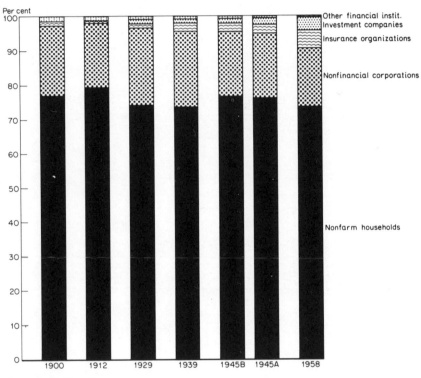

Source: Table 95.

7. More significant are changes in the share of corporate stock in the total assets of the main investor groups (see Table 96 and Chart 24). For households, the postwar level of about one-sixth is lower than the 30 per cent of 1929 when stock prices were extraordinarily high, and the 25 per cent of 1912, but it is very similar to the level of 1939 or of 1900.

8. For all financial institutions together, the share of stock in total

TABLE 96

SHARE OF CORPORATE STOCK IN TOTAL ASSETS OF HOLDER GROUPS, 1900-58

(per cent)

| | 1958 (1) | 1945A (2) | 1945B (3) | 1939 (4) | 1929 (5) | 1912 (6) | 1900 (7) |
|---|---|---|---|---|---|---|---|
| 1. Nonfarm households | 21.4 | 17.9 | 18.2 | 19.7 | 30.9 | 24.9 | 17.4 |
| 2. Nonfinancial corporations | 10.3 | 11.0 | 12.1 | 14.3 | 18.6 | 10.8 | 8.1 |
| 3. Federal government | 0 | 0 | 0.4 | 0 | 0 | 0.1 | 0 |
| 4. Financial institutions, total | 6.2 | 2.1 | 1.9 | 2.2 | 4.6 | 2.1 | 2.2 |
| a. Commercial banks | 0.1 | 0.1 | 0.2 | 0.9 | 1.8 | 1.3 | 1.0 |
| b. Mutual savings banks | 2.3 | 0.8 | 1.0 | 1.1 | 0.8 | 1.0 | 1.8 |
| c. Investment companies | 88.4 | 79.9 | 75.9 | 76.8 | 73.3 | | |
| d. Life insurance companies | 3.8 | 2.2 | 2.2 | 1.9 | 2.0 | 1.9 | 3.6 |
| e. Other private insurance | 3.2 | 2.6 | 2.5 | 1.0 | | 0 | 0 |
| f. Fire and casualty insurance | 32.5 | 31.4 | 31.1 | 29.9 | 32.0 | 23.0 | 25.0 |
| g. Noninsured pension plans | 38.8 | 10.8 | 12.0 | 20.0 | 20.0 | | |
| h. Government insurance and pension funds | 0.8 | 0.2 | 0 | 0 | 0 | | |
| i. Finance companies | 0 | 0 | 0 | 0 | 0.6 | | |
| j. Brokers and dealers a | 5.7 | 5.9 | 8.0 | 10.0 | 8.6 | 10.0 | 9.1 |
| 5. Total | 12.5 | 9.6 | 9.9 | 11.6 | 19.2 | 12.4 | 8.9 |

Source: National Balance Sheet, Vol. II, unless otherwise specified.

Lines 1-4: Tables I and Ia.

Lines 4a-4i, cols. 1-2: Tables III-5a through III-5ℓ.

Lines 4a-4i, cols. 3-7: Numerators from Table IV-b-17b, and denominators from Financial Intermediaries, total assets in Tables A-3, A-4, A-5, A-21, A-8, A-9, A-14, A-12, A-13, A-10, A-11, and total assets in Tables A-25, A-26, A-27, A-28 (total assets of mortgage companies only).

Line 4j: Table III-5m-1 and Study of Saving, Vol. III, Table W-37.

Line 5: Tables I and Ia.

a Cols. 1-2 include both incorporated and unincorporated brokers and dealers. Cols. 3-7 include only unincorporated brokers and dealers. See note to Table 55.

CHART 24

SHARE OF CORPORATE STOCK IN TOTAL ASSETS
OF MAIN HOLDER GROUPS, 1900–58

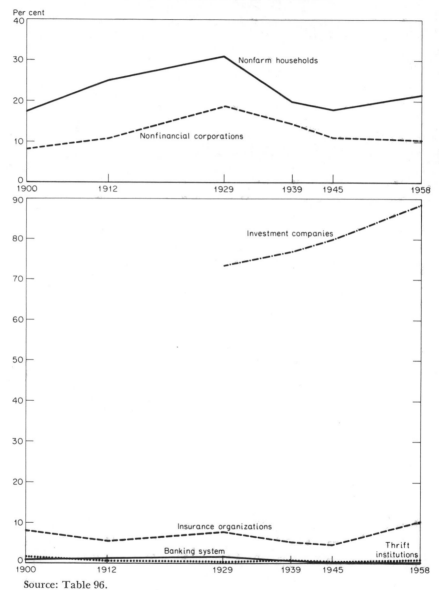

Source: Table 96.

assets just after the war was the same as at earlier benchmark dates. After 1948 it began to rise, reaching levels in the late 1950's that were considerably higher than even 1929. Even in 1958, however, the share of corporate stock in total assets was considerably above the prewar level only for pension funds and "other private insurance" (primarily fraternal organizations); it also increased somewhat for investment companies and mutual savings banks, but was not particularly high for life insurance and fire and casualty insurance companies. In the case of commercial banks, it was even lower than in the predepression period.

9. There is only indirect evidence on the trend of the distribution of stock ownership, and that is far from reliable. The share of the top 1 per cent of adults in total holdings of corporate stock has been estimated, mainly on the basis of estate tax returns, to have remained fairly stable at around two-thirds from 1922 to 1949, but to have risen to three-fourths in 1953.[34] This would indicate an increase in the concentration of stockholdings rather than the opposite, even if there should have been some reversal of the movement in the second half of the 1950's when the total number of stockholders increased substantially.

10. The share of stocks in the saving of individuals in the postwar period was considerably below the pre-1929 levels. For 1946–58 this share was 3.4 per cent (including investment company and unrecorded nonmarketable stock issues),[35] compared to ratios of one-fifth to one-fourth for the three predepression periods of 1897–1908, 1909–14, and 1922–29.[36] The decline in the share of stocks in individuals' total saving is more pronounced if both investment company and nonmarketable small issues are excluded, i.e., if the comparison is limited to publicly offered and traded noninvestment company securities. On that basis, the share of stock in individuals' total saving is 1.3 per cent,[37] against a ratio of 17 per cent before 1929 (1923–29).[38]

[34] Robert J. Lampman, *Changes in the Share of Wealth Held by Top Wealth-Holders, 1922–1956*, Occasional Paper 71, New York, NBER, 1960, p. 26.

[35] *National Balance Sheet*, Vol. II, Table VII-1.

[36] *A Study of Saving*, Vol. I, Tables V-1 and T-8.

[37] *National Balance Sheet*, Tables VIII-b-16 and VIII-b-17; and Table 88 (of this book).

[38] *A Study of Saving*, Vol. I. Numerator: Table T-8, col. 18, less the sum of Table V-17, cols. 12 and 13, and Table V-19, cols. 14 and 17. Denominator: Table T-8, col. 1.

# CHAPTER 10

# The Market for Residential Mortgages [1]

## Character of the Market

1. The market for residential mortgages does not yet meet the theoretical requirements of a perfect market nearly as well as the markets for government and corporate securities. It is still largely an aggregation of local markets, in contrast to the securities markets which are predominantly national in character. The residential mortgage is as yet much less of a fungible capital market instrument than government securities or corporate bonds and stocks. This market, however, advanced considerably toward true market status during the postwar period, particularly in the case of federally insured home mortgages.

2. The market for residential mortgages, apart from its local segmentation, can be divided according to three criteria. On the basis of the character of the property, it is divided into the markets for home mortgages (one- to four-family dwellings) and multifamily-structure mortgages; on the basis of the insurance status, into the markets for federally underwritten and for conventional mortgages; and on the basis of the rank of the lien, into the markets for senior and

---

[1] The organization and developments of the market for residential mortgages during the postwar period is discussed in detail in Saul B. Klaman's monograph which has been utilized here at various points (*The Postwar Residential Mortgage Market*, Princeton for NBER, 1960).

While this chapter deals with the entire market for residential mortgages, the discussion is concentrated, particularly in the nonstatistical part, on the market for first mortgages on single-family homes, which accounted for approximately three-fourths of the total volume of residential mortgages outstanding at the end of the period. Some background data on mortgage interest rates, maturities, and loan-to-value ratios are shown on an annual basis in Table 108.

274

for junior mortgages. The six segments, however, are of very different size. The market for home mortgages is almost eight times as large as that for multifamily mortgages; that for conventional mortgages is half again as large as the market for insured mortgages; the market for senior mortgages finally is probably ten times as large as that for junior mortgages, which are limited to conventional mortgages. (The size of net flows during the postwar period is used as the basis of measurement in all cases.)

3. The market for residential mortgages operates almost exclusively with a fairly standardized instrument—the amortizable long-term mortgage, usually with a final maturity of between ten and thirty years, commonly repayable at the borrower's option in advance of final maturity. It is only among junior mortgages that short-term obligations or contracts not providing for amortization are of substantial importance. The amortization feature has the important effect that large amounts of repayments become available fairly regularly to lenders. Another effect is the automatic decrease in the loan-to-value ratio which results from amortization schedules that usually exceed depreciation; this decrease is even greater in periods of rising real estate prices.

4. New home mortgages are acquired by lenders either directly through their head offices or their own branch organizations, or indirectly through real estate brokers or mortgage companies. Large institutional lenders often use such intermediaries also for servicing their mortgage portfolios at a fee of usually 0.5 per cent per year of the face amount of the mortgages.[2]

5. The distinction between direct and indirect acquisition and servicing of mortgages partly overlaps with another distinction, between mortgage lending at retail, where loans are made individually on specific properties, and lending at wholesale, where arrangements are made between a financial institution and a contractor or developer for a large number of loans of similar character, although each loan is legally secured only by an individual piece of property. Saving and loan associations and commercial banks operate mainly at the retail level, while a substantial proportion of the residential mortgage loans of life insurance companies, mutual savings banks, and pension funds are made on a wholesale basis.

[2] *Ibid.,* p. 244.

6. Advance commitments have become an important new technique connected chiefly with the wholesale activities of institutional lenders, particularly life insurance companies. They are in essence promises by a lender to purchase from a developer or builder directly or through an intermediary, usually a mortgage company, a specified amount of mortgages of more or less specifically defined characteristics during a specified period of time in the future, usually the next six to eighteen months. This promise then enables the developer or builder to obtain intermediate financing and to start construction. One of the main effects of the widespread use of advance commitments has been the introduction of a lag in the changes in the actual volume of construction behind the current supply and demand for funds in the residential real estate market, and a lag in interest rates on mortgage loans being paid out behind the market rates for current commitments.

7. Another result of wholesale lending is the development of "warehousing" operations. Here an institutional investor, usually a commercial bank, extends credit against the pledge of a substantial block of mortgages held either by an intermediary or by another institutional lender. Warehousing operations are usually resorted to when some lenders are temporarily overstocked with mortgages due to overcommitment.

8. Most institutional lenders acquire mortgages only in their final form which presupposes completion of the underlying structure. The need for financing while construction proceeds is met by intermediate financing in the form of construction loans. These are extended primarily by commercial banks, mainly large metropolitan institutions, and secondarily by saving and loan associations, which are then paid off by the financial institution which acquires the permanent mortgage.

9. Since construction loans usually are granted only if there is a definite commitment on the part of a lender to provide permanent mortgage financing, the practice has developed of stand-by commitments, which is particularly important when commitments for permanent loans are difficult to obtain. Stand-by commitments are a form of underwriting whereby a lender, usually a life insurance company, undertakes to make a permanent loan on terms more favorable to the lender than those prevailing at the time the agreement is made, or is entitled to a fee if he is not called upon to take up the permanent loan on the stand-by terms.

10. Mortgage companies became an important link in the market mechanism, their assets increasing from less than $0.2 to $1.8 billion during the postwar period.[3] The main function of mortgage companies is to act as agents for large organizations, particularly life insurance companies, who do not have a nationwide mortgage lending organization, in making insured home mortgage loans. In that function, mortgage companies usually carry a substantial portfolio of mortgages in different stages of completion which they finance by borrowing from commercial banks until the mortgages are taken over by the ultimate lender.[4]

11. In periods of tight credit, the residential mortgage market can find support in two federal credit agencies, the Federal National Mortgage Association (FNMA) which is authorized to acquire insured mortgages and the Federal Home Loan Bank which extends temporary credit to saving and loan associations. Although the FNMA was originally intended to be only a temporary holder of insured mortgages it was, by the end of 1958, holding a portfolio of $4 billion of insured mortgages, equal to 7 per cent of all insured mortgages outstanding and 3 per cent of the entire residential mortgage debt (Table 99).

12. The postwar market for residential mortgages was strongly influenced by the underwriting and lending and other activities of the federal government.[5] The government guarantee of residential mortgages, extended through the FHA and the Veterans Administration, undoubtedly increased the supply of funds for residential mortgages and lowered the rates. No quantitative estimate of these differentials is possible. In addition to the existence of government insurance of governmental mortgages, the operations of the FNMA and the FHA and many other interventions of the federal government in the residential real estate market deeply influenced many of the terms of residential mortgages, the distribution of holding of mortgages among institutions, the distribution of the mortgage debt and of mortgage holdings among borrowers, and the character and location of residential dwellings erected during the postwar period. The effects of government participation in the residential mortgage market were so strong,

---

[3] *Ibid.*, p. 20.

[4] On these companies, see Saul B. Klaman, *The Postwar Rise of Mortgage Companies*, Occasional Paper 60, New York, NBER, 1959.

[5] See, e.g., Leo Grebler, *The Role of Federal Credit Aids in Residential Construction*, Occasional Paper 39, New York, NBER, 1953, and *Housing Issues in Economic Stabilization Policy*, Occasional Paper 72, New York, NBER, 1960.

pervasive, and intricate that it is impossible to visualize the form this market would have had in the absence of government intervention.

13. The market for residential mortgages showed substantial cyclical fluctuations during the postwar period. These fluctuations, however, did not always coincide with the swings in the general business cycle, but to some extent were countercyclical. For example, the residential mortgage market reached a trough in 1949 but a peak in 1955 rather than in 1957, and did not show any evidence of the cyclical decline of 1954. On the other hand, the market was relatively depressed in 1951–53, as a result of government intervention, at the time when the economy was generally in a marked upswing.

14. The secondary market in residential mortgages, i.e., the sale and purchase of existing mortgages not immediately or shortly after their creation, is still unorganized and small. It is estimated that the annual volume of trading in residential mortgages does not exceed 10 per cent of the total amount outstanding. The majority of all residential mortgages probably never changes hands between the time the loan is originally made and the time it is retired through amortization or through prepayment of the outstanding balance.

## Developments During the Postwar Period

The market for residential mortgages during the postwar period is characterized by five developments: (1) the extraordinarily rapid rise of the volume of residential mortgage debt, slowed only from 1951 to 1953 because of the Korean War and government limitations on residential construction and mortgage lending; [6] (2) a persistent rise in interest rates; (3) a marked increase in the position of financial institutions as mortgage lenders; (4) the pervasive influence of the federal government on many aspects of the market, and the resulting tendency toward standardization of many aspects of the residential mortgage as a capital market instrument; and (5) the development of new techniques adapted to the special environment created by government interference and institutionalization.

The last two characteristics have already been touched upon in the preceding section. The first three will be discussed in this section.

[6] Raymond W. Goldsmith, Robert E. Lipsey, and Morris Mendelson, *Studies in the National Balance Sheet of the United States,* Princeton for NBER, 1963, Vol. II, Table VIII-b-11a.

# Market for Residential Mortgages

## THE ROLE OF RESIDENTIAL MORTGAGES IN THE MORTGAGE MARKET

Between the end of 1945, when the residential mortgage debt was no higher than in the mid-1920's, and 1958, the total mortgage debt on residential real estate increased by $110 billion. The rate of increase of 14.5 per cent per year was one of the highest, and the absolute increase was by far the largest among the main capital market instruments. Before briefly discussing some aspects of this immense increase, it is necessary to clarify the position of the market for residential mortgage within the total mortgage market, and of the main constituent of the residential mortgage market. The necessary data are shown in Table 97 and Chart 25.

During the postwar period the share of residential in total mortgage debt increased sharply, residential mortgages accounting for four-fifths of the net flow of funds into the mortgage market during the period. The absorption of funds by the residential mortgage market was more than five times as large as that by nonresidential nonfarm mortgages and seventeen times as large as the increase in farm mortgage debt. The share of residential mortgages showed no marked changes among the three postwar cycles. The two other sectors, however, differed in the movement of their share in the total flow of funds into mortgages. The share of nonresidential nonfarm mortgages fell considerably between Cycles I and II and recovered incompletely in Cycle III, while that of farm mortgages advanced considerably between Cycles I and II and remained at slightly beneath the higher level in Cycle III.

More significant differences occurred in the shares of the main components of the residential mortgage market. Of the total net absorption of funds of $110 billion, at least 90 per cent were accounted for by one- to four-family dwellings. Of these, in turn, approximately nine-tenths were made on single-family homes, which thus absorbed about four-fifths of the total net flow of funds into residential mortgages, leaving about one-tenth for multifamily dwellings. Almost one-half of the total increase in mortgage loans was insured by the Federal Housing Administration or the Veterans Administration, the share being quite similar for one- to four-family and multifamily dwellings.

The division of the total flow of mortgage funds between one- to four-family and multifamily dwellings was similar in Cycles I and II, in both of which the former accounted for more than 85 per cent of

TABLE 97

STRUCTURAL CHANGES IN THE MORTGAGE MARKET, BY TYPE, 1945-58

| Type of Mortgage | Outstandings | | Aggregate Net Flows, 1946-58 (3) | Net Flows (annual averages) | | |
|---|---|---|---|---|---|---|
| | 1945 (1) | 1958 (2) | | Cycle I 1946-49 (4) | Cycle II 1949-54 (5) | Cycle III 1954-58 (6) |
| | | | **BILLION DOLLARS** | | | |
| 1. Residential, total | 23.28 | 133.03 | 109.75 | 5.52 | 7.98 | 11.25 |
|    Homes | 18.59 | 117.69 | 99.10 | 4.88 | 7.09 | 10.44 |
|       Government-insured | 4.28 | 50.13 | 45.85 | 2.85 | 3.27 | 4.65 |
|       Conventional | 14.31 | 67.56 | 53.25 | 2.02 | 3.82 | 5.80 |
|    Multifamily | 4.69 | 15.34 | 10.65 | 0.64 | 0.89 | 0.81 |
|       Government-insured | 0.24 | 5.03 | 4.79 | 0.47 | 0.48 | 0.16 |
|       Conventional | 4.45 | 10.31 | 5.86 | 0.17 | 0.40 | 0.65 |
| 2. Nonresidential, nonfarm | 7.50 | 27.63 | 20.13 | 1.21 | 1.12 | 2.22 |
| 3. Farm | 4.76 | 11.25 | 6.48 | 0.20 | 0.52 | 0.71 |
| 4. Total | 35.54 | 171.91 | 136.37 | 6.93 | 9.62 | 14.18 |
| | | | **PER CENT** | | | |
| 1. Residential, total | 65.5 | 77.4 | 80.5 | 79.7 | 83.0 | 79.3 |
|    Homes | 52.3 | 68.5 | 72.7 | 70.4 | 73.7 | 73.6 |
|       Government-insured | 12.0 | 29.2 | 33.6 | 41.1 | 34.0 | 32.8 |
|       Conventional | 40.3 | 39.3 | 39.0 | 29.2 | 39.7 | 40.9 |
|    Multifamily | 13.2 | 8.9 | 7.8 | 9.3 | 9.3 | 5.7 |
|       Government-insured | 0.7 | 2.9 | 3.5 | 6.8 | 5.0 | 1.1 |
|       Conventional | 12.5 | 6.0 | 4.3 | 2.5 | 4.2 | 4.6 |
| 2. Nonresidential, nonfarm | 21.1 | 16.1 | 14.8 | 17.5 | 11.6 | 15.7 |
| 3. Farm | 13.4 | 6.5 | 4.8 | 2.9 | 5.4 | 5.0 |
| 4. Total | 100.0 | 100.0 | 100.0 | 100.0 | 100.0 | 100.0 |

Source:  National Balance Sheet, Vol. II.
Cols. 1-2, lines 1 and breakdown: Tables IV-b-11a, IV-b-11a-2,
  IV-b-11a-6,IV-b-11a-5, IV-b-11a-1, IV-b-11a-4, and IV-b-11a-3.
Cols. 3-6, lines 1 and breakdown:  Tables VIII-b-11a,
  VIII-b-11a-2, VIII-b-11a-6, VIII-b-11a-5, VIII-b-11a-1,
  VIII-b-11a-4, and VIII-b-11a-3.
Cols. 1-2, line 2:  Table IV-b-11b.    Cols. 3-6, line 2:  Table VIII-b-11b.
Cols. 1-2, line 3:  Table IV-b-12.    Cols. 3-6, line 3:  Table VIII-b-12.
Note:  Components may not add to totals because of rounding here and elsewhere in this chapter.

CHART 25

MARKET FOR NONFARM RESIDENTIAL MORTGAGES:
SUPPLY AND ABSORPTION BY SECTOR, 1946–58

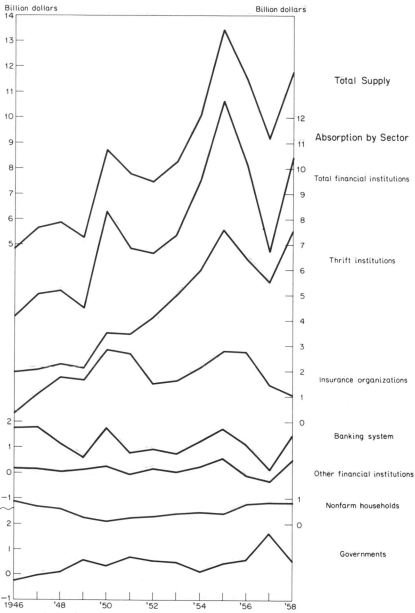

Source: *National Balance Sheet,* Vol. II, Tables VIII-b-11a, VIII-c-11a, and VIII-c-11b.

the total; but in Cycle III they accounted for over 90 per cent. One reason for the decline in the proportion of funds by multifamily dwellings was the reduced availability of government insurance during the latter part of the period.

More pronounced differences appear in the distribution of funds among insured and noninsured (conventional) mortgages. While insured mortgage loans accounted for three-fifths of the total funds absorbed by residential mortgages in Cycle I, their share declined to slightly less than one-half in Cycle II and to just over two-fifths in Cycle III. The shift was much more pronounced for multifamily dwellings, for which the share of insured mortgages dropped from more than two-thirds in Cycle I and less than three-fifths in Cycle II to less than one-fifth in Cycle III. The decline of the share of insured mortgages reflects the failure of the maximum interest rates permitted by legislation on insured mortgages to follow the rising trend in mortgage interest rates promptly or fully. Notwithstanding the decline in the share of total insured mortgages in the net flow of funds into residential mortgages between the early and the late part of the period, their share in total outstanding residential mortgage debt increased sharply from one-fifth in 1945 to more than two-fifths in 1958.

An important characteristic of the residential mortgage market in the postwar period is the association of certain groups of holders with certain forms of residential mortgages, which is summarized in the two following paragraphs. The detailed relations can be studied in Tables 98 and 99 for the beginning and the end of the period, and in Table 100 for the aggregate net flow of funds during 1946–58.

Saving and loan associations concentrated their mortgage investments to the extent of over three-fourths on unguaranteed home mortgages. Home mortgages also predominated, although in a less pronounced way, in the portfolios of mutual savings banks, but mostly insured mortgages since mutual savings banks were both authorized and willing to make home mortgage loans at considerable distances from their home offices where they did not need to investigate or directly supervise the loans if the loans were insured by the government. Mutual savings banks also invested in multifamily mortgages, about evenly divided between insured and conventional loans. Commercial banks and life insurance companies distributed their mortgage investments in about the same proportions, both putting more than two-thirds of total mortgage investments in home mortgages. Insured mort-

TABLE 98

DISTRIBUTION OF MORTGAGE LOANS AMONG HOLDER GROUPS,
END OF 1945
(billion dollars)

| Type of Mortgage | All Groups (1) | Federal Government (2) | Total (3) | Four Main Institutions (4) | Finance | | | | Other (9) | All Others (10) |
|---|---|---|---|---|---|---|---|---|---|---|
| | | | | | Life Insurance (5) | Savings and Loan Associations (6) | Commercial Banks (7) | Mutual Savings Banks (8) | | |
| 1. Residential | 23.3 | 0.9 | 16.1 | 15.8 | 3.7 | 5.3 | 3.4 | 3.4 | 0.3 | 6.3 |
| Homes | 18.6 | 0.9 | 12.5 | 12.3 | 2.3 | 5.2 | 2.9 | 1.9 | 0.2 | 5.3 |
| Government-insured | 4.3 | 0 | n.a. | 3.6 | 1.3 | 0.5 | 1.5 | 0.3 | | 0.6 |
| Conventional | 14.3 | 0.9 | n.a. | 8.6 | 1.0 | 4.6 | 1.4 | 1.6 | | 4.9 |
| Multifamily | 4.7 | 0 | 3.6 | 3.5 | 1.4 | 0.1 | 0.5 | 1.5 | 0.1 | 1.0 |
| Government-insured | 0.2 | 0 | n.a. | 0.1 | 0.1 | 0 | 0 | 0 | | 0 |
| Conventional | 4.4 | 0 | n.a. | 3.4 | 1.3 | 0.1 | 0 | 1.5 | | 1.1 |
| 2. Nonresidential, nonfarm | 7.5 | 0 | 4.1 | 4.0 | 2.2 | 0.1 | 0.5 | 0.8 | 0.2 | 3.4 |
| 3. Farm | 4.8 | 1.5 | 1.3 | 1.3 | 0.8 | 0 | 0.5 | 0 | 0 | 1.9 |
| 4. Total | 35.5 | 2.4 | 21.5 | 21.0 | 6.7 | 5.4 | 4.8 | 4.2 | 0.5 | 11.6 |

Source: See source to Table 97.

TABLE 99

DISTRIBUTION OF MORTGAGE LOANS AMONG HOLDER GROUPS,
END OF 1958
(billion dollars)

| Type of Mortgage | All Groups (1) | Federal Government (2) | Total (3) | Finance | | | | | | |
|---|---|---|---|---|---|---|---|---|---|---|
| | | | | Four Main Institutions (4) | Life Insurance (5) | Savings and Loan Associations (6) | Commercial Banks (7) | Mutual Savings Banks (8) | Other (9) | All Others (10) |
| 1. Residential | 133.0 | 5.1 | 113.5 | 110.0 | 25.9 | 44.7 | 18.4 | 20.9 | 3.5 | 14.4 |
| Homes | 117.7 | 4.6 | 101.3 | 98.4 | 22.4 | 42.9 | 17.5 | 15.6 | 3.0 | 11.8 |
| Government-insured | 50.1 | 3.6 | n.a. | 43.2 | 13.7 | 9.2 | 8.0 | 12.2 | | 3.4 |
| Conventional | 67.6 | 1.0 | n.a. | 55.2 | 8.7 | 33.7 | 9.4 | 3.4 | | 11.4 |
| Multifamily | 15.3 | 0.5 | 12.2 | 11.6 | 3.5 | 1.8 | 1.0 | 5.3 | 0.6 | 2.6 |
| Government-insured | 5.0 | 0.3 | n.a. | 3.6 | 1.2 | 0 | 0.7 | 1.7 | | 1.1 |
| Conventional | 10.3 | 0.2 | n.a. | 8.0 | 2.4 | 1.8 | 0.3 | 3.6 | | 2.1 |
| 2. Nonresidential, nonfarm | 27.6 | 0 | 17.7 | 17.0 | 8.5 | 0.9 | 5.4 | 2.3 | 0.7 | 9.9 |
| 3. Farm | 11.3 | 2.5 | 4.3 | 4.3 | 2.7 | 0 | 1.5 | 0.1 | 0 | 4.5 |
| 4. Total | 171.9 | 7.6 | 135.5 | 131.2 | 37.1 | 45.6 | 25.3 | 23.3 | 4.3 | 28.9 |

Source: See source to Table 97.

TABLE 100

DISTRIBUTION OF MORTGAGE LOANS AMONG HOLDER GROUPS,
NET FLOW, 1946–58
(billion dollars)

| Type of Mortgage | All Groups (1) | Federal Government (2) | Total (3) | Four Main Institutions (4) | Finance | | | | Other (9) | All Others (10) |
|---|---|---|---|---|---|---|---|---|---|---|
| | | | | | Life Insurance (5) | Savings and Loan Associations (6) | Commercial Banks (7) | Mutual Savings Banks (8) | | |
| 1. Residential | 109.8 | 4.2 | 97.4 | 94.3 | 22.2 | 39.4 | 15.0 | 17.6 | 3.2 | 8.1 |
| Homes | 99.1 | 3.7 | 88.9 | 86.2 | 20.1 | 37.7 | 14.6 | 13.8 | 2.7 | 6.5 |
| Government-insured | 45.8 | 3.5 | n.a. | 39.5 | 12.4 | 8.7 | 6.5 | 11.8 | | 2.8 |
| Conventional | 53.3 | 0.2 | n.a. | 46.6 | 7.6 | 29.0 | 8.1 | 1.9 | | 6.5 |
| Multifamily | 10.7 | 0.5 | 8.5 | 8.1 | 2.2 | 1.7 | 0.4 | 3.8 | 0.4 | 1.6 |
| Government-insured | 4.8 | 0.3 | n.a. | 3.4 | 1.0 | 0 | 0.6 | 1.7 | | 1.1 |
| Conventional | 5.9 | 0.2 | n.a. | 4.7 | 1.1 | 1.7 | -0.2 | 2.1 | | 1.0 |
| 2. Nonresidential, nonfarm | 20.1 | 0 | 13.6 | 13.1 | 6.3 | 0.8 | 4.5 | 1.5 | 0.5 | 6.5 |
| 3. Farm | 6.5 | 0.9 | 2.9 | 2.9 | 1.9 | 0 | 1.0 | 0 | 0 | 2.6 |
| 4. Total | 136.4 | 5.1 | 114.0 | 110.2 | 30.4 | 40.3 | 20.5 | 19.0 | 3.8 | 17.2 |

Source: See source tc Table 97.

gages, however, accounted for more than three-fifths of the home mortgages of life insurance companies, but for less than one-half of those of commercial banks, the difference possibly reflecting the stronger local connections of the latter. Life insurance companies extended about one-tenth of their residential mortgages on multifamily properties, which played only a much smaller role in the portfolio of commercial banks. Nonresidential nonfarm mortgages accounted for more than one-fifth of total mortgage investments in both institutions, and in both cases farm mortgages constituted about 5 per cent of this total. The mortgage investments by individuals are characterized by the high share of conventional home mortgages and of nonresidential nonfarm mortgages, each accounting for about one-third of total mortgage investment,[7] and by the relative absence of federally insured mortgages, the result of the legislative arrangements which throughout the period in practice limit the insurance to mortgages held by financial institutions.

Looking at the situation by type of mortgages rather than by lenders, life insurance companies and mutual savings banks were the main buyers of insured home mortgages, each accounting for more than one-fourth of the total. Commercial banks and saving and loan associations were next with one-seventh and one-fifth, respectively, and federal agencies with about one-thirteenth, leaving not much more than 6 per cent for all other holders.

Saving and loan associations were by far the most important lenders on uninsured home mortgages, accounting for more than one-half of the total. Commercial banks and life insurance companies followed at a great distance, holding about 15 and 13 per cent of the total, respectively, while noninstitutional lenders are credited with not much more than one-tenth of all uninsured home mortgages, a considerable part of which was represented by junior liens.

Mutual savings banks were the most important factor in the market for multifamily mortgages, absorbing over one-third of the postwar period total. Life insurance companies absorbed one-fifth, saving and loan associations, and noninstitutional lenders divided the rest about equally.

The sources of funds are quite different in the market for nonresidential nonfarm mortgages. The two main suppliers were life insurance companies and noninstitutional lenders, with more than 30 per

---

[7] *National Balance Sheet*, Vol. II, Tables VIII-b-11, VIII-b-11a-3, VIII-b-11a-5, VIII-b-11b, and VIII-b-12.

cent each of the total, followed closely by commercial banks with more than 20 per cent. The market for farm mortgages, finally, relied on noninstitutional lenders which supplied two-fifths of the total net funds during the postwar period and on federal agencies who provided almost one-seventh. Among private financial institutions, only life insurance companies, with almost one-third of the total net supply, and at a considerable distance commercial banks, with more than one-sixth, were of substantial importance.

### THE ROLE OF MORTGAGE CREDIT IN FINANCING RESIDENTIAL CONSTRUCTION AND TRADING

For residential mortgages, particularly those on single-family homes, the financing alternatives were simpler than for most other capital market instruments, particularly corporate stocks and bonds. The choice essentially is only between a mortgage loan and the owner's funds. There is no direct or comprehensive information on the share of these two forms of financing, but the order of magnitude can be ascertained with reasonable reliability (see Table 101).

During the postwar period, only a small proportion (around one-eighth) of all new residential structures was bought for cash.[8] In the remaining seven-eighths of purchases, mortgage credit constituted an essential part of financing, providing about seven-tenths of the purchase price, so that only about 30 per cent of the total cost of new residential structures was provided by owner's funds (current savings or realization of other assets).

The share of mortgages in financing is more difficult to determine, both for conceptual and statistical reasons, in the case of the change of hands of existing residential structures. It appears, however, that the contribution of buyers' own funds did not differ substantially here from the case of new residential structures. Mortgage loans, either new or in the form of the assumption of the mortgage outstanding on the property being acquired, apparently provided approximately 70 per cent of the funds needed by the buyers of existing residential real estate.

There are, however, two additional occasions on which existing home mortgages are created. The first is the financing of additions to and alterations of existing residential homes. The amounts involved are not recorded separately, but it is likely that a large proportion

---

[8] Leo Grebler, David M. Blank, and Louis Winnick, *Capital Formation in Residential Real Estate: Trends and Prospects,* Princeton for NBER, 1956, pp. 454–455.

TABLE 101

ROLE OF MORTGAGE CREDIT IN HOME FINANCING, ANNUAL AVERAGES, 1946-58
(billion dollars)

| | 1946-58 (1) | 1946-49 (2) | 1949-54 (3) | 1954-58 (4) |
|---|---|---|---|---|
| **I. All homes** | | | | |
| 1. Gross investment (line II-3 plus line III-1 plus line III-5) | 15.5 | 9.3 | 15.4 | 21.1 |
| 2. Depreciation allowances | 6.6 | 4.8 | 6.5 | 8.2 |
| 3. Net investment (line 1 minus line 2) | 8.9 | 4.5 | 8.9 | 12.9 |
| 4. Mortgages incurred (line II-4 plus line III-6) | 19.0 | 11.6 | 17.5 | 26.2 |
| 5. Mortgages repaid (line III-9) | 11.3 | 6.7 | 10.5 | 15.8 |
| 6. Net increase in mortgage debt (line 4 minus line 5) | 7.7 | 4.9 | 7.0 | 10.4 |
| 7. Net saving (line 3 minus line 6) | 1.2 | -0.4 | 1.9 | 2.5 |
| **II. New homes** | | | | |
| 1. Cost of construction | 10.3 | 5.7 | 10.4 | 14.1 |
| 2. Cost of land | 1.5 | 0.8 | 1.4 | 2.3 |
| 3. Total purchase price | 11.8 | 6.5 | 11.8 | 16.4 |
| 4. Mortgage loans | 8.1 | 4.4 | 8.0 | 11.5 |
| 5. Financing ratio (line 4 divided by line 3) | 0.69 | 0.68 | 0.68 | 0.70 |
| **III. Existing homes** | | | | |
| 1. Cost of additions and alterations | 2.7 | 2.0 | 2.6 | 3.5 |
| 2. Depreciation allowances | 6.6 | 4.8 | 6.5 | 8.2 |
| 3. Net depreciation (line 2 minus line 1) | 3.9 | 2.8 | 3.9 | 4.7 |
| 4. Purchases and sales | 16.5 | 9.4 | 15.6 | 22.7 |
| 5. Cost of transactions | 1.0 | 0.8 | 1.0 | 1.2 |
| 6. Mortgages made, total (line 7 plus line 8) | 10.9 | 7.2 | 9.6 | 14.8 |
| 7. Mortgages made, additional financing | 4.2 | 2.9 | 3.4 | 5.6 |
| 8. Mortgages made, refinancing | 6.7 | 4.3 | 6.1 | 9.1 |
| 9. Repayments, total | 11.3 | 6.7 | 10.5 | 15.8 |
| 10. Repayments, amortization | 3.9 | 1.9 | 3.5 | 5.7 |
| 11. Repayments, partial prepayments | 0.8 | 0.5 | 0.8 | 1.0 |
| 12. Repayments, full prepayments | 6.7 | 4.3 | 6.1 | 9.1 |
| 13. Increase in mortgage debt (line 6 minus line 9) | -0.4 | 0.5 | -1.0 | -1.1 |
| 14. Financing ratio, gross (line 6 divided by line 4) | 0.66 | 0.77 | 0.61 | 0.65 |
| 15. Financing ratio, net (line 8 divided by line 4) | 0.41 | 0.46 | 0.39 | 0.40 |

Source: National Balance Sheet, Vol. I, Part Three.

Lines I-2, III-2: Table 72.
Lines II-1, III-3, III-1, III-4, III-5, III-9 through III-12: Table 88.
Lines II-4, III-7, III-8: Table 87.

of them, often very small in absolute amounts, were financed by the home-owners without borrowing or with nonmortgage credit, and that where mortgage credit was used the ratio of loan to value was smaller than in the acquisition of entire structures. Since additions and alterations are estimated to have cost $35 billion during 1946–58, it may be estimated very roughly that they required about $10 to $15 billion of mortgages, probably nearer the lower limit.

The second addition to the home mortgage debt occurred in borrowing on existing structures not connected with a change of hands or with additions and alterations. Such additional borrowings were possible because the increases in real estate values, and to a lesser extent the reduction of mortgage principal, often reduced the loan-to-value ratio well below the customary limit, and some owners of residential real estate took advantage of this margin to raise funds for other purposes. This type of mortgage loan has been estimated at nearly $55 billion during the postwar period, which would amount to almost one-fifth of the average value of homes.[9] If this estimate is of the right order of magnitude, the question immediately arises of the use made by mortgages of these large sums—much larger, for instance, than individuals' net purchases of stocks and bonds. Unfortunately, no data exist to help us to answer this question.

We thus find that home mortgage loans made during the postwar period totaled almost $250 billion, of which approximately 40 per cent was on new structures, 5 per cent on additions and alterations, and 55 per cent on existing structures, mostly in connection with changes of hands. There were, however, also substantial repayments. First, regular amortizations are estimated at about $50 billion, or about one-fifth of total gross borrowing. Secondly, partial prepayments totaled about $10 billion. Thirdly, prepayments in full are estimated to have amounted to nearly $90 billion, most of which probably occurred when homes changed hands.

As a result, the net increase in the home mortgage debt between 1945 and 1958 amounted to just under $100 billion, or two-fifths of the gross mortgage loans contracted during the period. From Table 101, which shows these relations for each of the three cycles, it can be seen that the relation of mortgage loans made to the purchase price of new homes showed no substantial variations from the average of about 70 per cent for the entire period. The same ratio for

[9] *National Balance Sheet,* Vol. I, Part Three, Table 70.

old homes, which is statistically more tenuous, exhibited an irregular tendency. The ratio of repayments to new loans made for all homes rose from 58 per cent in Cycle I to 60 per cent in Cycles II and III. Notwithstanding this increase, the proportion of repayments to total mortgage debt outstanding declined from 15 per cent at the end of Cycle I to 12 per cent at the end of Cycles II and III.[10]

On the basis of these estimates, and from other figures shown in Table 101, it is possible to calculate alternative aggregate financial ratios for homes, always realizing that these ratios are averages that comprise a wide range of values.

From the point of view of the entire economy, probably the most important ratio is that of the total net investment in homes (i.e., the cost of new structures and of additions and alterations less depreciation) to the net increase in the mortgage debt outstanding. For the entire period, net investment, calculated on the basis of depreciation at replacement cost, amounted to about $104 billion. This means that the increase in the mortgage debt of $100 billion was about equal to net investment calculated according to national accounting procedures. Even if depreciation had been allowed only at original cost, net investment of about $150 billion would be only by about one-half above the increase in the home mortgage debt.

This ratio, of course, is not relevant from the point of view of the home-owners themselves, who are primarily interested in what happened to the equity in their homes. It is then found that owners' equity in homes increased from 1945 to 1958 by more than $160 billion,[11] notwithstanding an increase in the net mortgage debt of nearly $100 billion, but that this increase represented almost entirely realized and unrealized capital gains. The increase in the prices of homes, which in turn primarily reflects the increase in construction cost and land values, permitted an increase in debt almost equal to the net investment in homes, calculated according to national accounting principles, without impairing owners' equity, even taking into account the increase in the cost of living during the period. Thus, part of realized and unrealized capital gains on homes led to a write-up of the home mortgage debt, which, together with the effect of amortizations, raised the loan-to-value ratio on all homes at the end of 1958 to close to 30 per cent—compared to 13 per cent in 1945—although home buyers originally borrowed fully two-thirds of the purchase price of new

10 *National Balance Sheet*, Vol. II, Table IV-b-11a.
11 *Ibid.*, Vol. I, p. 311.

as well as old structures acquired during the period.[12] These relationships can be followed in more detail in Table 102 for the entire period as well as for the three cycles.

### DISTRIBUTION OF RESIDENTIAL MORTGAGE HOLDINGS AND INVESTMENTS

Annual changes in the distribution of the residential mortgage debt outstanding and in the flow of funds into it are shown for the main groups of investors in Tables 104 and 105,[13] while similar figures for the period as a whole and its three cycles are given in Table 103. The distribution between insured and noninsured mortgages is influenced to a considerable degree by the relation between the maximum interest rate permitted on insured mortgages and the market rate on conventional mortgages. When market rates are above the permissible maximum on insured mortgages, as has generally been the case in the late phases of cyclical upswings, there is some shift from insured to conventional mortgages, and the share in the total net flow of mortgages of institutions concentrating on insured mortgages tends to decline. This influence may, of course, be overridden by differences in the rates of growth of the total assets of different groups of institutional investors and by changes in their investment policies.

As a result of this relation, the share of insured mortgages showed a declining trend over the period, falling from three-fifths of all nonfarm residential mortgages in Cycle I to slightly under one-half in Cycle II and slightly more than two-fifths in Cycle III (see Table 97). The decline was considerably more pronounced in multifamily mortgages, from three-fourths to less than three-fifths and one-fifth, the particularly sharp fall in Cycle III being partly attributable to the cessation of insurance on new multifamily mortgages. Within the cycles the share of insured mortgages was usually highest in the middle phases of the upswing and lowest near its end (1952–53; 1956–57) when interest rates were generally highest. Fluctuations in absolute volume or in relative terms were more pronounced in the case of insured mortgages, and among them more for mortgages insured by the Veterans Administration rather than by the Federal Housing Administration. These differences in volatility can be explained by differences in permissible interest rates, other terms such as maturity, mini-

[12] *Ibid.*, Vol. I, Part Three, Table 69, and Vol. II, Table IV-b-11a-2.

[13] For separate data for one- to four-family and multifamily dwellings, on the one hand, and insured and noninsured mortgages, on the other, see *ibid.*, Vol. II, Tables IV-b-11a-1 through IV-b-11a-6 and VIII-b-11a-1 through VIII-b-11a-6.

TABLE 102

COMPOSITION OF CHANGES IN VALUE OF NONFARM PRIVATE RESIDENTIAL HOUSING, 1946-58

| | Aggregate, 1946-58 (billion dollars) (1) | Annual Averages (billion dollars) | | | Aggregate, 1946-58 (per cent) (5) | Annual Averages (per cent) | | |
| --- | --- | --- | --- | --- | --- | --- | --- | --- |
| | | 1946-49 (2) | 1949-54 (3) | 1954-58 (4) | | 1946-49 (6) | 1949-54 (7) | 1954-58 (8) |
| I. All residential structures | | | | | | | | |
| 1. Increase in value during period | 278.2 | 24.0 | 18.5 | 22.4 | 100 | 100 | 100 | 100 |
| 2. Net investment | 104.8 | 4.2 | 8.2 | 11.4 | 38 | 17 | 44 | 51 |
| Expenditures | 191.1 | 9.0 | 14.7 | 19.6 | 69 | 37 | 79 | 87 |
| Depreciation | 86.3 | 4.8 | 6.5 | 8.2 | 31 | 20 | 35 | 37 |
| 3. Capital gains (+) or losses (−) (line 1 minus line 2) | 173.4 | 19.8 | 10.3 | 11.0 | 62 | 82 | 56 | 49 |
| 4. Change in mortgage debt | 109.8 | 5.5 | 8.0 | 11.3 | 39 | 23 | 43 | 50 |
| 5. Increase in owners' equity (line 1 minus line 4) | 168.4 | 18.5 | 10.5 | 11.1 | 61 | 77 | 57 | 50 |
| II. One- to four-family homes | | | | | | | | |
| 1. Increase in value during period | 261.7 | 22.0 | 17.4 | 21.6 | 100 | 100 | 100 | 100 |
| 2. Net investment | 103.7 | 4.1 | 8.0 | 11.4 | 40 | 19 | 46 | 53 |
| Expenditures | 182.8 | 8.5 | 14.0 | 18.9 | 70 | 39 | 80 | 88 |
| Depreciation | 75.1 | 4.4 | 5.9 | 7.6 | 30 | 20 | 34 | 35 |
| 3. Capital gains (+) or losses (−) (line 1 minus line 2) | 158.0 | 17.9 | 9.4 | 10.2 | 60 | 81 | 54 | 47 |
| 4. Change in mortgage debt | 95.1 | 4.9 | 7.1 | 10.4 | 38 | 22 | 41 | 48 |
| 5. Increase in owners' equity (line 1 minus line 4) | 162.6 | 17.1 | 10.3 | 11.2 | 62 | 78 | 59 | 52 |

(continued)

TABLE 102 (concluded)

| | Aggregate, 1946–58 (billion dollars) (1) | Annual Averages (billion dollars) | | | Aggregate, 1946–58 (per cent) (5) | Annual Averages (per cent) | | |
|---|---|---|---|---|---|---|---|---|
| | | 1946–49 (2) | 1949–54 (3) | 1954–58 (4) | | 1946–49 (6) | 1949–54 (7) | 1954–58 (8) |
| III. Multifamily structures | | | | | | | | |
| 1. Increase in value during period | 16.5 | 2.0 | 1.1 | 0.9 | 100 | 100 | 100 | 100 |
| 2. Net investment | 1.1 | 0.2 | 0.1 | 0.0 | 6 | 10 | 9 | 0 |
| Expenditures | 8.3 | 0.6 | 0.7 | 0.7 | 50 | 30 | 64 | 78 |
| Depreciation | 7.2 | 0.4 | 0.5 | 0.7 | 44 | 20 | 45 | 78 |
| 3. Capital gains (+) or losses (−) (line 1 minus line 2) | 15.4 | 1.8 | 1.0 | 0.9 | 94 | 90 | 91 | 100 |
| 4. Change in mortgage debt | 10.6 | 0.6 | 0.9 | 0.8 | 64 | 30 | 82 | 89 |
| 5. Increase in owners' equity (line 1 minus line 4) | 5.9 | 1.4 | 0.2 | 0.1 | 36 | 70 | 18 | 11 |

Source: National Balance Sheet.

Lines I-1, II-1, III-1: Vol. I, Table 71.
Lines I-2, II-2, III-2: Vol. I, Table 72.
Lines I-4, II-4, III-4: Vol. II, Tables VIII-b-11a, VIII-b-11a-2, and VIII-b-11a-1.

TABLE 103

STRUCTURAL CHANGES IN OWNERSHIP OF NONFARM RESIDENTIAL MORTGAGES DURING POSTWAR PERIOD

| | Outstandings (billion dollars) | | Aggregate Net Flows, 1946–58 (billion dollars) | NET FLOWS (ANNUAL AVERAGES) | | | | | |
| | | | | Amounts (billion dollars) | | | Distribution (per cent) | | |
| | 1945 (1) | 1958 (2) | (3) | Cycle I 1946–49 (4) | Cycle II 1949–54 (5) | Cycle III 1954–58 (6) | Cycle I 1946–49 (7) | Cycle II 1949–54 (8) | Cycle III 1954–58 (9) |
|---|---|---|---|---|---|---|---|---|---|
| 1. Nonfarm households | 6.23 | 12.79 | 6.55 | 0.61 | 0.26 | 0.64 | 11.1 | 3.3 | 5.7 |
| 2. Finance | 16.08 | 113.52 | 97.44 | 4.84 | 7.23 | 9.87 | 87.7 | 90.6 | 87.7 |
| a. Government insurance and pension funds | 0.02 | 0.40 | 0.36 | 0 | 0.04 | 0.04 | 0 | 0.5 | 0.4 |
| b. Commercial banks | 3.38 | 18.41 | 15.04 | 1.35 | 1.02 | 1.07 | 24.5 | 12.8 | 9.5 |
| c. Mutual savings banks | 3.39 | 20.94 | 17.56 | 0.56 | 1.42 | 1.93 | 10.1 | 17.8 | 17.2 |
| d. Savings and loan associations | 5.27 | 44.72 | 39.44 | 1.54 | 2.56 | 4.60 | 27.9 | 32.1 | 40.9 |
| e. Investment companies | 0.09 | 0.24 | 0.12 | 0.05 | 0.01 | -0.01 | 0.9 | 0.1 | -0.1 |
| f. Credit unions | 0.03 | 0.35 | 0.34 | 0.01 | 0.02 | 0.04 | 0.2 | 0.3 | 0.4 |
| g. Life insurance | 3.70 | 25.92 | 22.22 | 1.24 | 1.99 | 1.98 | 22.5 | 24.9 | 17.6 |
| h. Fire and casualty insurance | 0.02 | 0.05 | 0.03 | 0 | 0 | 0 | 0 | 0 | 0 |
| i. Noninsured pension plans | 0.02 | 0.65 | 0.63 | 0 | 0.03 | 0.10 | 0 | 0.4 | 0.9 |
| j. Other private insurance | 0.07 | 0.27 | 0.20 | 0.01 | 0.02 | 0.01 | 0.2 | 0.3 | 0.1 |
| k. Finance companies | 0.07 | 1.40 | 1.35 | 0.05 | 0.09 | 0.11 | 0.9 | 1.1 | 1.0 |
| l. Other finances | 0.02 | 0.18 | 0.17 | 0.02 | 0.01 | 0.01 | 0.4 | 0.1 | 0.1 |
| 3. State and local governments | 0.06 | 1.61 | 1.55 | 0.02 | 0.09 | 0.21 | 0.4 | 1.1 | 1.9 |
| 4. Federal government | 0.90 | 5.10 | 4.21 | 0.06 | 0.40 | 0.53 | 1.1 | 5.0 | 4.7 |
| 5. Total | 23.27 | 133.03 | 109.75 | 5.52 | 7.98 | 11.25 | 100.0 | 100.0 | 100.0 |

Source: *National Balance Sheet*, Vol. II. Cols. 1–2 from Table IV-b-11a; cols. 3–9 from Table VIII-b-11a.

TABLE 104

DISTRIBUTION OF NONFARM RESIDENTIAL MORTGAGES, ASSETS, 1945-58

(per cent)

| | 1945 | 1946 | 1947 | 1948 | 1949 | 1950 | 1951 | 1952 | 1953 | 1954 | 1955 | 1956 | 1957 | 1958 |
|---|---|---|---|---|---|---|---|---|---|---|---|---|---|---|
| 1. Nonfarm households | 26.8 | 25.3 | 23.1 | 21.1 | 19.2 | 16.2 | 14.5 | 13.4 | 12.5 | 11.5 | 10.3 | 10.0 | 9.9 | 9.6 |
| 2. Finance | 69.1 | 72.1 | 74.9 | 76.9 | 77.8 | 80.6 | 81.6 | 82.4 | 83.1 | 84.4 | 85.7 | 86.0 | 85.0 | 85.3 |
| a. Government insurance and pension funds | 0.1 | 0.1 | 0.1 | 0.1 | 0.1 | 0.2 | 0.3 | 0.3 | 0.3 | 0.3 | 0.3 | 0.4 | 0.4 | 0.3 |
| b. Commercial banks | 14.5 | 18.2 | 20.4 | 20.2 | 19.2 | 19.3 | 18.2 | 17.5 | 16.6 | 16.1 | 15.6 | 15.0 | 14.0 | 13.8 |
| c. Mutual savings banks | 14.6 | 12.8 | 11.7 | 12.0 | 12.4 | 13.2 | 14.0 | 14.4 | 14.7 | 15.2 | 15.5 | 15.8 | 15.7 | 15.7 |
| d. Savings and loan associations | 22.6 | 24.9 | 25.7 | 25.5 | 25.4 | 25.0 | 24.8 | 26.2 | 27.9 | 29.3 | 30.6 | 31.2 | 32.3 | 33.6 |
| e. Investment companies | 0.4 | 0.5 | 0.6 | 0.6 | 0.6 | 0.6 | 0.5 | 0.4 | 0.4 | 0.4 | 0.3 | 0.3 | 0.2 | 0.2 |
| f. Credit unions | 0.1 | 0.1 | 0.1 | 0.2 | 0.2 | 0.1 | 0.2 | 0.2 | 0.2 | 0.2 | 0.2 | 0.2 | 0.2 | 0.3 |
| g. Life insurance | 15.9 | 14.3 | 15.0 | 17.1 | 18.7 | 20.7 | 22.2 | 21.8 | 21.5 | 21.3 | 21.1 | 21.2 | 20.6 | 19.5 |
| h. Fire and casualty insurance | 0.1 | 0.1 | 0.1 | 0.1 | 0.1 | 0.1 | 0.1 | 0.1 | 0.1 | 0.1 | 0.1 | 0 | 0 | 0 |
| i. Noninsured pension plans | 0.1 | 0.1 | 0.1 | 0.1 | 0.1 | 0.1 | 0.2 | 0.2 | 0.2 | 0.2 | 0.2 | 0.3 | 0.4 | 0.5 |
| j. Other private insurance | 0.3 | 0.3 | 0.2 | 0.2 | 0.1 | 0.3 | 0.3 | 0.3 | 0.2 | 0.3 | 0.3 | 0.2 | 0.4 | 0.2 |
| k. Finance companies | 0.3 | 0.6 | 0.7 | 0.6 | 0.7 | 1.0 | 0.7 | 0.9 | 0.8 | 1.0 | 1.4 | 1.1 | 0.8 | 1.1 |
| l. Other finance | 0.1 | 0.1 | 0.1 | 0.2 | 0.2 | 0.2 | 0.2 | 0.2 | 0.2 | 0.1 | 0.1 | 0.1 | 0.1 | 0.1 |
| 3. State and local governments | 0.3 | 0.2 | 0.2 | 0.2 | 0.4 | 0.4 | 0.5 | 0.5 | 0.6 | 0.7 | 0.7 | 0.7 | 1.0 | 1.2 |
| 4. Federal government | 3.9 | 2.4 | 1.9 | 1.8 | 2.7 | 2.8 | 3.4 | 3.7 | 3.8 | 3.4 | 3.2 | 3.3 | 4.1 | 3.8 |
| 5. Total | 100.0 | 100.0 | 100.0 | 100.0 | 100.0 | 100.0 | 100.0 | 100.0 | 100.0 | 100.0 | 100.0 | 100.0 | 100.0 | 100.0 |
| 6. Total (billion dollars) | 23.27 | 28.10 | 33.76 | 39.61 | 44.88 | 53.61 | 61.38 | 68.87 | 77.11 | 87.20 | 100.62 | 112.12 | 121.29 | 133.03 |

Source: National Balance Sheet, Vol. II, Table IV-b-11a.

## TABLE 105

### DISTRIBUTION OF FLOW OF FUNDS, NONFARM RESIDENTIAL MORTGAGES, 1946–58
(per cent)

| | 1946 | 1947 | 1948 | 1949 | 1950 | 1951 | 1952 | 1953 | 1954 | 1955 | 1956 | 1957 | 1958 |
|---|---|---|---|---|---|---|---|---|---|---|---|---|---|
| 1. Nonfarm households | 18.5 | 11.8 | 10.1 | 4.4 | 1.0 | 2.8 | 3.7 | 4.9 | 4.3 | 2.8 | 6.5 | 8.8 | 6.9 |
| 2. Finance | 86.3 | 88.9 | 88.2 | 84.6 | 95.1 | 88.3 | 89.0 | 89.2 | 94.5 | 93.9 | 88.5 | 73.4 | 88.6 |
| a. Government insurance and pension funds | 0 | 0 | 0 | 0 | 0.7 | 0.8 | 0.5 | 0.4 | 0.7 | 0.3 | 0.8 | 0.2 | -0.4 |
| b. Commercial banks | 36.1 | 31.4 | 18.9 | 11.4 | 19.8 | 10.4 | 12.3 | 9.0 | 12.2 | 12.7 | 9.7 | 1.5 | 12.1 |
| c. Mutual savings banks | 4.1 | 6.2 | 14.0 | 15.4 | 17.0 | 19.8 | 17.2 | 17.6 | 18.6 | 17.6 | 18.6 | 14.3 | 16.4 |
| d. Savings and loan associations | 35.9 | 29.7 | 24.2 | 24.3 | 22.9 | 24.1 | 37.2 | 42.5 | 40.2 | 38.7 | 36.8 | 45.7 | 46.9 |
| e. Investment companies | 0.8 | 1.2 | 0.7 | 0.4 | 0.3 | -0.1 | 0.1 | -0.1 | 0 | -0.1 | -0.1 | -0.2 | -0.3 |
| f. Credit unions | 0.2 | 0.2 | 0.3 | 0.2 | 0.1 | 0.3 | 0.4 | 0.4 | 0.3 | 0.2 | 0.5 | 0 | 0.7 |
| g. Life insurance | 6.4 | 18.7 | 29.4 | 30.4 | 30.9 | 32.8 | 18.7 | 18.3 | 19.8 | 19.8 | 22.0 | 13.6 | 7.9 |
| h. Fire and casualty insurance | 0 | 0 | 0.2 | 0.2 | 0.1 | 0.1 | 0 | 0 | 0 | 0 | -0.1 | -0.1 | 0 |
| i. Noninsured pension plans | 0.2 | 0 | 0 | 0.2 | 0.1 | 0.5 | 0.4 | 0.5 | 0.3 | 0.3 | 1.0 | 1.9 | 1.2 |
| j. Other private insurance | 0.2 | 0.2 | 0.2 | 0.4 | 0.3 | 0.4 | 0.3 | 0.2 | 0.2 | 0.2 | 0.1 | 0 | 0 |
| k. Finance companies | 2.3 | 1.2 | -0.2 | 1.7 | 2.4 | -1.0 | 1.9 | 0.4 | 2.2 | 3.9 | -0.9 | -3.5 | 3.9 |
| l. Other finance | 0.2 | 0.2 | 0.5 | 0.4 | 0.2 | 0.3 | 0 | 0 | 0 | 0.1 | 0.1 | 0 | 0.3 |
| 3. State and local governments | 0 | 0 | 0.2 | 1.7 | 0.6 | 0.9 | 1.1 | 1.7 | 1.0 | 0.9 | 1.0 | 3.9 | 3.6 |
| 4. Federal government | -4.8 | -0.7 | 1.5 | 9.3 | 3.3 | 8.0 | 6.1 | 4.2 | 0.2 | 2.4 | 4.0 | 13.8 | 0.9 |
| 5. Total | 100.0 | 100.0 | 100.0 | 100.0 | 100.0 | 100.0 | 100.0 | 100.0 | 100.0 | 100.0 | 100.0 | 100.0 | 100.0 |
| 6. Total (billion dollars) | 4.82 | 5.66 | 5.86 | 5.27 | 8.73 | 7.77 | 7.48 | 8.24 | 10.09 | 13.42 | 11.50 | 9.17 | 11.74 |

Source: National Balance Sheet, Vol. II, Table VIII-b-11a.

296

mum down payment, extent of support by FNMA, and other special factors. They indicate that the lenders tended to regard FHA-insured mortgages as the closest substitute for conventional mortgages and VA-guaranteed home mortgages as marginal investments.

Disregarding minor variations, it is evident from Table 105 that the main changes in the sources of funds for residential mortgages are the high shares of life insurance companies during the first part of the period (particularly 1948–51), of commercial banks (particularly in 1946–47), and of savings and loan associations especially during the second part of the period. These movements reflect, in the case of savings and loan associations, primarily an increase of the growth rate of total assets, since these institutions have always invested most of their assets in home mortgages (Table 106). In the case of life insurance companies, the fluctuations are due largely to the part of available total funds allocated to increases in the portfolio of residential mortgages (see Table 107). While on the average more than one-half of the total net funds available were allocated to residential mortgages from 1948 to 1951, the proportion declined to about one-fourth during the latter part of the period, except in 1955–56. These allocations, in turn, were largely determined by interest rate differentials, primarily that between mortgages and corporate bonds. Considerations of continuity of operation, such as keeping intact the company's own nationwide mortgage department or its correspondent system, were important additional factors in the allocation of funds.

Mutual savings banks showed no similar fluctuations. From 1948 to 1958, they absorbed in each year with only small variations between 14 and 20 per cent of the annual net supply of residential mortgages. This regularity, however, involved considerable fluctuations in the share of residential mortgages in total uses of funds, although the share never fell below 70 per cent from 1948 on. In several years early in cyclical upswings (1950–51, 1955–56), net investment in residential mortgages was even in excess of total funds used so that the absolute volume of other assets held was reduced. The increase in the proportional allocation to residential mortgages was influenced by changes in the law in most savings bank states in 1950 permitting the acquisition of out-of-state federally underwritten mortgages. Mutual savings banks thus were, during most of the postwar period, primarily investors in residential mortgages insofar as the use of their funds is concerned. Their allocation of 84 per cent of total net funds to resi-

TABLE 106

SHARE OF NONFARM RESIDENTIAL MORTGAGES IN ASSETS OF EACH SECTOR, 1945–58

(per cent)

| | 1945 | 1946 | 1947 | 1948 | 1949 | 1950 | 1951 | 1952 | 1953 | 1954 | 1955 | 1956 | 1957 | 1958 |
|---|---|---|---|---|---|---|---|---|---|---|---|---|---|---|
| 1. Nonfarm households | 1.0 | 1.0 | 1.0 | 1.0 | 1.0 | 0.9 | 0.9 | 0.9 | 0.9 | 0.8 | 0.8 | 0.8 | 0.8 | 0.8 |
| 2. Finance | 4.6 | 5.7 | 6.7 | 7.7 | 8.6 | 10.0 | 10.8 | 11.4 | 12.3 | 13.2 | 14.4 | 15.3 | 15.7 | 16.1 |
| a. Government insurance and pension funds | 0.1 | 0.1 | 0.1 | 0.1 | 0.1 | 0.2 | 0.4 | 0.4 | 0.4 | 0.5 | 0.6 | 0.7 | 0.7 | 0.6 |
| b. Commercial banks | 2.1 | 3.4 | 4.4 | 5.1 | 5.4 | 6.1 | 6.2 | 6.3 | 6.6 | 6.9 | 7.4 | 7.7 | 7.5 | 7.6 |
| c. Mutual savings banks | 19.9 | 19.1 | 19.9 | 23.0 | 25.5 | 31.0 | 36.3 | 38.8 | 41.4 | 44.7 | 49.3 | 52.6 | 53.6 | 55.0 |
| d. Savings and loan associations | 60.2 | 68.3 | 74.0 | 77.3 | 77.3 | 78.7 | 79.0 | 79.1 | 80.1 | 80.5 | 81.3 | 81.2 | 80.9 | 80.7 |
| e. Investment companies | 2.5 | 3.7 | 5.6 | 6.6 | 5.9 | 5.6 | 4.4 | 3.9 | 3.8 | 2.7 | 2.1 | 1.9 | 1.9 | 1.9 |
| f. Credit unions | 6.8 | 8.0 | 6.8 | 8.6 | 8.4 | 8.0 | 8.3 | 7.9 | 7.9 | 7.9 | 7.7 | 8.3 | 7.1 | 8.0 |
| g. Life insurance | 8.2 | 8.3 | 9.7 | 12.1 | 13.9 | 17.1 | 19.8 | 20.3 | 20.9 | 21.7 | 23.2 | 24.4 | 24.3 | 23.8 |
| h. Fire and casualty insurance | 0.3 | 0.2 | 0.3 | 0.3 | 0.3 | 0.3 | 0.3 | 0.3 | 0.3 | 0.3 | 0.3 | 0.3 | 0.2 | 0.2 |
| i. Noninsured pension plans | 0.9 | 0.9 | 0.9 | 0.8 | 0.8 | 0.8 | 1.2 | 1.4 | 1.5 | 1.4 | 1.4 | 1.7 | 2.3 | 2.3 |
| j. Other private insurance | 4.0 | 3.7 | 3.8 | 4.3 | 4.9 | 5.8 | 6.6 | 6.9 | 7.0 | 7.1 | 7.4 | 7.4 | 7.3 | 6.9 |
| k. Finance companies | 3.5 | 5.6 | 5.8 | 4.2 | 4.7 | 6.0 | 4.8 | 5.2 | 4.8 | 6.2 | 7.4 | 6.4 | 4.5 | 6.7 |
| l. Other finance | 0.3 | 0.6 | 0.9 | 1.1 | 1.4 | 1.5 | 1.8 | 1.7 | 1.6 | 1.3 | 1.6 | 1.7 | 1.5 | 1.5 |
| 3. State and local governments | 0.1 | 0.1 | 0.1 | 0.1 | 0.2 | 0.2 | 0.2 | 0.2 | 0.4 | 0.4 | 0.4 | 0.5 | 0.6 | 0.8 |
| 4. Federal government | 1.1 | 1.1 | 0.9 | 0.9 | 1.6 | 1.7 | 2.1 | 2.5 | 2.8 | 2.8 | 2.9 | 3.3 | 4.4 | 4.4 |
| 5. Total | 1.5 | 1.7 | 1.8 | 2.0 | 2.2 | 2.4 | 2.5 | 2.7 | 2.9 | 3.0 | 3.2 | 3.4 | 3.5 | 3.6 |

Source: National Balance Sheet, Vol. II, Tables III-1, III-5, III-5b through III-5m, III-6 and III-7; line 5 from Table I.

TABLE 107

SHARE OF NET PURCHASES OF NONFARM RESIDENTIAL MORTGAGES IN TOTAL NET USES OF FUND OF SECTORS, 1946-58

(per cent)

| | 1946 | 1947 | 1948 | 1949 | 1950 | 1951 | 1952 | 1953 | 1954 | 1955 | 1956 | 1957 | 1958 |
|---|---|---|---|---|---|---|---|---|---|---|---|---|---|
| 1. Nonfarm households | 2.3 | 1.6 | 1.4 | 0.5 | 0.2 | 0.4 | 0.4 | 0.6 | 0.6 | 0.4 | 0.9 | 1.0 | 0.9 |
| 2. Finance | 260.0 | 21.6 | 30.0 | 36.6 | 32.7 | 23.8 | 20.5 | 29.4 | 32.4 | 34.5 | 33.7 | 23.1 | 27.6 |
| a. Government insurance and pension funds | 0 | 0 | 0 | 0 | 4.6 | 1.5 | 0.9 | 0.9 | 2.6 | 1.2 | 2.5 | 0.7 | -4.1 |
| b. Commercial banks | -16.6 | 30.4 | -317.1 | 19.2 | 15.1 | 7.6 | 9.9 | 16.5 | 13.0 | 20.1 | 15.9 | 2.6 | 9.0 |
| c. Mutual savings banks | 11.6 | 34.7 | 82.0 | 79.4 | 160.9 | 155.6 | 72.9 | 75.9 | 87.9 | 116.8 | 105.4 | 71.2 | 73.7 |
| d. Savings and loan associations | 114.6 | 109.8 | 102.2 | 81.0 | 87.0 | 78.9 | 81.3 | 85.6 | 83.2 | 86.5 | 81.3 | 80.3 | 79.6 |
| e. Investment companies | 33.3 | 33.3 | 25.0 | 7.7 | 10.7 | -4.0 | 1.9 | -2.4 | 0 | -1.2 | -1.4 | -2.1 | -2.3 |
| f. Credit unions | 16.7 | 10.0 | 18.2 | 7.7 | 5.9 | 10.0 | 9.1 | 7.9 | 8.1 | 6.4 | 11.3 | 0 | 13.8 |
| g. Life insurance | 8.4 | 29.4 | 45.9 | 40.4 | 62.2 | 60.3 | 28.3 | 29.2 | 37.0 | 47.4 | 43.9 | 23.1 | 16.8 |
| h. Fire and casualty insurance | 0 | 0 | 0.9 | 0.9 | 1.0 | 1.0 | 0 | 0 | 0 | 0 | 0 | -1.0 | 0 |
| i. Noninsured pension plans | 1.1 | 0.6 | 0.6 | 0.8 | 0.7 | 3.1 | 2.1 | 1.9 | 1.6 | 1.7 | 4.2 | 5.9 | 4.5 |
| j. Other private insurance | 0 | 4.8 | 14.6 | 14.9 | 21.2 | 19.7 | 11.6 | 8.6 | 9.0 | 11.8 | 7.5 | -12.1 | 1.2 |
| k. Finance companies | 9.2 | 6.2 | -0.9 | 7.1 | 10.6 | -12.8 | 7.8 | 1.5 | 38.6 | 10.9 | -9.1 | -24.7 | -191.2 |
| l. Other finance | -0.6 | -1.2 | 5.1 | 3.4 | 2.8 | 200.0 | 0 | 0 | 0 | 10.0 | -25.0 | 0 | 1.8 |
| 3. State and local governments | 1.1 | 0 | 0.2 | 1.4 | 0.6 | 0.8 | 0.8 | 1.3 | 0.8 | 1.0 | 0.9 | 2.4 | 2.7 |
| 4. Federal government | 1.1 | -0.7 | 1.6 | 22.5 | 3.3 | 7.7 | 13.9 | 8.9 | -2.8 | 5.3 | 83.6 | 84.1 | 4.8 |
| 5. Total | 8.2 | 4.5 | 5.2 | 6.0 | 5.3 | 4.7 | 4.9 | 5.5 | 6.4 | 6.4 | 5.8 | 4.7 | 5.9 |

Source: National Balance Sheet, Vol. II, Tables VII-1, VII-5, VII-5b through VII-5m, VII-6, and VII-7; line 5 from Table V.

dential mortgages for the period as a whole is virtually as high as the comparable ratio for saving and loan associations (85 per cent), which are commonly considered as the typical investor in residential mortgages. The 1958 share of residential mortgages in total assets of mutual savings banks (55 per cent) was still considerably below that of saving and loan associations (81 per cent), but was far above that for all other major financial institutions such as life insurance companies (24 per cent) and commercial banks (8 per cent).

The predominance of the "big four" as suppliers of funds to the market for residential mortgages is evident from the fact that in no year of the postwar period did their combined share in the net flow fall below 75 per cent, and that it exceeded 90 per cent in two years (1950 and 1954). The only other investor groups of substantial importance at some periods were federal credit agencies who absorbed 9 per cent of the net supply of residential mortgages in 1949, 7 per cent in 1951–52, and 14 per cent in 1957; the years 1951, 1952, and 1957 were boom periods when market conditions were tight (see Table 108).

## Historical Background

The discussion of the developments in the market for residential mortgages during the postwar period has already indicated most points in which it differed from earlier periods, particularly in market organization and techniques. These differences may now be summarized and supplemented by indicating the main differences in the distribution of residential mortgages among holders and their relative importance in the portfolios of the main investor groups. The comparison will be made mostly with the period before 1929.

In market techniques, the basic difference between the postwar and the predepression periods, of course, is the substitution of the amortized long-term mortgage, often guaranteed by the federal government, for the unamortized, uninsured mortgage which was nominally short-term (three to five years) although in practice was often renewed. Other technical changes of importance are the development of advance commitments by large institutional lenders, the rise of mortgage companies, and the increasing importance of wholesale lending operations.

The first point where an important structural difference exists between the postwar and predepression periods is the role of mortgage credit in financing residential real estate, particularly one- to four-family structures. The postwar ratio for new homes of over two-thirds

TABLE 108

CREDIT CONDITIONS IN THE HOME MORTGAGE MARKET, 1946–58

| | Interest Rates (per cent) | | | | Maturity (years) | | Loan-to-Value Ratio (per cent) | |
|---|---|---|---|---|---|---|---|---|
| | Conventional Home Mortgage (1) | FHA Contract Rate (2) | VA Contract Rate (3) | **FHA** Secondary (4) | FHA New Homes[a] (5) | VA (6) | FHA New Homes[a] (7) | VA (8) |
| 1946 | 4.30 | 4.50 | 4.00 | n.a. | 21 | 19 | 84 | 93 |
| 1947 | 4.37 | 4.50 | 4.00 | n.a. | 20 | 20 | 81 | 90 |
| 1948 | 4.50 | 4.50 | 4.00 | 4.24 | 20 | 20 | 80 | 84 |
| 1949 | 4.61 | 4.50 | 4.00 | 4.28 | 23 | 21 | 84 | 86 |
| 1950 | 4.58 | 4.31 | 4.00 | 4.20 | 24 | 23 | 85 | 92 |
| 1951 | 4.64 | 4.25 | 4.00 | 4.36 | 23 | 24 | 83 | 90 |
| 1952 | 4.81 | 4.25 | 4.00 | 4.43 | 22 | 23 | 80 | 87 |
| 1953 | 4.93 | 4.44 | 4.38 | 4.74 | 22 | 23 | 83 | 89 |
| 1954 | 5.02 | 4.50 | 4.50 | 4.61 | 23 | 26 | 82 | 93 |
| 1955 | 4.92 | 4.50 | 4.50 | 4.70 | 26 | 27 | 85 | 95 |
| 1956 | 4.96 | 4.54 | 4.50 | 4.97 | 26 | 27 | 83 | 93 |
| 1957 | 5.88 | 5.08 | 4.50 | 5.65 | 26 | 27 | 82 | 92 |
| 1958 | 5.70 | 5.25 | 4.69 | 5.76 | 27 | 28* | 89 | 94 |
| Averages | | | | | | | | |
| 1946–49 | 4.44 | 4.50 | 4.00 | | 21 | 20 | 82 | 88 |
| 1949–54 | 4.75 | 4.35 | 4.13 | 4.44 | 23 | 23 | 83 | 90 |
| 1954–58 | 5.28 | 4.75 | 4.52 | 5.13 | 26 | 27 | 84 | 93 |
| 1946–58 | 4.86 | 4.55 | 4.24 | | 23 | 24 | 83 | 91 |

Cols. 1, 4: See source to Table 48.
Cols. 2–3, 1946–55: Klaman, <u>Postwar Residential Mortgage Market</u>, Tables A–4 and A–5,
  p. 285.
Cols. 2–3, 1956–58: <u>Annual Report of Housing and Home Finance Agency: Tenth</u>, p. 5;
  <u>Eleventh</u>, p. 4; <u>Twelfth</u>, p. 20; and <u>Thirteenth</u>, p. 19.
Col. 5, 1946–49: <u>Third Annual Report of HHFA</u>, p. 204, Table 16.
Col. 5, 1950–54: <u>Eighth Annual Report of HHFA</u>, p. 186, Table 59.
Col. 5, 1955–58: <u>Twelfth Annual Report of HHFA</u>, p. 105, Table III–39.
Cols. 6,8: Unpublished data in letter from VA.
Col. 7, 1946–49: <u>Third Annual Report of HHFA</u>, p. 204, Table 16.
Col. 7, 1950–52: <u>Sixth Annual Report of HHFA</u>, p. 273, Table 21.
Col. 7, 1953–54: <u>Eighth Annual Report of HHFA</u>, p. 193, Table 61.
Col. 7, 1955–56: <u>Tenth Annual Report of HHFA</u>, p. 105, Table III–43.
Col. 7, 1957–58: <u>Twelfth Annual Report of HHFA</u>, p. 107, Table IV–42.
[a]Arithmetic mean for new one-family houses.

(Table 101), implying that less than one-third of the purchase price is provided by the owner, is higher than the ratios prevailing before World War II. The contribution of mortgage loans toward the financing of new residential housing has been estimated at about three-fifths for the 1930's and 1920's, and at slightly more than two-fifths in 1911–18,[14] compared to over two-thirds in 1946–52. This is an important shift, since it means that the same dollar value of residential construction required about two-thirds more mortgage financing in the postwar period than before World War I, although only one-tenth more than in the 1930's.

[14] Grebler, Blank, and Winnick, *Capital Formation*, pp. 454–455, cols. 5 and 12.

TABLE 109

DISTRIBUTION OF NONFARM RESIDENTIAL MORTGAGES AMONG HOLDER GROUPS, **1900-58**

(per cent)

| | 1958 (1) | 1945A (2) | 1945B (3) | 1939 (4) | 1929 (5) | 1912 (6) | 1900 (7) |
|---|---|---|---|---|---|---|---|
| 1. Nonfarm households[a] | 9.6 | 26.8 | 29.8 | 28.2 | 34.2 | 37.6 | 54.3 |
| 2. State and local governments | 1.2 | 0.3 | 0 | 10.5 | 0 | 0 | 0 |
| 3. Federal government | 3.8 | 3.9 | 3.7 | 0 | 0 | 0 | 0 |
| 4. Financial institutions, total | 85.3 | 69.1 | 66.5 | 61.3 | 65.8 | 62.4 | 45.7 |
| a. Commercial banks | 13.8 | 14.5 | 15.0 | 13.5 | 13.3 | 11.9 | 6.6 |
| b. Mutual savings banks | 15.7 | 14.6 | 12.1 | 15.3 | 14.1 | 21.2 | 17.9 |
| c. Savings and loan associations | 33.6 | 22.6 | 22.2 | 18.0 | 24.8 | 17.0 | 12.6 |
| d. Life insurance companies | 19.5 | 15.9 | 15.8 | 12.3 | 10.9 | 9.4 | 6.2 |
| e. Fire and casualty insurance | 0 | 0.1 | 0.2 | 0.2 | 0.4 | 0.8 | 0.9 |
| f. Noninsured pension plans | 0.5 | 0.1 | 0 | 0 | 0 | | |
| g. Other private insurance | 0.2 | 0.3 | 0.5 | 0.4 | 0.3 | 0.1 | 0 |
| h. Investment companies | 0.2 | 0.4 | 0.3 | 0.4 | 0.1 | | |
| i. Mortgage companies | 1.1 | 0.3 | 0.5 | 1.3 | 1.9 | 2.0 | 1.5 |
| j. Credit unions | 0.3 | 0.1 | 0 | 0 | 0 | 0 | |
| k. Government insurance and pension funds[b,c] | 0.3 | 0.1 | 0 | 0 | 0 | | |
| l. Other finance | 0.1 | 0.1 | 0 | 0 | 0 | | |
| 5. Total | 100.0 | 100.0 | 100.0 | 100.0 | 100.0 | 100.0 | 100.0 |
| 6. Total (billion dollars) | 133.0 | 23.3 | 23.3 | 20.8 | 24.9 | 5.0 | 3.0 |

Source: *National Balance Sheet*, Vol. II. Cols. 1-2 from Table IV-b-11a; cols. 3-7 from Table IV-b-11-c-1.
For notes a-c, see notes to Table 110. Also, see note to Table 55.

The distribution of residential mortgages among the main investor groups, as seen in Table 109 and Chart 26, is characterized by a substantial, although not continuous, increase in the share of financial institutions. Financial institutions accounted for more than four-fifths of the increase in residential mortgage debt between 1900 and 1912, but for only two-thirds of the growth between 1912 and 1929. In the 1930's, when total residential mortgage debt shrank by about one-sixth, the holdings of private financial institutions declined by almost one-fourth. However, federal credit agencies, first entering the market during this decade, held one-tenth of the total residential debt in 1939, and the share of all financial institutions was three-fifths. The holdings of other investors, mostly individuals, declined from more than one-half in 1900 to two-fifths or less between 1912 and 1945. Thus the shrinkage in individuals' share in the residential mortgage debt and the concomitant rise in the share of financial institutions have been much sharper in the thirteen postwar years than in the preceding fifty years.

Among financial institutions, the main difference between the postwar and predepression periods is the sharp increase in the proportion of residential mortgages held by life insurance companies and saving and loan associations, and, to a much lesser extent, by commercial banks, and the decline in the share of mutual savings banks. The reasons for these shifts become clearer in Table 110 and Chart 27 which show the share of residential mortgages in the total assets of the main holder groups.[15] The share of residential mortgages in the total assets of financial institutions passed the highest prewar mark in 1953–54, and by 1958 was one-quarter higher than that.

In the period 1900–29, the increase in the share of assets allocated to residential mortgages was particularly marked for commercial and mutual savings banks. This was to a considerable extent the result of the relaxation of the statutory limits on holdings of mortgage loans, but it also reflected the residential building boom of the 1920's. In the case of life insurance companies, the increase in the share of residential mortgages was limited to the 1920's. Property insurance companies, in contrast, sharply reduced their share after 1900 and had almost liquidated their holdings by 1945.

---

[15] If federal corporations and credit agencies are included, the 1939 share of financial institutions is 8 instead of 7 per cent (see Table 110; Goldsmith's *A Study of Saving in the United States,* Princeton, 1956, Vol. III, Table W-40; *National Balance Sheet,* Vol. II, Table IV-b-11c-1).

CHART 26

DISTRIBUTION OF NONFARM RESIDENTIAL MORTGAGES
AMONG MAIN HOLDER GROUPS, 1900–58

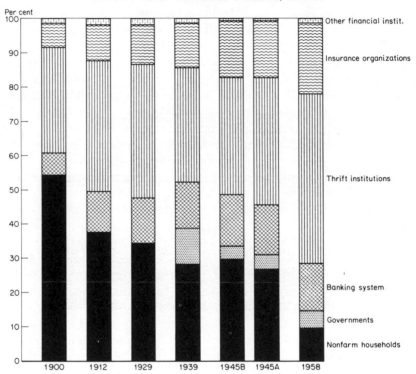

Source: Table 109.

TABLE 110

SHARE OF NONFARM RESIDENTIAL MORTGAGES IN TOTAL ASSETS OF HOLDER GROUPS, 1900-58

(per cent)

| | 1958 (1) | 1945A (2) | 1945B (3) | 1939 (4) | 1929 (5) | 1912 (6) | 1900 (7) |
|---|---|---|---|---|---|---|---|
| 1. Nonfarm households[a] | 0.8 | 1.0 | 1.1 | 1.6 | 1.9 | 1.6 | 2.6 |
| 2. State and local governments | 0.8 | 0.1 | 0 | 0 | 0 | 0 | 0 |
| 3. Federal government | 4.4 | 1.1 | 1.1 | 8.5 | 0 | 0 | 0 |
| 4. Financial institutions, total | 16.1 | 4.6 | 4.5 | 7.4 | 12.4 | 8.7 | 8.0 |
| a. Commercial banks | 7.6 | 2.1 | 2.2 | 4.2 | 5.0 | 2.7 | 1.9 |
| b. Mutual savings banks | 55.0 | 19.9 | 16.5 | 26.9 | 35.6 | 26.4 | 21.8 |
| c. Savings and loan associations | 80.7 | 60.2 | 60.0 | 69.7 | 83.4 | 89.0 | 75.7 |
| d. Life insurance companies | 23.8 | 8.2 | 8.2 | 8.8 | 15.5 | 10.6 | 10.5 |
| e. Fire and casualty insurance | 0.2 | 0.3 | 0.5 | 1.0 | 2.1 | 4.0 | 5.8 |
| f. Noninsured pension plans | 2.3 | 0.9 | 0 | 0 | 0 | | |
| g. Other private insurance | 6.9 | 4.0 | 6.2 | 6.3 | 8.4 | 4.3 | 4.0 |
| h. Investment companies | 1.2 | 2.5 | 3.0 | 5.0 | 0.5 | | |
| i. Mortgage companies | 87.5 | 70.3 | 71.3 | 64.5 | 61.7 | 27.3 | 24.2 |
| j. Credit unions | 8.0 | 6.8 | 0 | 0 | 0 | 0 | |
| k. Government insurance and pension funds[b,c] | 0.6 | 0.1 | 0 | 0 | 0 | | |
| l. Other finance | 1.5 | 0.3 | 0 | 0 | 0 | 0 | 0 |
| 5. Total | 3.6 | 1.5 | 1.5 | 2.4 | 2.6 | 1.6 | 1.9 |

Source: *National Balance Sheet*, Vol. II, unless otherwise indicated.

Lines 1-4, 5: Tables I and Ia.

Lines 4a-4h, 4i-4ℓ, cols. 1-2: Tables III-5a through III-5k and III-5m.

Lines 4a-4h, 4j-4ℓ, cols. 3-7: Numerators from Tables IV-b-11c-1; denominators from *Financial Intermediaries*, Tables A-3, A-4, A-5, A-1<u>5</u>, A-8, A-12, A-13, A-9, A-10, A-11, A-14, and A-21.

Line 4i, cols. 1-2: FRB unpublished worksheets.

Line 4i, cols. 3-7: *Study of Saving*, Vol. I, Table M-20 (numerator from col. 3 and denominator from col. 1).

[a]Cols. 1 and 2 include all nonfarm residential mortgages not included elsewhere.

[b]For cols. 3-5, small amounts of mortgages held by these groups are included in line 1.

[c]For 1929-45, mortgages held by government trust funds were recorded in *Financial Intermediaries*, Table A-11, but the figures were not comparable to the figures of the postwar period.

See note to Table 55.

305

CHART 27

SHARE OF NONFARM RESIDENTIAL MORTGAGES IN TOTAL ASSETS
OF MAIN HOLDER GROUPS, 1900–58

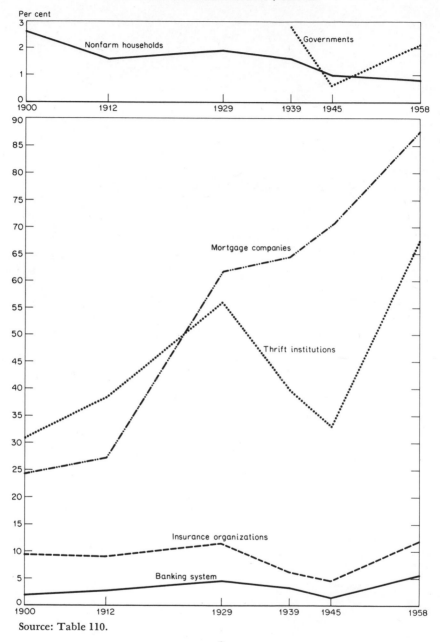

Source: Table 110.

Noninstitutional investors, whose holdings must be estimated as a residual and are therefore subject to a particularly wide margin of error, seem to have accounted for a relatively high share in the total increase of residential mortgage debt in 1900–29. For this period, a third of the total increase in residential mortgage debt is held by households, probably to a substantial extent in the form of junior mortgages. This compares with estimated shares of only about 15 per cent in 1900–12 and 40 per cent during World War II. Noninstitutional investors apparently also were heavily affected by the shrinkage in the volume of residential mortgages between 1929 and 1939. They are estimated to have borne more than one-half of the aggregate shrinkage, and they contributed to the decline in their share of total outstanding mortgage debt.

# Index

Agriculture sector:
  assets of, 49, 50
    financial, 127, 144
  balance sheets, 50, 51, 75, 76
  sectoring principles, 49, 51, 53, 58
  share of, in external financing, 6,
    118, 127, 144
  share of, in gross capital expendi-
    ture, 113, 123, 127
  share of internal financing, 124, 127
  sources of funds, 123, 124, 127, 128,
    133
  uses of funds, 6, 123, 127, 128
Assets, 28, 30
  in balance sheet, 75, 77
  corporate bonds, 221
  definition of, 44, 44n, 45
  financial, 30, 31, 33, 113, 244
    *See also* individual sectors
  liquid, 11, 33, 94
  in National Income Accounts, 81
  ratio of common stock values to,
    259, 267
  state and local government securi-
    ties, *see* State and local govern-
    ment securities
  tangible, 57
  Treasury securities, *see* Treasury
    securities

Balance sheet equation, 55, 61

Balance sheets, 34, 43–48, 51, 53, 76–
  78
  degree of netness in, 53–55, 57
  national, 77
  sectoral, 76, 77
Bjerve, Petter Jakob, 44n
Blank, David M., 287, 301
Bogen, Jules I., 238n
Bond issues, 110, 113, 210
  *See also* Corporate bonds
Borenstein, Israel, 232n, 268n
Business:
  share of, in capital expenditures,
    4, 5
  share of, in net capital formation,
    102

Capital consumption allowances, 22,
  45, 47, 57, 76, 81, 94, 98, 102,
  103, 105, 106, 119, 124, 140
  in federal government, 136
  in nonfarm households, 125
  share of, in total funds, 109, 111
  in unincorporated business, 127
Capital expenditures, 2, 5, 23, 24, 76,
  79, 95, 99–102, 108, 113, 119,
  123, 127, 132, 133, 217
  share of, in total uses of funds, 5
  *See also* individual sectors
Capital formation:
  and business cycles, 83–85, 88, 90,
  92, 95, 98

# Index

Copeland, Morris A., 45n

Corporate bonds, 8, 16, 17, 210, 212, 215, 216, 219, 220–222, 223, 228–229
  amount outstanding, 208, 211, 217
  as assets, 221
  compared with other capital market instruments, 190, 191, 240
  direct placement of, 11, 12, 209, 211–213, 230, 233
  public offering of, 209, 212–213, 230, 233, 238
  yield on, 8
    See also Capital market instruments; individual sectors; Sources and uses of funds

Corporate securities, 275

Corporate stock, 37, 46, 54, 57, 77, 108, 110, 151, 155, 246, 251, 253, 260, 263, 269, 270
  preferred stock, 234, 237, 265
  share of, in financing, 18, 249, 267, 268
    See also Capital market instruments; individual sectors; Sources and uses of funds

Corporations, treatment of, 48

Cost, as reflected by yield differentials, 28, 29

Creamer, Daniel, 232n, 268n

Credit unions:
  assets, 37, 40
  holdings of government securities, 187

Dawson, John C., 74n
Denizet, J., 45n
Dobrovolsky, Sergei, 232n, 268n
Dorrance, Graeme S., 45n

Earned depreciation allowances, 5, 6
Economies of scale, 29
Equities, 30–31

Equities (Cont.)
  corporate stock, 46, 123
  in nonprofit organizations, 46
  securities, 77, 110, 113
  share of, in external financing, 108, 110, 111, 123
  in source of funds, 124
  in unincorporated business, 46
  in uses of funds, 5

External financing, 7, 56, 79, 93, 94, 102, 106, 108, 116, 123
  corporate bonds in, 17, 214, 217, 232
  corporate stocks in, 248, 268
  gross, 108, 111
  long-term, 7, 110, 111, 248
  net, 108
  share of sectors in, 6, 7, 118, 214
  short-term, 7, 110

Fand, D., 74n
Farm households, treatment of, 48
Federal government sector, 51, 53, 58
  as debtor, see Treasury securities
  as holder and guarantor of mortgages, 20, 21, 277–279, 282, 287, 300, 303
  as holder of Treasury securities, 172
  as saving deficit unit, 24, 26
  balance sheets, 76
  capital consumption allowances, 136
  claims, long- and short-term, 123
  ratio of capital consumption allowances to net saving in, 124
  share of, in external financing, 6, 118
  share of, in gross capital formation, 90, 93
  share of internal financing, 124
  sources of funds, 133, 135, 136, 147, 148
  uses of funds, 6, 123, 133, 135, 136